THE SUBJECT APPROACH
TO
INFORMATION

••••••••••••••••••••••••••••••••

SECOND EDITION REVISED AND ENLARGED

A C FOSKETT
FLA
College of Librarianship, Wales

LINNET BOOKS & CLIVE BINGLEY

FIRST PUBLISHED 1969
REPRINTED 1970
THIS EDITION FIRST PUBLISHED IN USA 1972
BY LINNET BOOKS, AN IMPRINT OF
SHOE STRING PRESS INC, 995 SHERMAN
AVENUE, HAMDEN, CONNECTICUT 06514
PRINTED IN GREAT BRITAIN
0-208-01078-5

THE SUBJECT APPROACH TO INFORMATION

72 15473

Contents

Illustrations

LIST OF ABBREVIATIONS

ACS	American Chemical Society
AIP	American Institute of Physics
API	American Petroleum Institute
ASCA	Automatic subject citation alert
ASTIA	Armed Services Technical Information Agency (now DDC)
BC	Bibliographic Classification (Bliss)
BM	British Museum
BNB	British National Bibliography
BS	British Standard
BSI	British Standards Institution
BTI	British Technology Index
BuShips	United States Navy Bureau of Ships
CA	Chemical Abstracts
CC	Colon Classification (Ranganathan)
CDU	Classification Décimale Universelle (=UDC)
CFSTI	Clearinghouse for Federal Scientific and Technical Information (now NTIS)
CLRU	Cambridge Language Research Unit
CNRS	Centre Nationale pour la Recherche Scientifique
CLW	College of Librarianship Wales
COSATI	Committee on scientific and technical information
CRG	Classification Research Group
DC	Decimal Classification (Dewey)
DC&	Decimal Classification: Additions, Notes, Decisions
DDC	Defense Documentation Center
DK	Dezimal Klassifikation (=UDC)
DRTC	Documentation Research and Training Centre
EE	English Electric Company Limited
EJC	Engineers Joint Council
EURATOM	European Atomic Energy Community
ERIC	Educational Resources Information Center
FID	Fédération International de Documentation
FID/CCC	FID Central Classification Committee
IBM	International Business Machines Corporation
IEE	Institution of Electrical Engineers
IIB	Institut International de Bibliographie

IID	Institut International de Documentation
INSPEC	Information service in physics, electrotechnology and control
INTREX	Information Transfer Experiments
KWIC	Keyword in context
KWOC	Keyword out of context
LA	British Library Association
LC	Library of Congress classification
LCSH	Subject headings used in the Library of Congress
LISA	Library and information science abstracts
MAC	Multiple access computer; Machine aided cognition
MARC	Machine readable cataloguing
MARLIS	Multi-aspect relevance linkage information system
MEDLARS	Medical literature analysis and retrieval system
MeSH	Medical subject headings
MIT	Massachusetts Institute of Technology
NASA	National Aeronautics and Space Administration
NLL	National Lending Library for Science and Technology
NLM	National Library of Medicine
NTIS	National Technical Information Service
OECD	Organisation for Economic Cooperation and Development
OSTI	Office for Scientific and Technical Information
OTS	Office of Technical Services (later CFSTI, now NTIS)
P-Note	Provisional extension to the UDC
PCMI	Photo-chromic micro-image
PMEST	Personality, Matter, Energy, Space, Time
PRECIS	Preserved context indexing system
SC	Subject Classification (Brown)
SCI	Science Citation Index
SDI	Selective dissemination of information
SHARP	Ships analysis and retrieval project
SLIC	Selective listing in combination
SMART	G Salton's computer retrieval experiments
SYNTOL	Syntagmatic organisation language
TIP	MIT technical information project
UDC	Universal Decimal Classification
UKAEA	United Kingdom Atomic Energy Authority
UKCIS	United Kingdom Chemical Information Service
USAEC	United States Atomic Energy Commission
WRU	Case Western Reserve University

Author's preface

The author of yet another book on information retrieval is in duty bound to offer some sort of *apologia pro libro suo*. It is my hope that this work will help to fill a need which exists at present for a textbook which presents an integrated approach to the problems of retrieval of information about subjects. The impetus which persuaded me to write it came from the introduction in 1964 of a new syllabus for the (British) Library Association examinations.

The syllabus in force before 1964 drew a line between 'classification' (Ai) and 'cataloguing' (Aii); this line tended to separate the use of subject headings, which counted as cataloguing, from the use of classification schemes, which in their turn were separated from consideration of the classified catalogue. In the revised syllabus, a single paper covered both classification and cataloguing, enabling teachers and—more important—students, to avoid the previous unfortunate dichotomy. However, in teaching this new course, I became more and more convinced that it was possible and useful to establish a rather different kind of division: that between those factors such as author's names, or titles, which *identify* particular documents, and those such as subjects, where we have to scan our collections in some way before we can establish which documents are likely to provide the most satisfactory answer, and where the answer we provide will often be only tentative. This corresponds to the division between those readers who come to the library knowing what documents they require and interested only in whether we can supply them, and those who come seeking information and need some kind of assistance to help them to find it, that is, to identify the documents which will—or may—contain the information they seek. My experience in special libraries, where the second kind of reader is the norm, together with my personal predilections, led me to concentrate on this aspect.

Most textbooks on classification have ignored alphabetical headings and vice versa, and we have had to turn to a further set of texts to study post-coordinate methods. Yet the Cranfield Project showed that many of the intellectual problems were common to all three methods.

1*

I have also been concerned by the fact that it would be possible for a student following a 'conventional' cataloguing course to leave library school with little or no knowledge of coordinate indexing, though this is now commonly used in special libraries and in some bibliographical tools. I have therefore tried in this text to emphasize the similarities as well as the differences between the different methods of retrieving information, and to show the kind of situation where each is likely to prove of value.

Another important factor which has influenced my approach is the result of the trend in recent years towards full time library school as the normal means of education for librarianship, not only in Great Britain but in other parts of the world also. This has had two major consequences. The first of these is that, in line with general trends in higher education, the standard of students at entry to library school has risen, and it is now reasonable to expect students to assimilate a course with a good deal of theoretical content. The second is that students usually start their courses with a minimum of practical experience, and are therefore not set in the mould of a particular library system; no longer does Dewey or Sears represent the norm from which the teaching of classification theory is merely a temporary deviation.

The overall plan of this work has thus been developed over a period of several years, and I have had the opportunity of presenting a course based on it to students of the University of Maryland School of Library and Information Services, as well as to classes in this country. The reception of the first edition has shown that the integrated approach I have tried to present has been welcomed not only in this country but in the United States and other parts of the world as well. In this second edition I have therefore kept the same overall plan as in the first, but I have taken the opportunity of incorporating recent developments, notably those arising from the work of the Classification Research Group towards a new general classification scheme and the introduction of PRECIS as a method of indexing in the *British national bibliography*. There have of course also been new editions of such schemes as Dewey which have necessitated additions to the relevant chapters.

As this is a textbook intended to be used by students following courses in library schools, I have tried to devote particular attention to topics such as the Principle of Inversion which, though relatively unimportant in the overall scheme of things, seem to cause students a disproportionate amount of difficulty. I have concentrated everywhere on the modern approach, including terminology; I have never found it particularly useful for students trying to see the wood of classification to be distracted by the Tree of Porphyry. Existing schemes are judged by their ability to function well in present day libraries exploiting (and that is an important word) present day literature. A scheme may well have been very satisfactory in, say, 1910, or it may still appear to function adequately today, so long as nobody actually tries to *use* it; but today's libraries must be prepared to take an active part in seeing that information reaches those to whom it will be of value, and this requires tools which match today's needs, not yesterday's. I would also like to emphasize a point made in the text; it is not possible to study a scheme of classification, subject headings or co-ordinate indexing descriptors *at second hand*. Students should study *all* the schemes referred to for themselves, preferably under the direction of a tutor, with a certain amount of practical work. For this reason I have tried to concentrate on explaining why schemes are what they are and how their background and history affect their use today, rather than go into a lot of detail on their content.

Many of my examples are taken from science and technology. This again is to some extent the reflection of a personal predilection, but I make no apology for it. Many library school students have a non-scientific background (to put it charitably) and may find some of the terms used in the examples unfamiliar—but they will also find this situation repeated very frequently once they start practising their profession. I have tried to show that subject knowledge or the lack of it is not necessarily an important factor in the ability to index and retrieve information, a point first shown clearly by the Cranfield Project. Terminology and subject structure are usually reasonably well defined in science and technology, a state of affairs which does not always hold good in other subject areas, and examples taken from these other areas might well prove a great deal more difficult for students to grasp, even if the words used were more familiar (or perhaps *because* of this!). A final, and very significant, reason is that until quite recently most of the examples of modern indexing techniques had to be taken from the scientific and technical literature, since only there were they to be found. Anyone finding an example with unfamiliar words in it should not despair; in the first place, the examples demonstrate *structure* rather than terminology, and in the second—most of us have access to dictionaries.

My thoughts have obviously been influenced by many previous

writers, but it is perhaps fair to single out the following as being those to whom I am most deeply indebted: C W Cleverdon, under whose direction the Cranfield Project has given us all so much to argue over; E J Coates, whose work with the *British national bibliography* and *British technology index* has shown that theory can be put into practice; D J Foskett (who has of course been able to influence me for much longer than any of the others); J Mills, who for me as for many others was an inspiring lecturer as well as author; B C Vickery, whose writings have thrown light on such mysteries as the MARLIS; and A J Wells, who as General Editor of the *British national bibliography* has provided many library school lecturers with much of their most valued material. To E J Coates and J Mills, who very kindly agreed to read through my script before publication, I owe a special debt, for they have saved me from some errors and omissions; for the errors and prejudices which remain they are, of course, in no way responsible. I have also tried in this second edition to incorporate suggestions and comments made by my colleagues at the College of Librarianship Wales and by reviewers, many of whom have been most helpful in pointing out weaknesses in the first edition. If I have not adopted all the ideas put to me, I can only plead that an author should be permitted to retain *some* of his own prejudices. It is also no more than just that I should acknowledge the enormous debt I owe to my wife, without whose unstinting help and continuous encouragement this book would never have been written.

A C FOSKETT

February 1971

PART I: THEORY OF
INFORMATION RETRIEVAL SYSTEMS

CHAPTER I

Introduction

Libraries form an essential part of the chain of human communication. Before knowledge was recorded (and even to this day in very primitive societies), individuals formed the repository of knowledge, the bridge between successive generations and between those who generated new information and those who required to use it. The amount of information that can be passed on in this way is limited, and society began to move forward when information of various kinds began to be recorded in relatively permanent forms which could serve as a substitute for the ' wise man ' in person.

Nowadays, the quantity of new information being generated is such that no individual can hope to keep pace with even a small fraction of it, and the problem that we have to face is that of ensuring that individuals who need information can obtain it with the minimum of cost (both in time and in money), and without being overwhelmed by large amounts of irrelevant matter. Instead of the individual store of knowledge, we have the corporate store: the library; instead of the individual memory, we have the corporate memory: library catalogues and bibliographical tools. And just as the individual whose memory fails him cannot pass on wanted information when it is wanted, so a library whose corporate memory is inadequate will fail in its purpose.

THE IMPORTANCE OF CATALOGUES AND BIBLIOGRAPHIES

Libraries contain information in many different physical forms. While for many the book is still the major vehicle for the communication of information, for others the periodical or the technical report have taken its place; for yet others, newer forms such as films or gramophone records are the significant items. It is clear that the same work can appear in several different physical forms: for example, we may have Shakespeare's play *Hamlet* in book form, as a film, or on a record. The intellectual content will be the same in each case, but obviously it is not practical to try to arrange the different physical forms together. We cannot therefore rely on the physical arrangement of the items in a library to gather together different versions of the same work; we have to rely on a substitute—a set of records (surrogates) of the content of the library. In addition to the physical form, other factors may influence the place where we choose to keep any given item: we may decide that it should not be removed from the building, so it is placed in the reference section; or it may be suitable for children rather than adults, so it is placed in the children's section; or it may be a rarely used work which is placed in the stack rather than in the section open to the public. All of these factors emphasize the importance of the records, as opposed to the items themselves, for we can gather together in one place the records of items which themselves must perforce be scattered.

Suppose that our library only contains items of one kind, eg books. We can now attempt to arrange these in a way that will be useful, but we still cannot dispense with the records. For any particular book there will be several ways in which we might wish to find it: we may know the author, or the title, or we may need to find it because of its subject. The arrangement of books on our shelves may be by author, in which case we shall be able to find the required book if we know the author, but not if we only know the title or subject; equally, it may be by subject, in which case we shall not be able to find a book if we only know the author. But there is no such restriction when we consider the records we may make, for we can record a book by any and every factor which we think may prove to be of use when we are later searching for it. All we need is a fixed address to which each of these factors will lead us, so that we can locate the physical item no matter how we approach it. Once again, it is the records of the contents of our library which are the essential keys: the corporate memory.

The library's catalogue, however, is only one of the tools which serve as the corporate memory. A library containing large numbers of periodicals will not attempt to list every article in every issue it receives; instead, we rely on indexes, abstracts and similar bibliographical tools, which present the same kind of opportunity—and the same problems—as the library's catalogue, by enabling us to obtain access to any particular item through a number of different approaches.

FACTORS WHICH IDENTIFY

Some of these approaches *identify* the items they refer to. For example, if we state the number of a patent specification, there will only be one item corresponding to that description; if we name an author, we immediately limit severely the number of works which will satisfy us. Title, edition, date of publication, publisher, are all factors of this kind. We can therefore give a definite yes/no answer to an enquiry regarding one of these factors; either we can supply what our reader wants, or we cannot. A reader who asks for a copy of *Hamlet* may not mind which edition we give him very much, but he will certainly object if he is given *The alchemist*. An enquiry for AERE Inf/Bib 132 will not be satisfied by AERE Inf/Bib 125. Provided we have entries in our records which will lead us to the place where we can find these items, our search is straightforward.

FACTORS WHICH DO NOT IDENTIFY

There are, however, other approaches which do not identify the items which will answer them. If we are asked for a ' nice detective ' we have a wide choice of answers, any one of which may satisfy the enquirer. More seriously, if we are asked for something on a particular subject, we may be able to find a number of potential answers from which we shall have to ask our reader to make his own selection. Because authors write from within their own individual nexus of experiences, and readers read within their limits, there will seldom be the exact correspondence that we have with factors which identify; instead, we shall have to try to get as good a match as we can between our reader's needs and what we can supply, accepting that it is unlikely that we shall immediately find the same kind of yes/no answer as is possible when we can identify.

There is a further set of factors which do not identify particular documents but which are very important in selecting once we have identified potentially useful items. These include physical form—we may have the very thing, but only as a microfiche, useless without a reader; language—just what is wanted, but in Russian; level—we want an elementary introduction, but only have a doctoral thesis; intended audience—a book intended for one particular group of people (*eg* fluid mechanics for civil engineers) may not be well suited to the needs of another group; author's viewpoint—a Marxist history of Christianity may offend the practising churchgoer. It will be clear that we can only consider these factors when we have selected a set of documents which appear to match the reader's needs as far as their subject content is concerned.

This book is concerned with a discussion of the problems of optimizing our responses to requests for information on subjects. This is not to suggest that identifying factors such as authors' names do not present any problems; the fact that it took some twenty years of discussions to produce a new edition of the Anglo-American code[1] shows very plainly that they do! The problems of the subject approach to information, however, are more severe because they are more indeterminate; we never reach the stage of being able to say we have finished a search conclusively. A great deal of research has been done on these problems; much more remains to be done. This book is an attempt to show the present state of the art, in a way which will be acceptable as an elementary textbook; it does not pretend to be an advanced study, of which there are many, but rather to give beginners some understanding of present theories and ideas.[2]

BIBLIOGRAPHY

1 *Anglo-American cataloguing rules;* prepared by the American Library Association, the Library of Congress, the Library Association and Canadian Library Association. British text published by the Library Association, 1967. North American text published by the American Library Association, 1967. Work on the revision of the 1908 AA code took nearly twenty years.

2 There are a number of other works which are of value to the student who wishes to pursue the subject. The following are listed alphabetically by author:

Artandi, S *ed*: 'Rutgers series on systems for the intellectual organization of information'. This series includes volumes on UDC, SYNTOL, CC, faceted classification, coordinate indexing, and the alphabetical approach; all of them are of high standard and contain much original material. Advanced.

Bourne, C P: *Methods of information handling.* Wiley, 1963. Concentrates on the machine aspects, but has much of value on the theory. Advanced.

Coates, E J: *Subject catalogues: headings and structure.* Library Association, 1960. One of the few worthwhile books on the alphabetical approach. Not easy, but essential reading.

Foskett, D J: 'Classification'. (Chapter in Ashworth, W *ed*: *Handbook of special librarianship.* Aslib, third edition 1967). A concise but useful summary. Intermediate.

Foskett, D J: *Classification and indexing in the social sciences.* Butterworths, 1963. Discusses many general problems as well as those specific to the social sciences. Intermediate.

Foskett, D J: *Classification for a general index language*. Library Association, 1970. (LA Research pamphlet no 2.) An exposition of the theoretical development of the new general classification scheme being prepared by the CRG, this is of wider interest also as a statement of the problems to be dealt with. Elementary.

International study conference on classification research, Dorking, 1957: *Proceedings*. Aslib, 1958. Advanced.

International study conference on classification research, second, Elsinore, 1964. *Proceedings*. Copenhagen, Munksgaard, 1965. Advanced. (In general, the papers are beyond the scope of the student, but specific chapters, *eg* those on LC and UDC, are of value.)

Lancaster, F W: *Information retrieval systems: characteristics, testing and evaluation*. Wiley, 1968. A valuable new textbook by one of the Cranfield workers. Intermediate.

Library Association: *Some problems of a general classification scheme: report of a conference held in London, June 1963*. Library Association, 1964. Intermediate.

Mills, J: *A modern outline of library classification*. Chapman & Hall, 1960. One of the best textbooks available for its studies of the schemes of classification, though it is now somewhat out of date. Elementary.

Needham, C D: *Organizing knowledge in libraries: an introduction to cataloguing and classification*. Deutsch, second edition 1971. Useful though most of the emphasis is on cataloguing. Elementary.

Palmer, B I: *Itself an education*. Library Association, second edition 1971. The six lectures on various aspects of classification which formed the first edition published in 1962 are reprinted, together with a valuable new chapter on PRECIS by Derek Austin. Elementary.

Palmer, B I and Wells, A J: *The fundamentals of library classification*. Allen & Unwin, 1951. A very easy introduction to modern principles, especially those of Ranganathan, but now somewhat out of date. Elementary.

Ranganathan, S R: *The elements of library classification*. Asia Publishing House, third edition 1962. Obviously this presents its author's own ideas, but it is not the less useful for that. One of the best elementary texts available.

Sayers, W C Berwick: *Manual of library classification*. Fourth edition revised by A Maltby, Deutsch, 1967. The best presentation of the traditional approach to classification; this edition also goes some way towards presenting modern ideas. Elementary.

The Sayers memorial volume, edited by D J Foskett and B I Palmer. Library Association, 1961. A festschrift in honour of Sayers, who died before it could be published. Contains several chapters on modern developments of importance. Intermediate.

Sharp, J: *Some fundamentals of information retrieval*. Deutsch, 1965. Demonstrates the ways in which classification can cause difficulties in retrieval, and the methods which may be used to overcome these. Intermediate.

Sharp, J: 'Information retrieval'. (Chapter in Ashworth, W *ed: Handbook of special librarianship*. Aslib, third edition 1967.) Like the chapter on classification, this is a concise but valuable summary. Intermediate.

Vickery, B C: *Classification and indexing in science and technology*. Butterworths, second edition 1959. Of more general scope than its title implies, this work, like Coates, is not easy, but is essential reading.

Vickery, B C: *On retrieval system theory*. Butterworths, second edition 1965. One of the most satisfactory attempts to present a unified theory covering all IR methods. Advanced.

Vickery, B C: *Techniques of information retrieval*. Butterworths, 1970. Emphasizes the relationship between information retrieval and other aspects of library science, particularly bibliography. Intended as a textbook, it contains many valuable examples. Intermediate.

For developments over the past few years it is helpful to consult the chapters on classification in *Five years' work in librarianship; 1956-1960* by J Mills, *1961-1965* by A C Foskett. These chapters also have comprehensive bibliographies. Students should also note the series 'Progress in documentation' which now appears regularly in the *Journal of documentation* since 1969. This consists of a series of 'state-of-the-art' reviews covering, for example, 'Classification', and 'The automatic generation of index languages'.

For revision purposes, students will find it useful to consult Davison, K: *Theory of classification: an examination guidebook*. Bingley, 1966.

In the above list, 'elementary' indicates a work that can be read with profit by the novice; 'intermediate' indicates a work which should be read, but preferably after some preliminary grounding has been obtained; 'advanced', works which may be read by the student wishing to pursue the subject beyond the level of this text.

CHAPTER 2

Features of an information retrieval system

Authors generate large quantities of information every day. Estimates suggest that the number of useful (*ie* not merely repetitive) periodical articles published each year in science and technology alone is in excess of one million[1]; in Britain over 25,000 books are published every year. Libraries acquire a selection of this enormous output for the immediate use of their readers, and through the various schemes of inter-library cooperation they have access to a very much wider choice.

At the other end of the chain of communication we have readers, each with his own individual need for information which has to be selected from the mass available. In sum, readers will need all the information that we can collect (at least that is the hope of the authors!), but we cannot tell in advance what items of information we are likely to acquire that will be of value to any particular reader. What we have to do is organize our library in such a way that when we search for information for a reader we do not have to scan the whole contents in order to find what he wants, but can go with the minimum of delay to those items which will be of use. To look at it from another angle, our organization must permit us to eliminate what is *not* wanted. This idea introduces two very important concepts: recall and relevance.

RECALL AND RELEVANCE

For any particular reader who comes to the library with a need for information, there will be certain items in our collection which will be relevant. Among these it will be possible to establish some sort of precedence order; some will be definitely relevant, others will be useful, but less so, while others will be only marginally relevant. To take an example, a reader might want information on Siamese cats: in our collections we may have items dealing specifically with Siamese cats, and these will probably be highly relevant. There are however factors other than the subject alone which will influence this; these items may be too detailed, or not detailed enough; they may be written at the wrong level, or in a language which the reader does not understand. The reader's background will inevitably affect his decision as to which items he finds most relevant. To find more information we may broaden our search: that is, present to our reader those items which, though they do not deal specifically with the subject he is interested in, do include it as part of a broader subject. In our example, we may find items which deal with cats in general, not just with Siamese cats; or with pets in general, not just with cats. However, we must accept that the more we broaden our search—the more material we *recall*—the less likely it is that any given item will be *relevant*. At the extreme, we will find relevant information in a general encyclopedia, but it will only form a very small proportion of the total information therein. There is thus an inverse relationship between *recall*—the number of additional items we find in broadening our search—and *relevance*—the likelihood of their matching our reader's requirements.[2]

Normally, a reader will be satisfied with a few items, so long as they contain the kind of information he wants; that is to say, we need a system which will give us high relevance, even though recall will be low. But there will be situations when the reader will require high recall—as much information as possible—even though this means that he will have to look through a lot of items which will turn out to be of little or no value to him. We need to be able to vary the response of our system to cater for the kind of demand. It is also clear that relevance is a subjective factor depending on the individual; the same question, posed by two different readers, may well require two different answers. The problem arises from the fact that readers seek information which they can build into their own corpus of knowledge with the minimum of difficulty, whereas authors present information in a context dictated by *their* own background; the two will not necessarily coincide exactly. We must design our system to make the likelihood of achieving a match between reader's need and author's offering as high as possible, but we have to accept the fact that the match will not always be an exact one.

PROBABILITY OF ERROR

Indexers are human; so are users. Both are thus liable to make mistakes. Our system should be one which reduces the probability of error as far as possible. For example, research by Post Office engineers some years ago showed that the probability of incorrect dialling began to rise steeply if the length of the number increased to nine or more digits. (It is perhaps depressing to realize that most of us now have 9 or 10 digit telephone numbers.) If a system uses numbers for coding, mistakes may arise and probably will arise if the numbers grow beyond the limit indicated above; even if we use words, the likelihood of error still exists.[3]

Errors will have an effect on relevance, in that we shall get answers which are wrong; they will also affect recall, in that we shall miss items which we ought to find. We should therefore make sure that the system we use does not have a built in tendency to increase human error.

SPECIFICITY AND EXHAUSTIVITY

There are several other factors which affect the overall performance of an information retrieval system and its potential in terms of recall and relevance. First, we may consider *specificity*: the extent to which the system permits us to be precise when specifying the subject of a document we are processing. The higher the specificity, the more likely we are to be able to achieve high relevance, and conversely, with a system that permits us only limited precision we are likely to achieve reasonably high recall but correspondingly low relevance. In the previous example, if our system did not permit us to specify *Siamese* cats, we should have to look through all the items about cats before we could find out whether we had anything on that particular breed. Further, if the second item we found did relate to Siamese cats, there would be no guarantee that this would be the only one, or that any others would be found alongside it. If specificity is lacking, we are in fact reduced to the kind of sequential scanning that is necessary if our collections are not organized at all—though of course we have reduced the amount of material that we have to scan by partially specifying its subject content. If we are to obtain the maximum amount of control over our searching, the system must permit us to be precise in our specification of subjects; in fact, our specification should in every case be coextensive with the subject of the document. If we need to increase recall, we can always ignore part of our specification, but we cannot increase relevance by adding to it *at the search stage*. It is very important to keep clear the distinction between the INPUT to our system (*ie* the specifications of the documents we are adding), and the OUTPUT (*ie* the results of the searches we perform among these specifications). We cannot add to the input at the output stage; anything omitted at the input stage will remain outside the system, and will have to be replaced by sequential scanning of an unnecessarily large output. (We may however be able to use a systematic approach to help us formulate our search strategy, even though it is not part of the system used to specify the input.)

Specificity is a function of the system, but another important factor, *exhaustivity*, is the result of a management decision. This is the extent to which we analyse any given document to establish exactly what subject content we have to specify. We may distinguish between the overall theme of a document, and the subthemes which it may contain; for example, a description of a scientific experiment may be concerned overall with the purpose and results, but it will probably also contain a description of the apparatus used. In a large general library we may content ourselves with specifying the overall themes, giving perhaps an average of one to one and a half specifications per document, whereas in a small special library, anxious to exploit the stock to the maximum advantage, we may wish to index subthemes as well, giving perhaps dozens of specifications for every document. This is known as *depth indexing*, as opposed to the *summarization* of the first method. Depth indexing might indicate that a book is about Dryden, Wycherley, Congreve, Vanbrugh and Farquhar, while summarization might say that it was about Restoration drama. It would clearly be very difficult if not impossible to index *all* the subthemes in a document in a library catalogue or a bibliography (the index to the present work contains nearly 1,000 entries), so depth indexing is usually carried out in libraries where the needs of the readers can be foreseen fairly clearly; often depth indexing is applied to technical reports and similar documents which are relatively short and are therefore manageable. It involves the indexer in the exercise of judgment as to which themes and subthemes are worth noting. In choosing between depth indexing and summarization, the decision is ours and is not a function of the system. Recent research has shown, however, that there is a link between exhaustivity and specificity, in that there is little point in increasing exhaustivity unless the system being used has adequate specificity; depth indexing will not give improved access to the contents of a document unless the additional entries are specific.

A moment's thought should show that whereas specificity is a device to increase relevance at the cost of recall, exhaustivity works in the opposite direction, by increasing recall, but at the expense of relevance. A device which we may use to counteract this effect to some extent is *weighting*. In this, we try to show the significance of any particular specification by giving it a weight on a pre-established scale. For example, if we had a book on pets which dealt largely with dogs, we might give PETS a weight of 10/10, and DOGS, a weight of 8/10 or less. If it gave some information about dogs, but not much, we might give DOGS a low weighting of 2/10. The reader wanting high relevance now knows that this particular item can be ignored, at least for the time being, while the reader wanting high recall will have no difficulty in finding it.

EASE OF USE

Whatever system we choose to use, there are two persons who must find it usable: the person responsible for the input, *ie* the *indexer*, and the person trying to obtain an output, *ie* the *user*. At the input stage, how much skill does the indexer need to be able to use the system? Does it help to overcome deficiencies in his appreciation of the subjects he is dealing with? *Non omnia omnes possumus:* we cannot all be omniscient! Users often find it difficult to express exactly their needs; does the system help them to formulate a satisfactory search despite this? Is the physical form of the output acceptable? A system which presents the user with a set of documents, or at least abstracts, is likely to be more popular than one which gives merely a string of numbers.

TIME

Indexing takes time; searching takes time. By increasing our effort at the indexing stage—the input—we may well be able to reduce the amount of time we have to spend at the output stage in searching. On the other hand, in any given library situation, a proportion (which may be high) of the documents indexed will never be sought, and the effort used to index them will be wasted; if we concentrate our effort at the output stage by keeping our indexing to a minimum (for example by using abstracts or even whole texts for the input instead of subject specifications) and then perform complex searches to find relevant items, we can argue that we are eliminating a large amount of unnecessary work. As has already been mentioned, users cannot always specify exactly what it is they want, so any search will be a dialogue between the user and the system; the results of a first search will be used to modify or refine the question so that further searches can be per-

23

formed until such time as a satisfactory end point is reached. By concentrating our efforts on the searching rather than the indexing, we do not hamper this dialogue in any way, but we can very easily make use of such feedback in planning future search strategies. In a system where the effort is concentrated on the input, this may not be quite so easy, as the output cannot affect the input retrospectively; to take account of experience gained in searching we may have to re-index some items—*ie* increase the input effort still further.

At present, nearly all systems involve large amounts of input effort rather than transferring this to the output stage. As yet, the complicated search strategies necessary with the latter technique, together with the large amount of input information required, make it impractical in the normal library situation. The position may change as computers become more powerful and more commonly available, but even then questions of relative cost will arise.

ITERATIVE AND HEURISTIC SEARCHING

The idea of a dialogue between the user and the system is worthy of further examination. As has been pointed out above, users often find it difficult to express their needs precisely. In a conventional library, searches may be carried out by the user, or by the librarian acting for the user. When they are carried out by the user himself, the search will usually be modified as it progresses; each relevant document found tends to influence the user's decision as to what further information he requires. In many cases the clarification that results as the search is pursued leads to a situation where the user finishes up with an objective rather different from the one he started out with. Such a search, where the course of events is modified continuously in the light of knowledge being gained, may be described as *heuristic*. If on the other hand the search is carried out by the librarian, this continuous modification is not possible, since modifications of the librarian's knowledge do not affect the user. For this reason it is usual for the librarian to perform a first search and present the results to the user; the search strategy may then be modified in the light of the proportion of relevant documents among those resulting from this search. A second search may then be performed, and the process repeated until the user has what he wants. This kind of search, which is modified not continuously but at intervals, may be described as *iterative*. Both heuristic and iterative searches require

24

interaction between user and results, but heuristic searching eliminates the time delay between receiving the result of a search operation and using it to modify the search procedure.

Many information retrieval systems do not permit heuristic searching, for example most of those described in Part III of this book, whereas the conventional library card catalogue does. The importance of this should not be overestimated, but it is obviously a point to be considered when we are trying to estimate the relative value of different systems.[4]

BROWSING

We have assumed so far that the purpose of our system is to make it possible to find information on demand—that the users will approach it with some definite objective in mind, even though they may not, to begin with, have clarified this. However, this is by no means always the case; there will be many occasions when readers will approach the collection without any particular need in mind but wishing instead to be able to select items at random. To help in this situation, our system should permit *browsing;* a reader should be able to follow a casual train of thought as well as a planned search.

COST

Many of the factors affecting information retrieval systems are cost factors. We have to balance the cost of so organizing our libraries that we can find information when it is required, against the cost of not finding it at all, or finding it too late for it to be of use. In libraries serving industrial firms, for example, the cost of not finding information may be high; this is why ' hard headed businessmen ' add to their overheads by paying for extensive library services. (The term ' library services ' is here taken to include those denoted by the more elite term ' information services '.) On the other hand, public libraries have in the past tended to regard the exploitation of the information in their stocks as very much less important than its provision, because the cost to the community at large if one of its individual members fails to find information he requires is considerably less than the cost of organizing the material adequately. However, it is now being realized that the cost to the community of wasted information is in fact very high in terms of international competition, and more effort is being devoted to providing adequate services. We still have to find out a great deal about the cost effectiveness of various methods of organizing information, though we are beginning to learn something about their comparative efficiencies as systems. Despite our relative ignorance we must not ignore cost factors altogether, but they can usually only be studied in detail in a particular set of circumstances, and will therefore only be indicated in general terms in this text.

Modern trends in the evaluation of cost significance have been towards the idea of cost effectiveness. Most of the sophisticated devices developed in recent years have been aimed at improving relevance: reducing the number of unwanted documents revealed by a search, and thus reducing also the time taken to scan through the results and select those which are of use to us. However, if it costs more to use a sophisticated system for indexing than it would cost to look through the output of an unsophisticated system, there is no point in using the more advanced system. We have also to bear in mind that a relevance level which might be tolerable in a small system might well be quite unacceptable in a large nationwide mechanized system. If a search reveals ten documents, four of which are useful, this is not too bad; but if we have the same level with a collection a hundred times as large, we might well boggle at the thought of discarding six hundred documents from a total of a thousand. As yet only a limited amount of research has been carried out into this aspect of information retrieval, but it is obviously a field that is likely to be explored in more depth in the future, particularly with the development of the mechanized systems described in chapters 23 and 24.

PROBLEMS OF LINEAR ORDER

Knowledge is multi-dimensional: that is to say, subjects are related one to another in many different ways. In the example quoted earlier, it was assumed that Siamese cats were to be considered as pets, but it is obvious that they can be regarded in many other ways—as a branch of the zoological class *felidae,* or as originating in a particular part of the world, to name but two approaches. However, when we try to arrange items in our library or catalogue, we find that we are restricted to a linear, unidimensional, sequence, just as we are if we are reading a book. We cannot *display* multiple relationships and must therefore find some other means of showing them. If we have a book with no contents list and no index, the only way we can find a given item in it is to read it through. We have only one means of access: sequential scanning. However, we can overcome this problem by providing multiple access through the contents list and index, which permit us to go direct to the information we require; but the text of the book continues to display its information unidimensionally. The sequence in the book is chosen for us by the author and we cannot alter it, though we may to a large extent minimize the effect by adequate sign posting in the form of indexes and guiding.

We face exactly the same problem in organizing the information in our libraries. We can provide a sequence which we hope will be helpful to our readers, just as an author does, but we must recognize the need to cater for other modes of access. We must also realize that without these secondary modes of access we can only find information in one way, unless we are prepared to revert to sequential scanning. A simple example will demonstrate this in relation to a familiar tool, the telephone directory. These directories are arranged according to the surnames of the subscribers, set out in alphabetical order. Provided we know the subscriber's name, we can find his telephone number without much trouble, but we cannot perform the operation in reverse; we cannot find out the name of a subscriber whose number we know, unless we are prepared to look through the directory until we find it. To overcome this we can have a second sequence, arranged this time by number; but we still cannot find the number of a friend if we only know his forename and his address.

The problem is of course largely an economic one. We do not set up multiple sequences of books and other items in our libraries because it would cost too much to try to arrange a copy of a book at every point in the library where it might be related to other items. Nor can we afford to make multiple sequences in bibliographical tools which have to be printed and distributed. We might perhaps make several sequences in our records within the library, but even this will prove very expenpensive if we are to be consistent and comprehensive. However, just as we can overcome the problem in a book by providing multiple access through subsidiary sequences which lead us to the required points in our main sequence, so we can do the same thing in our information retrieval system. Different systems will permit us differing degrees of multiple access; the more flexible a system is in this respect, the more likely it is to be of value.

LITERARY WARRANT
No matter what our system may be, the information in it must be a function of the input; that is to say, our systems must take account of the relationships between subjects shown in the items we are in-

dexing. We may in addition build into it relationships between subjects of which we are aware *a priori*, through a study of knowledge *per se*, but if we restrict ourselves to a study of knowledge alone without taking into account knowledge as it is presented in recorded form, we shall find ourselves unable to specify subjects precisely. In other words, we are concerned with the organization of knowledge in libraries rather than the organization of knowledge on its own. The term *literary warrant* is used here to denote that our system must be based on the material we put into it rather than on purely theoretical considerations.

There is another aspect to this particular question. It is the output of the system which is important, since this is the whole purpose of the system. But we cannot know in advance what output will be required, at least not with any degree of precision, though we may be able to form an intelligent guess on the basis of past experience. So although it would be desirable to build up our system in such a way that it matched the required output, we are unable to do this since we do not know what the required output will be. We are obliged to use the input as our basis for building up the system, adding to this whatever is suggested by studies of knowledge outside the system. If we restrict ourselves to studies of knowledge outside the system we shall, by ignoring the input, be removing our system one stage further from the required output. In any subject area there will be an accepted corpus of knowledge, but each document we index may modify this; literary warrant implies a system that is able to accept this kind of change.

There is perhaps a danger that we may take a negative attitude to literary warrant: exclude from our system the possibility of catering for subjects which have not as yet appeared in our collections. This danger is usually associated with the older kind of enumerative system described below, but there have been more recent examples to demonstrate the problems that arise if we deliberately make our system a static one. Hospitality to new concepts as they are revealed by our collections is vital if we are to maintain the desired level of specificity.

The term literary warrant was used by Wyndham Hulme to denote a rather different kind of idea, though one basically similar.[5] He considered that if we have a document entitled, say, *Heat, light and sound,* then that represents a subject for which we should make provision in our system. However, most of these are not genuine subjects but aggregates of subjects resulting from the bibliographical accident

28

of being bound within the same pair of covers. They are better treated as separate topics and indexed as such. This situation should not be confused with that of a genuine interaction between subjects, *eg* the effect of heat on sound (discussed in more detail on p 125); this is a different kind of situation for which we do have to make provision. Hulme's use of the term is rarely found now, though his ideas were largely reflected in the practice of the Library of Congress, and have indeed developed into the modern theory already outlined.

HEADING AND DESCRIPTION

We use the terms in our indexing system to name the subjects of the documents in our collection, but obviously a user who has found the correct subject description will require in addition some details of the documents to which that description applies. We can therefore divide an entry in the system into two parts, the heading and the description.

The *heading* is the subject description which determines whereabouts in the sequence we shall find any given entry. (The present work is restricted to considerations of the subject approach; in a full catalogue, headings will include names of authors and titles as well as subjects.) In an alphabetical system, headings will consist of words, while in a systematic arrangement it is the notation that is used for the headings. The *description* is the part of an entry which gives us information about a document, and will therefore contain all those factors which serve to *identify*. There are various sets of rules for the compilation of document descriptions, *eg* those in the Anglo-American code, or the Library of Congress *Rules for descriptive cataloguing*, but for our purposes here we need only note their existence. The presence of a document description enables us to make a useful distinction: a *subject entry* consists of a heading from the index vocabulary together with a document description, while an *index entry* or *cross-reference* leads us from a heading with no document description to an entry. The heading from which we make a cross-reference may be one which appears only in the entry vocabulary, in which case the reference is a *see* reference, leading us from a heading not used to one which is used; or it may appear in both entry and index vocabulary, in which case the reference is a *see also* reference linking two headings which are both used, in order to show some kind of relationship.

It should be noted that in some systems the descriptions may be in the form of a number (an accessions number or document number) rather than the detailed information about author, title, imprint and so on which we find in, for example, a library card catalogue. The links between related headings may form an integral part of the main sequence of entries, as in the dictionary catalogue; part of a subsidiary sequence, as in the classified catalogue; or quite separate, as is usual in post-coordinate systems. These points will be clarified in due course; at this stage it is important to realize that these features, like the others in this chapter, are common to all information retrieval systems. Their presence or absence can make a great deal of difference to the ease with which we can retrieve information.

BIBLIOGRAPHY

1 Vickery, B C: *Techniques of information retrieval*. Chapters 1 and 2.

2 The concept of recall and relevance was introduced by the ' Cranfield project ' workers. The term relevance is used here in its subjective sense; in experiments designed to measure the effectiveness and efficiency of indexing systems it is usual to replace relevance as far as possible by an objective measurement, called *precision*. For further discussion of the project see chapter 23. Many of the ideas developed in this chapter owe their first formulation to this important project, which may be said to be the foundation of the integrated approach presented here.

3 Conrad, R and Hille, B A: ' Memory for long telephone numbers '. *Post Office telecommunications journal, 10,* 1957, 37-39.

4 Lancaster, F W: ' Interaction between requesters and a large mechanized retrieval system '. *Information storage and retrieval, 4 (2)* 1968, 239-252. The development of this idea arose during the survey carried out by Lancaster of the working of the MEDLARS project, discussed in chapters 23 and 24.

5 Hulme, E Wyndham: *Principles of book classification*. Association of Assistant Librarians, 1950 (AAL Reprints no 1). Originally published in the *Library Association record*, 1911-1912.

CHAPTER 3

The document as evidence

How can we establish the subject of a document so that we can specify it? The obvious answer is to read it, but this is not always as helpful as it might be. We do not have time to read the whole of every item we add to our stock, and even if we did we might not understand it. There are certain short cuts we may take; we may read the contents list, or the preface or introduction, or the publisher's blurb on the dustjacket; the author may have prepared an abstract if the item in question is a periodical article or technical report; we may turn to the claims in a patent specification. All of these will give some indication of the subject and will suggest certain lines of thought if we want to pursue the matter further, for example in a technical dictionary. Our system may itself give us some assistance by showing various relationships between subjects.

There is of course one part of the book in which the author himself usually tries to define the subject: the title. In many cases this will give us a very clear indication of what a book is about; however, there are also cases in which the title will not be of any great help, and some in which it is of no help at all because it has been chosen to attract attention rather than state subject coverage. In the first category we might place: *The heat treatment of metals,* and, *High-speed analogue computers;* in the second: *The teaching of commercial subjects in secondary schools* (what are ' commercial subjects '?), and *The opening of the Canadian West* (pioneering? transport?); and in the third: *Supper in the evening,* and *One pair of hands,* neither of which gives us any clue at all as to the nature of the subject. Authors often try to generalize in the titles they select, so that the subject area covered by the document may in fact be rather narrower than is implied by its title. So titles may be of help in tracing particular documents if the user remembers them, but are of more limited help as the basis of a complete system; they can suggest what subject it is we are trying to specify, but lack precision as specifications themselves. In addition, if we have two items on the same subject, the authors will almost certainly have tried to find two different titles, so any system based on their use is bound to have low recall, though it may give us high relevance.

However, though different authors may try to select different groups of words to name their books on the same subject, these different groups of words may well contain the same significant words. Consider the following titles:

Manual of library classification
Library classification on the march
Introduction to library classification
Prolegomena to library classification
A modern outline of library classification.

It is clear that the significant words in each title are the same, and might be used as the basis of a retrieval system. There are various methods of using the key words in titles for indexing, all of which depend on manipulation of the title to give multiple entries, one for each significant word.

CATCHWORD TITLE INDEXING

Catchword indexing has been used for many years in such bibliographical tools as *British books in print* and in the indexes issued by periodicals, for example *Nature*. The method may be rather haphazard if rules are not set down first; the title *Field plotting by Fourier synthesis and digital computation* needs careful manipulation if all the concepts present are to be used as index entry points:

Field plotting by Fourier synthesis and digital computation
Plotting, field, by Fourier synthesis and digital computation
Fourier synthesis and digital computation, field plotting by
Synthesis, Fourier, and digital computation, field plotting by
Digital computation and Fourier synthesis, field plotting by
Computation, digital, and Fourier synthesis, field plotting by.

It is clear that this requires rather more than a purely clerical operation, but gives a reasonable statement of the sense at each entry. Straightforward rearrangement would give the following:

Field plotting by Fourier synthesis and digital computation
Plotting by Fourier synthesis and digital computation, Field
Fourier synthesis and digital computation, Field plotting by
Synthesis and digital computation, Field plotting by Fourier
Digital computation, Field plotting by Fourier synthesis and
Computation, Field plotting by Fourier synthesis and digital.

Because this splits pairs of words like *field plotting* and *Fourier synthesis* when the second becomes the entry word, it gives entries which may be rather less helpful than the previous example, but this method does not require any intellectual effort.

KEY-WORD IN CONTEXT (KWIC) INDEXING

A method which does not require any intellectual effort may be used on a machine, and one particular development of catchword indexing is now widely used to produce title indexes on computers. The method was used by Crestadoro to compile a catalogue of the Manchester Public Library during the nineteenth century, but its value for computer manipulation was established by H P Luhn of IBM.[1] Each significant word in a title becomes an entry point, as in catchword indexing, but instead of appearing at the left hand side of the page the entry word appears in the middle, with the rest of the title on either side. A long title may have to be split, so that it appears with the end preceding the beginning, but having the filing word in the middle of the page helps to keep down the number of times this happens. The title used in the previous example will give rise to the following entries:

digital computation/	Field plotting by Fourier synthesis and
computation/ Field	plotting by Fourier synthesis and digital
Field plotting by	Fourier synthesis and digital computation/
plotting by Fourier	synthesis and digital computation/ Field
Fourier synthesis and	digital computation/ Field plotting by
synthesis and digital	computation/ Field plotting by Fourier.

As with catchword indexing, the entries resulting from the manipulation of the title are filed in alphabetical sequence of filing word. Insignificant words are ignored and do not give rise to index entries. A good example of a computer-produced KWIC index is *Chemical titles*, which indexes several hundred periodicals within a few weeks of publication.

KEY-WORD OUT OF CONTEXT (KWOC) INDEXING

Because the filing word is not in the normal place, KWIC indexing seems unfamiliar, and a further development of this kind of title manipulation is to move the key-word back to its normal place at the beginning of the line, but to follow it by the complete title, rather than by some altered form as in catchword indexing. This gives the advantage of having a familiar appearance—filing word at left—and also of presenting the whole title as it stands, but to set against this it is not so effective as KWIC indexing in bringing together titles which contains the same *pairs* of words. Consider the following titles:

Manual of library classification
Library classification on the march
Introduction to library classification
Prolegomena to library classification
A modern outline of library classification
The hospital library service in Lincoln
The National Library of Canada
Mechanized acquisition procedures in the University of Maryland Library
The King's Library in the British Museum
Library education
Public library administration

If we use catchword indexing and edit the titles, the five items on library classification will appear together under both library and classification; if we do not edit the titles, they will appear together under library but not under classification. If we use KWIC indexing, they will appear together under both; if we use KWOC, they will be scattered under both.

The following table sets out the index entries for these items that will appear at the word ' library ' :

1) *Unmanipulated catchword indexing*
Library administration, Public
Library classification, Introduction to
Library classification, Manual of
Library classification, A modern outline of
Library classification on the march
Library classification, Prolegomena to
Library education
Library in the British Museum, The King's
Library, Mechanized acquisition procedures in the University of Maryland
Library of Canada, The National
Library service in Lincoln, The hospital.

2) *Manipulated catchword indexing*
Library classification, Introduction to
Library classification, Manual of

Library classification, A modern outline of
Library classification on the march
Library classification, Prolegomena to
Library education
Library, The King's, in the British Museum
Library, National, of Canada
Library, Public, administration
Library service, hospital, in Lincoln
Library, University of Maryland, mechanized acquisition procedures
  in.

3) *KWIC indexing*

University of Maryland	library/ Mechanized acquisition procedures
Public	library administration/
Introduction to	library classification/
Manual of	library classification/
A modern outline of	library classification/
Prolegomena to	library classification/
	Library classification on the march/
	Library education/
The King's	Library in the British Museum/
The National	Library of Canada/
The hospital	library service in Lincoln/.

(NB When using a computer it is usual to restrict entries to one line
only; long titles may lose some words, as seen above and below.)

4) *KWOC indexing*

Library A modern outline of library classification
Library Introduction to library classification
Library Library classification on the march
Library Library education
Library Manual of library classification
Library Mechanized acquisition procedures in the University of
        Maryland
Library Prolegomena to library classification
Library Public library administration
Library The hospital library service in Lincoln
Library The King's Library in the British Museum
Library The National Library of Canada.

Using these systems, each title is liable to give rise to a number
of entries: as many as there are significant terms, in fact. For this

reason, they are normally used as indexes, *ie* guides leading to entries in a separate list, rather than as methods of arrangement of items or full entries.

Looked at according to the criteria established for information systems in general, those using titles for their sole source of information do not stand up very well. Though relevance may be high, in that a title found by looking for a particular word is likely to be useful, we may have to look through a number of entries at that word before finding a title that looks like the topic we want; in other words, once we have selected a set of titles, we are likely to find that a good proportion of them are useful, but we will probably have to search through quite a number of entries before we can select our set. Recall, however, is certain to be low; we have no means of linking related topics (other than our own knowledge, which is outside the system), and as we have already seen, in describing the same subjects, authors are likely to go out of their way to use different terms. We can only be as specific as the author permits, and in many cases a title gives only a broad description of the subject matter in an article. Similarly, we are limited as far as exhaustivity is concerned by the extent to which the author thinks it necessary to include detail in his title.

The major advantage of indexing systems based on titles is that little or no intellectual effort is involved in putting items into the system. Indeed, KWIC and KWOC were specifically intended for machine manipulation; all that is necessary is for the titles to be produced in machine-readable form, *eg* punched cards, and the computer can then generate the appropriate entries and print them out very speedily (KWIC is an unusually apposite homophonic acronym), without any of the delays associated with normal indexing processes. This does however raise a point which can be of some importance: how are the significant words selected? The discussion and examples cited earlier assumed that entry would be made under each significant word, but obviously a computer cannot select particular words unless it is previously programmed to do so. In practice, the method is inverted; instead of significant words being selected, non-significant words are rejected. A *stop list* is compiled of words which are of no value as indexing terms, *eg* a, the, and, very; the computer is then programmed to delete any entries which might arise under these terms. IBM has a standard stop list containing 17 such terms, which is supplied as part of the program. All other words will give rise to index entries, which may lead to a situation where useful entries are swamped by a mass of entries under terms which are of very dubious value; it is therefore usual to compile a second stop list, based on experience, of words unlikely to be useful in a particular subject area or library, and this can reduce substantially the number of unwanted entries in the index. IBM's own secondary stop list contains about three hundred words which they have found to be without value in their information retrieval operations, but this list might well include some terms which another library would find useful. There will also be words which occur so rarely that it is not thought necessary to include them in the stop list even though they are not useful; in such cases, one must be prepared to accept that there will be entries in the index which no one will find useful, but as a general rule we may accept that it is better to have a few entries which are not useful than to delete some which are.

The problems of exhaustivity and specificity can be overcome to some extent by using what is called *enriched* KWIC or KWOC. Additional terms are inserted into the title or added at the end to give further index entries. This method obviously involves intellectual effort in the selection of the additional terms and thus may be said to negate the advantage of speed, but work is at present in progress within the United Kingdom Atomic Energy Authority to evaluate an enriched KWOC index in comparison with the present system using UDC.

There are occasions when a reader can *identify* a document by its title; there are in fact indications that in many situations a reader is likely to remember a title more accurately than an author's correct name.[3] In such cases KWIC and similar indexes can serve both for subject information retrieval and document retrieval. The index entries, which are *headings,* must of course be linked to *descriptions* of the appropriate documents; this is usually done by means of a number which leads to a separate file of full entries. A typical KWIC index will thus consist of three parts: an accessions file, in which each item is given its identifying number; the keyword index based on the titles; and an author index. (In the case of a periodical, the page number might take the place of the accessions number.)

In recent years there has been considerable pressure on authors to give their papers meaningful titles which can be used in KWIC indexes. This has mainly been in the United States, where the lead was taken by the Engineering Societies and the American Chemical Society, and has been followed by the US Government. In science and technology generally it would seem that indexes using titles are likely to be more widely used in the future, because of the very large numbers of documents to be dealt with, though it is perhaps worth noting that KWIC indexes are rather unsuccessful with patents, where the title is often deliberately vague or misleading. In other subject areas, such as the social sciences, indexes based on titles are likely to be less useful because of the problems of terminology. They are also of very limited value if foreign language material is included in the collection, unless the titles are first translated.

The above discussion suggests that title-based indexes are better suited to *current notification, ie* informing readers of what is being published now and thus covering relatively small numbers of documents, than to *retrospective searching* among large collections, for which more tightly organized systems are probably more effective.[2]

CITATION INDEXING

Documents of value are likely to contain bibliographies; this is the way in which the author shows the foundations on which he has built. There is a link between the document and each item cited in its bibliography; we can invert this, and say that there is a link between the original item and the document citing it. By scanning a large number of documents we could establish a much larger number of such inverted links (since documents normally cite more than one item in their bibliographies). If we now file these according to the items cited, we shall bring together all the documents which have included a given item in their list of references. This is the basic principle of citation indexing.

Once again, though the idea itself is not new—it has been used in legal literature for many years—the use of computer techniques has led to the development of an important new service, Science Citation Index.[4] For this, some 2,000 scientific periodicals are scanned, including all those in the NLL's 'A' store—those most frequently borrowed —and all the bibliographic links found are fed into a computer. This then generates a citation index, corporate index, and source index. The stored information is also used for an SDI service, ASCA (Automatic Subject Citation Alert) and a subject index, the Permuterm index, which enters each item under pairs of significant words found in the title.

To use a citation index it is necessary to have the reference of a relevant document, but it is often the case that a search starts from such a basis. From the citation index we can find which more recent articles have cited the one we already know (assuming that it is not too recent to have been cited by others). We can then turn to the articles we have found; if they are not relevant we can discard them, but if they are relevant we can look to see what other articles they cite. With these citations we can go back to the citation index and continue to expand the search. By this process of re-cycling we can compile a large bibliography from our single starting point.

Since every item in the periodicals covered is entered, we can follow up corrections and amendments to previously published articles. These often contain important information, but tend to be ignored by conventional abstracting and indexing services. This advantage is of course not inherent in citation indexing, but reflects the cost of SCI when compared with conventional services in its field.

Compiling a bibliography manually using the re-cycling technique described above can be tedious, but it can of course be done quite simply by the computer. A development which is of interest is the idea of *bibliographic coupling*. Two articles which both cite another earlier article must have something in common; if they both cite two earlier articles, the linking is increased; while if their bibliographies had half a dozen earlier articles in common we should be justified in assuming that they covered very much the same subject. In other words, the articles cited by an author are to a considerable extent a reflection of the subject he is writing about. The idea of bibliographic coupling has been developed at MIT (Massachusetts Institute of Technology) in Project TIP.[5] In this, some 1,200 articles a month are entered; the information given for each includes author, author's affiliation, title, citations, and bibliographic reference. The system has been shown to give good results, relying on bibliographic coupling to reveal articles on the same subject.

The big advantage of such systems as Science Citation Index and Project TIP is that they require no intellectual effort at the input stage, but rely solely on the details to be found with each item—title, author, and citations. They do assume that authors are familiar with the literature of their subject and will cite it appropriately (though we should remember that what may seem to be an inappropriate citation may in fact be a very interesting example of interdisciplinary development), but require no indexing by human effort; their use thus requires no attempt on our part at formulating a subject description— often a difficult task when we are using conventional indexes. To search the literature using these tools, all we need is a relevant article to start with—to prime the pump, so to speak. It is likely that we shall see more tools of this kind in the future.

TEXT SEARCHING

Title indexing and citation indexing can be carried out by manual techniques, though we normally think of them now more in the context of computer processing. The kind of abstract or whole text searching mentioned earlier (p. 23) is essentially a computer technique. It is not unreasonable to argue that the clearest statement of the author's subject is his text, and that this therefore provides the easiest access to it. By searching the text or a detailed abstract, we again do away with the need for intellectual effort at the indexing stage. In view of the quantity of information to be processed, and the limited number of people qualified to handle it, any method of reducing the burden must be considered very seriously. However, we must still apply the same criteria as we would to any other system, and it seems possible that too high recall combined with too low a relevance level may be a problem with whole text searching. We can also not ignore the question of cost; most of the work that has been done on text searching has been carried out on collections which are relatively small. Computer techniques are discussed at greater length in chapter 24; those mentioned here are included because they represent methods which use only information given to us with the document.

BIBLIOGRAPHY

1 Luhn, H P: *Keyword in context index for technical literature*. IBM, 1959. See also chapter 24 ref 15, for the collected works of H P Luhn.

2 The NLL publishes a regular KWIC index to conference proceedings received, and there are other published services, *eg Chemical titles*. Students should scan one or more of these carefully to evaluate it. See also Vickery, B C: *Techniques of information retrieval*, p 188+.

3 Ayres, F H: 'Authors versus title: a comparative study of the accuracy of the information which the user brings to the library catalogue'. *Journal of documentation*, 24 (4) December 1968, 266-272.

4 Garfield, E: '*Science citation index*: a new dimension in indexing'. *Science, 144* (3619) 1964, 649-654.
Garfield, E: 'Primordial concepts, citation indexing, and historiobibliography'. *Journal of library history*, 2 (3) 1967, 235-249.

Cawkell, A E: 'Citations in chemistry'. *Chemistry in Britain*, 6 (10) 1970, 414-416.

Keen, E M: 'Citation indexes'. *Aslib proceedings, 16* (8) 1964, 246-251.

Martyn, J: 'An examination of citation indexes'. *Aslib proceedings 17* (6) 1965, 184-196.

Students should see either a set of *Science citation index* or (with caution) the publicity matter distributed by the Institute for Scientific Information.

5 Kessler, M M: 'The MIT technical information project'. *Physics today, 18* (3) 1965, 28-36.

CHAPTER 4

Subject analysis

We have seen in chapter 3 that systems which rely on the document itself, particularly those using the title, tend to be unsatisfactory in many ways. We are thus obliged to devise our own system of headings, and the most satisfactory way of doing this is to begin by analysing the subjects that we meet in a collection of documents in order to determine exactly what subjects we can identify and what the relationships between them may be. We soon find that subjects in documents fall into two large categories: those in which only one concept is involved, which we may call *simple* subjects, and those in which more than one concept is involved, which we may call *composite* subjects.

PARADIGMS AND SYNTAGMAS

If we study table 1 carefully, we shall see that the subjects listed there show various kinds of relationship, but that whereas some of these are permanent (aluminium is always a non ferrous metal; polyethylene is always a plastic) others are of a rather different kind (heat treatment is something done to aluminium, windows are something made of aluminium; film is a form of polyethylene) in which subjects which are normally distinct are brought together to form a composite more specific than any of its elements considered separately.

1 Metals	10 Plastics
2 Ferrous metals	11 Plastic films
3 Iron	12 Polyethylene
4 Non-ferrous metals	13 Polyethylene films
5 Aluminium	14 Plastic bags
6 Heat treatment of metals	15 Polyethylene bags
7 Heat treatment of non-ferrous metals	16 Welding of plastics
	17 Welding of plastic bags
8 Heat treatment of aluminium	18 Welding of polyethylene bags
9 Aluminium windows	

TABLE 1 : Related subjects

J C Gardin[1] has introduced the grammatical terms *paradigms* and *syntagmas* to distinguish between these two kinds of relationship. It will be seen that whereas paradigmatic relationships can be established without reference to any particular collection of items, the syntagmatic relationships arising in such a collection may well be restricted to that collection. What we can do is to establish the kinds of syntagma which may arise in any given subject area, but we cannot prophesy exactly which individual syntagmas may arise as we build up our collection; that is to say, provision for syntagmas must essentially be based on literary warrant.

Paradigms show the various aspects of *genus-species* relationships: one subject (non-ferrous metals) may include another (aluminium), or form part of another (metals), or be of equal rank with another (ferrous metals). In this work, the term genus-species will be preferred, to avoid confusion with the grammatical meaning of paradigm, *ie* a set of words having the same stem. On the other hand, syntagmatic relationships may be of various kinds and are directional; when a dog bites a man it isn't news, and an album of photographs is not the same as photographs of an album. Our system should therefore permit us to show not only subjects, but also the relationships between them, if we are to achieve specificity. The relationship is in fact part of the specification, and to specify a composite subject precisely we need the individual subjects involved, the relationship between them and its direction.

Relationships can be of many kinds and are often difficult to specify precisely. In some systems discussed later, notably those of Farradane (p 74) and Gardin (p 379) it is the relationships which are emphasized, whereas in others they are completely ignored. In any case, relationships on their own are of very limited value; we use them to link subjects we have named, rather than as retrieval factors in their own right. But how do we set about naming subjects? Table 2 shows that there are a number of problems which arise when we try to carry out this apparently simple operation.

SYNONYMS

The English language is rich in synonyms and near-synonyms, because it has roots in both Teutonic and Romance languages. While it is true that Wordsworth's ode would sound less impressive as *Hints of deathlessness* than it does as *Intimations of immortality*, the former is as correct a formulation of the subject as the latter. Should we try to eliminate synonyms and thus achieve a higher degree of consistency?

1 Dictionary of applied chemistry
2 Encyclopedia of chemical technology
3 Glossary of industrial chemistry
4 Automation in business and industry
5 Automatic production methods
6 The technical illustrator
7 Graphic science: engineering drawing
8 Engineering graphics
9 A survey of astronomy
10 The earth, the planets and the stars
11 The moon
12 Electronic computers
13 Highspeed analogue computers
14 Understanding digital computers
15 Screw extrusion of plastics
16 Heat treatment of metals
17 The ballet in Britain
18 Local government in Great Britain
19 The inheritors: the story of man and the world he has made
20 Let's learn to fly

1, 2 and 3 Synonyms; order of concepts; order of terms
4 and 5   Synonyms
6, 7 and 8 Synonyms (US and British terminology differ)
9, 10 and 11 Is a book about the moon a book about astronomy?
12, 13 and 14 Order of terms: Computers, analogue, or Analogue computers
15, 16, 17, 18 Order of concepts: Metals, heat treatment, or Heat treatment of metals?
19, 20 Choice of most appropriate term: civilization, culture, history of technology, anthropology—all very broad terms with correspondingly shallow meanings.

TABLE 2: Problems of naming subjects

There are many situations where we have to make this decision; for example, many subjects have both a common name and a scientific one, American terminology differs from English, authors differ in their usage. For example, a technical article will use technical terms, whereas a popular article on the same subject will use popular terminology; by not merging synonyms, we will in effect be keeping these

44

two papers on the same subject apart. A search based on the technical terms will retrieve technical papers only, while one based on popular terms will retrieve only those using that set of terms. If we do not merge the various synonyms into one preferred form, we shall lower the recall of our system, though we will probably get high relevance.

A further problem arises when we attempt to deal with paradigms in the strict grammatical sense, *ie* different forms of the same stem. Weld, welding, welded, welder all have the same basic concept as their root, but the first may be a noun describing the join made by this process, or it may be a verb denoting the process; the second is a verbal noun denoting the process; the third is an adjective describing an object treated by the process; and the fourth is a noun denoting someone using the process. We only need to define the first of these terms; the others are then defined for us by their grammatical relationship to the first. A user may well think in terms of one of these when his interests are actually rather wider; he thinks of the process, but is interested in the results of the process also, or vice versa. By using only one form we can increase recall while still maintaining a high relevance in the items we find. However, we may well find a conflict between the use of only one form and the need for specificity. We may also find it useful to merge antonyms; there are occasions when material on a topic is relevant to a study of its opposite, for example indulgence and abstention.

HOMOGRAPHS

The same spelling is sometimes used for different words, which may or may not be pronounced the same, *eg* sow and sow, China and china. This may arise by a figure of speech such as metonymy, in which we use part of a description to mean the whole; it may be through analogy, for example when terms such as ' filter ' from hydraulic engineering are used by electrical engineers; or it may be simply an etymological accident. Whatever the cause, there is likely to be confusion if we do nothing to distinguish such words. One way of doing this is to qualify each by another word in parenthesis to show the context and thus the meaning, *eg*

PITCH (Bitumen)
PITCH (Music)
PITCH (Football)
PITCH (Baseball).

45

If we do not distinguish homographs we shall get reduced relevance; the seriousness of this will depend on the coverage of our system. For example, if our collection only covers music there will be no problem with the word Pitch, since other meanings than the musical are unlikely to arise at the input stage.

ONE WORD OR MORE

We have already seen that in any given entry in the telephone directory we can find only the first word, the surname, but there are in fact additional problems if our subject names are more than one word long. In order to separate them, we may need to introduce other symbols, for example the comma; we may be in some doubt as to what to do with insignificant words such as prepositions and conjunctions. Where do we find *Smith's* in relation to *Smith, Smithers* and *Smithson*? Where do we find *Galliher & Huguely* in relation to *Galliher Chas E*? These are simple examples taken from a telephone directory, and the rules governing their filing can soon be learnt—but we do have to have rules. Similarly, we must have rules if the subject specifications we use contain more than one word; the simplest arrangement is one where all the entries contain one word only.

Unfortunately, this is not possible. Many concepts cannot be expressed in one word; new subjects often grow out of old and are described, at least to start with, by a phrase, *eg* solid state physics. In some cases a new word is coined to describe the new topic: television, nucleonics; in other cases we are likely to have to continue to use a phrase indefinitely: mother of pearl, electrical engineering.

If we do use one word, it is often preferable to use the plural form of a noun. We tend to think of things rather than actions, so nouns are preferable to verbal forms; and if we think of something in general terms, we usually denote it by the plural: birds rather than bird, capacitors rather than capacitor. However, there are occasions when the plural has a slightly different meaning from the singular; war represents a generalized concept, whereas wars refers to a series of events. If we do specify an action, this again will be in the singular, usually the present participle of the verb: sailing, teaching; here again the plural has a rather different connotation.

COMPOSITE SUBJECTS

So far we have been discussing only single concepts, but we have already seen that our system must be prepared to accept subjects in

46

which more than one basic concept is present: not merely aluminium, polyethylene, windows, films, heat treatment, but also heat treatment of aluminium, aluminium windows, polyethylene films. These present us with a further set of problems, since we now have to decide not only the form of the individual elements in a subject but also the order in which we put them. This is very important, since we must help our users as much as possible by filing subjects where they will look for them; we must also be consistent, so that we and the users know what the rules for finding any given subject are. Finally, we must realize that any element in a heading other than the first is hidden unless we take steps to reveal it by making it, in its turn, the first element in a heading. We have to discover some means of telling us which is the element in a composite subject most likely to come to a user's mind if he is looking for the subject: a significance order. In a special library this may not be too difficult; we can establish in many cases a significance order which will reflect the known usage of our readers. But what of the general library, attempting to serve each and every user? We have to try to find rules which will be valid in this *neutral* situation, bearing in mind that some part of the meaning may be inherent in the order in which the concepts involved are presented. For example, *guide dogs* for the *blind* does not mean the same thing as *blind guide dogs,* though the words involved are the same. In effect, in addition to the problems involved in the selection of terms, we have to look at the problems involved in syntagmatic relationships, since these can affect the meaning of the terms we have selected.

INDEXING LANGUAGES

A system for naming subjects in the way we have described is called an *indexing language,* and, like any other language, it will consist of two parts: *vocabulary* and *syntax.* If we use terms as they appear in documents without modification, we are using *natural language.* However, as has been seen, this can lead to many problems, such as those arising from the use by different authors of different words to denote the same idea—synonyms—which lead to a decrease in recall. Another problem is that we can often express the same idea in more than one way using the same or similar words but altering the kind of phrase: child psychology or psychology of children; adult education or education of adults. For these reasons, nearly all systems introduce a measure of control over the terms used; that is to say, we use a *controlled vocabulary.* We often find also that the flexible syntax of natural lan-

47

guage is formalized to permit only certain constructions; instead of heat treatment of aluminium we use aluminium, heat treatment; instead of children's libraries and libraries for children we use libraries, children's. We are then using a *structured* language. A controlled vocabulary is part of an *artificial* indexing language, as is a formalized structure. The extreme example of an artificial language is the notation of a classification scheme; instead of the natural language terms heat treatment of aluminium, or the more formalized aluminium, heat treatment, we use 669.71.04.

The use of an artificial language enables us to use *concept indexing* rather than *term indexing*. In term indexing, we rely on the words used by each author to give us the subject descriptions we require, and hope that when we are trying to find information we can match the different terms used by different authors. In concept indexing, we try to establish a standard description for each concept and use that description each time it is appropriate, whether it has been used by the author himself or not. When we are searching our files, we again use the standardized descriptions, and should be able to match these much more consistently and reliably. Natural language is very flexible, particularly in a highly developed language such as English; this is a tremendous advantage for the author, who can vary his terminology to maintain the reader's interest, but is a handicap to the indexer, who is more concerned with the ideas conveyed than with the niceties of a graceful literary style.

If we use words for our subject descriptions, then the only way in which we can arrange them is alphabetically; if we try to arrange them any other way we shall not be able to find them when we want them, except by sequential scanning. But there are many occasions when an alphabetical order may not be particularly helpful to us; for example, if we want to follow the progress of a railway train, an alphabetical list of stops and the time the train arrives at each will be much less use than a list in chronological order. An artificial language such as the notation of a classification scheme can permit us to arrange concepts in any order we wish; in particular, it permits us to group similar concepts together to show a relationship between them. We can show that metals, ferrous metals, iron, aluminium, non-ferrous metals and similar terms denote concepts which are closely related, by actually bringing them together in our arrangement.

It is possible to take concept indexing a stage further than the simple standardization of subject descriptions. We can identify the same basic concept wherever it occurs, even though it may not have any common factor in the terms used for it. We might connect stream, current, flux, flow and evolution as being manifestations of motion; expurgation, disinfection, refining, Bowdlerization and whitewashing as being manifestations of cleaning. A list of terms showing their classification according to the ideas they represent is called a *thesaurus*, and the two examples quoted are taken from perhaps the most famous example, Roget's *Thesaurus of English words and phrases*. Such a list can only be compiled by concept indexing, and can form the first stage of development of a completely artificial indexing language. It should be noted that the term thesaurus has been somewhat abused by compilers of subject headings lists for post-coordinate indexing (*cf* p 317); the closest approach to a thesaurus in Roget's sense is a faceted classification scheme with its index rather than an alphabetical system.

PRE-COORDINATE AND POST-COORDINATE SYSTEMS

We have to be able to index both single concepts and composite subjects using our indexing language, but there are two ways of approaching this. The first is to treat composite subjects as units. To do this, we first analyse them into the single concepts, then select the 'correct' term from the vocabulary (this may be a piece of notation, or a preferred synonym) for each concept, and finally arrange these in a particular order dictated by the structure of the language. The resulting heading represents the subject as a whole, and we file an entry under it in the system with descriptions of any documents to which it applies. When we are searching, we formulate headings in the same way, and use these as a basis for matching what we can find in the system. However, this can lead to difficulties, particularly when the headings we use as a basis for searching differ slightly from those used already in the system; these difficulties arise from the structure that we have imposed, and are discussed later under the headings CITATION ORDER (p 89) and MULTIPLE ENTRY SYSTEMS (p. 179). One solution is to abandon the use of structure altogether, and this is the second way of approaching composite subjects. The process of analysis is the same, and the selection of the correct term is the same, but we no longer combine these terms in a pre-determined order; instead, we file descriptions of the appropriate documents under each single concept. In searching, we have to have some method of combining concepts, or *coordinating* them, so that we can perform the required matching operation, and this second method is often known as *coordinate* indexing. It is however more useful to call it *post-coordinate*, to

49

contrast it with the first method which we may call *pre-coordinate*. This emphasizes the fact that coordination takes place in both systems, but at a different stage of the proceedings. As a reflection of the history of the subject, pre-coordinate systems are dealt with first in this book, and the discussion of the problems which arise in their use leads logically to the section on post-coordinate systems.

If we are to be consistent in the use of an indexing language, we must record somewhere any decisions we take, for example on the choice of preferred synonyms or significance order. The record thus compiled becomes our *authority file*, and it may be our own entirely or it may be based to a greater or lesser degree on a published list. In the interests of standardization, it is usual for libraries to make use of published lists, and indeed Part II and Part IV of the present work are given over to descriptions of such schemes. However, they may present a problem summed up in Ranganathan's phrase: *autonomy for the classifier*.

Knowledge, as we have stressed, is not static, and an indexing language needs continuous revision if it is to remain current. Furthermore, since general schemes may not relate to the literary warrant of any particular library, they may exclude some subjects which we find represented in our collections. What are we to do if we find that this is the case? Can we insert a new heading in the authority list ourselves, or must we wait until the compilers have produced a new edition or an amendment sheet? If the first of these is the case, the system is said to be *open*, while the second situation is a *closed* system. Dewey saw the problem at an early stage, and suggested that if a particular topic was not represented we should classify a document at the nearest inclusive heading, on the theory that new subjects usually grow from the splitting up, or ' fission ', of already existing subjects. The central compilers would then make a specific place in a subsequent edition for the new topic, an optimistic hope which has not always been borne out by practice.

Since alphabetical order is self-evident, it is rather easier to insert a new heading in an alphabetical list than in one systematically arranged; all that we need to know is the form of a heading, *eg* whether we should use the singular or plural form of a noun. Alphabetical lists such as Sears and LCSH have rules for the insertion of headings for named individuals of a species, *eg* persons, flowers, places, animals. It is rather more difficult to establish in advance the correct piece of notation for a new topic in a classification scheme, since we are dealing with a wholly artificial language, and no satisfactory solution has been proposed. Ranganathan's *seminal mnemonics*, discussed on p 136, offer a temporary solution, but one in which the arrangement is dictated by the notation rather than the needs of the subject. It is for this reason that the method of revision adopted by a classification scheme is so important, and this point is discussed in relation to each of the schemes studied in Part II.

ENUMERATION AND SYNTHESIS
In a pre-coordinate indexing language we have to provide for both single concepts and composite subjects, and the problem of a closed system becomes that much more acute. Older systems set out to list, or *enumerate*, all the subjects which seemed appropriate, both single concepts and composite, leaving the individual classifier no autonomy to insert new subjects which might be found in his collection.

More recent systems have tended to be of the *synthetic* kind. These list only single concepts, but give the indexer rules for the construction of headings for composite subjects. The method is obviously a great deal more powerful than the purely enumerative, but does depend on the individual concepts being listed, or there being rules for construction of headings for them. A synthetic language is thus a great deal more open than an enumerative one, but may still not give the indexer complete autonomy if he is relying on a published list. It is for this reason that many special libraries have constructed their own indexing language; they have avoided being tied to a possibly out of date published list.

There is of course no hard and fast line between the two types of system; we may expect to find a complete range between the closed enumerative system where the indexer has no freedom at all, and the open synthetic system which permits the indexer to specify any subject he wishes. Most systems fall somewhere between the two extremes, and it should perhaps be mentioned that although one of the advantages often claimed for post-coordinate systems is that they are much freer than pre-coordinate systems, this is not necessarily the case; a language such as that used in BTI can be almost unrestricted, while the ERIC *Thesaurus*[2] offered its users a very limited vocabulary indeed.

It is perhaps significant that the systems giving the extreme of complete freedom of input (the computer systems using natural language

51

text mentioned in chapter 3) do require greater effort at the output stage than do those systems which have imposed a measure of organization at the input stage. On the other hand it may be argued that the greater the degree of organization we impose on our collection of information, the less likely we are to achieve that felicitous concatenation of hitherto unrelated subjects known as *serendipity*. Since many of the most important advances in science have been the result of serendipity rather than deliberate effort, we may perhaps be cautious of a system which excludes it altogether. However, it is doubtful whether we can in fact consider this factor in a system intended for the *organization* of knowledge—though subject analysis may itself reveal hitherto unsuspected relationships!

CRITICAL CLASSIFICATION
The indexer is serving as intermediary between authors and users; to what extent is he justified in interposing his own ideas and prejudices? The immediate answer is, not at all, but in practice this is found to be the case very rarely. An indexing language inevitably reflects to some extent the social and cultural background of its compiler, and while it serves users of a similar persuasion this is not necessarily a bad thing; it is when we try to impose one culture on users of another that problems are likely to arise, in a variety of ways. We may find examples of chauvinism:

Women's periodicals, American *See* Women's periodicals (LCSH)
Africa—discovery and exploration (Sears) [*ie* by Europeans]
World War II: Germany's Conquest of Europe, Rescue by the
    United States (BC)
or genuine differences of approach:
compare the schedules for *government* in, say, LC and CC
or *education* in UDC (European continent) and DC (US)
or intellectual arrogance:
821.9 Minor poets [*eg* John Donne!] (early editions of DC)
or euphemism:
Vulgar fractions *use* Common fractions (ERIC Thesaurus)
Voluntarily idle *use* Labor force non-participants (ERIC Thesaurus).
Whatever the reason, *critical classification*—the imposition of the indexer's viewpoint on the user—is found rather more widely than we would like to admit. Even such schemes as UDC, which has a definite international policy, are not entirely free from bias. The indexer should be careful not to introduce bias needlessly, and the user has to

be made aware of its possible existence, if our systems are to achieve their objective of making information available freely.[3]

CONCLUSION

We have seen that there are various kinds of indexing language: pre-coordinate and post-coordinate, closed and open, enumerative and synthetic, with syntax and without, biased and highly biased. This variety should not blind us to the fact that the collection of documents we are indexing does not change if we change the method of indexing, nor do the demands made on it by the users. No matter what system we use, it must measure up to the same criteria.

BIBLIOGRAPHY

1 Gardin, J-C: *SYNTOL*. Rutgers, State University, Graduate School of Library Science, 1965. (Rutgers series on systems for the intellectual organization of information, *ed* Susan Artandi. Vol 2.)

2 US Educational Resources Information Center: *Thesaurus of ERIC descriptors*. USGPO, 1967. The first edition has now been replaced by the second edition, discussed in Part IV.

3 Foskett, A C: 'Misogynists all: a study in critical classification'. *Library resources and technical services, 15* (4) 1971.

CHAPTER 5

Alphabetical subject headings

CUTTER: The first attempt to establish a generalized set of rules for alphabetical subject headings was Charles Ammi Cutter's *Rules for a dictionary catalogue,* published in 1876[1] (the year which also saw the first edition of Dewey's *Decimal classification*: truly an *annus mirabilis!*). Cutter laid down several rules which went some way towards solving the problems, but was handicapped by his acceptance of natural language as the only possible kind of terminology. For Cutter, subject names existed only insofar as they were generally accepted and used by educated people. This reliance on what H E Bliss was later to name the ' scientific and educational consensus ' meant that a new subject could not be named specifically until it was, in effect, no longer new. Accepted names were to be used very much as they stood; consistency was secondary to familiarity. When a choice arose, as in headings containing more than one term, Cutter's solution to the problem of significance order had the sublimity of innocence: put the more significant term first. Only if the second term in a heading was definitely more significant than the first was natural language order to be abandoned; a useful rule, but one which still leaves the definition of ' significant ' to the indexer. Double entry was recommended to help overcome the difficulties caused by lack of specificity, an inadequate solution which has been followed by most lists of subject headings since Cutter; according to *Sears list of subject headings* a subject such as Medieval church architecture must be entered twice, once under Church architecture, the other under Architecture, medieval. Neither heading is specific, so relevance is low.

In some situations Cutter does give more definite rulings, as for instance when there is a clash between subject and place. Here we are instructed to enter under subject, qualified by place, in scientific and similar areas, but under place, qualified by subject, in areas such as history, government and commerce where the country might reasonably be taken to be the main focus of interest. For the humanities—literature, art—we are recommended to use the adjectival form of

54

the country or language as the entry word: English drama, French painting.

To link related subjects, Cutter recommended a network of references giving a *syndetic* catalogue. He also recognized that to be able to compile such a network we need to have some sort of systematic approach to the subject; a purely alphabetical approach will not indicate genus-species relationships, though we can see syntagmatic links when two unrelated terms are used together in a heading. For example, the heading English drama itself shows the need to show a link with the related subject Drama, but does not show the relationship with the broader subject Literature; to reveal this, we need to study the whole subject area in a systematic way. However, Cutter restricted the links shown in practice to downward references, *ie* from broader to narrower subjects, and suggested that we should ignore on economic grounds both upward links (from narrower to broader subjects) and collateral (sideways) links from one term to another of equal rank. Thus Cutter would have cross-references such as

Literature *see also* drama

but not

Drama *see also* Literature

or

Drama *see also* Poetry.

Now it is certainly true that many users begin a search by specifying a much broader subject than they in fact want; needing information on the Moon they ask for information on Astronomy. A lead from Astronomy to Moon is therefore very valuable in helping users to clarify their specific needs. But suppose that after searching the system at a heading which is specific we still do not find what we need? We need to be able to broaden the search to include broader subjects, and we can only do this systematically if the system includes upward and collateral references as well as the usual downward ones. Like Cutter's advice to make double entry to overcome lack of specificity in the kind of headings he found acceptable, this practice tends to hamper the easy use and development of alphabetical indexes but is standard practice despite this. The cost of making the network of references complete would in most cases be prohibitive, and we therefore have to accept the fact that the alphabetical subject catalogue does not lend itself to the kind of search strategy which involves looking systematically for broader headings.

Cutter's *Rules* have been the basis of United States practice in subject cataloguing during this century, and are best exemplified in Sears and LCSH, which between them govern the methods used in all but a tiny fraction of US library catalogues. Their use in the Library of Congress has meant that they have appeared on the printed cards used by most US libraries, while the fact that the Library adopted a dictionary catalogue has meant that this has been the norm. As is shown in chapter 17, LCSH shows many inconsistencies and inadequacies, a reflection of the fact that, though the *Rules* may have been adequate to deal with nineteenth century literature, they are so no longer. Yet despite some dissatisfaction, there has been little progress in the US on the development of any kind of new theory, while the enormous size of the catalogues in the Library of Congress has itself been a weighty factor on the side of inertia. It should also be pointed out that the problems of size associated with a very large library catalogue are the cause of many of the defects found in LCSH, rather than any fundamental errors in the *Rules*.

We should not blame Cutter for not solving all our problems, or for not even being aware of some of them. The information we have to deal with is greater in quantity, and individually more complex, than anything Cutter envisaged his rules applying to. What he did do was bring order into a previously haphazard process, and in doing so point the way forward for later developments; his *Rules* can still be read with profit (and, more unusual in such works, pleasure) today.

KAISER[2]

In 1911 J Kaiser published a work entitled *Systematic indexing*, which took the practice of alphabetical subject indexing an important step forward. His ideas formalized the practices he had developed in trying to index information relating to business and industry, and to that extent are limited in their application; but they represent the first attempt to find a sound and consistent answer to the problem of significance order, and are still valid and useful in many cases. Kaiser pointed out that many composite subjects can be analysed into a combination of a *concrete* and a *process*, and stated the rule that in such a combination it is the concrete which is the more important and which should be cited first. This means that *Heat treatment of metals* and *Screw extrusion of plastics* are entered respectively:

METALS—Heat treatment
PLASTICS—Screw extrusion

If *place* is involved, Kaiser makes double entry, once under concrete and once under place; entry for localities is indirect, *ie* under country subdivided by more specific locality. Thus *Steel production in Sheffield* would be entered:

STEEL—Great Britain, Sheffield—Production

GREAT BRITAIN, Sheffield—Steel—Production

Concretes are linked by a complete network of cross-references, to superordinate and coordinate as well as subordinate headings. An index constructed along these lines will contain a large number of cross-references, but this is not necessarily a bad thing; Cutter's objections were on economic grounds, not theoretical, and it is unfortunate that most libraries using the alphabetical approach do limit their references to the ' downward ' kind. Concretes are often specified by more than one word, *eg aluminium windows*, and here Kaiser uses natural language order; however, many topics have now reached a degree of complexity when natural language is not necessarily much of a help, *eg Gas-cooled natural-uranium fuelled nuclear power reactors*, where natural language permits more than one arrangement.

Kaiser realized that many terms apparently denoting processes in fact could be analysed into the standard concrete-process formula; thus *cataloguing* could become *Catalogues—construction*. This kind of analysis can present problems, particularly those of inconsistency, in that it might well be possible to analyse the same subject in different ways on different occasions. In addition, the concrete revealed by this analysis might well be found in quite a different part of the alphabet from the original term, which would be the one normally sought by users: *welding* and *soldering* might both be found under *Metals* (Metals—welding, Metals—soldering), which would show their relationship but would not give direct entry.

This process of analysis is an important one, which has been carried further in classification than in alphabetical indexing, the most nearly complete example being the *semantic factoring* of the Western Reserve University system. Consideration of the problems that arise is therefore deferred here. Kaiser himself did not explore the possibilities very deeply, and his use of it is mainly to avoid having process terms standing alone.

Another important point which Kaiser illustrated clearly in his examples is the effects of introducing systematic arrangement of sub-headings as opposed to straightforward alphabetical filing. For any given concrete there may well be composites including place, as well as composites including both place and process; when one comes to arrange these, there are two possibilities—to use a strictly alphabetical sub-arrangement, or to group places together and processes together. The first approach gives:

STEEL—Great Britain, Sheffield—Production
STEEL—Smelting
STEEL—United States of America, Pittsburgh—Smelting
STEEL—Welding

while the second groups the processes *before* the places:

STEEL—Smelting
STEEL—Welding
STEEL—Great Britain, Sheffield—Production
STEEL—United States of America, Pittsburgh—Smelting

A further sequence may arise if we include bibliographical forms as subdivisions, *eg* Periodicals, Dictionaries, Indexes *etc,* as once again it may be helpful to avoid interfiling these with other kinds of subheading. The principle followed by Kaiser has been more fully investigated in the field of classification and will be considered later under the heading *Principle of inversion* (page 96). However, the idea of grouping subheadings is followed by most alphabetical subject catalogues, as is shown, for example, by the following headings from the Library of Congress *Subject headings :*

Sales	(Single term)
Sales—periodicals	(Bibliographical form)
Sales (Roman Law)	(Context)
Sales, conditional	(Qualification)
Sales accounting	(Two or more terms)

The problem with introducing systematic arrangement into an alphabetical catalogue is that the order is no longer self-evident, and in consequence a user following up a cross-reference may find himself lost.

RANGANATHAN

Kaiser's three categories, Concrete, Process, Place, are satisfactory as far as they go, but for modern literature they frequently do not go far enough. S R Ranganathan, in his *Dictionary catalogue code*[3] has suggested the use of five ' Fundamental categories ' as the basis for order in composite headings. These are: ENERGY MATTER PERSONALITY SPACE TIME. Thus welding of steel, which Kaiser would enter as

STEEL—Welding

would be entered by Ranganathan in the reverse way as

WELDING, Steel

It has proved very difficult to define what is meant by *Personality*, and in practical applications the very generality of Ranganathan's categories can cause doubts as to their precise mode of use. They do however solve some of the problems left unsolved by Kaiser, and can prove effective in a limited subject field such as Architecture, as has been shown by A Thompson in compiling the catalogue of the library of the Royal Institute of British Architects.[4]

COATES

Undoubtedly the most important contribution to the theory of alphabetical subject headings for many years is the work of E J Coates. In his book, *Subject catalogues*,[5] Coates has summarized succinctly the previous approaches, both theory and practice, and put forward his own theories as to the correct formulation of specific subject headings. He has also had the challenge of putting his ideas into practice on a large scale in the *British technology index*, of which he has been editor since its inception—an opportunity of a kind which rarely presents itself to the theorist.

He begins his study of order in composite headings by trying to establish the reason for Kaiser's selection of Concrete rather than Process as the entry point, and suggests that there is a sound psychological basis for this. If we try to visualize an action out of context, it is very difficult; we normally think of some ' thing ' which is involved in the action. For example, we can visualize a piece of steel or aluminium undergoing heat treatment, possibly glowing, changing shape and so on; but it is much more difficult to visualize *heat treatment* on its own. We can therefore establish an order of *significance* reflecting this, and for this simple case it is of course the same as Kaiser's Concrete-Process. Coates uses the terminology *Thing-Action*, but this is simply a new way of naming the same idea. However, Coates develops his ideas much further. If we think of a Thing and the Material of which it is made, it is once again the Thing which is more significant, because it conjures up a more definite mental image. So we can develop our significance order one stage further, to give us *Thing-Material-Action*; from here we can again move forward to incorporate *Parts*, which must depend on the *Things* to which they belong, thus

59

giving us *Thing-Part-Material-Action*. Coates also shows how other variants can be built up by following the same principle.

If we had to try to establish the significance order every time we wished to establish a subject heading, it would take a great deal of intellectual effort, but Coates has pointed out a very valuable corollary of his ideas on significance order. When we translate the idea of a *Thing* being acted upon by an *Action* into natural language, we can very often do so by using a prepositional phrase, in the form *Action-Preposition-Thing*. To obtain a subject heading in accordance with the *Thing-Action* significance formula, all that we have to do is to reverse the phrase, omitting the preposition. Thus *Heat treatment of aluminium* becomes *Aluminium, Heat treatment*. These ideas enable us to establish a heading for very complex subjects, such as the following two examples taken from the *British technology index:*

1 Manufacture of multiwall kraft paper sacks for the packaging of cement.

2 Determination of the temperature of combustion of coal particles.

1 We can split this into two parts, Manufacture of multiwall kraft paper sacks, and, Packaging of cement. In the first part, the *Thing* is sacks, and the *Action* manufacture, giving us Sacks, manufacture. Paper is the *Material,* giving us Sacks, paper, manufacture, while kraft and multiwall are obviously type-specifying terms for paper, giving us for the whole of this part Sacks, paper, kraft, multiwall, manufacture. In the second part, we can easily derive the heading Cement, packaging. To link the two, we think of sacks for packaging, giving us Packaging, sacks; so for the whole heading we have:

Cement, packaging, sacks, paper, kraft, multiwall, manufacture.

2 Coal particles are clearly the *Thing* involved here, but is the entry term Coal or Particles? The phrase may be expressed as Particles of coal, leading us to Coal, particles; from here we have a series of similar prepositional phrases, which we reverse in order, giving:

Coal, particles, combustion, temperature, determination.

These headings are not natural use of language; they are lengthy and complex, and they are not obvious. (It is, however, fairly simple to learn to read the line from back to front with a little practice.) To set against these disadvantages we have the very real advantages of consistency and specificity, and—if Coates' ideas are correct—the first element of the heading is the one most likely to come into the mind of the enquirer seeking information on these topics. Coates distinguishes twenty different kinds of relationship, including Thing-

Action, and tabulates these to show their relation to the corresponding prepositional phrase; there are a few exceptions to the reversal rule, for example Thing-Material, where the heading agrees with the amplified phrase order (sacks [made] of paper gives Sacks, paper, not Paper, sacks), but once these are known the rule is a very simple one to follow. As has already been mentioned, Coates has been able to put his ideas into practice in the *British technology index*, and some critics have complained that the kind of entry demonstrated here is no longer a direct entry to the specific subject. It is difficult to see how the entries could be made more direct; once we try to be specific, and name composite subjects—syntagmas—we must inevitably group to some extent under the first element in a heading. For example, as well as Cement, packaging, we may have Cement, manufacture. giving us a certain amount of grouping at the word cement—but this does not make either of the entries any the less direct. If we require specificity, we have at the same time to accept the concomitant complexity of headings and the occurrence of grouping. It must however be stressed that the grouping arises out of the need for a significance order, not from any attempt to bring together related subjects in a systematic way. The words at which grouping occurs are stated directly: Aluminium, heat treatment, *not* Metals, aluminium, heat treatment.

A catalogue of this kind shows the problems of related subjects in an acute form. We not only have to establish a network of genus-species relationships, but must also cater for those who approach a composite subject through a term other than the one we have used as entry word. The heading

ALUMINIUM, Heat treatment

involves us in both kinds of link. We must make cross-references

METALS *see also* NON-FERROUS METALS

NON-FERROUS METALS *see also* ALUMINIUM

and possibly also

FERROUS METALS *see also* NON-FERROUS METALS

MAGNESIUM *see also* ALUMINIUM

to express the permanent relationships within the field of metallurgy. These can only be established by a study of the subject in a systematic way, and the BTI in fact relies to some extent on the Universal Decimal Classification to suggest this kind of link. For this particular heading, another cross-reference suggests itself without much difficulty to take care of the hidden element Heat treatment:

HEAT TREATMENT *see also* ALUMINIUM, Heat treatment

Alternatively, we may make a direct cross-reference from the inverted heading as does BTI:

HEAT TREATMENT, Aluminium *see* ALUMINIUM, Heat treatment.

But what are we to do with the much more complex heading we arrived at earlier:

CEMENT, packaging, sacks, paper, kraft, multiwall, manufacture? There are two considerations here. In the first place, although we hope that our significance order will enable users to find this straight away, there is no guarantee that this will succeed every time, and we therefore must cater for the user who looks under one of the hidden words. In the second place, users who are primarily interested in paper sacks may very well wish to know of the existence of at least one document on their use in the packaging of cement.

There are various ways in which we might approach this problem. One would be to *permute* the terms in the heading, that is, to make a cross-reference to the chosen heading from every possible arrangement of the terms. To give an example in symbolic form, if we chose a heading ABCD we would make references to it from

ABDC	BCDA	CDAB	DABC
ACBD	BCAD	CDBA	DACB
ACDB	BACD	CABD	DBCA
ADBC	BADC	CADB	DBAC
ADCB	BDAC	CBDA	DCAB
	BDCA	CBAD	DCBA

Twenty three cross-references in all! The number of permutations that can be made of n things is n! (factorial n) or

$$n \times (n-1) \times (n-2) \times \ldots \times 3 \times 2 \times 1.$$

For our symbolic heading containing 4 elements, n! is 24 ($4 \times 3 \times 2 \times 1$), giving us one heading and twenty three cross-references; but the example we are looking at from BTI contains seven elements, which would give us one entry and no less than 5,039 cross-references! This is obviously impractical, so we are faced with the problem of selecting which of these entries and cross-references we are to make.

It is important to distinguish here between an entry and a cross-reference. Suppose that we have one document, and we are faced with the choice of making one entry and four cross-references or five entries; either way will give us the same number of cards in the catalogue (assuming that physical form is used). But if we should add to the collection another nine documents on the same subject, the first method would give us ten entries and four cross-references (the same four, of course) while the second would give fifty entries. If we now think in terms of twenty similar subjects, the first method would give us 200 entries and eighty cross-references, but the second would give us 1,000 entries. The distinction is that an entry contains information about a document, and can therefore relate only to that one document, whereas a cross-reference links related headings and thus relates to everything filed at those headings. Both are, however, entry points into the sequence, and we have to provide an entry point under each term that the user is likely to use in his search, insofar as we can establish this in advance.

If for the moment we disregard genus-species relationships and concentrate on the problems of syntagmatic links in composite headings, a moment's thought should show that if there are n significant elements in a given heading, then $(n-1)$ of them will be 'hidden' and ought to form additional entry points. Obviously, we must then make at least $(n-1)$ cross-references, for if we make fewer than this we must be overlooking one of the hidden elements. We have already seen that if we permute we have to make $(n!-1)$ if we wish to cover every possible variation, so there will be a wide margin between the minimum and the maximum as n increases; but when $n = 2$, $(n-1)$ and $(n!-1)$ are both the same: 1. The problem of having to find an economic means of selecting which cross-references to make only becomes acute when we use composite headings with more than two elements.

CHAIN PROCEDURE

Ranganathan has suggested a method whereby we can make the minimum number of cross-references, yet still be sure that readers will find an entry point under every significant term in a composite heading. We begin by writing down the 'chain' of terms:

CEMENT, packaging, sacks, paper, kraft, multiwall, manufacture.

We now write down the last term in the chain, following it by each of the preceding terms in turn; this forms the entry point under that word, and refers us to the full heading in its preferred order:

MANUFACTURE, multiwall, kraft, paper, sacks, packaging, cement
    see

CEMENT, packaging, sacks, paper, kraft, multiwall, manufacture.

We have now covered the approach through this word, and can move on to the next-to-last, following exactly the same procedure for this:

MULTIWALL, kraft, paper, sacks, packaging, cement

    see

CEMENT, packaging, sacks, paper, kraft, multiwall.

We follow this procedure through until we have made the necessary $(n-1)$ cross-references, in this case six:

KRAFT, paper, sacks, packaging, cement

    see

CEMENT, packaging, sacks, paper, kraft

PAPER, sacks, packaging, cement

    see

CEMENT, packaging, sacks, paper

SACKS, packaging, cement

    see

CEMENT, packaging, sacks

PACKAGING, cement

    see

CEMENT, packaging.

Every hidden term now forms an entry point which will lead us to the correct part of the catalogue, *ie* the preferred heading. Note also that if we next have to deal with a document on Plastic sacks for the packaging of cement, we shall make an entry for this

CEMENT, packaging, sacks, plastic

but we shall only need *one* more cross-reference because the network we built up for the similar subject earlier will serve for the rest:

PLASTICS, sacks, packaging, cement

    see

CEMENT, packaging, sacks, plastic.

This method of compiling a network of cross-references is called *chain procedure;* we make a cross-reference from each link in the chain. It is a very economical method; we can in effect make fewer than the minimum number $(n-1)$ of cross-references because some will serve for more than one heading. To set against this is the disadvantage that only the first is specific; the others do not lead us to the full heading we have used.

The point is shown by the sample references already worked out; for example, the word SACKS does not lead us to the specific subject

CEMENT, packaging, sacks, paper, kraft, multiwall, manufacture but to the much broader heading

CEMENT, packaging, sacks.

To overcome some of these problems, BTI uses a modified form of chain procedure, in which type-specifying words (such as 'paper' in relation to 'sacks') are not detached from their words they refer to; in the above example, BTI would make a reference

SACKS, paper, packaging, cement
    see

CEMENT, packaging, sacks, paper.

To facilitate this using computer processing, BTI introduced differential punctuation in the 1968 issues; the above heading would now appear as

CEMENT: packaging: sacks; paper

in which the semi-colon indicates that the inversion reference will not be in strict accordance with chain procedure. The punctuation marks used are the colon, comma, double comma, double point and semicolon, in accordance with the following schema:

Thing—Action, Property, Part or Auxiliary   :

eg MOTOR VEHICLES: Bodies

   PACKAGING: Labelling

   PLYWOOD: Building materials [*ie* Plywood as a building material]

Thing—Material   ;

eg BOTTLES; Polythene

Thing or Action—Kind   ,

eg MIXING, Batch

   ATOMISERS, Air blast

Thing—Material—Kind of material   ; ,

eg BOTTLES; Polythene, Blow moulded

Thing—Kind—Material   , ;

eg PLATES, Clamped; Steel

Thing—Kind—Kind of kind   , ,

eg MOTOR CARS, Three wheeler, Types, Bond

Thing—Kind + Kind   , „

eg PLATES, Circular,, Anisotropic

Thing—Material—Kind of thing   ; „

eg ELECTRODES; Glass,, Ion selective

Thing—Place   ..

eg MOTORWAYS.. Belfast

By replacing some of the syntax which is lost in headings of the earlier type, some ambiguities can be removed. For example, we can now distinguish

STRUCTURES; Steel (meaning Steel structures)

from

STRUCTURES : Steel (meaning Steel used in structures)

Some still remain; for example,

METALS: Extrusion: Presses

can mean either the action 'Extrusion of metals using presses' or the thing 'Presses for the extrusion of metals'. However, as Coates points out, it is often very difficult to distinguish these in the reader's approach anyway; thing and action are so closely linked that it is hard to think of one without the other.

The punctuation is ignored in the arrangement, since its purpose is to operate the computer program for the generation of cross-references.[6] However, though the network is now more satisfactory with a lower expenditure of effort than it was previously, there are still problems arising from the fact that many of the references are not specific. For example, suppose that a user wanting *Determination of neutron flux in a boiling water reactor* looks under the word REACTOR; all that he will find will be a reference

REACTORS, nuclear

see

NUCLEAR REACTORS

When he turns to this heading, say in the annual volume of BTI, he will find a very large number of entries, all beginning NUCLEAR REACTORS, and will have to work his way through these without being certain of the next term to look for. It might well be BOILING WATER, or perhaps WATER—but it might be that the only information on this subject in that particular year dealt with Boiling water reactors for power generation, in which case the next word after REACTORS might well be power. The price of economy here is loss of specificity, which leads to an increase in the amount of searching that has to be done when part only of the wanted heading is known.

There is no doubt that the ideas put forward by Coates and their implementation in BTI have been a solid step forward in the theory of alphabetical subject headings. So far, we have only seen these ideas in use in the field of science and technology. Indexing services in the social sciences and humanities are, in general, less well organized than those in science and technology, and this applies to their indexing just as it does to their other features. It will be interesting to see whether detailed application in these fields leads to any important additions or modifications to the significance formulae suggested by Coates. It should also be stressed that—as has already been mentioned—generalized rules for significance order are intended for the neutral situation; in a situation where it is possible to establish in advance the likely needs of the users, we may well need to use quite different rules.

PRECIS

The MARC (MAchine Readable Cataloguing) project, discussed in chapter 24, has led to a new awareness of the need for international standards, and to this end BNB has adopted DC18 as its classification scheme. The chain procedure used previously to generate the subject index entries was exactly the same as that just described for BTI; it was based on a statement of the specific subject in words, and only one of the series of references was specific. In order to obtain the original statement in words, the class number was 'translated', but for this to be satisfactory the classification scheme itself must be satisfactory. As is explained in chapter 12, BNB often found it necessary to expand the detail found in DC, but even this does not solve the problem of anomalies in the scheme; quite often it is found that very similar subjects are treated quite differently, and this makes consistent indexing impossible. Unless the original statement is satisfactory, and consistently formed, it is not possible to mechanize the production of chain index entries, and anomalies have to be resolved by 'special treatment', which is very inefficient in a mechanized system.

There has thus been considerable pressure to devise a means of obtaining a subject statement in words in a form lending itself to machine manipulation. This has been combined with the study by the CRG of the development of a new general classification, discussed in chapter 7, and has led to the development of a new indexing technique known as PRECIS (PREserved Context Indexing System).[7] With the adoption in January 1971 of DC18, BNB has gone over to the use of PRECIS to produce its monthly subject index, but the method would appear to have much wider significance than this, and to be in fact a completely new approach to the generation of subject headings. While it is as yet too early to estimate its final significance, there are many indications that it may represent a basic step forward in our understanding of indexing problems. There appears to be also the possibility that, because it is based on fundamental characteristics of language, it may be independent of the original language, in that it may be possible to take the strings of terms used in one language and translate them into the comparable terms in another language and still be able to use the same manipulation to give meaningful index entries. Such a development would clearly revolutionize our approach to abstracting and indexing services, since it would be possible to mechanize not merely the production of indexes in English but also in a number of other languages, by feeding in interlingual dictionaries in addition to the manipulation program. The possibility has already been demonstrated on a small scale by D W Austin, who has himself carried out most of the PRECIS research.

The preliminary subject analysis recognizes two large categories of concept: entities and attributes. Entities are things, which may be mentefacts (mental constructions) as well as artefacts or concrete objects. Attributes are properties of things, or activities, or properties of activities. Four different fundamental relationships between concepts may be distinguished. The first of these is the genus-species type —the permanent relationships which we can establish by a study of knowledge. In order to cover these relationships, we have to build up a network of *see also* references which may be based on literary warrant, or our own knowledge, or other external sources. These relationships are not generated as part of the PRECIS manipulation and would of course appear in the final index only if they were inserted by the indexer, just as in any other system.

The second type of relationship is the attributive: the relationship between entity and attribute, or attribute and attribute. The rule here is that in the basic statement, an attribute always *follows* the entity to which it is linked. This is the same as Kaiser's rule, concrete-process, except that Kaiser did not permit processes to stand on their own; they had to be related to a concrete. In PRECIS, an attribute which is of general application may stand alone, *eg* Advertising, but in practice this is found to happen relatively rarely.

In the third and fourth types of relationship, more than one entity is present, in the possessive (thing-part) and interactive (thing-thing) modes. To clarify our approach to these two relationships, it is useful to introduce the idea of general systems theory, which enables us to state that in the possessive example, it is the possessing system which should come first, while in the interactive case it is the passive system which comes first.

So far, we have an indexing system rather like that of Coates, giving us similar rules for combination order, *eg*

Thing—action (attributive)

Thing—property (attributive)

Thing—part (possessive)

Thing—thing (interactive)

We may also distinguish another relationship noted by Coates in the form thing—kind, for which PRECIS uses the terms *focus* and *difference*. A difference is the quality or property which serves to define the context within which we are studying the focus, *eg* Electrodes, glass; Plates, clamped. In many cases, a difference can be identified because we use the adjectival form to express it. The same concept might also be an entity, in which case we would use the noun form, *eg* Glass for electrodes (NB in English, no difference in form); Clamps for plates. Or it might be an attribute, in which case we use the verbal noun form, *eg* Plates, clamping. Focus and difference may also be shown by a prepositional phrase, *eg*

Welfare for old people

Boys on probation

Transportation of animals

where a rearrangement omitting the preposition might lead to ambiguity.

The real advance in PRECIS is that it enables us to be much more precise about the kind of relationship between concepts, and in doing so to generate a basic statement that can be manipulated by a computer to give a complete set of headings. Unlike the secondary entries generated by chain procedure, all PRECIS statements are completely specific, and the layout is designed to aid the user to appreciate the complete sense of each heading, no matter which term is used as the lead term which determines the filing position.

To construct a primary PRECIS statement, *ie* the one on which all the rest are based, we write down the concepts involved in a composite subject in the order dictated by the relational operators which we insert between the concepts. The set of operators is still being developed, but at present is as shown in Table 3. The rule is that operators must appear in decreasing numerical order from left to right; non-numerical operators are inserted at the correct logical point in the sequence, *eg* a property immediately follows the concept to which it belongs.

69

(a) Form; physical, *eg* microfilm, or bibliographical, *eg* journal
(b) Target; *eg* for librarians [cf bias phase, chapter 7]
/ Field membership, quasi-generic relationship
, Difference
(p) Subsystem, structure, material
(q) Property, percept
(o) Study region, sample population
(1) Viewpoint, perspective
(2) Active system
(3) Effect, action
(4) Key system
(5) Discipline
(6) Environment
(v) Coordinate concept
(w) Coordinate correlated subject [cf comparison phase, chapter 7]
(x) Coordinate subject in same document

TABLE 3 : PRECIS operators

The headings are set out according to the following two-line pattern:

Lead term   Qualifier(s)
Display

From the primary statement, using the combination order determined by the rules, we can generate as many secondary statements as are necessary to bring each significant term to the lead position; non-significant terms will appear in each statement but will not form the lead term at any time. The whole process, including the alteration of prepositions to maintain the correct sense, is completely automatic once the primary statement has been prepared for entry into the system. Some examples will demonstrate the method.

'Remuneration of teachers in French universities' gives us the primary statement with operators

(6) France (4) Universities (p) Teachers (3) Remuneration

which gives us the index heading

France
Universities. Teachers. Remuneration

From this we also obtain the three secondary statements

Universities. France
Teachers. Remuneration
Teachers. Universities. France
Remuneration.
Remuneration. Teachers. Universities. France

It is interesting to note that the final statement, in which there are no display terms left, coincides with the natural language order (omitting prepositions)

Remuneration (of) teachers (in) universities (in) France

Note also that except in certain clearly defined cases the noun form France is preferred to the adjectival French; this is very similar to Cutter's suggestion, and in the BNB index we find such entries as **' English costume '**, **' French drawings '**, **' Germany. Politics '** and **' Ireland.** Socialism ', showing the kind of situation where one or the other is preferred.

For our second example, let us consider one of the items used to demonstrate Coates' methods, ' Determination of the temperature of combustion of coal particles '. This gives us a primary statement with operators

(4) Coal (p) Particles (3) Combustion (q) Temperature (3) Determination

This however breaks the rule that it is not possible to have the operator (3) twice in the same string, and we therefore rewrite it

(4) Coal (p) Particles (q) Temperature of combustion (3) Determination

Coal and particles form an aggregation which we can usefully treat as a unit, while ' determination ' is a nonsignificant word which we do not want as a lead term. We therefore finish up with the primary statement

Coal particles

Temperature of combustion. Determination

from which the computer can derive the secondary statements

Particles

Coal particles. Temperature of combustion. Determination

Combustion. Coal particles

Temperature of combustion. Determination

Temperature of combustion. Coal particles

Determination

Logical analysis on the above lines may sometimes lead us to include redundant terms in our string, which may be deleted before we build up the headings. This can happen when we have an activity followed by a tool, when the tool implicitly defines the activity. For example, in the string ' Metals. Pressing. Presses ' which we build up with operators (4) Metals (3) Pressing (2) Presses, we must include Pressing because the rules do not permit (4) to be followed by (2) with no intervening (3); however, it is fairly obviously unnecessary as an indexing term, and can be suppressed.

PRECIS is concerned with the syntactic organization of subject statements, but in addition we need to be concerned with semantic organization—Gardin's paradigmatic relationships as well as syntagmatic. As has been pointed out, these do not arise from the PRECIS analysis but have to be built up externally; in fact, the PRECIS team at BNB are building up a thesaurus which will be stored in the computer, and drawn on as necessary to supplement the index statements generated by manipulation. In addition to the genus-species relationships already mentioned, five categories of concept involving these external relationships have been defined:

1 Synonyms (*eg* **Speech sounds** *see* **Pronunciation**
                Sphenisciformes *see* **Penguins)**

2 Wider group terms not included in the string (examples will be shown from BNB)

3 Partial synonyms, or 'overlapping coordinates' (terms whose meanings are very similar but not identical, *eg* Legends and Folktales). These have to be linked by *see also* references in both directions.

4 Elided concepts (*eg* Demography, which is a single term for the two concepts Population and Statistics)

5 Discipline concepts. Such terms as Economics, which are very broad, are related to very large numbers of other concepts, many of the relationships being ill-defined. Although these terms cannot be included in the subject statement, *see also* references may be useful.

Over the years, it is hoped to build up a very large and comprehensive thesaurus of such relationships, using such tools as Webster's *Dictionary*. However, it is interesting to note that several months of experimental work have led to the inclusion of no more than some 4,000 words so far, and it may well be the case that we can construct a complete indexing system using a very much smaller vocabulary than one would assume to be necessary. It must be remembered that the number of *combinations* of terms is enormously greater than the actual number of terms, a point to which we shall return in chapter 7.

As yet we have had little opportunity to see how PRECIS will work out in practice, but it would seem that, apart from a few minor difficulties, it has worked well both in trial runs and in the first two production runs in January and February 1971. OSTI is supporting further research over the next few years to see whether the initial high promise can be realised in full by extending the method to other services as well as BNB.

Some examples taken from the January issue of BNB will show how it works out in practice.

1 Primary statement
Crops
Pollination by insects
Secondary statements
Pollination of crops   [NB change of preposition]
By insects
Insects. Pollination of crops

2 Primary statement
Comprehensive schools
Administration. Role of heads of departments
Secondary statements
None. There are no other terms which would be of value as lead terms.
Additional cross-references
Education *see also* **Schools**
Schools *see also* **Primary schools**
Secondary schools
Secondary schools *see also* **Comprehensive schools**

3 Primary statement
Vertebrates
Nervous system. Drug receptors. Molecular structure and properties.
— *Conference proceedings*
Secondary statements.
Nervous system. Vertebrates
Drug receptors. Molecular structure and properties—
Conference proceedings
Drug receptors. Nervous system. Vertebrates
Molecular structure and properties — *Conference proceedings*
Molecular structure and properties. Drug receptors. Nervous system. Vertebrates
— *Conference proceedings*
Additional cross-references
Chordates *see also* **Vertebrates**
Living systems *see also* **Animals**

73

Animals *see also* **Vertebrates**
Biology *see also* **Living systems**
Structure *see also* **Physical structure**
Physical structure *see also* **Molecular structure**

It is evident that much of the total PRECIS system is not new, but represents rather a refinement of previous practice. The use of such analytical tools as general systems theory has enabled a more precise approach to the formulation of subject statements to be made, and the objective of computer manipulation has made consistency not just desirable but essential. It would seem that in PRECIS in its fully developed form we shall have a tool with all the qualities that have been postulated in earlier chapters as desirable, and its practical realization in BNB subject indexes must be studied very carefully.

FARRADANE

Another kind of indexing system using relational operators is that devised by Farradane.[8] He has based his system on ideas of the learning process. By studying the psychology of childhood we can begin to understand how children, and thus all human beings, learn by developing powers of discrimination in time and space; we can then establish stages of discrimination in each of these areas. In time, the first stage is ' non-time '—the co-occurrence of two ideas without reference to time; the second stage is ' temporary '—the co-occurrence from time to time, but not permanently, of two ideas; and the third is ' fixed '—the permanent co-occurrence of two ideas. In space, the stages of discrimination are: first, ' concurrent '—two concepts which it is hard to distinguish; second, ' not-distinct '—two concepts which have much in common; and third, ' distinct '—two concepts which can be completely distinguished. These two sets of gradations can be used to form a matrix, the points of intersection denoting nine different kinds of relationship. Concepts may be joined by operators to give *analets,* which are in effect very similar to the subject statements generated by PRECIS. The problem that has been found with Farradane's system (and to a lesser degree with PRECIS also) is that the generality of the operators at times makes it difficult to see which is the correct one to choose; it is difficult to get agreement among a group of indexers as to the correct form of the analets. This is of course a serious drawback to a system intended for general use. However, Farradane has claimed that his methods have given very good results under experimental conditions, and some of the recent develop-

74

ments are of interest, for example the use of two-dimensional indexing statements, *eg*

Authors/ : Books
/θ   *ie* Books by English authors
Nationality / = English
Steel/ : Plates / — Clamping
/;   *ie* Clamping of hardened steel plates
Hardening

which can be filed under any or all of the concepts involved, or could be found additionally through the operators in a computerized system.

	NON-TIME RELATION	TEMPORARY	FIXED
CONCURRENT	Concurrence /θ	Comparison & Self-activity /*	Association /;
NOT-DISTINCT	Equivalence /=	Dimensional & State /+	Appurtenance /(
DISTINCT	Distinctness /)	Reaction /—	Causation or Functional Dependence /:

FIGURE I : Farradane's operators

ARTICULATED SUBJECT INDEXES

A rather different approach has been made by M F Lynch[9], relying to a much greater extent on the use of natural language, in particular the prepositional phrase. The project, which was intended to devise a method of generating subject indexes by computer manipulation of a simple sentence-like statement, began with a study of the indexes to *Chemical abstracts*. Based on skills acquired over the years, these indexes set a very high standard, and the first step was to find out whether they were based on any implicit logical analysis which could form the basis of a computer program (which must necessarily be *explicit*). A method was found of transforming an index entry back to a 'title' which worked in a high proportion of cases, some 60 percent. Of the remainder, nearly half could be treated in the same way if a simple set of procedures was followed. The method is to treat prepositions as points at which the phrases can be pivoted; often a comma will appear in the final index entry in association with the preposition. A phrase beginning with a preposition is designated o, one ending with a preposition, 1. A type o phrase is now placed after the entry word, while type 1 phrases are placed before it, and the original 'title' (a descriptive statement, not necessarily the title of the work) can be regenerated. Take, for example, the index entry:

Insects
    pollination by, of crops
'Pollination by' is a 1-phrase, while 'of crops' is a o-phrase. By following the simple rule, we can derive the statement

Pollination by   insects   of crops.
This very simple example shows how the method of regeneration works, but it is effective for much more complex index entries than this.

The analysis of *Chemical abstracts* entries led to the development of methods for the generation of index entries from a title statement, based on the logic discovered in the reverse process. As might be expected, some modifications were found to be necessary to avoid the generation of 'awkward' entries, but it has proved possible to compile computer programs which will work very satisfactorily, and articulated indexes are used in *Food technology abstracts* and the Safety in Mines Research Establishment abstract bulletin. The method avoids the necessity for the somewhat complicated process of subject analysis required for indexes of the Coates or Austin type, since all that the indexer has to do is to write a statement in the approved format, using merely a rather stylized form of English. Like PRECIS, the method gives a complete subject statement at every entry point; a simple example from a demonstration index is as follows:

Character recognition by computer (title from *Documentation abstracts*)

Index entries :
Character recognition
    by computer
Computer(s)
    character recognition by

It remains to be seen, however, whether the method is as powerful as PRECIS in arriving at adequate index entries for every situation. If we are thinking on the national scale, it may well be worth while to employ indexers with the skills required by PRECIS and BTI, but Lynch's method is certainly attractive for the smaller organization.

ALPHABETICO-CLASSED ARRANGEMENT

All of the systems described so far in this chapter have used what is called *direct* entry; that is to say, a topic is entered directly under the term or terms which most closely correspond to the subject. Another approach is to use *indirect* entry: a topic is entered under a broad heading which includes it, if necessary using a whole series of intermediate divisions of the broad subject. For example, instead of

    Aluminium
we might find
    Metals—non-ferrous—aluminium
Instead of
    Cans
we find
    Containers: tinplate: food: cans

The advantage to be gained from indirect entry is that related subjects are grouped together; in the above examples, everything on Metals will be together, as will everything on different kinds of container. However, there are certain difficulties associated with indirect entry which have led to its general rejection, though some examples are to be found, *eg* the Metal Box Company's card index to periodical articles closed some years ago but still used for older materials) and some published bibliographies. In the first place, how does one decide at what point to open the chain of division? And how many steps of division does one include? Should we have

    Astronomy—solar system—sun
or
    Science—astronomy—stars—sun
or perhaps
    Science—physics—astronomy—stars—solar system—sun?

While we are still thinking of alphabetical arrangement rather than systematic grouping, such decisions are likely to be made on an *ad hoc* basis rather than in a consistent theoretical fashion. The second point is that this kind of indirect entry is only helpful if we arrange the resulting headings systematically. For example, alphabetical arrangement of a series of subheadings under Physics would give

Physics—electricity

Physics—heat

Physics—light

Physics—magnetism

The amount of grouping that can be achieved is too limited to be of any great value, and the objective is more satisfactorily attained by adopting systematic arrangement completely. However, both BTI and LCSH occasionally use headings of this kind, *eg*

MOTOR CARS, Types, Aston Martin DBS (BTI)

Shakespeare, William, 1564-1616—Characters—Falstaff (LCSH)

though one could argue strongly that these are out of place in direct entry methods.

Since the direct entry terms are hidden in indirect entry, it is necessary to build up a large network of cross-references in order to make sure that readers can find the topics they are looking for. This can be done by chain procedure, which is probably reasonably effective in this situation. On the other hand, we can cut down on the number of *see also* references we need to link related terms, since we do not need to link those which are brought together by the indirect mode of entry. For example, we need an entry

Cans: Food: Tinplate: Containers

see Containers: Tinplate: Food: cans

but we do not need a reference

Containers *see also* Cans;

Aluminium

　see Metals: Non-ferrous: Aluminium

Non-ferrous metals

　see Metals: Non-ferrous

but we do not need

Metals *see also* Non-ferrous metals

or

Non-ferrous metals *see also* Aluminium.

We have already mentioned that some simple filing rules are necessary even in a telephone directory, and as headings in an alphabetical catalogue get more complex it is often necessary to introduce quite complex rules to govern the overall arrangement. The first decision is whether filing is to be *letter by letter* (all through) or *word by word*. The index to the present work is word by word: thus 'index vocabulary' is found *before* 'indexing'; in a letter by letter arrangement the converse would apply. A good example of a letter by letter index is that to the *Encyclopaedia Britannica*. There are arguments on both sides, and the case for each has been put forward in the *Indexer*.[10] A lot depends on whether hyphens are taken as splitting or joining words; for example, in the index to this work they are taken as joining words into one whole, so that 'cross-references' follows 'Crossley', whereas 'cross references' without the hyphen would precede 'Crossley'. The reverse convention is used by LCSH, where we find the sequence

Pitch pine
Pitch-pipe *see* Pitchpipe
Pitching
Pitchpipe

in which the hyphen is in effect deleted altogether.

The second decision is the one already mentioned in our consideration of Kaiser's rules: the problem of grouping. Again we have two possibilities; either we can use a strict alphabetical order, or we can group certain subheadings to give what may be a more helpful arrangement. The punctuation in headings consisting of more than one word can be highly significant, or it may be ignored, or there may be a difference between the filing position of two words separated by punctuation and two not separated. The following examples from Sears and BTI will illustrate this, though the convention adopted is the exact reverse in the two cases.

Sears:

Advertising
Advertising, Art in *see* Commercial art
Advertising—Libraries
Advertising, Television *see* Television advertising
Advertising as a profession

Ability
Ability—testing
Ability grouping in education
BTI:
MIXING ENGINES
MIXING: Animal feedstuffs
MIXING, Batch
MIXING: Fluids

Apart from this both BTI and Sears use strict alphabetical order, ignoring the punctuation, but this is not the case with LCSH; in that list a considerable amount of grouping takes place at some headings, and the punctuation used is given a filing value, as can be seen from the following examples and from the example Sales on p 58.

Shakespeare, William, 1564-1616
  — Characters
    — Welshmen
    — Women
    — Falstaff [Margaret of Anjou, etc]
  — Chronology
Shakespeare, William, 1564-1616.
    Paraphrases, tales, etc.
Shakespeare, William, 1564-1616, in
    fiction, drama, poetry etc.

Women
  — Portraits
Women, British
Women, delinquent *see* Delinquent women
Women and socialism
Women and the sea
Women as statisticians
Women delinquents *see* Delinquent women
Women statisticians *see* Women as statisticians
Women's colleges

Pipe
Pipe — Welding
Pipe (Musical instrument)
Pipe, Aluminium
Pipe, Wooden
Pipe bending

Pipe-fitting
Pipe music
Piperonal
Pipes, Deposits in

(In the above examples, a selection of the headings is given to illustrate the filing order; there will be other headings in the lists at the points shown)

It is evident that LCSH is not alphabetically arranged, and one may question the purpose of the groupings illustrated.[11] The value of the direct alphabetical approach is that, given a working knowledge of the alphabet, one can find a heading for a specific subject very quickly; to gain this advantage one has to accept the consequential alphabetical scattering. If we want the advantages of grouping, we have to accept that access will become less direct unless we go over to systematic arrangement with its notation to guide us. Without a considerable knowledge of LCSH it is difficult to see how a user could find ' Falstaff ' in the above arrangement, for example, while the deviation from strict alphabetization is highlighted by the need for the two references to ' Delinquent women ' from ' Women, delinquent ' *and* ' Women delinquents '.

The early part of this chapter was devoted to the construction of alphabetical headings, and means of devising rules for this. We also have to have rules for filing, otherwise we may not be able to find the headings we have constructed, but their existence suggests that even those who favour alphabetical headings may see some point in systematic arrangement!

BIBLIOGRAPHY

1 Cutter, C A: *Rules for a dictionary catalog.* Washington, Government Printing Office, fourth edition 1904 (reprinted by the Library Association).

2 Kaiser, J: *Systematic indexing.* Pitman, 1911.

3 Ranganathan, S R: *Dictionary catalogue code.* Madras, Thompson & Co Ltd; London, Grafton, 1945 (Madras Library Association publications series, 14).

Ranganathan, S R: *Classified catalogue code, with additional rules for dictionary catalogue code.* Asia Publishing House, fifth edition 1964.

4 Thompson, A: ' Rules for subject headings, periodicals subject index, Royal Institute of British Architects library '. *Journal of documentation,* 9 (3) 1953, 169-174.

5 Coates, E J: *Subject catalogues.* LA, 1960. The first six chapters are essential reading. Students should also study carefully Coates' principles as they are practised in BTI, preferably contrasting one of the earlier volumes with one published 1968-, after the introduction of modified punctuation and computer production.

6 Coates, E J and Nicholson, 1: '*British technology index*—a study of the application of computer typesetting to index production'. (*in* Cox, N S M and Grose, M W: *Organization and handling of bibliographic records by computer.* Oriel Press, 1967, 167-178).

7 Palmer, B I: *Itself an education.* Second edition. Chapter on PRECIS by Derek Austin.

Austin, D and Butcher, P: *PRECIS: a rotated subject index system.* Council of the BNB, 1969 (BNB MARC Documentation Service publication No 3). Deals in detail with the computer codes necessary, as well as the basic theory.

Austin, D: 'An information retrieval language for MARC'. *Aslib proceedings, 22* (10) 1970, 481-491.

Foskett, D J: *Classification for a general index language.* Discusses the problems of subject analysis involved.

8 Farradane, J E L: 'Fundamental fallacies and new needs in library classification'. (Chapter 9 in the *Sayers memorial volume.*)

Farradane, J E L: 'Analysis and organization of knowledge for retrieval'. *Aslib proceedings, 22* (12) 1970, 607-616.

Farradane, J E L *and others*: *Report on research into information retrieval by relational indexing.* Part 1: methodology. London, City University, 1966. Though not as widely available as the other two references, this is probably the most detailed statement of the way in which Farradane intends his operators to be used.

9 Lynch, M F: ' Subject indexes and automatic document retrieval: the structure of entries in *Chemical abstracts* subject indexes '. *Journal of documentation, 22* (3) 1966, 167-185.

Armitage, J E and Lynch, M F: 'Articulation in the generation of subject indexes by computer'. *Journal of chemical documentation, 7* (3) 1967, 170-178.

Armitage, J E and Lynch, M F: ' Some structural characteristics of articulated subject indexes '. *Information storage and retrieval, 4* 1968, 101-111.

10 *The indexer, 3* 1962-3, 15, 21, 93-95, 158.

11 American Library Association: *ALA rules for filing catalog*

cards. Chicago, ALA, second edition 1968. Opts for strict alphabetical order.

Horner, J L: *Cataloguing*. AAL, 1970. Chapter 24.

Section 3 of J L Horner's *Cataloguing* is valuable background reading for this chapter.

CHAPTER 6

Systematic arrangement

We have seen that to construct an adequate network of genus-species cross-references for an alphabetical subject catalogue, we need to have some sort of systematic approach to the subject. The question that arises from this is whether we would not do better in the first place if we used a systematic arrangement which brought related subjects together. If we use such an arrangement, we must have some authority to turn to which tells us what the system is; we do not want to have to keep making the same decisions as to which subjects are related over and over again. Such an authority, listing subjects systematically and showing their relationships, is generally known as a *classification scheme,* and consists of four parts: *schedules,* in which subjects are listed systematically; *notation,* to enable us to use an arrangement which is no longer self-evident; *alphabetical index,* to enable us to find a given topic without having to scan all the schedules; and an *organization* to keep it current. These will now be considered in detail, but it must always be remembered that it is the schedules which are the essential core of the scheme.

SCHEDULES

Before we can start to arrange subjects systematically we have to establish what exactly are the subjects we wish to arrange; we have to carry out the same process of analysis as with alphabetical arrangement, but this time with the object of grouping the subjects rather than establishing which is the most significant element. Consider the titles enumerated in table 4. It quickly appears that they fall into two main groups, literature and metallurgy, and that these groups are homogeneous and distinct; such distinct, homogeneous subjects are called *basic classes.* If we want to arrange these titles systematically, then obviously the first move is to group them into the two basic classes. The next step is to consider each basic class separately, to see what principles we can use to arrive at a useful order within them.

84

1 The study of literature
2 Select methods of metallurgical analysis
3 The growth of the English novel
4 Elements of heat treatment of metals
5 Modern drama 1800–
6 A textbook of metallurgy
7 Playwriting
8 Methods for the analysis of aluminium
9 The poet's task
10 Iron and steel
11 The French drama of today
12 The metallurgy of beryllium
13 The literature of the Spanish people
14 The manufacture of iron and steel
15 A history of English drama 1600-1900
16 Equipment for the thermal treatment of non-ferrous metals
17 English literature of the twentieth century
18 Rare metals handbook
19 The background of modern English poetry, 1901-1915
20 Methods for the analysis of raw copper
21 Latin literature
22 Heat treatment of aluminium alloys
23 English literature and its readers
24 Heat treatment of steel
25 Some principles of fiction
26 Copper: the science and technology of the metal
27 A short history of German literature
28 Methods for the analysis of iron and steel
29 The temper of the seventeenth century in German literature
30 Twentieth century German verse
31 A few facts about aluminium
32 The decline of the Spanish novel, 1516-1600

TABLE 4: Facet analysis

We therefore need to study the titles carefully to see whether any further groups suggest themselves. We find that in literature, such terms as German, French, English, Spanish and Latin occur and form a group of *languages;* drama, poetry, novels suggest a group characterized by *literary form;* while seventeenth century, 1901-1915, and 1840's are clearly periods of *time.* If we now go through the whole of the group, we will find that all the important concepts fall into one or other of these groups; no matter how many more similar titles we take, they will still repeat this pattern. In metallurgy, we find a number of terms denoting *metals*, either individual or families (*eg* non-ferrous), and others which indicate that some sort of *operation* is carried out, *eg* heat treatment.

We can analyse any basic class into a limited number of such groups. Ranganathan, to whom much of the terminology in this area is due, named these groups *facets*, because each represents a particular facet or aspect of a subject. If we consider a topic such as copper, we can place it in a number of different contexts; for example, there will be a metals facet in metallurgy, as we have already seen, but there will also be a materials facet in engineering, a substances facet in chemistry and so on. Copper as a topic taken out of context is an *isolate*, but if we place it in context in a facet in a particular basic class we can refer to it as a *focus* in that facet (plural *foci*). We can tell if we have carried out our analysis adequately by the fact that the foci within a facet should be mutually exclusive; that is, we cannot envisage a composite subject which consists of two foci from the same facet. We cannot have the seventeenth century 1840's, or German English, or copper aluminium, but we *can* have composite subjects consisting of combinations of foci from different facets: English novels, seventeenth century German literature, analysis of copper, heat treatment of aluminium.

We have to make two important decisions before we can start to write down our classification scheme. We have to decide on the order within a facet, and we have to decide on the order in which we cite the facets in a composite subject—the citation order.

ORDER WITHIN FACETS

Whereabouts in the sequence does any given subject appear? We are trying to arrange subjects systematically, but it is important to remember *why* we are doing this; it is because we believe that by arranging related subjects together we will be helping our users. Our efforts to find a sound systematic arrangement must therefore be directed to finding a *helpful order*. There are a number of general principles which may be appropriate, particularly in the neutral situation where we cannot foresee the needs of the users.

Chronological: This is obvious where arrangement in periods may be envisaged, such as in literature, but it is also applicable where operations may be considered sequentially, *eg* Natural gas technology, where we find:

processing
storage
transportation
distribution
use.

Evolutionary: This is frequently similar to, or identical with, the previous arrangement. It suggests itself for the biological sciences, but may also be used elsewhere, and is also related to the next principle.

Increasing complexity: In many subjects we find a steady development from basic ideas to their most complex application, a good example being mathematics:

arithmetic
algebra
geometry
  Euclidean
  non-Euclidean
  trigonometry
  descriptive
  coordinate
calculus
  differential
  integral

Size: Many subjects lend themselves to a quasi-arithmetical arrangement, *eg* music:

solos
duets
trios *etc*

and government:

central/federal
regional/state/provincial
metropolitan/city
urban/town
rural/village

Spatial: This is the obvious choice for place, where we would try to arrange together countries which are contiguous, but it may also be used elsewhere, *eg* transport:

```
ground
  railway
  car etc
water
  inland
    rivers
    canals
  marine
air
  balloons
  aircraft
space
  rockets
```

Preferred category: We often find that our users are likely to be interested in one or a few of the foci within a facet far more than in the rest. The normal approach is to begin at the beginning of a sequence, and work through it from left to right (on the shelves), or forward (in a catalogue or bibliography). It will therefore be helpful if we arrange our sequence so that the most wanted items are at the beginning rather than in the middle or at the end. We may remove the *preferred category* from its normal place in the sequence and bring it to the beginning; for example, in Linguistics or Literature we may begin with English (or the mother tongue), even if this means that it will not fall into its logically correct place according to whatever principle we are using. It must be remembered that we are aiming at a *helpful* order, not necessarily a logical one (though in general of course a clear principle of arrangement logically followed *will* be helpful). An example of spatial arrangement with an exception made for preferred category may be found in astronomy:

```
Planets
  Earth (preferred)
  Mercury
  Venus
  Mars
  Jupiter    etc
```

Canonical: In some subjects we find a traditional order, named by Ranganathan *canonical order;* this will often in such cases form a useful basis for our arrangement, particularly as it will almost certainly be reflected in literary warrant. For example, in Physics we often find in textbooks the sequence Heat, Light, Sound, and unless we wish to use a different principle we can usefully follow this order in our arrangement. The archetypal canon is of course that of the books of the Bible, which are gathered together in a fixed and unchanging order. However, we must be prepared for the fact that where subjects are concerned, few groupings are likely to show this kind of permanence; new approaches call for different groupings from the traditional, and other arrangements are likely to prove more helpful.

Alphabetical: If we are arranging individual topics each of which has a distinct name which is likely to be used to identify it, there is a strong argument for using these names and arranging them in alphabetical order. The obvious examples are found in Biography, where the individual topics are people, and Literature, where we reach a point where we need to arrange by author's name but still need to subarrange each author's works systematically. Individual makes of car form another group where alphabetical arrangement may be helpful.

There will be occasions when it is difficult to see any helpful principle; for example, in what order should we arrange grain crops, root crops, legumes, *etc* in the crops facet in Agriculture? If after careful study we are unable to establish any principle to guide us in our choice of a helpful order, then it is equally unlikely that our users will expect any particular order; we should choose one of the general principles listed above and use that. In other cases, there will be an order which is unique to a particular subject, and is suggested by the structure of the subject itself. The careful study of the literature which is necessary before we start our analysis will reveal this.

CITATION ORDER

We have already seen that it is very important when using alphabetical headings to choose the most significant item in a composite heading as the entry word. We have exactly the same choice to make with systematic arrangement, but this time the effects are if anything even more important. The links in the chain forming a composite heading must come from different facets (foci from the same facet cannot be combined), so we are faced with the problem of deciding which facet is the most important, which is next most important, and so on down to the least important. This order of precedence—the order in which we cite the facets—is called the *citation order*. The effect of the citation order is to group material on topics which fall into the *primary facet*, but to scatter information on topics which fall into any of the other facets. Table 5 shows the effect of changing

the citation order in Literature, using the titles from the list we have
already studied in table 4.

Literature grouped by language, then by literary form :
    Playwriting
    Modern drama, 1800-
    The poet's task   (no language specified)
    Some principles of fiction

    English literature and its readers
    English literature of the twentieth century
    The growth of the English novel
    A history of English drama, 1660-1900
    English poetry, 1901-1915

    German literature, a short history
    The temper of the seventeenth century in German literature
    Twentieth century German verse

    The French drama of today

    The literature of the Spanish people
    The decline of the Spanish novel, 1516-1600

Literature grouped by literary form, then by language :
    English literature and its readers
    English literature of the twentieth century
    German literature, a short history   (no form specified)
    The temper of the seventeenth century in German literature
    The literature of the Spanish people

    Some principles of fiction
    The growth of the English novel
    The decline of the Spanish novel, 1516-1600

    Playwriting
    Modern drama 1800-
    A history of English drama 1660-1900
    The French drama of today

    The poet's task
    The background of modern English poetry, 1901-1915
    Twentieth century German verse

            TABLE 5 : Effect of citation order on grouping

The first section shows the groupings which result from citing Language first, then Literary Form, then Period, while the second shows the effect of citing Literary Form first, then Language, then Period. In the first case, the user interested in English literature, French literature, or the literature of any language group, will find all his material together; but the student of Poetry will have to look in several different places. In the second case, the user interested in a particular Literary Form, *eg* Poetry, will find all his material together, but the student of English literature will have to look in several different places. Whichever citation order we choose, we have to accept the fact that we cannot please all of the people all of the time. Systematic arrangement brings related subjects together only if they fall into the primary facet. We accept the fact that secondary topics will be scattered because we consider that the groupings brought about by systematic arrangement will be helpful to an extent which will outweigh the disadvantages.

There is another point to having a definite citation order; this is, to provide one, and only one, unambiguous place for any given composite subject. Suppose that we have a document dealing with the Heat treatment of aluminium, and we do not have a fixed citation order; we do not know whether this item ought to go with other works on Heat treatment, or with those on Aluminium. Suppose again that we decide that this particular document ought to go with others on Heat treatment; next week, we may have another document on the same subject, but because of its different treatment of the subject we may decide to place it with other items on Aluminium. We now have two items on the same subject in two different places; the user trying to find information will find one, and assume that he has now found all that we have. The system has an inbuilt tendency to error which will cause us to miss items which we should find; the potential for recall will be greatly lowered. Placing the same composite subject in more than one group is known as *cross-classification,* and it cannot happen if we have a clearly defined citation order to which we adhere. If we are using an enumerative classification, we may have to make up our own rules if it does not cater for the composite subjects we have to deal with.

An important corollary of a fixed citation order is the factor of *predictability.* Not only can the classifier avoid cross-classification, by having one and only one possible place for any given composite subject, but the users can begin to recognize the pattern themselves. This can help in two ways; it can make using the arrangement easier, but it can also help in those situations where the users are not sure exactly what it is they want. In such cases the existence of a predictable pattern is an aid in the formulation of a satisfactory search strategy.

As with order within facets, there are some general principles which will help when we are trying to establish the correct citation order.

Subject before bibliographical form: In general, the subject of a work is more significant than the bibliographical form in which the information is presented, *ie* an encyclopedia of chemistry should be grouped with other works on chemistry, not with other encyclopedias; *New society* should be grouped with other works on the social sciences, not with other periodicals. However, there will be occasions when we will disregard this principle in favour of grouping by bibliographical form. We may have a periodicals room where we keep all periodicals, or perhaps only current issues; we may have an abstracts and indexes room where we keep all our tools for bibliographical searching, rather than scatter them by subject; if we have an active translations section associated with the library, as is the case in many special libraries, we may decide to keep all our technical dictionaries together; or we may decide to keep all ' quick reference ' works together so that people using them do not disturb other users of the collections. All of these decisions relate to the locating of physical items within the library, but will be reflected in the catalogue; we can however make additional entries in the catalogue using the preferred citation order.

Purpose/product: Many basic classes represent subjects in which the objective is to construct some particular product, or achieve some particular purpose. In such cases, the primary facet will normally be the end product or purpose. For example, the purpose of agriculture is to produce crops; the crops facet will therefore be the primary one in the basic class Agriculture. This principle may be used throughout most of Technology.

Dependence: It is difficult to imagine such operations as Heat treatment without the materials they are applied to, as we have seen earlier when discussing Coates' ideas on significance order. These operations are in fact *dependent* upon the existence of the material; without the materials, there would be no operations. In such cases, the dependent facet should follow the one on which it depends.

Whole-Part: An extension of the idea of dependence is that of Parts being subsidiary to the Wholes to which they belong. Thus in the various branches of Engineering, Machines are more important than Parts, so the Machines facets should precede Parts facets in the citation order. In general, *kinds* of things are more important than *parts*. For example, in Packaging, kinds of container (cans, composites, paper boxes) is the primary facet, with parts (bodies, ends, lids) subsidiary to it.

Decreasing concreteness: Ranganathan has suggested that one, and only one, correct citation order for every basic class can be established, reflecting an order of decreasing concreteness. This order is usually known as PMEST, from the initial letters of Ranganathan's *fundamental categories*, Personality, Matter, Energy, Space, Time. These will be studied in more detail in the chapter on colon classification; for the present, we should note that, as has already been mentioned in considering Ranganathan's ideas on the use of these categories to establish significance order in the alphabetical catalogue, their generality frequently leads to doubt as to their precise mode of application, particularly in the case of Personality. In addition, a facet which is Matter in one basic class *eg* Materials in Library science, may become Personality in another basic class, in this case Bibliography; other similar changes are possible.

The above lines may be followed to give a generalized facet order: Things—Kinds—Parts—Materials—Properties—Processes—Operations—Agents. However, it is by no means obvious how we can apply this to Literature, or some of the social sciences. We are faced with the same problem as in alphabetical order: what exactly is the most significant part of a subject? Once again we have to restate the purpose of systematic arrangement: to provide an order which will be helpful to the user. We must try to group together those foci which a user is likely to want to find grouped; if we can discover this, we have established at least the primary facet. As with significance order in alphabetical headings, it is when we have difficulty in establishing users' needs that we are obliged to rely on general principles, in the hope that these will prove valid for a good proportion of our users.

The idea of one place and one place only for any composite subject is central to the idea of shelf arrangement, or ordering of items in a bibliography. However, the essential corollary of the one place requirement, a fixed citation order, can lead to problems, and has been the source of most of the criticism of systematic arrangement and pre-coordinate systems. It assumes that we can satisfy our users by one fixed grouping, but as has been pointed out, we cannot please all of the people all of the time. Two examples may help to demonstrate this, one from Literature, the other from Engineering.

In a general library, the user's approach to Literature will usually be primarily through language, secondly through literary form. Our readers often take it for granted that all the English literature is together, and ask for novels, or plays, or whatever form is of interest to them. Period is usually less important, but has a role in that most readers are interested in *modern* literature. The situation in an academic library is rather different; here, students will usually be interested primarily in a particular language, as before, but within that language are likely to be studying a particular period rather than a particular form. Indeed, it can be argued that division by literary form is a hindrance to them, because it separates the works of an author who has written in more than one form. We have here two situations which differ in that the need of the users in one is for a different set of groupings from that required by users in the other. One citation order cannot cater for both, and it is interesting to note that the Dewey decimal classification (DC), which is directed mainly toward the general, public, library situation, has the language, form, period, citation order first outlined, whereas the Library of Congress classification (LC), intended to arrange a library for scholars, to a very large extent ignores form in its Literature schedules.

A fixed citation order implies that there is a ' standard ' approach to a subject; but what of the situation in a library serving a research establishment? The essential characteristic of research is that it is intended to upset the accepted order of things, and we must therefore expect research workers to find an arrangement based on the old order something less than helpful. Such a situation arose in the Central Library of the English Electric Company, where a classified catalogue was in use, arranged by the library's own classification scheme for Engineering. This has a citation order Machines: Parts: Materials : Problems; thus a topic such as fatigue, which assumed a new importance in the 1950's as the unexpected cause of at least two major air disasters, is a Problem, and falls into the least important facet. For most of the users of the catalogue this is acceptable; the company produces machines, and most of its research is concerned with these— motors, generators, nuclear reactors, aircraft. However, this citation order does mean that fatigue is scattered at a very large number of places in the classified sequence, simply because it falls into the least important facet and is thus not used for grouping; in fact, more than 300 places. This is hardly likely to appeal to the groups of engineers who are working on this very problem; they cannot be expected to regard as helpful an arrangement which scatters their interests to over 300 different places. A similar difficulty was met in the Library of the Atomic Energy Research Establishment, Harwell, where it proved impossible to find a satisfactory citation order in some subject areas covered by the catalogues. Some solutions to the problem are discussed later under the heading Multiple entry systems (chapter 10); we may assume for the time being that, for the general library at least, it *is* possible to find a citation order which will result in groupings helpful to the great majority of users, while remaining aware of the fact that in certain situations this is less likely to be the case.

FILING ORDER

We have now established the need for a careful study of the literature of a subject to determine the concepts likely to arise, and the facets into which we can group these concepts; the need for order within the facets; and the need for a citation order which will determine the order of precedence of facets in composite subjects. We now have to study the way in which we must write out the schedule which will show clearly whereabouts in the sequence any given subject—simple or composite—will be found.

It is a commonly accepted principle of systematic arrangement that general should precede special. This can apply both to subjects related as genus to species and to those in which the relationship is syntagmatic. For example, Metals should precede Non-ferrous metals, which in its turn should precede Aluminium (though this does not indicate whether Aluminium should precede or follow Ferrous metals—aluminium does not lie in the same chain of subdivision). At the same time, Aluminium should precede Heat treatment of aluminium, as should Heat treatment, since both are more general than the composite subject of which they form part. But should Aluminium precede Heat treatment, or *vice versa*? We cannot say that Aluminium is more general than Heat treatment since we have no basis of comparison; we cannot determine a special/general relationship between foci from different facets, only between those within the same facet. We have determined the order of facets when more than one is represented in a composite subject, but we still have to determine the order in which the facets themselves should be written down so that we can arrange simple subjects in which only one facet is represented. The citation order, together with the general principle enunciated above, that general should precede special, will enable us to do this.

Consider the following seven titles, falling within the basic class Literature:

The English novel
Trends in twentieth century literature
The novel as a literary form
Twentieth century English literature
English literature
The English novel in this century
The modern novel, 1900-

Using the citation order Language—Literary form—Period, we can re-state these subjects in the formal manner:

English: novel	(1)
Twentieth century	(2)
Novel	(3)
English: twentieth century	(4)
English	(5)
English: novel: twentieth century	(6)
Novel: twentieth century	(7)

Having done this, we can group them according to the citation order into those in which a language is specified; those in which no language is specified but we have a literary form; and those in which neither language nor literary form is specified but we have a period.

Group A	English: novel	(1)
	English: twentieth century	(4)
	English	(5)
	English: novel: twentieth century	(6)
Group B	Novel	(3)
	Novel: Twentieth century	(7)
Group C	Twentieth century	(2)

Now, however we arrange them, we must keep the groups intact, because this is the purpose of having a citation order. Consider the three subjects (6), (7) and (2); if we are to arrange these so that general precedes special, it must be in the order (2), (7), (6).

Twentieth century	(2)	Group C
Novel: twentieth century	(7)	Group B
English: novel: Twentieth century	(6)	Group A

If we are to keep the groups intact, then equally group C must precede group B, which in turn must precede group A. Within group B, clearly (3) must precede (7). Within group A, (5) must come first, since it is more general than any of the others, and (6) must come last, as being more special than any. This leaves us with (1) and (4) to sort out, but (1) must be grouped with (6), since within the general group English literature they both deal with the novel, which is in the next facet to be considered. So we end up with the arrangement:

Group C	Twentieth century	(2)
Group B	Novel	(3)
	Novel: twentieth century	(7)
Group A	English	(5)
	English: twentieth century	(4)
	English: novel	(1)
	English: novel: twentieth century	(6)

We have now followed the two guidelines we established to begin with, the citation order Language, Literary form, Period, and the general-before-special principle. If we now study the result, we find that (perhaps contrary to expectation) it is the least important facet Period which comes first, with the most important, Language, coming last; that is to say, the filing order is the reverse of the citation order. This effect, which arises because we wish to preserve the idea of general before special for both genus-species and syntagmatic relationships, is known as the *Principle of inversion*. If we do not follow this principle, then we shall find that general precedes special for genus-species relationships, *ie* relationships between foci within the same facet, but that for some syntagmatic relationships general will follow special.

The principle of inversion is in conflict with the suggestion put forward under the heading *Preferred category* (page 88) that users like to find the material of most interest to them at the beginning of the sequence. In the example worked out above for Literature, before we come to any particular language (English will probably be the first), we shall have to scan through entries relating to the whole of Literature limited only by Period, and entries relating to particular literary forms—yet we have said that Language is the most important element. For this reason, some classification schemes have ignored the principle of inversion, for example the English Electric Company's scheme for *Engineering* previously mentioned, and the scheme for *Occupational safety and health* devised by D J Foskett. However, the introductions to editions of the English Electric scheme after the first have pointed out that in practice this has not worked satisfactorily, and if the scheme were to be started again from the beginning there is little doubt that the editors would decide to follow the principle of inversion.

A rather different way of showing the principle has been demonstrated by Palmer and Wells. If we indicate when a facet is present by a 1, and absent by a 0, we can write down a formula for each title in the form of a binary notation, using the citation order:

	L	F	P	
English: novel	1	1	0	(1)
Twentieth century	0	0	1	(2)
Novel	0	1	0	(3)
English: twentieth century	1	0	1	(4)
English	1	0	0	(5)
English: novel: twentieth century	1	1	1	(6)
Novel: twentieth century	0	1	1	(7)

If we now arrange the titles by the notation, we find that we get the order that we arrived at previously: (2) (3) (7) (5) (4) (1) (6). The notation has made the rearrangement simpler, but does not show quite so clearly *why* we get the result we do.

The principle of inversion is one that often causes students an unnecessary amount of difficulty. The easiest way to understand it is to arrange a set of examples using first a scheme following the principle, then a scheme ignoring it. The difference in the overall arrangement will then become clear. In the example used above to demonstrate the principle, we used the citation order Language: Literary form: Period. This gave us the groups A, B and C, since this is the function of the citation order; we chose that citation order because it would give us those groups, which represent the kind of grouping that we think our readers will find useful. If we ignore the principle of inversion, we will make our filing order also A B C, so let us consider the effect this will have on the overall filing order. In Group B, if general is to precede special, Novel must precede Novel: twentieth century. For the same reason, in the Group A (ignoring title 4 for the moment) we shall have the sequence

English

English: novel

English: novel: twentieth century

and since period now follows literary form we can add title 4 at the end of this sequence. The overall order will thus be

98

English
English: novel
English: novel: twentieth century
English: twentieth century
Novel
Novel: twentieth century
Twentieth century

It will be seen that the result here is not the orderly progression from general to special that we had before, but a progression which moves from general (English) to less general (English novel) to least general (English: novel: twentieth century), then back to more general (English: twentieth century) to more general (Novel) to less general (Novel: twentieth century) to more general (twentieth century). The same kind of result will occur whenever the principle is not followed. Later in this chapter a schedule is worked out for Library science, using a particular citation order, the way in which the principle of inversion works can be seen very clearly if the titles on p 105 are arranged first using the schedule with the citation order suggested, then using it with a different citation order but keeping the same filing order. (The exercise is easier if the schedule is given a notation, but can be carried out without this. The method is outlined within the next section, schedule construction.) The principle will be ignored if we keep the same citation order and alter the filing order, as we did just above, or keep the same filing order but alter the citation order, as is suggested for the exercise. In both cases the result is the same; instead of an orderly progression in which a general heading always precedes headings more specific, we shall find an order in which it is difficult to predict exactly whereabouts a particular degree of generality is to be found. We shall still be able to find subjects, and the order will still give us the groupings which we have decided are likely to be most helpful, but if we do not find what we want straight away, altering our search strategy is likely to be confusing.

SCHEDULE CONSTRUCTION
We have now established all the information that we need to enable us to construct a schedule, or table, in a given subject area. We have decided on the order of importance of the facets of the subject—the citation order; the order of foci within each facet; and, using the principle of inversion, we know that the order in which the facets should appear in the schedule is the reverse of the citation order.

We now have to make a decision as to whether our schedules should be enumerative or synthetic; since the latter are very much easier to construct and use, let us consider them first.

In a synthetic schedule we need only list simple subjects; we do not try to list any composite subjects. All that we need to include in the schedule will be the foci within the various facets; the citation order tells us how to combine these whenever this is necessary. To write down the schedule, all that has to be done is to write down the facets, beginning with the least important and ending with the most important. Within each facet, the foci will of course be arranged according to whatever principle we have adopted.

To arrange composite subjects using such a schedule, we must first analyse them into individual foci, and rearrange these according to the citation order, so that the most important focus in each case is the first in the formal statement. Taking some of the titles from table 4 and using the citation order Language, Literary form, Period, we arrive at the following formal statements:

3 English: novel
5 Drama: 1800-
7 Drama: techniques
9 Poetry: criticism
11 French: drama: twentieth century
15 English: drama: 1600-1900
17 English: twentieth century
19 English: poetry: 1901-1915
25 Novel
29 German: seventeenth century
30 German: poetry: twentieth century
32 Spanish: novel: 1516-1600

(Note that in addition to putting these into our preferred citation order we have eliminated various synomyms, *eg* fiction, verse, plays). Using the schedule we have constructed, we can put the primary foci into order:

Novel   25
Drama   5, 7,
Poetry   9
English 3, 15, 17, 19
German   29, 30
French   11
Spanish 32

We have thus settled the order for some but not all of our examples. We still have to sort out those which have the same primary focus, once again using the schedule, but this time applying it *within* each group of items.

Drama : techniques   7
        1800-   5

(because techniques comes from a facet less important than period and thus precedes it), and

English : twentieth century   17
         novel   3
         drama   15
         poetry   19
German : seventeenth century 29
         poetry   30

We now have arrived at the correct placings for each of the subjects in our list:

25 Novel
 7 Drama: techniques
 5 Drama: 1800-
 9 Poetry: criticism
17 English: twentieth century
 3 English: Novel
15 English: drama: 1600-1900
19 English: poetry: 1901-1915
29 German: seventeenth century
30 German: poetry: twentieth century
11 French: drama: twentieth century
32 Spanish: novel: 1516-1600

In this particular case we did not have to go beyond the second concept in any of the statements, but if we had been obliged to do so the procedure would have been exactly the same. Suppose for example that we had reached a stage where we had

English : drama : Restoration
English : drama : Jacobean
English : drama : techniques
English : drama : 1800-
English : drama
English : drama : 1840-1890

We should now have to arrange these according to the third concept in the formal statement, to give us

English: drama
English: drama: techniques
English: drama: Jacobean
English: drama: Restoration
English: drama: 1800-
English: drama: 1840-1890

and so on, until we had arrived at the most complete systematic arrangement possible. In a normal library situation, there will of course be more than one item at most points in our systematic arrangement, and these can then be arranged according to author's name, in chronological sequence, or by some similar characteristic additional to the subject specification.

The schedule is thus very simple, yet from it we are able to find an unambiguous place for any given composite subject (provided of course that the concepts involved in it are listed in our schedule). Because we list only single concepts, with none of their possible combinations, the schedule can be very brief, yet be as powerful in arranging our collections as a much longer enumerative schedule.

If, however, we decide to compile an enumerative schedule, we have to follow a similar procedure, but this time for any and every composite subject. For each focus in the primary facet we have to envisage which foci from the second facet will be likely to co-occur in a composite subject, and list these; in addition, for each of these we have to consider which foci from the third facet are also likely to co-occur, and then list the composite subjects formed in this way. Then, when we come to classify by the scheme, we do not have to build up the composite subject represented in the item we are dealing with, but will instead find it, ready made, in the scheme.

An example will help to make the distinction clearer. If we are using the Universal Decimal Classification (UDC), we find that in the basic class Literature we have a completely synthetic schedule, which occupies about a page of the schedules; to classify a composite topic such as *The English novel of the 1840's* we have to find English, novel and 1840's, and combine these elements. If we are using an enumerative classification such as the Bibliographic Classification (BC), we turn to Literature, then find English literature, then find nineteenth century English literature, and finally the period 1837-1870, which is the closest we find to the precise one we require; then we find listed under that period: novelists (as well as the other literary forms). Problems of synthesis are mainly notational: can we combine the notation for the various elements to give us the correct composite notation? These are discussed in a later section. The problems of enumeration, on the other hand, are mainly those of quantity: can we enumerate all the composite subjects we are likely to need, or do we make a selection? LC is an enumerative scheme, and its schedules for language and literature occupy some 2,000 pages of print, as opposed to UDC's one; but even this is a selection of the possible combinations, because LC only includes subjects if there is literary warrant for them in the Library of Congress *and* it is thought that they need to be specified for the shelf arrangement. What usually happens in enumerative schemes is that a rather limited selection of composite subjects is listed and that others which are not listed have to be accommodated with their most important focus but without specifying other foci. In addition, enumerative schemes do not usually have a clear facet structure, so that one is often left in doubt as to which is the most important focus.

Consider the subject *Gothic mural painting in Bohemia and Moravia;* there are three foci here, *Gothic,* from the Time facet, *mural,* from the Form facet, and *Bohemia and Moravia* from the Place facet, all three facets within the basic class *Painting.* If we turn to DC16 to classify this, we find that we can classify any of the foci singly, but have no means of combining them, nor is there any clear indication of which is to be considered the most important. We find an instruction that place is more important than time, but no instruction is given as to priority between place and form. Not only can we not classify this topic precisely, we do not even know which focus to classify it with as being the most important. This is a criticism of one particular enumerative scheme, DC; it is however typical of the kind of criticism that inevitably arises with this kind of scheme, from the impossibility in practice of listing all the composite subjects that have occurred or may occur in the future.

Another problem that is often found in practice in enumerative schemes, despite the fact that theoretically it cannot occur, is that concepts of different kinds are found to be mixed up, so that cross-classification becomes not so much a danger, more a way of life. Consider the following excerpt from the abridged UDC schedules:

628	PUBLIC HEALTH ENGINEERING
628.3	Sewage, rain-, foul-water. Purification, etc.
628.33	Physical and mechanical treatment
.334	Screening. Grit and grease removal

.335	Flocculation: tanks, etc.
.336	Sludge: handling, disposal
.337	Electrical treatment of sewage
.34	Chemical treatment processes *etc*

It will be seen that in the middle of a series of methods of treatment (Actions, Operations, Processes) we find a material 'sludge' which is the result of a process of settling, not mentioned in the schedule. In another example we find:

361	SOCIAL RELIEF IN GENERAL
.9	Relief or aid in emergencies, disasters
.91	Earthquakes, storms, hurricanes
.92	Floods
.93	War, civil war
.94	Epidemics
.95	Famine
.96	Fires, conflagrations
.98	Technical (volunteer) relief services

Either technical (volunteer) relief services are to be regarded as disasters in themselves, or we are faced with considerable problems in finding the correct place for technical (volunteer) services for earthquake relief. We shall be in the same position as we found in the last paragraph, uncertain of the correct place to choose for a composite subject not specifically listed in the schedules.

As has already been indicated in chapter 4, all systems enumerate to some extent; a synthetic classification scheme has to list the foci in each facet, and if it fails to list the particular focus we are searching for on some occasion we shall again be faced with the problem of lack of specificity. For example, the subject *Design and construction of transistor superhets* implies a specification

Communications engineering-radio-apparatus-receivers-
superheterodyne-using transistors.

If we are using the Colon Classification (CC), which is as completely synthetic a scheme as possible, we find that this can only be classified with radio engineering; the scheme simply does not enumerate anything more detailed in this subject area. Even with UDC we find (using the abridged edition) that we can only specify receivers, not superhets, and are thus unable to be specific.

It should be remembered that we have been thinking so far of the classifier trying to find a place in the overall arrangement for each new subject as it arises. From the point of view of the user, who only sees the results of the classifier's work, there is no difference between a synthetic scheme and an enumerative, except in those instances where the enumerative scheme has failed to foresee a composite subject. If we were to write out all the possible combinations of concepts arising from the use of a synthetic scheme, we should have an enumerative scheme. The real problem for the classificationist, *ie* the compiler of a classification scheme, is that the number of possible combinations is enormous. Mathematically speaking, if we have a schedule containing four facets, with four foci in each facet, the number of possible subjects we can specify is 624! And this from a ridiculously simple schedule containing only sixteen concepts! It is small wonder that an enumerative scheme usually only lists a selection—but provided that it lists the *right* selection, it will prove just as effective as a synthetic scheme, and the user will have no means of telling the difference. The real problem lies in the fact that enumerative schemes are usually *closed*; if we do have to deal with a subject not enumerated, we have to wait for the compiler to tell us where we can put it in the schedule, rather than insert it ourselves as we can in a synthetic scheme.

CONSTRUCTION OF A CLASSIFICATION SCHEDULE

It may be helpful to demonstrate how we may set about constructing a classification schedule in a limited subject area, in this case Library science. By studying the following list of titles carefully, we can establish certain facets; we can then decide on a citation order and helpful order within each facet. Finally we can write down the schedule and use it to arrange the items (titles taken from *Library science abstracts*).

1 Progress of the Universal Decimal Classification in the USSR
2 Baltimore County Public Library initiates book catalog
3 An art reference library for children
4 Automation in the Detroit Public Library
5 Cooperation in government libraries
6 Non-standard material at the National Lending Library for Science and Technology
7 The National Library of Canada
8 Libraries and librarianship in Saskatchewan
9 Book selection tools for agricultural documents
10 An information retrieval system for maps
11 Aspects of recent research in classification

12 La Roche College classification scheme for phonograph records

13 The economics of book catalog production

14 Classification of law books in the University of South Africa Library

15 Book selection and acquisition processes in university libraries

16 Administrative problems of university libraries

17 Revision of classification schemes for Nigerian needs

18 Acquisitions

19 School libraries

20 Federal assistance to special libraries

21 The hospital library service in Lincoln

22 A mechanized circulation system

23 Automation in university libraries

24 Newspapers in technical college libraries

25 Library services to the blind in New Zealand

26 Public libraries in the New York metropolitan area

27 Metropolitan areas growing and under stress: the situation of the Detroit Public Library.

If we try to group the concepts arising from the titles, we find that a first approximation gives us four groups:

Libraries	*Materials*	*Operations*	*Common facets*
special	non-standard	cooperation	
government	newspapers	administration	automation
university	books	selection	research
technical	phonorecords	acquisition	revision
college	(*ie* records)	cataloguing	economics
public	maps	catalogues	various places
municipal	agriculture	bookform	
county	law	classification	
national		schemes	
hospitals		UDC	
blind		circulation	
children		finance	
reference		Federal aid	
art			
science			

It is clear that there is a group of 'Libraries' but that these fall into more than one subfacet:

kind	people served	mode of use	subject coverage
special	hospitals	reference	art
government	blind		science and
academic	children		technology
university			
technical college			
school			
public			
municipal			
county			
national			

We can of course extend the above lists even without literary warrant, by the addition of *eg*, lending, under mode of use, or industrial, under kind, once we have identified the facets.

We can also subdivide the Materials facet into two groups:

subject
law
agriculture
form

books	maps	non-standard
newspapers	records	

Within the Operations facet we find some concepts which depend on others, *eg*

classification—schemes
cataloguing—catalogues

In each case further subdivision by kind can be made. It would be possible to separate these into another facet, but for the time being we may keep them with the operations to which they belong.

We find a group of topics which may appear in any basic class, called common foci; as we shall see in the next chapter, there are usually four of these groups, but in the present example only two are represented, place and common subjects.

Having identified the facets, we need to decide on a citation order. For the neutral situation, this might well be Libraries—Materials—Operations, though in the context of a library school a citation order which brings Operations to the most significant place might well be more useful. Within Libraries, we may decide that kind is most important, then population served, then mode of use and finally subject; Materials may be arranged primarily by subject, then by physical form. Of the two common facets, place is more important than common subjects. This gives us an overall order:

Libraries—kind—population served—mode of use—subject—Materials—subject—form—Operations—Place—Common subjects.

If we decide to follow the principle of inversion, we shall arrive at a schedule outline as follows:

Common subjects
Place
Operations
Materials
  by form
  by subject
Libraries
  by subject
  by mode of use
  by population served
  by kind

Within each facet we need to arrive at some helpful order. In the Common subjects none suggests itself; for Place, we may use the schedule from an existing scheme; those Operations which form a logical sequence in time may be arranged chronologically, with circulation perhaps moved to a place under administration rather than its chronological place following technical services; in Materials, books, as the preferred category, begin the sequence; in kind of library, a progression by size of population served is a possibility. We can thus build up a schedule as follows:

FIGURE 2: Tentative schedule for library science

Common subject subdivisions
  revision
  research
  automation
  economics
Common place subdivisions
  (no schedule needed)
Operations
  Administration
   selection
   acquisition
   circulation

```
Technical services
  cataloguing
    catalogues
      book form
  classification
    schemes
      UDC
  Cooperation
  Finance
    government aid
Materials
  Books
  Serials
    periodicals
    newspapers
  non-standard (ie non-printed word)
    records
    maps
  by subject
    (no schedule needed)
Libraries
  by subject
    (no schedule needed)
  by mode of use
    reference
  by population served
    children
    hospitals
    handicapped
      blind
  by kind
    special
      government
    academic
      school
      technical college
      university
    public
      municipal
      county
      national
```

There are several points to note from this schedule. The first is that it is very incomplete in its listing of foci, but that despite this it probably covers most of the facets of library science. The more literature we study, the more foci we can insert, but additional facets will be few. Secondly, we can show some hierarchical (*ie* genus-species) relationships by the layout, though if we apply the schedule to shelf or catalogue arrangement it will not be possible to do this. Thirdly, we need to carry our analysis rather further than we have; for example, we could have blind children as the population served—but we have said that it is not possible to combine foci from the same facet! We may need to introduce subfacets here, to distinguish persons by age (and sex also, perhaps). Experience may also suggest modifications to the facet order suggested here. A scheme of the kind adumbrated here has been compiled by the Classification Research Group, and is in use in the libraries of the College of Librarianship Wales, the Polytechnic of North London School of Librarianship, and the Library Association. It is also being used to arrange the entries in *Library and information science abstracts* (LISA); largely as a result of studies of user reactions to this, the citation order was changed from the original Library—Materials—Operations to Operations—Materials—Libraries at the beginning of 1971.

BIBLIOGRAPHY

1 Several of the items mentioned in the bibliography for chapter 1 contain sections on facet analysis, *eg*

Vickery, B C: *Classification and indexing in science and technology.*

Foskett, D J: *Classification and indexing in the social sciences.*

Mills, J: *A modern outline of library classification.*

See also the following items:

Vickery, B C: *Faceted classification.* London, Aslib, 1960.

Vickery, B C: *Faceted classification schemes.* Rutgers, State University, Graduate School of Library Science, 1966. (Rutgers series on systems for the intellectual organization of information, *ed* Susan Artandi, vol 6.)

Mills, J: *Guide to the Universal Decimal Classification.* British Standards Institution, 1963. A valuable introduction to facet analysis, this work also shows how it may be applied successfully in a scheme which is basically one of the older enumerative kind.

Students should also look at examples of faceted schemes, *eg*

Foskett, D J: 'The London education classification'. *Education libraries bulletin*, Supplement 6, 1963.

English Electric Company Ltd: *Thesaurofacet*. 1970.

Classification Research Group: Bulletin no 7: *Four faceted schemes of classification. Journal of documentation, 18,* 1962, 65-88.

It is a useful exercise to construct a schedule by examining the literature of a subject, as found for example in an abstracting or indexing service, identifying the concepts present, grouping them into facets and deciding on a citation order, in the same way as we have demonstrated for library science.

CHAPTER 7

General classification schemes

So far we have been considering the problems that arise within a particular basic class. If we wish to include more than this, we have to face additional problems, in particular the one of overall order; in what sequence do we arrange a collection of basic classes? In the early years of library classification in the modern sense (*ie* from Dewey's introduction of his decimal classification in 1876) it was assumed that the order of main classes was the one important feature of a scheme, and such classification theorists as H E Bliss devoted much time and thought to this. When Ranganathan introduced the idea of consistent facet analysis applied to all basic classes in the first edition of CC, published in 1933, interest began to concentrate on the development of ' special ' classifications, *ie* those applied to a particular, limited, subject field, usually a single basic class, and during the 1950's the Classification Research Group in Britain devoted most of its thought to this problem. Techniques of analysis and synthesis, and the notational devices required to permit them, were developed, and several notable schemes were produced. In the 1960's there has been a swing back towards the general scheme and its problems, with the objective of developing a new classification of the whole of recorded knowledge, and some practical work has been done with the aid of a grant from NATO. We have therefore to consider now the problems of arranging basic classes in a helpful order, and the additional features which we must provide in a general scheme if it is to function properly.

COMMON FACETS

If the titles listed in table 6 are studied carefully, it will appear that there are certain kinds of concept which keep recurring, and which may be found in any basic class. We find for example dictionary, periodical, illustration, encyclopedia: all kinds of bibliographical form. Statistics, law, societies, research: all kinds of subject which exist in their own right, yet may be found as features within other subjects as well. We also find that all subjects may be considered from the historical and geographical points of view, or to use the more common terms, time and place. There are in effect four groups of subjects which may occur within any basic class: four common facets. In providing a schedule for a basic class, we may decide that it is not appropriate to include these common subdivisions, but obviously in a general scheme they must appear.[1]

1 *Metal industry* handbook and directory
2 Glossary of terms relating to iron and steel
3 English poetry and prose: an anthology
4 Metallurgical dictionary
5 British miniature electronic components data annual 1967-68
6 Colliers encyclopedia
7 The Oxford English dictionary
8 *Life* magazine
9 XIX century fiction: a bibliographical record
10 Cassell's encyclopedia of literature
11 *Washington post*
12 Bibliography on steel converter practice
13 Instrumentation in the metallurgical industry
14 The *voice of youth*: the Poetry Society's junior quarterly
15 Aluminium Development Association: Directory of members
16 Winston Churchill: the early years
17 The Highlands of Scotland in pictures
18 The rules of the game of netball
19 Statistical assessment of the life characteristic: a bibliography
20 A year with horses: John Beard's sketch book
21 American scientists of the 19th century
22 Handbook of chemistry and physics
23 Education in Scotland
24 Scientific and learned societies of Great Britain
25 Annual abstract of statistics
26 International who's who

TABLE 6: Identify the common factors

The titles in table 6 indicate that in some cases the bibliographical forms and the common subjects may be applied to the whole of knowledge as a unit, not just to a limited area such as a single basic class. A general encyclopedia presents information on the whole of knowledge in a particular form; a general periodical may treat of any or every subject. In a general scheme we shall therefore find it necessary to make provision for this, in what is known as a generalia class. Some general schemes also include in this class topics which may be regarded as pervasive or tool subjects; DC includes Library science and Documentation, while Brown included a number of subjects such as Logic, Mathematics, and Education in the Generalia class in his Subject Classification (SC) which are more helpfully arranged elsewhere.

MAIN CLASS ORDER

In a general scheme, we have to continue our process of grouping by arranging related basic classes together in sequence and imposing some sort of overall plan. To start in this way with the elements and build them up into larger groups is the inductive approach; in the past, the deductive method of taking the whole of knowledge and dividing it up into smaller areas has been the one more often used. The results are similar, but we find in many cases that the number of areas discovered by the deductive approach bears a close relationship to the number of notational symbols available, the most striking example of this being DC, where Dewey freely admits that ' Theoreticly division of every subject into just 9 parts is absurd ', but nevertheless goes ahead to do just that. By using induction we are more likely to avoid this kind of trap.

A major problem has always been to define the term main class, which is commonly used for these large areas or groups. We can see that heat, light, sound, electricity and magnetism can be grouped with various other basic classes to form a group of subjects which we call physics; but physics can itself be grouped with such subjects as chemistry and astronomy to form the group of physical sciences, while these can further be grouped with the biological sciences to form the natural sciences group. Finally, we can group this with a similar large assembly to form science and technology. We can carry out a similar series of groupings in other disciplines, ending up with three assemblies: science and technology, social sciences, and humanities. At what point do we stop? Or do we conclude that there are only three main classes? The question is evidently one of terminology, and in practice we find no agreement between the compilers of general classification schemes as to what constitutes a main class. Ranganathan defines main class: ' any class enumerated in the first order array of a scheme of classification of the universe of knowledge. This definition is valid only for the scheme concerned '.[2] Elsewhere he suggests that main classes are conventional, fairly homogeneous and mutually exclusive groups of basic classes, and also introduces the idea of ' partially comprehensive ' main classes as a means of differentiating the ' supergroups ' such as physical sciences. The idea that main classes are merely conventional groups may serve to free us from having to find any theoretical justification for our selection and ordering, and it emphasizes the fact that there is unlikely to be long term stability in any particular selection we may make. However, it is important to study the arguments which have been advanced to justify one order or another of main classes, and to see what effect this factor has on the overall arrangement given by a scheme.

DEWEY

Dewey credits his arrangement of main classes to ' the inverted Baconian arranjement of the St Louis library . . .', but also points out that ' everywhere filosofic theory and accuracy hav yielded to practical usefulness '. Palmer[3] suggests that if literary warrant be taken as the criterion BNB has identified no less than fifty four main classes in DC, rather than Dewey's nine. In many ways, the order in DC is poor, separating language (400) from literature (800), and history (900) from the other social sciences (300). It also reflects the state of knowledge of the latter half of the nineteenth century, with, for example, psychology shown as a division of philosophy. It illustrates quite well the point that an order of main classes which may be justified at one point in time may well cease to be acceptable as time passes; despite its grounding in Bacon's theory, nobody would now claim that Dewey's order is particularly helpful or theoretically valid.

BROWN

The order of main classes in the *Subject classification*[4] fits into the overall pattern :
  Matter and force
  Life
  Mind
  Record
which may be said to have some logical validity. However, Brown did not worry unduly about this aspect, and indeed placed the graphic and plastic arts in his generalia class, because he had some spare

notation there which was not available under the 'record' section. Brown is however interesting in that he introduced a principle which is still somewhat controversial but seems to be useful: the grouping of a science and its technology. Dewey had grouped all 'sciences' together and all 'technologies' together (with the exception of medicine, where both science and technology appear together). Brown instead placed each technology with the science upon which it depended, so that electrical engineering is found with electricity in physics, for example. This can be a helpful approach, particularly in such subjects as electronics, where the technology of solid state devices is hard to differentiate from their fundamental physics. However, Brown allowed himself to be carried away by this idea, linking music and acoustics, horseracing and zoology and so on in a way which is clearly unhelpful.

BLISS

Bliss devoted a great deal of time to establishing the correct order of main classes, and the introductions to the two volumes of his scheme contain much that is of value in this discussion, as does his other work.[5] He introduced several ideas which are still of value. Perhaps the most basic of these is the idea of the 'educational and scientific consensus'. Bliss thought it vital that a classification scheme for recorded knowledge should reflect the structure of knowledge as recognized and taught by scientists, philosophers and educators, and that the more knowledge we acquire, the more clearly we shall see this desired structure. Unfortunately, this is not the case: knowledge changes, the structure of knowledge changes, and any widely accepted pattern is likely to be out of date, for the purpose of research is indeed to change the structure of knowledge as well as to expand it. Bliss himself recognized that 'the old order changeth', and that any classification scheme will inevitably become gradually more and more divorced from helpful order; what he does not seem to have recognized is the speed with which this process can take place.

To establish the order of subjects within the educational and scientific consensus, Bliss used three main principles. The first of these is *collocation of related subjects*. For example, Bliss considers that Psychology is related to both Medicine and Education, so that the relevant part of his outline is as follows:

Anthropological sciences
   medicine

Psychology
Education
Social science

Here it will be seen that psychology is linked to both of these other topics. However, it may also be seen that Bliss did not follow his own second principle, *subordination of specific to general,* for in order to collocate it with psychology, education has to precede the more general heading social science. However, in general these two principles are sound and can give a helpful arrangement.

The third principle Bliss called *gradation in speciality,* and it relates to what is in effect a kind of progression of dependence. If we compare mathematics and physics, we can see that though we use the ideas of mathematics in physics, the converse is not true; we do not use the ideas of physics in mathematics, and to this extent therefore physics depends on and should follow mathematics. If we now compare physics and chemistry we find that on similar grounds chemistry should follow physics. We can arrive at an order within the sciences which can be justified in this way:

logic
mathematics
physics
chemistry
astronomy
geology
geography

It becomes rather more difficult to apply this idea to the biological sciences and social sciences, but within its limitations it is a valuable principle.

Apart from Bliss we find few efforts to produce a philosophically justifiable order of main classes. Ranganathan has argued the case for his own order in CC, but without conveying any great conviction; he clearly recognizes the fluid nature of such groupings, and is in any case more concerned with order within classes. LC does not claim any sort of theoretical basis—it reflects the holdings and use of that library and is thus justified for its own purposes. UDC is based on DC, but is trying to arrive at a more satisfactory order by a slow process of change; so far there has been one major relocation, placing language together with literature, and others are foreshadowed.

DC and UDC	LC	BC	CC
Psychology	Ethics	Anthropology	Recreation
Ethics		Recreation	Humanities and
	Anthropology	Psychology	Social sciences
Social sciences	Folklore	Education	
Sociology	Manners and customs	Social sciences	Psychology
Statistics	Recreation	Sociology	Social sciences
Politics	Social sciences		Education
Economics	Statistics	Social welfare	
Law	Economics	Ethics	Politics
Government	Transport	Politics	Economics
Military science	Commerce	Law	Transport
Social welfare	Sociology	Economics	Commerce
Education	Social groups	Business methods	Sociology
Commerce	Welfare		Anthropology
Transport	Political science		Social work
Folklore and customs	Law		Law
	Education		
Anthropology			Statistics is a
	Military science		common focus
Business methods			
Recreation			

TABLE 7a: Comparative classification: social sciences

NB A line between two subjects indicates that they are separated by a subject from some other area. Two lines indicates a considerable gap.

DC	UDC	LC	BC	CC
Philosophy	Philosophy	Philosophy	Philosophy	Humanities and Social sciences
Philosophy—topics	History of Philosophy	Logic	Logic	Spiritual experience and Mysticism
	Philosophy—topics			Humanities
Logic		Religion		Fine arts
History of Philosophy	Logic		Religion	Literature and Language
Religion	Religion	Recreation		Literature
			Fine arts	Language
Language	Fine arts	Music	Literature and Language (together)	Religion
	Photography	Fine arts		Philosophy
Fine arts	Music	Literature and Language (sometimes together, sometimes not)		Logic
Photography	Recreation			
Music	Literature and Language			
Recreation	Language			
Literature	Literature (or together)			

TABLE 7b: Comparative classification: humanities

NB Opinions differ as to whether a subject such as 'recreation' is in the humanities or the social sciences; it is included here if that appears to be the intention of the scheme. LC treats 'language' and 'literature' separately for the major Western languages; UDC permits either approach.

DC and UDC	LC	BC	CC
Science	Science	Science	Science
Mathematics	Mathematics	Mathematics	Mathematics
Astronomy	Astronomy	Physics (including some applications)	Astronomy
Physics	Physics	Chemistry	Physics
Chemistry	Chemistry	Chemical technology	Engineering
Crystallography	Geology	Astronomy	Chemistry
Mineralogy	Natural history	Geology	[Chemical] Technology
Geology	Botany	Geography	Biology
Biology	Zoology	Biology	Geology
Botany	Anatomy	Botany	Mining
Zoology	Physiology	Zoology	Botany
Technology	Medicine	Anthropology	Agriculture
Medicine (including scientific aspects)	Agriculture	Medicine	Zoology
Engineering	Technology		Animal husbandry
Agriculture	Engineering	Useful arts	Medicine
Domestic economy	Building	Agriculture	Useful arts
Business methods	Mechanical engineering	Engineering	
Chemical technology	Electrical engineering	Manufactures	
Manufactures	Chemical engineering	Domestic arts	
Building	Manufactures	Building	
	Domestic economy		

TABLE 7c: Comparative classification: science and technology

NB Two approaches are shown: 'science' as a whole followed by 'technology' as a whole, or each individual science followed by its related technology. DC in 'medicine' and BC in 'physics' depart from their normal practice of separating the two.

Traditional classification schemes rely on main classes which represent the traditional disciplines. Modern developments in all areas of knowledge tend to cross the boundaries between disciplines; that is, new topics develop not merely by *fission*—the splitting up of established subjects—but also by *fusion*—the merging of previously distinct subjects. It is very difficult to accommodate interdisciplinary subjects in a conventional classification scheme, just as it is difficult to take account of changes in relationships between existing subjects. The Classification Research Group has been working for some years now on the problems of developing a new general classification scheme, with mechanization particularly in mind, and though we have as yet no final results, the achievements of the group so far have made a very real contribution to classification thought. Basically, the principle of facet analysis is applied to the whole of knowledge, with rather interesting results.

We have seen that if we analyse the concepts which we find in the literature of a given basic class they can usefully be grouped into facets consisting of ideas which have some common link. We have seen in this chapter that in addition to those which relate specifically to a particular basic class there are others which are common to the whole of knowledge. The four common facets described are those which have been identified as the result of several years' experience in classifying for BNB, but in addition we find that there are others which apply to substantial parts of knowledge though not the whole of it. For example, in UDC there is a ' persons ' facet which can be used throughout the social sciences but is unlikely to be of much significance in science and technology, and in engineering there is a ' parts ' facet which is of wide applicability. Because these quasi-common facets are still discipline-oriented, they do not cause any problems, but we also find that there are certain facets which can occur in more than one place but are not discipline-oriented. For example, ' lamb ' is a concept falling into an ' animals ' facet which may be found in both science (zoology) and technology (agriculture), but also in social sciences (animals in folklore), as well as in various other contexts.

The position becomes even more confused if we look at something like ' tobacco ' in a conventional scheme such as DC. We find that it may be regarded as a plant, in Botany; or as a crop, in Agriculture; as a raw material, in Manufactures; as a drug source, in Medicine and in Ethics; as a habit, in Customs; and in other places according to the point of view we adopt to study it. We have at once a problem: which discipline is the correct one to select for this concept in a particular document? And how do we deal with the documents which deal with several aspects of ' tobacco '? DC solves this problem on an *ad hoc* basis; for each such topic we find a place in the schedules which has the tag ' comprehensive works '. This works for those topics specifically dealt with in this way, but it gives us no guidance for those which are not.

While we are still thinking of manual systems such problems are a nuisance, but we can overcome them by the expenditure of more effort. If however we start to think in terms of mechanization anomalies of any kind become intolerable; we are trying to base our system on the use of simple repetitive rules which can be easily programmed for the computer, and we do not wish to have to write a separate program for each anomaly. Quite apart from the added expense involved, we would be relying on enumeration of a closed system, and would sooner or later come across documents which could not be dealt with by the system.

In a discipline-oriented scheme, it is concretes which are scattered; if we gave up disciplines as our primary basis of division we could compile a scheme in which there would be one place, and only one place, for each concrete; the disciplines would now be scattered, but on balance it is more useful to have things this way round. The idea of concrete as primary concept was used by Brown in his *Subject classification,* and we have already seen how it has been the normal approach in systems for alphabetical headings such as those of Kaiser, Ranganathan, Coates and others. If we are to apply the idea to a general classification scheme, two problems have to be solved: how do we arrive at our sets of concretes and subsidiary concepts, and how do we arrange them in a helpful order?

FACET ANALYSIS
The Kyle classification for the social sciences[6] demonstrated that it was possible to analyse the whole of that area into two large facets, persons and activities. The logical development of this line of thought has been the analysis that we have already seen in discussing PRECIS, which is based on the postulate that we can allot any concept to one of two facets; it must either be an entity or an attribute. These terms are necessarily rather vague, but have a very respectable ancestry (they

go back to Aristotle); for practical purposes we have to be more precise. Entities can be divided up according to the following schema:

Physical entities
Chemical entities
Heterogeneous non-living entities
Artefacts
Biological entities
Man
Mentefacts

while attributes fall into three categories which may themselves be further organized:

Relative and positional terms
Properties
Activities.

This analysis has now been carried further than any comparable research, and appears to be yielding useful results, but it does not in itself lead to progress in the search for a helpful order.

INTEGRATIVE LEVELS

The philosophical theory of integrative levels[7] suggests that there is a recognizable order in nature which consists of a progression from lesser to greater levels of organization. If we consider sub-atomic particles in their own right, we find that they have certain properties, but if we consider them as united to form an atom we find that the atom forms a new *level of integration* which has its own set of properties. A car is more than a collection of parts; they have an organization imposed on them which means that the whole is greater than the sum of its parts. We can therefore use this principle to arrange the entities in our list in order; as a beginning we arrive at the order outlined in the previous section, which may be expanded to give a more detailed schedule[8]:

Physical entities
Level   I   Fundamental particles
       II   Atoms, isotopes
      III   Molecules
      IV   Molecular assemblages
Chemical entities
Level   I   Elements
       II   Compounds
      III   Complex compounds

Heterogeneous non-living entities
Level I   Minerals
    II   Rocks
   III   Physiographic features
   IV   Astronomical entities   *etc*

When we come to look at terms for activities, we can use the principle of general to special to give us an order in which static conditions precede dynamic, on the assumption that they are more general, and the overall order is one in which activities of the dynamic kind are ranked according to whether they lead to a mixing of entities, or aggregation, or integration, with the forming of a new whole. This gives, in outline:

General activity concepts	
General static and kinetic conditions	static
Equilibrium	
General kinetic conditions	mixing
Contacts and disturbances	
Motions and transfers	aggregation
Assembly and disassembly	integration

We thus have a method of constructing a schedule which will give a unique place for each concept. To use the schedule, the methods already described under PRECIS are employed: relational operators, systems theory, and entity-attribute rule.

The situation is somewhat fluid, in that research is still in progress, and very little of the scheme has been worked out in detail, largely because of the lack of funds. However, if PRECIS proves to be as successful as is hoped in indexing BNB it will provide a great deal of the analysis needed to construct the schedules of the new classification, and the next few years may well see the project nearing completion, insofar as any scheme intended to cover the whole of knowledge can be complete in an everchanging situation.

The one serious objection seems to be that the research is producing a classification of knowledge rather than one directed at documents. The vast majority of documents do fit, even if a little uncomfortably, into a conventional framework; disciplines, ill-defined though they may be, do exist; there *is* an educational and scientific consensus. We may well be moving into an era in which we use one scheme to arrange the documents in our library, and another quite different one to index them—but then that is already the position in BNB, so perhaps we shall have less difficulty than is anticipated by some in coming to terms with the new order.

It can be seen that the problem of finding a satisfactory overall order that will last for anything more than a few years is one of the most difficult problems facing systematic arrangement. Traditional approaches do not serve as a helpful basis for placing new interdisciplinary subjects in relation to the disciplines from which they arise; novel methods may fail to accommodate the mass of published information that still falls into the conventional framework. As Mr Bennet observed, ' it seems an hopeless business '[9]. The solution may lie in the recognition of the fact that any user of a scheme can only be aware of a relatively small part of it at any time, even in a small library; the overall order will in practice not be visible. It seems likely that information will continue to be presented in conventional ways, even though the conventions may change from decade to decade; the problem lies perhaps more in the area of keeping up to date than in that of theoretical study.

PHASE RELATIONS

Assuming that we use the synthetic principle and thus restrict our needs to those of listing simple subjects in our schedules, we can compile a classification scheme that will now serve most purposes. We can analyse basic classes into facets, list the foci in each facet and state the citation order; the basic classes themselves can be grouped into a helpful order, with a generalia class and common facets added. We have accounted for genus-species relationships by showing related subjects together in the sequence, and we have allowed for syntagmatic relationships within the basic classes, by permitting the combination of foci from different facets.

If we consider table 8, however, we can see that the kind of relationship demonstrated is one that we have not yet made provision for. We may use Ranganathan's term *phase relationships* to denote these, though the four kinds identified here do not entirely coincide with those in cc[10]. In the first group we see a subject treated with a particular audience in mind; it remains the same subject, but we will find that the examples used for discussion will come from the subject interest of the intended audience. Thus *multi-variate statistical analysis for biologists* is a book about a branch of statistics, using examples from biology; the essential point is that this work might well be of use to a nuclear physicist, (failing a work on multi-variate statistical analysis for nuclear physicists) but it is unlikely to be of any use to a taxonomic botanist. In these examples of *bias phase*, the subject is the subject treated, not the audience for whom it is intended.

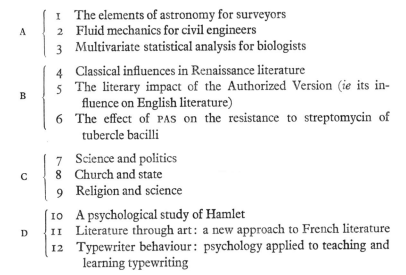

A
1 The elements of astronomy for surveyors
2 Fluid mechanics for civil engineers
3 Multivariate statistical analysis for biologists

B
4 Classical influences in Renaissance literature
5 The literary impact of the Authorized Version (*ie* its influence on English literature)
6 The effect of PAS on the resistance to streptomycin of tubercle bacilli

C
7 Science and politics
8 Church and state
9 Religion and science

D
10 A psychological study of Hamlet
11 Literature through art: a new approach to French literature
12 Typewriter behaviour: psychology applied to teaching and learning typewriting

TABLE 8 : Phase relationships
Group A Bias; Group B Influence; Group C Comparison or interaction; Group D Exposition.

In the second group, we see one subject influenced by another; in examples of *influence phase*, it is the subject influenced that is the core. In the fourth, *exposition phase*, it is the subject expounded, not the 'tool' subject, which is the important one. The third group, showing *comparison*, presents a rather different problem; here we have no indication which is the primary phase, because both phases are equal. Most general schemes of classification have a simple rule that in this situation, the primary phase is to be the one appearing first in the schedules. This is an arbitrary rule intended to save the trouble of making a decision on merit each time the occasion arises; it means that using DC, 'Science and politics' will be classified with politics, whereas using CC, it would belong with science. In each case it would be necessary to make provision for the secondary phase, for example by making an added entry in the catalogue.

The examples given of phase relationships in Table 8 all illustrate the linking of concepts from essentially different basic classes, but this is not necessarily the case. Phase relationships can occur between foci in the same facet, *eg*

The influence of Goethe on Sir Walter Scott

Town and gown.

We have pointed out that foci from the same facet cannot normally be combined, indeed this is the criterion by which we judge whether we have carried our analysis to the point where foci in one facet are mutually exclusive. Phase relationships are obviously one kind of relationship in which foci cannot be mutually exclusive. This also illustrates the point that phase relationships do not in general present serious problems in alphabetical systems, except that it may be necessary to use a phrase to specify them; it is in systematic arrangement that we have to make special provision for them.

There is one very important point about phase relationships which it is essential to grasp. They are necessarily *ad hoc* relationships : though we can tell in advance that books will be written in which one subject is treated in comparison with another, or to show how it has been influenced by another, or with a particular audience in mind, we cannot know which subjects will be so treated. Indeed, phase relationships are becoming more and more common now; bias phase may be the first indication of the growth of a new interdisciplinary subject, as may comparison, while influence and exposition clearly also may lead in this direction. Phase relationships cannot be foreseen; all that we can do in our system is to make adequate provision for them by some kind of synthetic device. It is in fact here that we see the final distinction between the enumerative and the synthetic approach. In an enumerative scheme, all that we find will be provision for phase relations that existed before the scheme was compiled; *eg* in DC we find *science and religion* listed (the Darwinian controversy) but not *science and politics*. Phase relations can only be accommodated as they arise in a synthetic scheme; even here there is a need to recognize the different kinds, *eg* in UDC the colon, :, is used to link the notation for the two phases in this kind of relation, but it is used for all four kinds and is thus not very precise. CC is the only scheme to set out detailed provisions for phase relationships, though the four given here are in fact taken from the BNB supplementary schedules rather than CC. It is important to emphasize the *ad hoc* nature of these relationships; for example, it is essential that we distinguish *science and politics, ie* the interaction between two normally distinct topics, and the *science of politics, ie* politics as a discipline. In the first case, we are studying the effect that political decisions may have on science (in determining, for example, which projects are to receive government funds, which may alter the whole direction of scientific progress) and conversely, the effect that scientific advances may have on politics (for example, by making it possible for politicians to reach an enormous audience, which may alter the whole direction of political progress). In the second case, we are studying the structure and mechanics of politics: how decisions are reached and implemented. Where two subjects are permanently related, *eg* when one forms an aspect of the other as does science of politics in the second case above, this should not be considered as a phase relationship.

Having seen the need to include them, we now have to decide whereabouts in the order we want to insert them. Here cc and BNB again differ slightly; cc files all phase relationships immediately after the subject treated generally, whereas BNB files bias phase here, then common facets, then comparison, exposition and influence, followed by the least important facet of the basic class. DC makes provision for bias phase by a standard subdivision, but this places such items in the middle of ' miscellany ', with ' the subject as a profession ' on one side, and ' directories ' on the other. Other kinds of phase are enumerated occasionally in DC, but no consistent provision is made for them.

BIBLIOGRAPHY

1 Grolier, E de: *A study of general categories applicable to classification and coding in documentation.* Paris, Unesco, 1962.

2 In the rules for main classes in cc.

3 Palmer, B I: *Itself an education.* 1971. Chapters 2 and 3.

4 Brown, J D: *Subject classification.* Third edition revised by J D Stewart. 1939. This edition was very similar to the first, 1906, and second, 1914, and retained all of Brown's novel features. However, though it survived in a few British libraries till recently, it became too outdated to be usable and has been replaced.

5 See chapter 14 for details of Bliss's writings.

6 Kyle, B: ' Towards a classification for social science literature '. *American documentation, 9* (4) 1958, 168-183. This is also discussed by D J Foskett in his *Classification and indexing in the social sciences.*

7 Foskett, D J: ' Classification and integrative levels.' (Chapter *in* the Sayers memorial volume, 1960.)

8 Coates, E J: ' CRG proposals for a new general classification ' (*in* Library Association: *Some problems of a general classification scheme.* 1964. 38-45).

Foskett, D J: *Classification for a general index language.* This is the most up to date commentary on the CRG work at present available, and is intended for the student.

Austin, D W: ' Prospects for a new general classification '. *Journal of librarianship, 1* (3) 1969, 149-169.

Classification Research Group: *Classification and information control.* LA, 1970 (LA Research pamphlet no 1). This sets out the reports produced during the development period of the new classification. It is very interesting to see how the ideas of the group clarified as the discussions proceeded.

9 Austen, J: *Pride and prejudice.* 1813. Chapter 20.

10 The phase relationships identified here are those used by BNB.

5

CHAPTER 8

Notation

Unlike alphabetical arrangement, systematic order is not self evident, and indeed there may be differing views as to the best order at any given point. It would be tedious in the extreme if we had to consult the schedules every time we wished to find a subject in the catalogue or on the shelves, and search for it by following through the overall order; even if the catalogue and shelves were guided to a very high standard, in a large library searches for specific subjects would be impossible if we had to rely on the systematic arrangement on its own. To make it a practical proposition we must add to the arrangement a set of symbols—a *notation*—which does have a self evident order; we can then use the notation to find out the position in the catalogue or on the shelves of the subjects we want[1].

There are two important points here. The first is that the notation is something *added* to the schedules; it is the schedules which give the systematic arrangement, and only when we have decided on the arrangement can we start to think about the notation. It is an unfortunate fact that notation is often assumed to *be* the systematic arrangement, and classification schemes have been criticised for poor arrangement when it has been the notation which has failed, not the schedules. The notation cannot turn a bad schedule into a good one, but a poor notation may so hamper a good schedule that it becomes a bad one. To quote H E Bliss, ' notation . . . does not make the classification, tho it may mar it '[2].

The second point is that the notation has to show the order: that is its function. The notation itself must therefore have a self evident order, otherwise it will not serve its purpose. If we adopt a notation which does not have a self evident order, we may well find that we are no better off than we were with no notation at all; taken to its logical extreme, this would mean giving each subject in the schedule a symbol and then allocating to these symbols an arbitrary order reflecting the order of the schedules, a procedure which would not really be very helpful. The Chinese system of ideographs is such a set of symbols; in order to produce quite simple messages on a typewriter it is necessary to remember the position of some 2,000 separate keys. This is obviously not a practical means of finding our way round the library.

There are two sets of symbols which have a widely recognized order: arabic numerals, and the roman alphabet. (Roman numerals are not widely known, nor are they so easy to manipulate as arabic; and while the greek and slavonic alphabets do have a self-evident order, it is not nearly so well known as that of the roman.) Using letters, we have the choice of lower or upper case (small letters or capitals) which means in effect that we have the choice of three sets of symbols rather than just two. A notation which uses only one set of symbols is called a *pure* notation, while one which uses more than one kind is known as a *mixed* notation. It is clear that only a pure notation will give us the completely self evident order we have stated to be necessary, but other factors enter into the picture which indicate certain superiorities on the part of a mixed notation, which may make it worth while accepting the loss of consistency.

MEMORABILITY

We have to *use* notation; it is the means by which we move from a subject expressed in words in an alphabetical index to that same subject in its context in the systematic arrangement; it has to appear on catalogue entries, backs of books, entries in bibliographies, stock records, shelf guides—anywhere, in fact, where we may have to find our way through a systematic arrangement. We must therefore be able to carry it mentally with ease, write it and type it without error, inscribe it on book covers which may be relatively narrow. The notation must lend itself to these activities; to do so it must possess a number of qualities which between them add up to what we call *memorability*.

The first quality is *simplicity,* by which we mean that it must be easy to grasp mentally. Consider the following ten digit number:

7382159142.

This looks much too long, and most people would find it difficult to grasp as a unit, but if we split it up into three shorter sections:

738 215 9142

it at once becomes much simpler. We are all familiar with ten digit numbers split up in this way, for the vast majority of telephone dialling codes are of this length or even slightly longer. By splitting the number up, we have increased its length by two digits (counting each space as a digit) but this leads to an increase in the ease with which we can grasp it.

This leads us to a consideration of the effects of mixing different kinds of notation. The following pieces of notation are all the same length, but clearly some of them are much easier to grasp than others:

1 738215914237
2 738LIN914237
3 738/215/9142
4 738:215:9142
5 BD7382GS5738
6 7382(159)142
7 73k,BD24:Kaw
8 TipModHafDun
9 TrdMbhHloDfx

We find that on the whole devices which normally act as separators —*ie* punctuation marks—are psychologically acceptable for this purpose in notation; on the other hand, a notation using punctuation marks solely as separators must be longer than one without separators; these are *empty digits* which convey structure but not meaning. Mixed notation *may* be easier to grasp than a pure notation of the same length, but only if we can grasp some sort of pattern to the mixing; and numbers are for most people more acceptable as an ordering device than letters. Example 8 (above) shows a recent trend in notation towards the idea of organizing letters into recognizable groups, in this case pronounceable syllables.[3] The object is to provide a notation which is easily grasped, and in this it is obviously successful, though one has to remember that combinations of letters have semantic content and it may be preferable not to use some of the possibilities. Numbers do not in general have any semantic content, though we may have to except from this such notations as 007!

The second quality which is important is *brevity*. Other things being equal, a brief notation is more easily grasped than a long one; as we have seen, other things are not always equal, but there is no doubt that brevity is important. For example, it becomes difficult to write a long piece of notation on the spine of a book, unless we can split it up into shorter units. Brevity depends mainly on two factors: the *base* of the notation, and the *allocation*. The base is simply the number of symbols available in the system; for numbers this is ten (0/9) or nine if we ignore the zero, while for letters it is twenty six.

If we mix the notation by using numbers and letters we may have thirty-five (it is not possible to use both O (capital letter o) and o (zero) without confusion), while if we use both upper and lower case letters and numbers we will have slightly less than sixty. (On many type-writers l (lower case L) is also used for 1 (one) and there is the possi-bility of confusion between written b and 6, or i and l, or o and O.) If we use numbers, we shall have longer symbols than if we use letters. For example, if we have about 2,000 items in our schedule and we want to show their order, we shall have to use up to four digits if we use numbers only, but only three if we use letters (base 26), while if we use numbers and upper and lower case letters we shall only need two digits ($57^2 = 3,149$). The longer the base, the larger the number of items that can be arranged by a given length of symbol; mathematically, if the base contains x symbols, then by using up to n digits we can construct

$$x^n + x^{n-1} + x^{n-2} + x^{n-3} + \ldots x^3 + x^2 + x$$

different notational symbols. The general preference for numbers has to be set against the fact that letters will in general give shorter symbols.

Another factor affecting brevity is the way the notation is allocated. Some subjects are static; they have not developed in recent years. For example, the schedule for Logic in Dewey's first edition is almost the same as that in his seventeenth edition, eighty nine years later. Compare this with a dynamic subject such as Engineering; here the growth of the subject is increasing almost exponentially, and whereas Dewey's first edition gave this subject less than a page, his seventeenth takes up ninety pages to cover it. When we allocate the notation for a classification scheme, we should try to make sure that it gives a large share to dynamic subjects, even if this means fairly long notation for some static subjects to start with; after a few years, the notation for static subjects will not be any longer, while that for dynamic subjects will inevitably have grown. Of course, we cannot tell in advance which particular subjects are likely to grow most in years to come, but we can at least make some sort of intelligent guess, bearing in mind that if we could indeed foretell the future the construction of classification schemes would probably not be our chosen profession.

In his first edition, Dewey gave the same spread of notation to Logic as he did to Engineering: ten three figure numbers. As a con-sequence, in the seventeenth edition, we still find three figure numbers in Logic (which has been static now for the best part of 2,000 years), but in Engineering, particularly those branches which have had to be inserted since the scheme was first drawn up, we find that six digits are common, and ten digit numbers are by no means uncommon. What makes the situation worse is that the great majority of libraries have a lot of items dealing with engineering but relatively few on logic—so the short pieces of notation are rarely used. It must be remembered that, although we can provide for the growth of subjects to a certain extent it is not possible to make sure that dynamic subjects will retain a brief notation indefinitely; as we have already seen, any systematic arrangement will need revision over the years to keep pace with the growth of knowledge, and it may well be that in some areas knowledge is growing so fast that we cannot hope to keep pace with it and still retain a convenient notation.

A further factor affecting brevity is *synthesis* of notation. We have seen the contrast between enumerative and synthetic classification schemes; in the latter, only simple subjects are listed, and the classifier has to select the appropriate ones for any subject he has in hand and combine them according to the specified citation order. This means that the notation for the individual elements must also be combined to specify a composite subject, and this will usually lead to longer notation than if the symbols had been evenly distributed over all the required subjects, simple or composite. For example, the Library of Congress classification rarely uses more than two letters and four figures for any subject in its schedule—though it is only fair to point out that the schedules often lack specificity where composite subjects are concerned. UDC has often been criticized for the length of its notation for this reason; synthesis leads to very long numbers, but it must be pointed out that in many cases this is because the notation was not designed with synthesis in mind, and in consequence the results are often clumsy, repeating certain sections of the notation. For example, at one time the notation for the subject

Power supplies for the electromagnet of a proton synchrotron
was 621.384.61:539.185:621.318.3:621.311.6. Nobody can claim that this is brief or memorable, and it repeats 621.3 (Electrical engineering) three times. It is however specific, and UDC is the only classification scheme which is detailed enough to specify this subject and others like it. If we want specificity, we have in general to accept long notations; if in addition we are using a scheme in which the allocation of notation is poor in relation to modern needs, we must expect this to have a further adverse effect on the length of the symbols

we have to use. It is not possible to avoid this kind of conflict eventually, no matter how carefully the notation is allocated in the first place; all that we can do is to try to minimize the problems by accepting the necessity for fairly drastic revision from time to time, a topic which is discussed at more length under ' Organization ' (chapter 9).

It is often suggested that *mnemonics* in notation are an aid to memorability—as indeed they should be! Mnemonics may be of two kinds, systematic and literal. A systematic mnemonic is found when the same piece of notation denotes the same topic wherever it occurs; for example, in UDC Great Britain must always be denoted by (42), USA by (73). In DC there are several mnemonics which fall into this category, but in a limited way; for example, in Literature, within a particular language ' drama ' is always denoted by 2 :

English literature	820	English drama	822
French literature	840	French drama	842
German literature	830	German drama	832

However, 2 does not by any means always mean drama, even within Literature. Great Britain is often denoted by 0942, but it may be shown by 942, 42, 042, or even 2, and while 0942 does nearly always mean Great Britain, the other symbols usually do not. So we do not have the consistency which is necessary if a piece of notation is to be truly mnemonic.

Literal mnemonics are associated with letters, and the theory is that by using the initial letter of the name of a subject for its notation we shall aid the memory. Thus in the Bibliographic classification Chemistry is C (but Physics is B); in LC Music is M (but Fine arts is N). This kind of mnemonic is so haphazard that it has little value; it only works for a very limited number of subjects, and then only for one particular term. For example, BC has U for Useful arts, while LC has T for Technology—but Dewey in his schedule now calls Technology the class which used to be called Useful arts!

It is clear that literal mnemonics depend completely on language; a piece of notation which is mnemonic in English may not be so in, say, French, but it may also not be so in American, since usage on the two sides of the Atlantic frequently differs. What could one use as a literal mnemonic for Lifts/Elevators, or Films/Movies? However, provided that the striving for mnemonic value does not distort the schedules of the classification, there would appear to be no harm in them; unfortunately, one gets the impression that in some cases the mnemonic value has led to the use of alphabetical order where a systematic order might be more useful, for example in the Generalia class in LC.

The value of mnemonics is doubtful. The non librarian user will not come across them sufficiently often to become aware that they are 'helping his memory', while the classifier using a particular scheme will have little difficulty in remembering large amounts of its notation, whether they are 'mnemonic' or not. On no account should the schedules of a classification scheme be modified in order to gain some dubious advantage of this kind.

Seminal mnemonics form a third kind, rather different in their intention from the other two in that they are wholly classifier-oriented. Suppose that we have a schedule that needs expansion; we have the choice of attempting an expansion ourselves, with the attendant risk that we shall clash with a future expansion published by the compilers of the scheme, or of abandoning specificity for the time being, until such time as an approved expansion is available. If we could be sure of drawing up the same schedule as the compilers, and allotting it the same notation, the dilemma would be resolved, and seminal mnemonics are an attempt to permit us to do this. The numbers 1 to 8 are given a fundamental significance: 1, for example, means first, unitary, one-dimensional; 4 means malfunction, disease, *etc.* Ranganathan developed the theory of seminal mnemonics after a careful study of the way that he had used notation in the early editions of CC, and we owe the name to Palmer and Wells in their *Fundamentals of library classification.* However, although their use may give a measure of autonomy to the classifier, it would appear to be a very clear example of notation dictating order, and to be suspect for that reason. Seminal mnemonics can in practice only be studied in the context of CC, and they are discussed further in chapter 15.[4]

Memorability is important, and the factors contributing to it must be carefully weighed when a notation is selected for a classification scheme. There is no doubt that much of the success of DC is owed to its simple, easily understood and widely known notation, rather than to any theoretical excellence in its schedules. Despite this, it is important to reaffirm that notation is subsidiary to the needs of the schedules, and that it is possible to worry too much about the difficulties caused by long or complicated symbols. Far more important is the need for the notation to possess other qualities, of which the most important is hospitality.

Notation shows the order of the schedules, but the schedules are merely a helpful way of listing subjects; since knowledge is not static, our schedules cannot be static—we must be prepared to add new subjects as they arise, in the correct place (as far as we can see it) in the overall order. The notation must therefore also be able to accommodate insertions, at any point where we find it necessary to make them. We will most often need to insert a new topic within a facet, but we may occasionally need to develop a new facet, and we may well have to find room for new basic classes. The notation must not prevent us from accommodating any new subject in the correct place: *ie* it must be hospitable.

If we are using arabic numbers, we may use them as integers (whole numbers) or we may use them as decimals. Integers give a clear order which is known to everybody; 12 comes later than 2 but earlier than 115, for example. But suppose we have a series of foci in a facet, and we give them the numbers 1 to 7; if we now require to insert a new topic between the third and fourth we cannot do so, for there is no whole number between three and four. One solution is to leave gaps when we are allocating the notation originally, but of course this is only postponing the time when we run out of places; there is also the temptation to insert new subjects in the schedules at points where we have left gaps in the notation, rather than in their correct, systematic, positions in the schedules. And since it is very difficult to foresee where new subjects are going to arise, we shall often leave gaps in the wrong places, but none where they are necessary.

If however we use numbers as decimals, we can insert new symbols at any point in the sequence. Between 3 and 4 we can insert 31, 32, 33 . . . 39; between 33 and 34 we can insert 331, 332, 333 and so on. Now there is no longer any need to worry about leaving gaps in the right places, or to waste notation by leaving gaps in the wrong places. The facility of decimal numbers to incorporate new symbols at any point was seen by Dewey, and proved to be one of the most vital parts of his scheme—indeed, it gave the scheme its name.

The term decimal applies to arabic numbers and relates to division by ten. The idea can of course be applied equally well to letters, where it will mean division by 26, so the term decimal is no longer correct, and instead we should speak of 'radix fraction'. As the term decimal is widely understood it will be considered to apply to letters as well as numbers in this text. In a letter notation used fractionally, between

137

B and C we can insert BA, BB, BC . . . BZ; between BB and BC, we can insert BBA, BBB, BBC and so on.

If we wish to have complete hospitality at any point, we must never finish a piece of notation with the first symbol of the base, 0, A or a; unless we follow this simple rule we will find that we cannot insert new items at the beginning of a schedule. For example, if we use all twenty six letters A to Z, we cannot in the future file anything before the established sequence, but if we begin at B we shall be able to insert AB/AZ before B and still maintain hospitality at all points. Similarly, between 2 and 3 we can insert the ten numbers 20 to 29, but if we use 20 we shall not in the future be able to insert anything between 2 and 20; if we restrict ourselves to the nine numbers 21 to 29, we can now insert 201 to 209 between 2 and 21. The effect of this is to reduce the length of the base by one digit; numbers to 9, letters to 25. In practice this loss is not likely to be serious, provided we make provision for allocating the notation adequately, whereas lack of hospitality may lead to distortion of the schedules—notation dictating order—which we must avoid.

EXPRESSIVENESS

There is another quality which notation is often expected to have, *expressiveness*. This means that the notation reflects the structure of the scheme, and such a notation is known as a *structural* or *hierarchical* kind, as well as expressive. This quality is a valuable one because it helps the user to find his way about the systematic order. We have to remember that the order of items on the shelf or in a bibliography, or the arrangement of cards in a catalogue, is perforce a single linear sequence which cannot show any kind of structure, and though we can (and should) do as much as possible to make the structure clear by guiding, an expressive notation is an added help. Unfortunately, we find that expressiveness and hospitality are mutually exclusive; sooner or later one or the other breaks down. The reason for this becomes clear if we consider a practical example such as the schedule for Engineering in DC. In the first edition, Electrical engineering was omitted, but this was included in the second edition as a subdivision of mechanical engineering; while this may have been an acceptable subordination at the time, it would not now find general agreement. However, by 1900 the motorcar was beginning to develop its own peculiar form of engineering, and since then we have had aviation engineering, nuclear engineering and control engineering.

600	Technology
620	Engineering
621	Mechanical
621.3	Electrical
622	Mining
623	Naval
624	Civil
...	
628	Sanitary

Clearly, car engineering and aviation engineering are similar to mechanical engineering rather than civil or sanitary, while control engineering, as one of the more theoretical studies, surely belongs at the beginning of the schedule with the other theory subjects rather than with the more practical branches of engineering listed later. Equally clearly, if branches of engineering of equivalent status to those listed are to be shown as equivalent by the notation, we cannot insert any of these subjects unless we use 629, for this is the only three figure number left vacant. Dewey realized this, and left 629 open for ' Other ' branches of engineering, so that is where we find car engineering, aviation engineering and control engineering, while nuclear engineering appears at 621.48, which may be approximately the correct place in the schedules, but certainly does not show the relative importance of this new discipline.

In recent editions DC has introduced the idea of ' centred headings ' to help in its retention of an expressive notation, and has also introduced new terminology. For example, Christian religion is now 220-289, instead of being equated with Religion generally as it was in the early editions, and many other cases of a similar kind can be found. The ' inserted ' heading is centred on the page, and the use of the notation is not recommended, since it includes a hyphen and is thus not in the completely pure tradition of DC. (UDC is able to achieve the same end by using the stroke / : thus Science and technology 5/6.) An example of updated terminology is the substitution of Applied physics for Mechanical engineering at 621. This removes the anomaly of describing Electrical engineering as a subdivision of Mechanical, but carries with it the implication that the rest of 620 (eg Control engineering in 629) is *not* Applied physics. It may thus be as difficult to justify the amendment as the original, but the intention is sound. It seems a pity that the notation of centred headings remains in disfavour.

The fact is that immediately we start to require our notation to be expressive, we limit ourselves to an integral use of the final digit; in the example above, Dewey had only the nine numbers 1, 2, . . . 9 to list all the branches of engineering and at the same time show their equal status. As we have already seen, an integral notation cannot be hospitable; for the same reason, an expressive notation cannot be hospitable. Hospitality is more important than expressiveness. In effect, hospitality is the quality which allows us to govern the notation according to the needs of the schedules, instead of having the notation dictate the order within the schedules. Sooner or later, all notations which set out to be expressive break down; DC and UDC, both originally expressive, do not show structure in their notation in a number of places in the schedules, while Ranganathan has introduced two devices to overcome the problem in CC without completely achieving his objective.

The first of these devices is the *sector device*. This was first known as the octave device, as it was applied only to the numbers 1 to 9, but its wider use with letters as well has led to the change of name. It consists of using the final digit of the base, 9 or z, solely as a repeater; the sequence of numbers now runs:

1, 2, 3, . . . 7, 8, 91, 92, 93, . . . 97, 98, 991, 992, 993 . . . (*ie* in octaves) while with letters the ' extended ' alphabet is:

a, b, c, d, . . . y, za, zb, zc, . . . zy, zza, zzb, zzc . . . etc.

The repeater digit shows us the place in the sequence where we will find a given symbol, but when estimating the ' status ' of the topic denoted by this symbol we are to ignore the repeater.

As in many other instances, it would seem that Ranganathan's theory makes explicit and formalizes what had already been the practice, though unrecognized, in other schemes. We have already noted the use by Dewey of 9 to denote ' other . . .' in Engineering, but in fact he used the device throughout his scheme. (In the early editions he tended to use the word ' minor ' instead of ' other ', as has been mentioned in chapter 4 under the heading Critical classification.) A related though not entirely similar use of the 9 was the development in DC13 and UDC of a new schedule for Psychology at 159.9, first published in 1931, before the first edition of CC had appeared.

The second of these devices is *group notation*, or in its application to UDC, *centesimal notation*. In this, instead of showing subordination by adding one digit to the base notation (62 leading to 621, 622, etc) we add *two* digits. By so doing, we give ourselves 100 numbers (00 to

99) or 676 letters (AA to ZZ) instead of 10 and 26 respectively, so that we can show a great many more topics as being of equivalent status. However, neither of these solutions can really be said to be satisfactory. Sector device enables us to add *at the end of the array*, but not in the middle; we can extrapolate the series indefinitely but we cannot insert an expressive piece of notation between 3 and 4, or anywhere else within the array. Group notation merely gives us a longer base to start with, but is liable to run out of hospitality eventually, just as is any other integral notation. We can add at the end of the sequence or in the middle, but only for as long as we have gaps in the appropriate places.

Another possibility which has been suggested, and indeed is used in CC, is the introduction of symbols from another series, for example, greek letters. Ranganathan uses Δ (capital delta) to denote Mysticism, which has the status of a main class in CC. Other main classes are all given roman letters (1963 reprint of the sixth edition), and we thus have the very real problem of determining whereabouts in the sequence we are to find Mysticism. There is no external guidance which tells us whereabouts in the sequence A/Z we are to find Δ; in fact, the scheme itself seems to be somewhat uncommitted. In the fifth edition we find

M   Useful arts
μ Humanities and social sciences together
Δ   Mysticism
ν Humanities
N   Fine arts

In the sixth edition (1960 printing) we find

M   Useful arts
Δ   Mysticism
μ Humanities and social sciences
ν Humanities
N   Fine arts

and in the sixth edition (1963 reprint) this has become

M   Useful arts
Δ   Mysticism
MZ   Humanities and social sciences
MZA   Humanities
N   Fine arts

The filing value of Δ lies between MY and MZ, which can hardly be said to be self evident, nor is it clear from a study of the schedules that it is the correct place, since we are given to understand that Mysticism is to be considered among the humanities and should therefore follow the general heading, not precede it.

It is evident that no satisfactory solution to the problem of reconciling hospitality and expressiveness is to be found. If we insist (as we should) on hospitality, sooner or later we shall have to abandon expressiveness; if we insist on expressiveness we are likely to find ourselves either abandoning hospitality altogether or else introducing devices which permit a degree of hospitality by maintaining a semblance of expressiveness only. We may take the argument further by considering whether we *ought* to seek expressiveness in the notation. As has already been mentioned, the order of items or entries cannot show any kind of structure: it is a linear sequence. The purpose of the notation is to show the order within the sequence; should we in addition expect it to show the relationships which the order does not show? The argument for expressiveness is that it helps users to find their way through the systematic arrangement, which is sometimes puzzling to them; the argument against expressiveness is that it conflicts with hospitality. We can help users to find their way around by guiding the library, the bibliography, the catalogue; we cannot help them by distorting the systematic arrangement to fit in with the needs of the notation.

If on the other hand we abandon expressiveness, we give ourselves a valuable degree of freedom which can be put to good use. It is the case that in a systematic arrangement the schedule has to include some steps of division which are logically necessary but are represented by little or no literature. If we use an expressive notation, these steps of division will inevitably be given a shorter notation than their heavily used subdivisions; we shall be 'wasting' short symbols by never using them. Consider the following schedule:

MUSIC
  Individual instruments and instrumental groups arranged according to their basic mode of performance
    Keyboard instruments
    Piano
    Organ
    String instruments
    Bowed
     Violin
     Viola
    Plucked

If we apply an expressive notation to this schedule, Violin and Viola will have the same length of notation, which will be three digits longer than the notation for the general heading at the beginning; Piano, Organ, Bowed and Plucked string instruments will all have a notation two digits longer than the heading; and Keyboard and String instruments will have notation one digit longer. Now this is already inconsistent, for it means that individual instruments do not all have the same length of notation, depending on the number of steps it takes to define them by a process of division. More seriously in practice, it means that the short symbols will hardly ever be used (how many items are we going to need to place at the general heading, which has the shortest notation?) while the vast majority of items—those dealing with specific instruments—will have to be given a long notation. This is obviously an inefficient use of notation.

If we abandon expressiveness as a requirement, we can allocate the notation far more satisfactorily:

MUSIC

PVV	Individual instruments and instrumental groups arranged according to their basic mode of performance
PW	Keyboard instruments
Q	Piano
R	Organ
RW	String instruments
RX	Bowed
S	Violin
SQ	Viola
T	Plucked

Now, although the notation bears no relation to the significance of the subject in terms of extension, it does show the order, and it does bear a close relationship to the significance of the subject in terms of literary warrant.

This example, taken from the *British catalogue of music classification*,[5] shows the gain in efficiency that can result from the abandonment of expressiveness. Most classification schemes which set out to have an expressive notation have at some stage had to give up the idea; even Dewey, who started with a completely structured notation, was forced to accept that in some places he would not be able to maintain this. For example, 439.7 *Swedish language* is a subdivision of 439.5 *Scandinavian languages*, while in *Metal manufactures*, *Tin* 673.6, *Mercury* 673.71 and *Magnesium* 673.723 are all individual metals and are thus coordinate. In some of the schedules in the Natural sciences, *eg Botany* 582-589, changes in the accepted order of plant species have meant that the notation now bears no relation to the structure of the schedules.

Although it is true that this loss of expressiveness makes the overall arrangement that much harder to follow, we can overcome this problem by adequate guiding of catalogues, bookshelves and indeed whole libraries. It can be argued that every time we use a class number we should also produce a guide showing the ' translation ' of that number into words. This would mean a much higher concentration of guide cards in a card catalogue than is customary—but perhaps users would not then complain so often that they do not understand the catalogue. The *British national bibliography*, with its ' feature headings ' for each class number used, shows very well what can be done to make a systematic arrangement intelligible.

SYNTHESIS

Synthesis has already been mentioned as one of the factors influencing the length of notational symbols, but we must now consider in more detail the problems that arise if we try to synthesize notational symbols for composite subjects from the symbols used for their elements. If we take the schedule for Library science that we constructed and go through it giving the facets an expressive notation, we shall finish up with something like the result shown in figure 3. Here we see that *History* (the generalized Time facet) is 3 and *Academic libraries* is 75; so the notation for *History of academic libraries* ought to be 753. But we can see at once that this will not do; 753 is the notation for *Technical college libraries*. We are of course trying to divide the heading *Academic libraries* in two different ways using the same notation, and this cannot be done because it causes ambiguity: the same piece of notation might mean more than one subject. What we have to do to remove this is to label not only the foci within a facet, but also the facet itself; if we do this, we can combine elements of notation from different facets to denote composite subjects without any risk of ambiguity.

There are various ways in which we can do this. We may use different kinds of notation for different facets; for example, BC uses lower case letters only for *Place*, while CC uses them only for common facets of *bibliographical form* and *subject*. In both cases it is possible to add these symbols directly to another piece of notation without confusion.

BC	Cricket (sports)	HKL
	Australia	ua
	Cricket in Australia	HKLua

CC	Physics	C
	Encyclopedia	k
	Encyclopedia of physics	Ck

This method is clearly limited by the fact that there are only three kinds of notation we can use.

A more practical method is shown by the fourth column in figure 3. In this, capital letters have been used to denote the facets, with lower case used to denote foci within the facets. We can now combine notational symbols for foci without any possibility of confusion. In column 5 the method has been used with some modifications to give pronounceable syllables, which again may be combined unambiguously.

History	Q	Fab
Academic libraries	Qh	Ped
History of academic libraries	QhC	Ped Fab
Technical college libraries	Qm	Peg

The same results could be achieved by using letters and numbers instead of two kinds of letters. Letters were used in this way by the English Electric Company's classification for engineering,[6] while pronounceable syllabic notation is used in the London Education Classification.[7]

FIGURE 3

The seven columns to the left show how various kinds of notation might be allocated to the schedule for Library Science. Since the schedule itself is tentative, so are the attempts at allocation of notation. Some kinds lend themselves more easily to leaving gaps than others, and letters give a longer base to start with.

Column 1 is a simple expressive notation. The facets need indicators
2 is the same, using letters
3 is a non-expressive notation which tends to assume that the schedule is now fixed. It is usually shorter than 1 and 2
4 uses capitals for facets, l/c for foci. Non-expressive.
5 is similar, but uses pronounceable syllables
6 is a non-expressive retroactive notation, using numbers :

(see explanation on p 150)

7 is similar, using letters. No facet indicators needed.

1	B	1	A	B	1	B	Common bibliographical
2	C	2	B	D	15	C	Common subject
21	CB	21	Bb	Dad	16	CC	revision
22	CF	22	Bf	Dal	17	CF	research
23	CJ	23	Bj	Dat	178	CJ	standards
24	CN	24	Bm	Deb	18	CM	automation
25	CR	25	Br	Dib	19	CP	economics
3	D	3	C	F	2	D	Time
4	E	4	D	G	3	E	Place
5	G	51	E	H	4	EZZ	Operations
51	GB	52	Eb	Had	44	F	administration
511	GBB	53	Ec	Haf	444	FG	selection
512	GBF	54	Ed	Hag	446	FK	acquisition
513	GBJ	55	Ee	Haj	454	FM	circulation
52	GF	56	Eh	Heb	459	FZ	technical services
521	GFB	57	Ei	Heg	46	G	cataloguing
5211	GFBM	58	Ej	Hel	465	GG	catalogues
52111	GFBMB	59	Ejz	Hep	4659	GL	by physical form
521113	GFBMBJ	60	El	Het	467	GP	book
522	GFF	61	En	Hid	47	H	classification
5221	GFFM	62	Eo	Hif	475	HG	schemes
52215	GFFMJ	63	Er	Him	478	HP	UDC
53	GJ	64	Ew	Hod	48	J	cooperation
54	GN	65	Ex	Hom	49	K	finance
541	GNF	66	Ey	Hop	495	KG	funding
5413	GNFF	67	Ez	Hot	498	KJ	Federal
6	K	69	F	J	5	LZZ	Materials
61	KB	70	Fb	Jad	55	M	Books
62	KF	71	Ff	Jag	56	N	Serials
621	KFB	72	Fj	Jak	565	NN	periodicals
622	KFF	73	Fm	Jal	566	NP	newspapers
63	KJ	74	Fpz	Jed	57	NZZ	non-standard
631	KJB	75	Fr	Jeg	575	O	maps
632	KJF	76	Fw	Jel	576	P	records
69	L	77	G	K	58	Q	by subject
7	P	78	H	L	66	QZ	Libraries
71		79	J			R	by subject

72	Q	80	L	M	67	RZ	by mode of use
721	QB	81	Lb	Mad	677	SS	reference
73	R	83	N	N	68	SZ	by population served
731	RB	84	Nb	Nad	687	T	children
732	RF	85	Nc	Nag	688	TT	hospital
733	RJ	86	Nd	Ned	689	TU	handicapped
7331	RJB	87	Ne	Nep	6897	TV	blind
74	S	88	Q	P	7	TZZ	by kind
741	SB	89	Qb	Pad	77	U	special
7411	SBF	90	Qc	Pal	777	UU	government
7412	SBJ	91	Qe	Pam	778	V	industry
75	SF	92	Qh	Ped	78	W	academic
751	SFB	93	Qi	Pef	787	WU	school
753	SFF	94	Qm	Peg	788	WX	technical college
757	SFJ	95	Qr	Pem	789	X	university
76	SJ	96	Qu	Pib	8	Y	public
761	SJB	97	Qv	Pif	88	YY	municipal
762	SJF	98	Qw	Pil	89	YZ	county
77	SN	99	Qx	Pod	9	Z	national

As mentioned, notations 1 and 2 require facet indicators; we can use Ranganathan's , for the Libraries facet, ; for Materials and : for Operations. For the common facets we can use . for Place, ' for Time, - for subjects and " for bibliographical forms. We can use these also for 3, but the rest do not need facet indicators separate from the notation. Independent facet indicators do permit us to change the facet order and the filing order; notice also that once we have introduced the idea of facet indicators, we can use the whole of the notational base in each facet. This will usually allow us to reduce the notation by one digit, to make up for the extra digit (the indicator).

Samples from the list of titles:

3   An art reference library for children
731,721,71(Art) RB,QB,P(Art) 84,81,79(Art) NbLbJ(Art)
NadMadL(Art) 68767766(Art) TSSR(Art).

12   La Roche College classification system for phonograph records
757;632:522.4(LaR) SFJ;KJF:GFF.E(Lar) 95;76:61.4(LaR)
QrFwEnD(LaR) PemJelHidG(LaR) 789576473(LaR) XPHE(LaR).

These examples show that allocation has an important effect on length of notation, and that length itself is not the only factor involved in memorability.

We can remove the ambiguity in the notations shown in columns
1 to 3 by using arbitrary symbols as facet indicators. We could use,
say, " to introduce bibliographical form

–	common subjects
'	time
.	place
:	operations
;	materials
,	libraries.

We would normally not use the , to introduce the libraries facet,
because the fact that we use no label is itself a label. We would have
to use the comma if we wished to combine concepts falling within the
libraries facet, *eg* Children's reference library on art 731,721,71. If
we do introduce such a system of facet indicators, we must lay down
a filing order for them, which will normally (following the principle
of inversion) be the reverse of the citation order of the facets they
introduce, and we shall have to accept the fact that this order will no
longer be the self evident kind that we have previously stated to be
desirable. However, UDC and CC both function satisfactorily using
punctuation marks for facet indicators, and they do have the advantage
of being expressive. BC also uses punctuation marks as indicators, but
Bliss does not seem to have fully realized the implications of this for
filing order.

FLEXIBILITY

The use of arbitrary symbols for facet indicators may in fact be of
some value. We have seen that for any given situation, it is important
to have a fixed citation order, so that there will be one, and only one,
place for a composite subject, but that different situations may call
for different citation orders, for example in Literature, where DC and
LC differ because they are intended to serve different groups of users.
If we use capital letters to introduce facets, we immediately determine
the filing order for them, so that if we wish to follow the principle of
inversion we are limited to one citation order—the reverse of the
fixed filing order. (Note that it is the filing order which is fixed here;
we can alter the citation order if we accept the loss of the general-
special progression.) We are thus obliged in effect to accept the citation
order laid down for us by the compiler of the scheme, but this may
not serve our particular needs as well as might some other.

Now if we have used arbitrary symbols as facet indicators, their filing order has to be laid down as a special rule, for they have no accepted order among themselves. We can alter the filing order to suit our own needs, and can therefore also alter the citation order and still follow the principle of inversion; we have introduced the element of flexibility. To illustrate this we may take two examples from UDC, which has a very flexible notation. The first of these is the literature class, where we find language shown by direct subdivision, literary form introduced by the hyphen - and period shown by quotation marks " . . . ". We can accept that language is always the primary facet and therefore needs no indicator (though even this may be altered if necessary by using the facet indicator for language, the equals sign $=$). For the second facet we may have either form or period; we can ignore form altogether as does LC; we can use the same facet order as DC, language—form—period; in short, whatever arrangement will best suit our needs can be selected.

The second example is taken from Political science, where we find a subdivision Political parties. Within this basic class we find that there are three facets: place, party and party organisation. For most purposes the last of these will be the least important, and we can consider the others on their own. Direct division in the notation is used for the party facet, and this then would normally be the most important, with place second, shown by the use of curves (. . .). However, for perhaps the majority of libraries it would be more helpful to find place as the primary facet; readers are likely to be interested in the parties within a particular country and will wish to find them grouped, rather than in particular parties regardless of country. The notation permits either approach; we can choose a citation order to give us the arrangement we want and still follow the principle of inversion, for although there is a suggested filing order for the facet indicators in UDC, it is not mandatory.

Flexibility is a valuable quality in notation, but few schemes possess it. Even CC, which uses arbitrary symbols, has fixed filing and citation orders, while enumerative or semi-enumerative schemes usually give no flexibility at all. Bliss recognized the need for different approaches in different libraries, and in BC there are some subjects where it is possible to select one of several facet orders; however, the scheme itself is not clearly enough structured to give a great deal of potential for alterations of this kind. The most detailed example is once again Literature, where Bliss gives the classifier the choice of four ' modes '.

It is essential to realise that even if a scheme allows us to decide which of several alternatives we are going to adopt, once we have made that decision we must remove all the other options from the scheme. It is not possible to use one citation order one week, and then a different one the next week. Flexibility in the notation of a scheme enables us to make a choice, but once made that choice becomes unalterable.

The term flexibility is used by some writers to denote the ability to accommodate new concepts, for which we have used the term hospitality, an interesting example of a problem which has already been discussed at some length in chapters 3 and 4. With this term, as is unfortunately the case with many others, it is important to make sure of an author's meaning if misunderstandings are to be avoided.

RETROACTIVE NOTATION

Mixed notation has some advantages in its potential for giving memorable notation, for flexibility and for *synthesis*. However, it loses the great advantage of pure notation, which is its completely self evident order. Is it possible to devise a pure notation which will permit synthesis without introducing as facet indicators symbols of another kind? A hint of the answer to this question is found in the use in DC of a zero o to introduce the standard subdivisions; here we have synthesis with a pure notation, achieved by reserving the symbol o to act as a facet indicator.

If we have a subject with, say, three facets, we may use 1 to introduce the least important, which ought to file first. We can now use 2 to introduce the second, and combine notation from the two facets according to the citation order, *provided that we never use the figure 1 in the notation for the second facet*. Similarly, we can use 3 to introduce the primary facet and still achieve complete synthesis, provided that we do not use either 1 or 2 in the notation for this facet. The penalty that we have to pay for the ability to synthesize within a pure notation is a progressive diminution of the base available; in the second facet above, the base is no longer 1-9 but 2-9, while in the third it is 3-9. If we continue, in a subject with nine facets we could end up with the single digit 9 as the base in the primary facet, with the only possible subdivisions 9, 99, 999, 9999 *etc*. This is clearly unacceptable; in fact, if we wish to use this idea we must begin by allocating an adequate amount of the base to the primary facet, and work back to the least important. Also the method is likely to prove more successful if we use letters, where the base is much longer to start with, than if we use numbers. Provided that we observe this precaution, we can devise a pure notation that will permit us to combine elements from different facets to give notational symbols for composite subjects; this notation need not be expressive, so that composite subjects which occur frequently may be given reasonably short symbols; and we can retain the advantage of pure notation, a completely self evident order. Examples of such notation are found in the *British catalogue of music* classification and in the *British national bibliography* supplementary schedules. Because the elements must be combined in order, beginning at the end and working backwards, it is known as *retroactive* notation. The rigid combination order does not permit any degree of flexibility, but apart from this limitation retroactive notation measures up well to the requirements we have discussed. The last two columns of notation in the sample library science schedule indicate how both letters and numbers may be used in this way, with letters having more potential because of the longer base.

HOSPITALITY IN CHAIN AND IN ARRAY

In the foregoing discussion we have treated expressive as being synonymous with hierarchical, but it is in fact possible to differentiate between the two in a manner which recognizes the distinction between genus-species and syntagmatic relationships. A notation which reflects genus-species divisions may be denoted hierarchical, while one which reflects syntagmatic relationships is expressive or structured. For example, in DC17 the convention of using an asterisk to show points at which notational synthesis is possible was introduced. This is usually found to apply where there is a general heading with several subdivisions; because the notation for the general heading is extended *hierarchically* to show its subdivisions, it is not possible to extend it *expressively* to show synthesis. On the other hand, the notation for the subdivisions is *not* extended hierarchically, so it is possible to use syntagmatic extension by synthesis. An example will make this clearer: in Agriculture, we have the general headings

633   Field crops
633.4 Root crops

Both of these are extended by genus-species division, 633 obviously to include root crops and other kinds of crops at 633.1, 633.2 and so on, and 633.4 to specify particular types of root crop, *eg* 633.49 Tubers, which is itself extended to specify Potatoes at 633.491*. It is therefore not possible to extend any of these numbers for general headings to indicate the composite subject 'injuries to . . .' since this would lead to ambiguity. To synthesize a piece of notation for 'injuries to . . .' we are told to add a 9 to the notation for the crop, then add the appropriate number from 632 Plant injuries, diseases, pests and their control. Injuries to crops in general is 632.1, so to specify diseases of root crops we would take the base number 633.4, add 9, then add 1 (taken from 633.*1*; this would give us 633.491, which is the notation for Potatoes! Because the notation is divided hierarchically we cannot divide it syntagmatically. However, when we get to the end of the chain of division, at potatoes, we *can* synthesize a number for 'diseases of potatoes' because there are no hierarchical subdivisions; to 633.491 we add 9, then 4, to give us 633.49194 Diseases of potatoes. The asterisk is used to show that we can use synthesis at 633.491*.

The problem arises because of the lack of facet indicators in DC; there is no means of distinguishing genus-species division in the notation from synthetic division at the same point, and since genus-species division is considered to be more important, this takes precedence. Although we can add more crops if any should arise, we cannot devise specific numbers for many composite subjects. The scheme may be said to be hospitable *in array*, but not *in chain*. In order to be completely hospitable in chain, a scheme must have notational means to permit synthesis as well as genus-species division, and will thus have an expressive notation. On the other hand, as we have already seen, it is quite possible for a scheme to permit synthesis and yet have a completely non-hierarchical notation, for example the BCM classification. We end up with a tabulation as follows:

Hierarchical but not expressive
    permits genus-species but not syntagmatic division (*eg* DC in part)

Non-hierarchical and expressive
    permits genus-species division and syntagmatic, but does not display genus-species (*eg* BCM)

Hierarchical and expressive
    permits both kinds of division and displays both (either explicitly or implicitly) (*eg* most of CC)

Non-hierarchical and non-expressive
    permits genus-species division but not systematic synthesis, and displays neither (*eg* LC)

(A scheme in the last category, such as LC, does permit some syntagmatic division; a glance at the schedules will show composite subjects enumerated on nearly every page. However, it does not permit *systematic* synthesis; each and every composite subject has to be fitted into the schedules as it occurs.)

Because a synthetic scheme lists only single concepts, and has to provide means for notational synthesis of composite subjects, it makes the distinction between hierarchical and expressive notation in the above sense very obvious. The limitations on hospitality concomitant with the use of hierarchical notation have already been discussed, as have those relating to synthesis, but since we have already emphasized the importance of the distinction between genus-species relationships and syntagmatic it may be useful to carry this distinction over into the discussion on notation.

The distinction between hospitality in chain and in array has also been applied to a purely hierarchical notation, *ie* one applied within a single facet, but here it has no meaning. Logically, we obtain a species by adding a difference to a genus; in any chain of division, we shall have a number of steps between the *summum genus* and the *infima species*, each step representing a stage at which a species itself is regarded as a genus which can be further divided. That is to say, at each stage of division we generate an array of new species, each of which forms part of a chain of division from summum genus to infima species. We cannot distinguish between hospitality in chain and in array. A hierarchical notation must be hospitable in chain *and* array or in neither; in practice, it usually begins by having room to be both and ends up either by losing its hierarchical nature or by ceasing to be hospitable to new concepts at all.

SHELF NOTATION

Up to this point we have been working on the assumption that the arrangement of books on the shelves of a library would parallel exactly the arrangement of entries in a classified catalogue or bibliography. However, whereas there are no real limits to the length of notation we can use on a catalogue or bibliography entry, to put a long piece of notation on the back of a book may be difficult. For this reason there has been for many years now a divergence of opinion between those who believe that shelf arrangement should be as specific as possible and those whose believe that this is not necessary. The introduction to DC always includes a section on how to cut back class numbers from their full length without changing the meaning, and much of the controversy over the relative merit of DC and LC seems to arise from the idea that DC numbers have to be studied carefully with a view to cutting back whereas LC numbers do not.[8] On LC cards, DC17 numbers are set out in up to three segments, so that libraries can use as long or short a notation as they think fit. UDC numbers tend to be very long, and some libraries using this scheme compile a parallel set of shelf marks which may conveniently be placed on the backs of books, while retaining the full notation for the catalogue.

It is certainly easier to scan a series of books on a shelf than a series of cards for the same books in the catalogue. Whether this is a sufficient reason for abandoning specificity is not so clear. Notation can often be split up in such a way that it can be placed on the spines of books without causing any problems; a full LC call number may be quite long, *eg* Z695.1.E5E5 1967, but if this is set out in groups it is not inconvenient:

Z
695
.1
.E5E5
1967.

The notation from other schemes may be similarly treated.

One scheme was compiled solely with brevity of notation in mind; this was Fremont Rider's *International classification for the arrangement of books on the shelves of general libraries,* published by the author in 1961. Rider set out to provide a scheme which could be used for shelf arrangement and would never require more than three digits in its notation; he chose letters rather than numbers because of the longer base, but avoided mixed notation (which would have given a longer base still) because he felt that it was confusing for the users. However, Rider's allocation of the notation was in some cases ill-judged, and in many places brevity was achieved simply by ignoring composite subjects. As has been seen, this can cause cross-classification if no citation order is stated, but Rider seems to have ignored this also. The scheme was published as a preliminary edition, and unfortunately Rider died before he could take note of any comments or prepare any revisions. The scheme remains outside the mainstream of library classification, interesting because it illustrates the logical conclusion of the demand for brevity in shelf notation.

Although we stated earlier that there were no real limits on the length of notation that could be used on a catalogue card or a bibliography, there may in practice be certain limitations of convenience. To discover what piece of notation it is we require we have to look in an index of some kind, and then go to the main sequence, and this may prove difficult if the piece of notation we have to remember is long and complicated. There is no real solution to this problem in the card catalogue, but on the printed page it may not be quite so acute if we concentrate on the first one or two elements and then rely on our ability to scan a page quickly. LISA[9] is using the CRG classification for library science to arrange its entries, and to solve the problem of lengthy numbers it prints the first section only of each class number in the index so that it can be easily remembered. The first element is not in itself sufficient to get us to the specific place we want, but the layout on the printed page permits us to scan quickly over the entries at the point where we enter the sequence and thus find what we are looking for. This demonstrates in a rather satisfactory way that the function of the notation is to mechanize the arrangement, and in expecting it to do this *and* to be convenient as well we may be asking too much of it.

BIBLIOGRAPHY

1 There are several useful accounts of notational problems, *eg*

Coates, E J: 'Notation in classification'. (Chapter *in* International study conference on classification research, Dorking 1957. *Proceedings*.)

Vickery, B C: *Classification and indexing in science and technology*. Butterworths, second edition 1959. Chapter 3.

Foskett, D J: *Classification and indexing in the social sciences*. Butterworths, 1963. Chapter 9.

2 Bliss H E: *The organization of knowledge in libraries*. H W Wilson, second edition 1939. Chapter 3.

3 Foskett, D J: 'Two notes on indexing techniques'. *Journal of documentation, 18* (4) December 1962, 188-192. Also 1 above.

4 Ranganathan, S R: *Prolegomena to library classification*. Asia Publishing House, third edition 1967. Parts H, J, K and L deal with notation; seminal mnemonics are explained in chapter KE.

5 Coates, E J: *The British catalogue of music classification*. Library Association, 1960.

6 English Electric Company Ltd: *Classification of engineering,* third edition 1961. The latest edition, *Thesaurofacet,* uses uppercase letters only, which suggests that the mixed notation of upper and lowercase letters did not prove satisfactory.

7 Foskett, D J: ' The London Education Classification '. *Education Libraries bulletin,* Supplement 6, 1963.

8 Gore, D: 'A neglected topic: the COST of classification '. *Library journal, 89* (11) 1964, 2287-2291. Many recent discussions on reclassification have illustrated the same point.

9 *Library and information science abstracts,* published bi-monthly by the Library Association, supersedes the earlier *Library science abstracts,* which was arranged under very broad alphabetical headings.

CHAPTER 9

Alphabetical index

Systematic order is not self evident; we need notation to show
whereabouts in the sequence we shall find a particular subject. However, we also need some means of finding the notation, and this must
be through an alphabetical sequence, for we inevitably use words in
our first approaches to the system. A classification scheme must therefore have an alphabetical index to serve as its entry vocabulary, leading
us to the notational symbols which form the index vocabulary.[1]

The obvious place to find the required words is in the schedules,
where we have listed all the terms we wish to arrange. As a first
approximation, we can indeed take all the words in the schedules,
together with their appropriate notation, and simply rearrange them
in alphabetical order. This is however something of a simplification,
for we find many of the problems that we have already seen under
alphabetical arrangement recurring. The first of these is *synonyms*.
In the schedules we shall normally use only one term for a particular
focus, but there may well be others; both the preferred term and its
synonyms must form part of the entry vocabulary. For example, in
the index to UDC we find:

Sleep-walking	159.963.5
Somnambulism	159.963.5
Arachnida	595.4
Spiders	595.4

The second problem is that of *homographs*. With systematic arrangement we have to distinguish the same word used with different
meanings, just as with alphabetical arrangement, but in addition we
need to realise that the same word may occur in a number of places
in the schedules, denoting the same concept but in different contexts.
The context may in some cases so affect the meaning of the concept
that we can regard the different occurrences as 'pseudo-homographs'.
An example of the first kind, taken from UDC:

| Waders (birds) | 598.3 |
| Waders (footwear) | 685.315 |

157

An example of the second kind, taken this time from DC16:

Tobacco		
botany	583.79	
field crops		
agriculture	633.71	
economics	338.173	71
hygiene	613.8	
products		
manufactures	679.7	
social customs	394.1	
use ethics	178.7	

Here we have an example of a word that occurs several times in the schedules of a general classification scheme; it is represented by several pieces of notation, but each of these represents it only in one particular context. In indexing such a word, it would be less than helpful to give merely the word and several pieces of notation—though this would certainly lead us to all the places in the schedules where the word may be found. To make the index more precise, we give the context in which a particular piece of notation denotes the word we are interested in. There is really no need to distinguish these two kinds of homograph typographically in the index; the earlier example might equally well have been set out:

Waders	
birds	598.3
footwear	685.315

In both examples, the qualifying words show the context which links word and notation.

Related subjects are not normally a problem with systematic arrangement, for this is itself intended to arrange related subjects together; however, we can only display relationships in one way, by juxtaposition, so that if a subject has more than one link we cannot show the others. It is possible to overcome this in two ways; one is to make cross-references in the schedules, for example (DC16)

550   Earth sciences

Study of all earth materials, forces, processes
Including geology
For astronomical geography, see 525; geography 910; mineralogy, 549; paleontology, 560.

(Most of these cross-references have been dropped from DC17.) The other way is to make the cross-references in the index, as does UDC:

Geology 55 *Cf.* Palaeontology; Surveying.

We do not normally make *see* references within the index, because this means referring the user to a heading which is still not the one he wants, and which will in its turn refer him to a piece of notation. However, there are some occasions when this is permissible, as for example when a common word which can appear in a number of contexts has a synonym. The following illustration is from UDC:

Marriage(s), customs, forms, etc.	392.5
hygiene (guidance, etc.)	613.89
insurance	368.45
law	347.3
registers	929.3
sacraments	265.5
statistics	312.3

Weddings. *See* Marriage (s).

COMPOSITE SUBJECTS

If we are using a synthetic scheme, it will list only single foci, which are relatively simple to index. An enumerative scheme will include composite subjects, and we have to face similar problems in indexing these to those that were discussed in relation to alphabetical headings. Since every entry in the index is in the entry vocabulary and has to lead to the index vocabulary (the notation), we shall require $n!$ entries for a composite subject of n elements if we permute, rather than $(n!-1)$; again, an unacceptable number when n is more than 2 or 3. We can however use exactly the same kind of chain procedure to reduce the problem to manageable proportions. We make an index entry for each term in the chain, qualifying it by as many of the previous terms as necessary to show the context, and ignoring terms after it. The notation may help us here if it is expressive, but we can use the procedure whether it is or not; the important thing is to ensure that the chain of division is correctly written down in the first place.

Even if we use a synthetic scheme, we shall of course have composite topics in the catalogue which we shall have to index. We must draw a distinction between the index to the scheme and the index to a catalogue compiled by using it. Although the difference is most clearly seen with a synthetic scheme, where the catalogue will obviously include subjects not enumerated in the scheme, it is equally present when an enumerative scheme is used. Even with a completely enumerative scheme there will always be some individual topics which are not named in the scheme, but which we shall wish to index; on the other side, there will always be a number of topics listed in the scheme but not represented in our collection and therefore not in our catalogue. They will appear in the index to the scheme, but should not appear in the index to our catalogue. The practice found in some libraries of using the index to the scheme as an index to the catalogue is a makeshift expedient, by penury out of ignorance, and must be condemned.

We may find that chain procedure is not entirely an automatic process because of the nature of systematic arrangement. To refer back to an example used earlier to demonstrate a notational principle, *violins* are a subdivision of the broader heading *Individual instruments and instrumental groups arranged according to their basic mode of performance.* If we were to index this chain of division, we should have to make an entry for that heading, but it is most unlikely that anyone would try to find it through the heading. Although it is necessary to insert it in order to achieve a proper progression from general to specific, we do not need to index it: it is an *unsought link*. It is normal to omit also, as being unsought, such weak entry points as periods of time, and common terms of wide application but low significance such as Methods, Equipment, Production, Calculations, Research, and so on; in practice, to index in detail bibliographical forms would lead to a large increase in entries in the index without a corresponding increase in its value, and they too are treated as unsought.

It should be clear from this that the problem is not an easy one to solve. To exclude unsought links requires an intellectual effort, which negates one of the big advantages of chain procedure; it also involves a decision as to whether a particular link in a given chain is sought or not, and there will be many occasions when a term falls into the borderline area of ' possibly sought '. By excluding a term we may be reducing the potential for recall significantly; we normally leave unsought terms unindexed because they do *not* have a significant effect on recall, but we cannot always be certain that we are doing the right thing. On the other hand, to index all unsought links would add considerably to the bulk of the index, without a corresponding increase in effectiveness.

Another kind of problem, that of *false links*, may arise if we place too much reliance on the notation to indicate the chain that we have to index. Ranganathan considers facet indicators to be false links, though they may more usefully be regarded as unsought, and in any case will not even be considered if we refer to the chain of division rather than the notation. Another kind of false link arises from errors on the part of the compiler of the scheme, or changes in the structure of knowledge, so that subjects appear to be subdivisions of other subjects when in fact they are not. DC shows several examples of this in the notation of the sixteenth edition, but the majority of them are shown correctly by the schedules. If we rely on the notation, we may go wrong, but this cannot happen if we rely as we should on the systematic chain of division. The following example shows this clearly:

600	Technology
620	Engineering
621	Mechanical
621.3	Electrical

If we rely on the notation, we will index the false link mechanical as part of the chain from engineering to electrical engineering, but this cannot happen if we rely on the schedules. The converse effect may also be seen if we rely on the notation and it is not expressive:

400	Language
430	Germanic
439	Other Germanic
439.5	Scandinavian
439.7-439.8	East Scandinavian languages
439.7	Swedish

Though the last example is untypical of DC, in which the notation is made expressive as far as is possible, it is the norm in a scheme such as LC in which a largely integral notation is used. Once again, provided that we follow the chain of division carefully through the schedules, we can apply chain procedure, as the following examples show:

ND	Painting
ND1700-2399	Water-color painting
ND2290	Still life
ND2300	Flowers
ND2305	Reproductions. Facsimiles

which would give index entries

Reproductions: flowers: still life water-color painting ND2305
Flowers: still life water-color painting ND2300
Still life: water-color painting ND2290

Water-color painting ND1700-2399
Painting ND

NB   Sculpture
NB60-198   History
NB69-169   Ancient
NB135-159   Special materials
NB145   Terra-cottas
NB150   Figurines
NB155   Greek
NB157   Tanagra
which would give index entries
  Tanagra figurines: ancient sculpture NB157
  Greek figurines: ancient sculpture NB155
  Figurines: ancient sculpture NB150
  Terra-cottas: ancient sculpture NB145
  [Special materials—unsought]
  Ancient sculpture NB69-169 [possibly unsought]
  History: sculpture NB60-198
  [or History of a subject *see* the subject]
  Sculpture NB
The problem in applying chain procedure to a scheme with a non-expressive notation is that it is sometimes difficult to follow all the steps of the division through the schedules, particularly if they are not clearly set out, as is the case with, for example, BC. It will also be clear from the above examples that although chain procedure can sometimes be completely mechanical, as it is with BTI, it is sometimes necessary to modify the method to take account of unsought links and redundant qualifiers, and this means intellectual effort in a procedure which should be at the clerical level.

DISTRIBUTED RELATIVES
We have already seen in chapter 6, particularly table 5, that systematic arrangement only brings together the topics which we have decided shall form our primary facet; all the rest are systematically scattered. It is therefore useful to make explicit a point which is implicit in the earlier part of this chapter, *ie* that foci which are scattered by the systematic arrangement are brought together in the alphabetical index. These *distributed relatives* (concepts which are related but scattered) are shown clearly in the index, as is demonstrated clearly in the

'tobacco' example from DC. The index to a classification scheme or classified catalogue thus has a dual role; not only does it enable us to find the notation for a particular topic and thus its place in the overall arrangement, it also shows all of the several places where a particular concept is to be found even though they are scattered throughout the arrangement.

The index is thus much more than a convenience; it is an essential, integral part of a classified arrangement. As is emphasized in chapter 12, Dewey realized the importance of the index to his classification scheme from the very beginning, but all too often compilers of classified catalogues appear to regard an index as an expensive luxury. Chain procedure is one method of compiling an index, but there are of course others; in addition to the 'pot luck' method which some indexers seem to favour, we now have the use of PRECIS to serve as the indexing method in BNB, and with it the use of specific index entries at each point rather than the less satisfactory general headings generated by chain procedure. Whichever method we adopt, it is vital that we should not underestimate the importance of the alphabetical index.

ORGANIZATION

Knowledge does not stand still, and a classification scheme left un-revised will, sooner rather than later, become unusable. There are several implications here which we must consider, beginning with those for the compiler. In the first place, continuing revision implies some sort of organization, rather than an individual, to carry it through. Individuals are mortal, but an organization can continue indefinitely. We find that those schemes which have relied on the genius of their compilers, without the backing of an adequate organization, have gradually fallen into obsolescence, whereas those schemes which have adequate backing continue to progress. Examples of the first kind are SC and BC, both interesting and successful in their day; SC is now to all intents and purposes of historical interest only, and while renewed efforts are being made to keep BC up to date, it is doubtful whether these are sufficient. In the second category we find DC, LC and UDC, which have the backing of the Library of Congress and the FID; despite the fact that they have serious theoretical deficiencies, and may in some ways be compared to their detriment with BC, they are likely to remain important practical schemes, largely because of their successful organization. It should go without saying that one feature—perhaps the most important—of such an organization is a sufficiency of funds; the Revision Committee for BC set up by a group of users in Britain certainly does not lack the ability to revise the scheme, but at present it does lack the funds necessary to put its proposals into effect, though this situation may be changing, as is indicated in chapter 14.

There are various ways of keeping a scheme up to date. The most obvious is to publish a new edition from time to time, but this may not necessarily be the best way. In a large and detailed scheme, some sections may need revising fairly frequently, eg science and technology (and within these areas particular topics may present more problems than the areas as a whole), whereas other sections will need little or no revision. It may therefore be better to issue the scheme in parts, and revise each part on an *ad hoc* basis, in this way keeping the whole scheme current with the minimum of publishing effort. DC is an example of a scheme which appears in a new edition at regular intervals (the editorial policy is to publish a new edition every seven years), while LC exemplifies the policy of piecemeal publication. UDC is interesting in that it uses both methods: for the full editions, publication is in fascicules, while for the abridged editions, the whole text is published anew at intervals. CC is also intended to fit into this pattern, but the publication of the full edition (' depth schedules ') appears to be on a rather more haphazard basis. A limited number of subjects having been covered so far in *Annals of library science* and *Library science with a slant to documentation.*

Whichever of these methods is adopted, with a well organized scheme revision will be continuous, and it is therefore useful to have some means of publishing current revisions at regular intervals, so that users do not have to wait until the new schedules are published formally. DC is kept up to date through *Decimal classification: additions, notes, decisions* (DC&); UDC through *Extensions and corrections to the UDC;* and LC through *LC Classification—additions and changes.* Revision must also be planned, and must bear a close relationship to the needs of users. Editions of DC up to the fourteenth showed very clearly the problems of haphazard revision; for example, in DC14 Medicine occupied some eighty pages of the schedules, while the equally important topic Chemical technology (including fuel, food, industrial oils, and metallurgy, among other things) was given so little detail that it occupied only two pages; the most detailed schedule in DC2 was for Sanitary engineering, because Dewey had a friend who worked out the expansion. Later editions have shown the editors' concern that detail should be appropriate to the needs of the literature. UDC's revision is based to a much greater extent on the expressed needs of users, but the fact that much of the work is done voluntarily has, in practice, led to the same kind of inconsistency, with the social sciences generally lacking in detail in comparison with science and technology.

From the point of view of the person trying to use the scheme to arrange a library or catalogue, revision presents several other problems. Once a scheme has been adopted, the library begins to build up a vested interest in the scheme as it stands; there will be ever increasing numbers of cards, books and other documents and records with pieces of notation on them. If the scheme is changed, the librarian has to consider whether he can afford the effort needed to alter all these records, and rearrange them, in accordance with the new schedules. Dewey recognized this very early, and in his second edition adopted the policy of 'integrity of numbers': a piece of notation will not be reused with a changed meaning, and topics will not be relocated in such a way as to require a change of notation, though there may be expansions involving longer notation. There is no doubt that this statement contributed to the success of the scheme; librarians, who are by nature conservative (for many years the main duty of librarians has been seen as the need to preserve documents), welcomed this concession to administrative convenience. However, there is equally no doubt that its effect over the years was to remove the structure of DC further and further from the present day approach to knowledge; indeed, we have seen quite substantial amounts of reordering in all the editions since the fifteenth, to bring the structure more into line with modern thought despite the principle of integrity, and these changes have in many cases been the subject of strong criticism by users.

One means of incorporating changes while avoiding clashes with past practice is the UDC policy of 'starvation'. If a new schedule is drawn up, the notation previously used for that topic is left vacant, and may be used again if required after not less than ten years. It is felt that after a period of ten years, any material in a library still classified by the old notation will be of historical interest only and may be ignored for current purposes. This is probably true in some areas of science and technology, though by no means all; it is very doubtful if it is the case in the social sciences, and it is certainly not the case in the humanities, which are essentially cumulative, *ie* new writings add to, but do not necessarily supplant, older work. However, since most libraries using UDC are science and technology oriented, in practice the method seems to work without too much difficulty. Take for example the subject ' particle accelerators '; the schedule for these used 621.384.61 and 621.384.62, so when a new schedule was drawn up these numbers were not used, the new schedule being based instead on 621.384.63-621.384.66. Should it prove necessary to revise the schedule once again in the 1970's, the first two numbers may be reused with new meanings. The method is rather wasteful of notation, but as UDC notation in science and technology tends to be very long anyway (owing to its original basis of Dewey's allocation), users do not seem to be unduly worried by this prodigality.

The problem of keeping pace with knowledge is not restricted to systematic arrangement, of course. Terminology changes, new terms have to be introduced, new relationships arise, and all of these changes must be taken into account in any system. The problem is more acute with systematic arrangement because of the inflexibility of notation, which tends to crystallize (fossilize!) the arrangement in a structure reflecting the approach to knowledge at one particular time, and to make more difficult the process of changing. One suggestion that has been made is that libraries should begin a new catalogue at regular intervals introducing changes that become necessary in each new sequence. Each of the BNB five year cumulations has differed from its predecessors, but as far as possible changes of practice are not made within the five year periods. The United Kingdom Atomic Energy Authority started a new catalogue of technical report literature at the beginning of 1959, and took the opportunity of introducing a number of changes; by 1960, the previous catalogue was used only rarely, illustrating very well the rapid decay of interest in scientific and technical subjects. It would be much more difficult to introduce a similar method into a large general library, where users might find themselves obliged to look through several sequences, but of course this is exactly the method used by all abstracting and indexing services and similar bibliographies, which rarely cumulate beyond five yearly periods. Users do not find this intolerable, so it may be that we tend to exaggerate the hostility that would be aroused by a similar approach in library catalogues.

There is no easy solution to this problem, but a policy of starting a new catalogue at regular intervals would at least recognize the impossibility of reconciling tradition and the need for change.

One way of facilitating revision is to link it to the current indexing operations of a service such as BNB, and thus making it a continuous process. This is the method adopted by LC, but many users complain that keeping pace with all the alterations is very time consuming, and impractical in a busy library. (It should be remembered here that nearly all libraries in the USA use the dictionary catalogue; the task of changing class numbers in the catalogue and on the shelves is much easier when a classified catalogue is in use.) As with so many library problems, the root of the matter is economic; can the library afford the effort of keeping pace with changes, either continuous or at periodic intervals? Administrative procedures may hinder revision, for example if class numbers are used widely in administrative records as well as in the catalogue and on the shelves. Whatever methods we adopt, we cannot afford to ignore the fact that knowledge is changing all the time; if we do, we may end up by finding that people who need information are ignoring us.

RECLASSIFICATION

A library which uses any scheme which is kept up to date will need to change its classification practice from time to time or even continuously, depending on whether the scheme itself is revised at intervals, *eg* DC, or continuously, *eg* LC. However, for many libraries a quite different decision has to be faced at some point in time : should the library adopt an entirely new scheme and reclassify all its material? This position was reached by a number of libraries in this country some years ago, when it became clear that we could not expect a new edition of Brown's *Subject classification,* and the result was a gradual change to DC which is now complete. The reason for this change is fairly obvious; a scheme which must have had a curiously oldfashioned look even in 1939, when the third edition was published, proved to be less and less useful for the arrangement of post-war literature. This is not a reflection on Brown's theoretical ideas, many of which have formed the basis of modern theory, but of the practical fact that a scheme must be kept up to date, especially in today's rapidly changing scene. In recent years, however, there has been a move to use LC rather than DC, particularly noticeable in the USA, and in academic rather than in public libraries. There are a variety of reasons for this which are worth examining; some of them appear to be less justifiable than others.

It is important to remember that DC and LC are very largely intended for different sets of users. DC, though it began as a scheme used in a small university library, has developed into one which is aimed almost entirely at the general reader: the non-specialist using the public library. (The specialist tends to get his specialist materials from other sources.) LC has been developed over the years since 1900 with one particular set of users in mind: the readers served by the Library of Congress. We have already seen the difference in approach between the two schemes where Literature is concerned, and this difference is found in many other subjects areas as well. Because LC is aimed at a largely academic audience, it is likely to be more satisfactory for academic libraries serving the same kind of audience than is DC with its bias towards the non-specialist reader. On these grounds, there may well be a good case for changing classification.

There is however another reason, which seems to be rather more suspect. The vast majority of libraries in the USA use Library of Congress printed catalogue cards, and while all of these carry an LC class number, not all have a DC number. Financial and other problems meant that for some years the proportion of cards with DC numbers was relatively low; in order to concentrate the effort where it was most useful, numbers were given as a first priority to those works likely to be found in the majority of public libraries, while more esoteric works were left unclassified. It is of course precisely these esoteric works which are most likely to find a home in academic libraries, which may well ignore more run-of-the-mill publications. In consequence, libraries found that they had to classify a substantial proportion of their intake if they were using DC, but very much less if they used LC. In the interests of work load reduction, they decided to change to LC; however, administrative expediency may not be a very satisfactory reason for changing the arrangement of books on our library shelves.

Another reason which has been advanced is that each new edition of DC introduces major changes; for example, DC16, DC17 and DC18 have introduced new schedules for Chemistry, Psychology, and Law and Mathematics respectively. Libraries using LC cards and the DC numbers on them are obliged to accept these changes, which can lead to a substantial amount of work. However, this reason ignores the fact that LC is changing all the time, and often the only indication of change is that a different class number appears on a card for a book on a subject already represented in the library. Keeping pace with these changes may well mean more work than the seven year hitch experienced by DC users. In any case, this is again a case of administrative convenience dictating order, which may be hard to justify on the grounds of service to users.

The only real ground for reclassification is that a different scheme will give a more satisfactory arrangement. If we reclassify on grounds that it will be easier for the librarian, we may be in some danger of forgetting that the person who is meant to benefit from the arrangement is the user. This said, we may well agree that LC is likely to be more satisfactory in the academic environment than DC, though whether it is so much better that it justifies the effort of reclassification is by no means so certain. The problems of reclassification have been discussed at some length at conferences and in the professional press; since many of them relate to the practical implementation rather than theoretical considerations, they will not be further discussed here.[2] The principle which we should always bear in mind is that we use systematic arrangement for the benefit of our users; if a change is to their advantage we should make it, but not otherwise.

BIBLIOGRAPHY

1 Coates, E J: *Subject catalogues*. Library Association, 1960. Chapters 8 and 9.

Foskett, D J: *Classification and indexing in the social sciences*. Butterworths, 1963. Chapter 10.

Mills, J: ' Chain indexing and the classified catalogue '. *Library association record*, 57(4) 1955, 141-148.

Horner, J L: *Cataloguing*. Chapter 16 has some useful examples demonstrating the fallibility of completely mechanical use of chain procedure.

Wilson, T D: *An introduction to chain indexing*. Bingley, 1971.

2 Perreault, J M, ed: *Reclassification: rationale and problems. Proceedings of a conference on reclassification . . . April 1968*. College Park, Md, School of Library and Information Services, 1968.

Samore, T, ed: *Problems in library classification: Dewey 17 and conversion*. University of Wisconsin, School of Library and Information Science, 1968.

CHAPTER 10

Kinds of precoordinate index

We are now in a position to compare the ways in which precoordinate systems are used, and to point out the relative advantages and disadvantages of different methods. There are three basic areas to be considered:

1 Shelf arrangement of books
2 Library catalogues and bibliographies
3 Book indexes

All of these depend very largely on the fact that precoordinate indexes are ' one-place ' indexes in that they can give us a single place which can be regarded as the primary statement of the subject, though they may well require also various secondary statements, *eg* in the form of supporting sequences in a different order.

SHELF CLASSIFICATION

We have seen in chapter 1 that there are a number of factors to be taken into account when considering the arrangement of documents in a library, and that we may finish up with several different sequences, some of which will be in an order dictated by their physical form, or mode of presentation, or identifying number. However, when all these things are taken into account, they still leave most libraries with a substantial collection of books which it is desirable to have on *open access*: that is to say, we permit the users to get at the books themselves and choose what they want, rather than have them come to us with the details of a book which we must then fetch from the bookstacks. (The idea of open access is now so widely accepted that it is salutary to remember that when J D Brown allowed the public of Islington to get at the books in the 1890's he was regarded by many of his colleagues as mad!) If we are to have open access, then presumably we should at least try to arrange the books in a way which will be helpful to the readers. There are various ways in which they might be arranged: size, author, title, alphabetically by subject, systematically by subject. Of these, it seems probable that the most helpful arrangement is one in which related subjects are brought together, *ie* systematic or classified arrangement.[1] Most of the major classification schemes have in fact been devised with this objective in mind; Dewey intended his scheme to be used for this from the beginning, though he was also an advocate of its use in the catalogue, while LC is intended solely for this purpose and it is only outside the USA that one finds it used for catalogue arrangement.

We have already seen in previous chapters some of the problems that arise in shelf classification. If the scheme we are using is one that permits us to be specific, then its notation may well be long; if so, it may be inconvenient to inscribe it on the spine of a book, or—worse still—a pamphlet. Immediately we have put a piece of notation on the back of a book we have a vested interest in obsolescence: we do not want relationships between subjects to change because it may mean altering what we have done in the past. Unless we guide the shelves adequately, readers will find it difficult to follow the notation, especially if it is mixed.

Additional problems arise in a lending library. A good part of the stock will be on loan at any given time, the actual books involved changing of course from week to week. Under these circumstances it becomes difficult to maintain a classified sequence in good order, and there will be gaps and 'bulges' which will involve moving the overall sequence around on the shelves; this means that a reader accustomed to finding 'his' books on a particular shelf may well be aggrieved to find that they have been moved somewhere else. In a reference library, the main problem is that of an ever increasing stock, which can involve almost as many problems of location as in a lending library.

Despite the problems, there seems to be a general consensus that we should make the effort and provide our readers with an open access stock in classified order, though one gets the impression in some libraries that classification is merely a device to 'mark and park': a convenient piece of notation to stick on the back of a book so that we can locate it. If this is indeed all we require from shelf classification it would be a great deal cheaper to use some other method entirely—perhaps go back to fixed location and closed access!

We have already seen that with any kind of retrieval system it is not possible to please all of the people all of the time. A particular classified shelf arrangement may well suit a high proportion of our readers, but there will be some who will find it unhelpful. The shelf arrangement can usefully be backed up by a continuing series of displays bringing together subjects which are scattered by the classification. For example, DC scatters concretes such as Steel and Transport; these can form the topic of displays from time to time so that users of the library become aware of the fact that the primary arrangement on the shelves is not the only one possible. Many libraries do of course have a semi-permanent display of 'recent additions'; while this display is not subject-oriented, it is a very accurate reflection of the fact that for many readers novelty is more significant than subject matter. Since the whole object of our shelf arrangement is to help readers, we should not permit theoretical considerations to prevent our providing this useful service. When the novelty has worn off, the books can be returned to the normal sequence, as they can after any other kind of display.

LIBRARY CATALOGUES AND BIBLIOGRAPHIES

A library catalogue is intended to record the stock of that library; a bibliography, on the other hand, is not limited to the stock of any one library, but usually has some other kind of limitation, eg national, language, or subject. As far as the subject approach is concerned, both are very similar and can be considered together. For example, the theory of subject headings developed by Coates has been applied so far in BTI, a bibliography, but could also be applied in a library catalogue. Many libraries use UDC for their catalogue, and for their shelf arrangement (often in an abbreviated form), but UDC is also used by some bibliographies for their primary arrangement. LCSH is intended for use in library catalogues, but will be equally effective in a bibliography, and is in fact the basis of headings used in several indexing services. This point has been stressed by Vickery in his recent *Techniques of information retrieval*,[2] which goes a long way towards eliminating the gap which all too often exists between 'subject bibliography' and 'information retrieval'.

Bearing this point in mind, we can evaluate the different kinds of subject catalogue so far described, and point out the relative advantages and disadvantages. It must be stressed that if we start with systems having the same degree of specificity, and adopt the same policy with regard to exhaustivity, there will be no difference in the information that can be found through the systems; what will differ is the ease with which the systems will give answers to particular types of enquiry. All systems are equal overall, but in any given situation, some are more equal than others.[3]

The alphabetical subject catalogue contains subject entries and cross-references arranged alphabetically in one sequence. As we have seen in chapter 2, subject entries consist of a heading, from the index vocabulary, and a description which identifies the item being catalogued. Cross-references are of two kinds: *see* references, which lead from headings which appear only in the entry vocabulary (*ie* terms which users may think of but which are not part of the preferred index vocabulary) to headings in the index vocabulary; and *see also* references, which serve to link related headings within the preferred index vocabulary, either to show genus-species relationships or to reveal 'hidden' terms in a composite heading, as discussed in the section on chain procedure in chapter 5.

Headings for the index vocabulary must be carefully chosen, to correspond as far as possible with the approach of the user. Where a heading contains more than one word, it is necessary to lay down a significance order, to bring to the front the word most likely to be sought. Entry should be direct, *eg* aluminium is entered as aluminium, not as metals—non-ferrous—aluminium. The order in which headings are arranged will have to be dictated by a set of filing rules unless all of our entries follow exactly the same pattern, which in practice is impossible. Two tools are almost essential: a source of headings—an index vocabulary—and an authority file showing our particular usage. The index vocabulary may be enumerative, *ie* may list composite headings as well as simple, and show a selection of ready made references from which we can choose the ones that are relevant at any given time; such lists as *Sears list of subject headings* and the more detailed *Subject headings used in the dictionary catalogs of the Library of Congress* are of this kind. It is possible to use the list itself as the authority file, by marking in it those headings and references we have used; *Sears list* is designed to make this easy, by having only one column of print to a page and thus leaving the right hand half of the page blank for annotations.

Alternatively we can compile an authority file separately on cards, on which we will note headings used, references made to them, and headings not used. It is possible to use the catalogue itself as the authority file; it certainly shows past practice, but it is rather more difficult to show references made to a heading clearly in the catalogue than in a separate file.

If we use a synthetic approach, then our index vocabulary will consist largely of rules as to the construction of headings, rather than the headings themselves. The compilation of an authority file is thus rather more important, for not only will we not find any composite subject headings in the index vocabulary—we may well not find many single terms either. We must however have a source for *see also* references; this will normally be a systematic listing, and has already been mentioned, BTI rely to some extent on UDC for this purpose.

We may summarize the advantages and disadvantages of the alphabetical approach as follows.

Advantages: Self evident order (within limits—it is sometimes helpful to depart from strict alphabetical arrangement).

Hospitality—we can insert new topics at any time simply by filing the headings in the appropriate places, provided that the index vocabulary that we are using permits us to add terms.

Flexibility—we can show more than one genus-species relationship in exactly the same way, by making *see also* references; this freedom can be important when we are dealing with interdisciplinary subjects, though it can equally be misleading if we do not carry through an adequate analysis of the structure of the subjects we are dealing with.

Disadvantages: To set against the above advantages we have to consider the following points.

Alphabetical scatter—if we look under Zoology, we may be referred to Animals; having made our way to the other end of the catalogue we may find that really the heading we should have been looking for was Zebras. In other words, related subjects are not found together, but are scattered according to the accident of their names.

Conflict with natural language—if we are to be consistent in our selection of headings, we shall be forced to abandon natural language in favour of an artificial index vocabulary: artificial in the sense that the choice of terms will be strictly controlled, and headings will not conform to normal usage. The simplest example of this is the elimination of synonyms, but equally, or more, important are the problems that arise from the use of insignificant words. These form an essential part of natural language but are not always used consistently: a periodical may be ' Journal of . . .', or ' Journal for . . .' or ' Journal on . . ', for example. We therefore try to avoid their use in headings, and if we are obliged to use them there is always the problem of whether they are ignored in the filing or not. Conflict arises because our controlled vocabulary still consists of words taken from natural language. However, users are accustomed to finding artificial conventions in catalogues; how many authors put their names on the title pages of their books with the surname first? So perhaps we should not exaggerate the importance of this point.

Generic searching is tedious—if we wish to pursue a subject in depth, it can become quite difficult to follow up all the references that might be relevant; there is no question of finding the whole of a topic displayed at one point in the sequence.

Alphabetical arrangement works well in a situation where terminology is well defined, and where users are mainly concerned with requests for information on specific subjects; it does not lend itself so well to broad generic searching. It has, however, the advantage that the subject catalogue can be combined with the author/title catalogue to give a dictionary catalogue in one single sequence; this brings together works by and works about a given author, individual or corporate.

CLASSIFIED CATALOGUE[4]

Systematic arrangement brings related subjects together by using notation as its index vocabulary; there is therefore no question of combining the subject and author/title sequences in one. Entries consist of a heading, which in this case is a notational symbol, and a document description. References are necessary from the entry vocabulary to the index vocabulary, *ie* from the names of subjects in words to the correct notational symbol; we need an alphabetical subject index to the classified sequence. There are therefore essentially at least two parts to a classified catalogue: the systematically arranged sequence and the alphabetical index. In addition, we may have a third sequence of authors and titles, though BNB has shown that it is quite feasible to combine this with the subject index.

Genus-species relationships and syntagmatic relationships are both shown by a combination of juxtaposition in the classified sequence and juxtaposition in the alphabetical index, but whereas in an alphabetical arrangement it is difficult to show *kinds* of relationship (the syntax of the indexing language), in a classified arrangement these are shown by the notation in many cases as well as by the arrangement, which groups together foci bearing the same relationship to the basic class containing them.

In a systematic arrangement, it is the notation which forms the index vocabulary, *ie* the headings by which subject entries are arranged, but this is merely a convenience, to make the act of finding a subject in the sequence easier. It does not help the user when he finds a piece of notation if he does not know what it stands for. Suppose that a user thinks of too broad a subject and finds the notation for this through the index; he now has to find his way through the systematic arrangement to the specific subject that he wants. The arrangement is intended to help him to do this, but if all he has to guide him are notational symbols this will not be of much help. This point was noted by Dewey, the first librarian to use a notation in the sense in which we now use the word, and he put forward the very simple solution of *feature headings*. A feature heading consists of a ' translation ' of the notation back into words; it is not used for arranging purposes but simply to guide the user. A very good example of the use of feature headings is the *British national bibliography,* where in the classified section we find a liberal use of words to clarify the systematic arrangement. Feature headings are an obvious source for index terms, and were used for this purpose by BNB.

If we are using a published scheme, *ie* one where we have to rely on some external agency to publish expansions, we may find that the scheme is not specific enough for our needs. We can find notation for part, but not all, of our subject specification. Rather than lose specificity we may decide to use the feature heading to state the subject precisely, despite the fact that some of the terms we write down in the heading will not be represented by notation. These terms are *verbal extensions;* we can use them for indexing, but it is rather more difficult to use them in the arrangement, for this would mean that we had a systematic arrangement not shown by notation. Again, the best example of the use of verbal extensions is BNB; using DC14 to classify a very large collection of literature in detail quickly revealed deficiencies, which have been overcome to a large extent by this device. Its use is indicated by [1] and is demonstrated by the following examples :

630   AGRICULTURE
631—FARM EQUIPMENT & OPERATIONS
631.2—Buildings
631.2[1]—Lighting

| 400 | LANGUAGES |
| 420 | ENGLISH |

428—ENGLISH SCHOOL BOOKS
428.[1]—Comprehension tests
428.[1]—Precis writing

| 330 | ECONOMICS |

333—NATURAL RESOURCES, LAND, REAL ESTATE
333.3—PRIVATE OWNERSHIP OF REAL ESTATE
333.33—REAL ESTATE TRANSACTIONS
333.33[1]—Surveying. *Reports*
333.33[1]—Houses. *Europe. Periodicals*
333.33[1]—Houses. *Great Britain*
333.33[1]—Houses. *Great Britain. Law*
333.33[1]—Investment in real estate

The third example shows the practice of arranging systematically despite the lack of notation; if there are a lot of specific subjects arranged in this way, as was the case in the first two five year cumulations of BNB, then even when the notation has been found through the index, the user has to search through perhaps several pages of entries, systematically arranged in an order which may be helpful but is unknown to the searcher. The advantages are those of helpful order and specificity; the searcher will find related topics together, and if there are two books on the same specific topic they will be found together. Without the use of verbal extensions these two advantages would have been lost; the user would still have had to look through as many entries, with no guarantee that if he found one on a subject he had found them all.

Feature headings and verbal extensions, as well as being the major source of indexing terms, will indicate the terms which should be used for guiding, both in the catalogue and on the shelves. In general, libraries provide quite inadequate guides to their systematic arrangement, assuming that readers can find their way through the catalogue with a minimum of help. Readers do not make much use of library catalogues. It may be thought extreme to make a guide out for every feature heading, but this is what is done in BNB, and there is no doubt that it makes the systematic arrangement a great deal easier to use. Students should compare the careful guiding of BNB with, say, *American book publishing record*, in which the guiding is minimal; the superiority shows up very clearly in the cumulations. The use of verbal extensions to make up for the deficiencies of the classification scheme can be studied in the BNB cumulations for 1951-54 and 1955-59, at, for example, 656 or 791.4.

A practical problem can arise if we try to guide a card catalogue on the lines recommended above. Guide cards project above the body of the cards, and if there are a lot of them in a drawer they tend to obscure each other, and also to wear out—a point which does not diminish their theoretical efficiency but does affect the enthusiasm with which readers use the catalogue. On the printed page, as in BNB, guiding is far more satisfactory: a reflection of the superiority of the user-oriented printed catalogue over the indexer-oriented card form.

We may summarize the advantages and disadvantages of the classified catalogue as follows:

Advantages: Helpful order—the arrangement, though not self evident, is designed to bring related subjects together in a way that will help users.

Search strategy is simple—to broaden a search we need only look at the headings in the same part of the catalogue, while it is equally simple to do the same thing to find more specific subjects.

Disadvantages: Indirect access—because the order is not self evident, we have to have a secondary file in alphabetical order to gain access to the main sequence; any search, no matter how simple, thus involves two steps, whereas with an alphabetical catalogue the user who knows the correct terminology can go straight to the heading he requires.

Systematic scattering—in any basic class, only the foci in the primary facet will have all the relevant entries at one point; foci in the secondary facets will be scattered. Furthermore a subject which can appear in more than one discipline will be scattered by the normal classification scheme, in which the primary arrangement is by discipline rather than by concrete.

The classified catalogue works well in a situation where users are not sure of their approach and need help from the arrangement; it is best suited to searching for information on broad subjects, and to browsing, but may involve the user in an extra step in the situation where he knows the subject and the heading he requires. To set against this is the fact that if the shelf arrangement of books is systematic, the alphabetical index to the catalogue will also direct users to the correct place on the shelves; it is thus possible to bypass the catalogue if the user wishes to browse among the books on the shelf at the moment rather than scan the complete set of entries in the catalogue.

If a dictionary or other alphabetical catalogue is in use, the headings used in it will differ obviously from the notation used for shelf arrangement. If a classified catalogue is in use, this may still be the case, particularly if we use a shelf notation as described in chapter 8. However, future trends may tend to accentuate this division; it seems likely that a system which works well for shelf arrangement will be inadequate for information retrieval, while a scheme designed for information retrieval may not give a helpful shelf arrangement. We may have to accept the fact that two different objectives are involved, which cannot be attained by the use of only one system.

ALPHABETICO-CLASSED CATALOGUE

We may attempt to combine the self evident order of the alphabetical approach with the helpful groupings of the systematic approach by using an alphabetico-classed arrangement. In this, headings are indirect, in contrast with the direct headings we have been considering; aluminium is entered under Metals—non-ferrous—aluminium, not under Aluminium. Everything on metals will be grouped, just as with the systematic approach; equally, we need a system of references to serve as an entry vocabulary, to lead us from the specific terms to the broader heading under which they are subsumed. Within each heading, subheadings are arranged alphabetically, not systematically, so that subgroups may not be arranged in a helpful order.

In trying to get the best of both worlds, we may have finished up with the worst. We no longer have the direct entry of the alphabetical (or, more precisely, alphabetico-direct) sequence, nor have we the helpful order of the systematic. The alphabetico-classed catalogue has in practice few of its theoretical advantages and has found few advocates. In Britain and indeed Europe generally the classified catalogue is most popular, while in the USA it is the dictionary catalogue which is most commonly found.

MULTIPLE ENTRY SYSTEMS

In the discussion of citation order, we saw that there are likely to be situations where users are badly handicapped by insistence on one fixed citation order; the same is of course true of the alphabetical catalogue with a fixed significance order. The reason for having one, and only one, such order is to ensure that the same topic is not entered under more than one heading at different times, introducing an element of inconsistency which leads to lowered recall, and also to provide a definite place for the shelf arrangement. We can only put a document in one physical place, and there must be definite rules to make sure that we are consistent in choosing this one place; but there is no reason other than economics to stop us making additional entries in the catalogue. However, the economics of multiple entry are important; as has already been pointed out, permutation of all the elements in a composite subject may lead to a quite unacceptable number of entries. We have to find methods of increasing the number of entries to a level which is acceptable; these methods must be consistent, and simple to apply. Haphazard selection from the mass of potential permutations will not help the users; the penalty of inconsistency here, as everywhere, is sequential scanning of a much larger number of entries than is necessary if strict rules are followed.

CYCLING

We saw that to construct a KWIC index, each significant element of the title had to be made the filing word in turn. If we consider our subject specification as a 'title' consisting of several elements, it becomes clear that we can construct the same kind of index, using these elements instead of words. This practice is closely associated with UDC; here it is common to build up class numbers for composite subjects by linking the notations for the elements, using the colon. The elements can then be cycled, to give as many entries as there are elements. To illustrate this symbolically, let us take a composite subject represented by the five notational symbols ABCDE, representing the words abcde. One-place entry means one entry at ABCDE and five index entries:

edcba	[see]	ABCDE
dcba	[see]	ABCD
cba	[see]	ABC
ba	[see]	AB
a	[see]	A

Cycling involves five entries, and also five index entries, but this time the index entries are for the individual elements only, not for any composite subjects:

entries	index entries
ABCDE	a [see] A
BCDEA	b [see] B

CDEAB	C [see] C
DEABC	D [see] D
EABCD	E [see] E

This means that no matter what composite subjects may occur in the future, it will not be necessary to make any further index entries for these elements; using one-place entry and chain procedure, new composite subjects may involve extra chain index entries.

Cycling is frequently used with UDC, where numbers may be combined by using the colon; when only two numbers are concerned the cycled entry is simply the reverse of the primary entry, and the technique is often known as *reversing*. An example will show the effects of the technique in terms of indexing and number of entries.

Let us suppose that documents are received on the following topics

Steel pipes for fluid distribution	669.14 : 621.643.2
Copper pipes	669.3 : 621.643.2
Aluminium pipes	669.71 : 621.643.2
Steel saucepans	669.14 : 643.352.3
Copper saucepans	669.3 : 643.352.3
Aluminium saucepans	669.71 : 643.352.3
Steel conductors (Electrical)	669.14 : 621.315.5
Copper conductors	669.3 : 621.315.5
Aluminium conductors	669.71 : 621.315.5
Welding of steel	669.14 : 621.791
Welding of copper	669.3 : 621.791
Welding of aluminium	669.71 : 621.791
Annealing of steel	669.14 : 621.785
Annealing of copper	669.3 : 621.785
Annealing of aluminium	669.71 : 621.785

Assuming that we have one document on each topic, and that we reverse colon combinations, there will be fifteen pairs of entries in the classified catalogue, thirty in all, and eight entries in the alphabetical index (ignoring for simplicity the entries for superordinate terms in the chain for each term, *eg* Metals):

Aluminium	669.71
Annealing	621.785
Conductors : electrical engineering	621.315.5
Copper	669.3
Pipes : fluid distribution	621.643.2

Saucepans	643.352.3
Steel	669.14
Welding	621.791

If we now add documents on brass pipes and brass conductors:

669.35.5 : 621.643.2 and reversed   621.643.2 : 669.35.5

669.35.5 : 621.315.5   621.315.5 : 669.35.5

Another four entries for the classified file, but only one for the index:

Brass   669.35.5

Seventeen documents have now given rise to thirty four entries in the classified file, nine in the alphabetical index. But if instead of one we have thirty documents on each of these subjects, there will be the same nine entries in the index, but 1,020 entries in the classified sequence—a drawer full of cards. If we add another document on the annealing of copper pipes, this will give rise to three cycled entries in the classified sequence:

621.643.2 : 669.3 : 621.785

669.3 : 621.785 : 621.643.2

621.785 : 621.643.2 : 669.3

but will give no further index entries. There are thus two advantages to cycling: it makes the indexing simpler, and it means that any user can find all his information at one point in the sequence.

If we have the same fifteen subjects, but decide that instead of reversing we will have a fixed citation order and detailed indexing, the results will be rather different. Assuming that we adopt the citation order Product: Material: Process we shall have entries at the following points (note that these are in every case *one* of the entries we make in reversing):

621.643.2 : 669.14

621.643.2 : 669.3

621.643.2 : 669.71

643.352.3 : 669.14

643.352.3 : 669.3

643.352.3 : 669.71

621.315.5 : 669.14

621.315.5 : 669.3

621.315.5 : 669.71

669.14 : 621.791

669.3   : 621.791

669.71 : 621.791

669.14 : 621.785
669.3 : 621.785
669.71 : 621.785

Fifteen entries to be inserted in the classified sequence, but more than this for the alphabetical index:

Aluminium	669.71
Aluminium : conductors	621.315.5 : 669.71
Aluminium : pipes	621.643.2 : 669.71
Aluminium : saucepans	643.352.3 : 669.71
Annealing : aluminium	669.71 : 621.785
Annealing : copper	669.3 : 621.785
Annealing : steel	669.14 : 621.785
Conductors : electrical engineering	621.315.5
Copper	669.3
Copper : conductors	621.315.5 : 669.3
Copper : pipes	621.643.2 : 669.3
Copper : saucepans	643.352.3 : 669.3
Pipes : fluid distribution	621.643.2
Saucepans	643.352.3
Steel	669.14
Steel : conductors	621.315.5 : 669.14
Steel : pipes	621.643.2 : 669.14
Steel : saucepans	643.352.3 : 669.14
Welding : aluminium	669.71 : 621.791
Welding : copper	669.3 : 621.791
Welding : steel	669.14 : 621.791

Twenty one entries in the alphabetical sequence, compared with eight, but only fifteen in the classified sequence compared with thirty. If we now add documents as before, on brass pipes and brass conductors, we shall have the following entries:
classified sequence

621.643.2 : 669.35.5
621.315.5 : 669.35.5

alphabetical sequence

Brass : pipes	621.643.2 : 669.35.5
Brass : conductors	621.315.5 : 669.35.5

This will raise the number of entries in the alphabetical index to twenty three, with seventeen entries in the classified file. If however we have thirty documents on each of these subjects, we shall still have twenty three index entries, but only 510 in the classified file instead of 1,020. We have economized to the extent of half a drawer of entries; the penalty we pay for this is that we can no longer tell our readers that everything on their topic will be found in one place, unless it happens to be a Product. Furthermore, if we add a document on annealing of copper pipes, this will mean only one new entry in the classified sequence, but also one in the alphabetical index:

Annealing: copper: pipes   621.643.2:669.3:621.785

Every new composite subject will give rise to additional index entries, even if the elements of which it is composed are already indexed.

Cycling is thus a partial solution to the problem of systematic scatter, but it tends to increase the bulk of the classified file; it also may have other shortcomings. To consider again our symbolic example ABCDE, let us assume that we add another document, this time on ABCD. The cycled entries for this will be as follows:

ABCD

BCDA

CDAB

DABC

If we interfile these with the cycled entries arising from ABCDE, we find that only at the primary entry are they certain to be found in the same place; at D, for example, the first will be under the heading DEABC, while the second will be under DABC, and these two entries could well be separated by a number of other entries at D. While it is true that cycling brings together at one place all the information to be found on any given topic, it does so at the cost of making us search the whole body of entries at that heading instead of being able to go to the specific ones we want. In this example, we shall have to scan every entry at D to make sure that we have found something on DA; to quote the detailed example worked out earlier, if we want to find everything on copper pipes, we shall have to search every entry under copper, because although there is a heading for *copper pipes,* it is not the same as the heading for *annealing of copper pipes*:

669.3:621.643.2

669.3:621.785:621.643.2

ROTATING

A method of overcoming this problem is to *rotate*[5] instead of cycle; in this, the citation order is retained, but entries are made under each element:

*A*BCDE
A*B*CDE
AB*C*DE
ABC*D*E
ABCD*E*

Here the filing element is in each case the one in the same position as
A in the first, but the relative position of each element with respect
to the others remains unchanged. The method has been demonstrated
with the London education classification by D J Foskett. It gives the
same advantage as cycling, but without the problem of scattering;
thus recall is as good but relevance is likely to be much higher. Both
cycling and rotating have been discussed here with reference to classified order, but of course there is no reason why they should not be
used with alphabetical indexing. It is important not to confuse these
with permuting, an error into which a number of writers have fallen
in the past. Permutation, as has been stressed, will normally involve
an unacceptable number of entries, whereas cycling or rotating, though
it will increase the number of entries we make, will not do so in-
tolerably.

SLIC INDEXING

Cycling and rotating are means of ensuring that all material on one
particular focus can be found in the same place in the classified
sequence, but they achieve this at the cost of giving the user a certain
amount of sequential scanning to do. Further, they do not help the
user who is interested in a combination of foci which are kept apart
by the citation order. For example, if we use the English Electric
citation order Machines : Parts : Materials : Problems, we shall build up
a series of subject specifications of the following kind:

Dynamos : bearings : steel : fatigue

Generators : bearings : bronze : fatigue

Motors : bearings : nylon : fatigue

Alternators : bearings : white metal : fatigue

It is plain that anyone interested in bearings will have to look in
a number of places, perhaps as many as there are machines in the
catalogue; it will be possible to find these places through the alphabetical index. Anyone interested in fatigue will have to look in a
great many more places, for this focus may be scattered under every
metal or other material, which in turn may be scattered under every

part of every machine; once again it will be possible to find all these places through the alphabetical index, though the task will almost certainly be very tedious and for human reasons is unlikely to be completed. Cycling and rotating will both ensure that everything on bearings will be found at one point, and everything on fatigue will be found at one point also; but what of the reader who is interested in fatigue in bearings? Neither of these methods will bring together these two concepts; they are separated by the citation order, with material specified between them, and even cycling does not help, for now they will be separated by machine.

To demonstrate this using symbolic notation, B and D will always be separated in ABCD if it is rotated, while cycling will bring both to the front but does not bring them together: BCDA and DABC. If we use single entry and chain indexing, then we will not find any index entries linking them under the word bearings, though this will lead us to all the places where bearings forms part of the heading; if on the other hand we look under fatigue, we shall have to search through every entry at that point, *selecting* those which also contain the word ' bearings '. The probability of error in such an operation is obviously high if there is any considerable number of entries under fatigue; in the catalogue of the English Electric Company there were in fact over 300, and the likelihood of anyone successfully completing such a search is small. A computer might well be able to carry out this kind of search with no difficulty, but human error would almost certainly invalidate results obtained by manual searching.

Permutation would bring the two terms together in every case, but at the cost of too many entries. However, a mathematician normally associates permutations with *combinations;* whereas permutations are the different ways of arranging things, combinations are the ways in which groups may be selected. If we have two things, A and B, we can arrange them in two ways, AB and BA, but we can only select one group containing both of them; it does not matter whether we select A first or B, the final result will be that we have them both. For example, if we have n things we can arrange them in n! ways, but we can only select one group of n; we can select n groups containing (n-1) things, because we can remove each of the n things in turn to give us a different group of (n-1). If we consider all the possible groups, containing n, (n-1), (n-2) . . . 3, 2, 1, things, then, for each group a particular thing is either in that group or it is not, *ie* there are two states for each thing with regard to each group. There are n things, so that the total possible number of states is 2^n, but this includes the state where none of the things is present, which is not of interest. We therefore arrive at the figure 2^n-1 as the total number of combinations of n things taken any or all at the time. When n is 5, the number of possible permutations is 120, but the number of possible combinations is 31.

If we could use combinations instead of permutations, we could reduce the total number of entries required by a substantial amount, but the total would still be rather large. J R Sharp[6] has pointed out that in fact we do not need to use all of the possible combinations; for indexing purposes, some of them will be included in others and will therefore be superfluous. By eliminating these superfluous combinations we can reduce the total to $2^{(n-1)}$ from 2^n; in figures, when n is 5, we can reduce the number of entries from 31 to 16, compared with 120 for permutation. When we consider that chain indexing, the most economical method, would involve at least 5 entries, it begins to look as though the use of selected combinations might give a tolerable increase in the number of entries, at least in situations where n is fairly small. Sharp suggests 5 as the limit; when n is 6, the number of entries is 32—too many; higher values of n simply increase the number of entries by a factor of 2 each time. Sharp calls the method Selective Listing In Combination or SLIC indexing.

We may list all the possible combination of five things:

ABCDE	ABCD	ABC	ADE	AB	BD	A
	ABDE	ABD	BCD	AC	BE	B
	ACDE	ABE	BCE	AD	CD	C
	ABCE	ACD	BDE	AE	CE	D
	BCDE	ACE	CDE	BC	DE	E

five (1)	four (5)	three (10)	two (10)	one (5)

Total: 31 groups all told.

We can rearrange these to show the ones which are included in larger groups by marking the latter *ABCDE*:

ABCDE	*ABDE*	*ABCE*	*ABE*	*BCE*	*CDE*	*E*
ABCD	ABD	*BCDE*	*ACE*	*BDE*	CD	
ABC	*ACDE*	BCD	*ADE*	BD	C	
AB	ACD	BC	AD	*BE*	*DE*	
A	AC	B	*AE*	*CE*	D	
1	2	2	4	4	2	1

Total: 16 groups which are not contained in any larger group.

One thing which characterizes all the combinations shown above is that they all follow the same internal order; we do not write down a group such as DABE. If we are to apply the SLIC principle to indexing, we must begin by laying down the internal order of our headings. Sharp originally applied the idea to alphabetical headings, using alphabetical order as his internal arrangement; a heading such as

  Dynamos : bearings : steel : fatigue
would be written down in the form
  Bearings : dynamos : fatigue : steel
and will give rise to the following additional headings:
  Bearings : dynamos : steel
  Bearings : fatigue : steel
  Dynamos : fatigue : steel
  Bearings : steel
  Dynamos : steel
  Fatigue : steel.
  Steel.

Bearings and fatigue, separated by the fixed order, and impossible to bring together by cycling or rotating, are assembled by the SLIC technique, as is shown by the second added heading above. Alphabetical order in this context is an arbitrary order, but the citation order of a classification scheme is intended to be helpful, and can very well serve as the fixed order required.[7] In fact, with this technique as with any of the other methods of multiple entry, we are unlikely to obtain a worthwhile return for the additional cost unless the composite heading that we are manipulating is itself a valid and useful statement of the subject.

To make even 16 entries manually for each document would involve a great deal of work, but it is straightforward to program a computer to generate and file the appropriate headings. Unfortunately there has been no large scale use of SLIC, and it is difficult to tell how well it compares with other methods from the cost point of view. It achieves its objective, to bring together elements separated by the citation order, but it does so at the cost of loss of specificity; in the example given above, one of the headings is simply Steel, and there will be numerous entries at that heading to look through, the majority of them about far more specific topics.

PHYSICAL FORM OF INDEX

Although in theory the physical form of the indexing system should not affect its performance, in practice it does, to quite a large extent. There are two aspects to this: firstly, input problems; secondly, those to do with output.

In any system that is open ended, we need to be able to insert new items as necessary. If we have a fixed location serial file, ie one in which we give each item a permanent place, there is only one place that we can add new items: at the end. We cannot add in the middle, because that would disturb the items already filed. The only kind of arrangement that can be displayed is thus a chronological one, with the latest always at the end. Such a file is the accessions book in a library, or a file of data on magnetic tape, and to find entries by any but the chronological approach involves sequential scanning of the whole file; we do not have *random access,* ie the ability to go direct to any particular access point we may require.

The most popular form of catalogue in libraries is the card catalogue. This consists of a set of cards, usually of standard 12·5 × 7·5 cm size; the cards are arranged according to the indexing system headings. New cards can be added wherever they are needed, and we can go direct to any access point we want, provided that it is used as a heading. As has already been mentioned, we normally make a distinction between the headings, *ie* those points where we want to be able to find information, and the description, *ie* the information which identifies the document; we cannot find our way to any information in the description which is not used as a heading. For example, the date of publication forms part of the description, but it is not normally used as a heading; we cannot then find all the entries in the catalogue representing documents published in a given year, unless we are prepared to scan every entry. In a card catalogue, we need a drawer for every thousand cards; if we have 100,000 documents in our collection, and we decide to make an entry for each using the date of publication as the heading, we shall require another 100,000 cards, or 100 drawers. There is a limit to the convenient height for a set of card catalogue drawers; the users have to be able to see what is in the top drawer. Equally, it is not usual to have drawers so near the ground that users have to kneel to be able to use them. If we allow users to remove the drawers from their place in the cabinet, we can use more vertical space, but there is still a limit at top and bottom; in consequence, when we increase the size of the catalogue, we have to think in terms of horizontal expansion. Space for 100 drawers might be five feet long; in depth it will have to be large enough for us to use with the drawers pulled out to their maximum depth, say three feet. This gives fifteen square feet as the requirement for the extra 100,000 cards, a not inconsiderable amount of floor space. Thus we may find that we are constrained in the number of entries we make in a card catalogue by the economic factor of space costs.

Filing entries in a card catalogue also costs money; although it is strictly speaking a clerical operation, it is usual for filing to be checked before the cards are finally inserted into the sequence. Furthermore, the larger the catalogue is, the more difficult it is to use; this is particularly noticeable with an alphabetically arranged catalogue, where we may have to go from one point in the sequence to another some distance away through the accident of alphabetical scatter of related subjects. It is therefore clear that there are quite strong arguments in favour of keeping the number of entries in the catalogue as low as possible, and that these are economic arguments rather than intellectual ones. In practice, the figure of (very approximately) one and a half subject entries per document has been suggested as being the average. This could mean that we make fewer entries than are justified for a particular document, but it is important to realise that this is an economic restriction, not an intellectual one; the card catalogue permits us to make as many entries as we like for any and every document, without any restriction other than the economic and practical ones outlined above.

On the output side, a drawback to the card catalogue is that it is only possible to see one entry at a time; to see a number of entries under one heading we must leaf through them singly. This can be a relatively slow process, even if we take a bundle of cards out of a drawer and turn them over one by one on a desk—a procedure which would normally be frowned upon, because of the danger of getting the cards out of order. It is possible to turn over two cards at once, particularly if the cards have been well thumbed in the past; in this way, important entries might be missed, and the searching process is necessarily slowed down by the attempt to avoid this.

To sum up, the card catalogue is very flexible; it permits us to arrange any number of entries in any way we wish, and to insert new entries as required. To set against this, it is relatively expensive, both in capital cost and in upkeep, it is not convenient to scan, and it is essentially a single copy device; it costs twice as much to maintain two copies as to maintain one. There is also the very practical problem of wear and tear. We have already pointed out that guide cards, which project above the main body of the cards in the catalogue, are liable to deteriorate fairly quickly, but over a period of time the same is true of the whole set of cards. For example, in 1965 it was estimated that the card catalogue of the New York Public Library contained eight million cards and was growing at the rate of two million cards a year —but that of the cards in the catalogue some 30 percent (nearly two and a half million!) were either worn out or illegible and ought to be replaced. Readers are reluctant to make use of a tool which is in poor physical condition, no matter how excellent its intellectual content.

The sheaf catalogue is akin to the card form in that entries consist of individual, independent, pieces of paper, but whereas in the card catalogue these are standard size pieces of thin card, in the sheaf catalogue thin paper is used, and there is no standard size; slips may vary from, say, $4in \times 2\frac{1}{2}in$ to $6in \times 4in$ of usable space. The slips are held in stout covers known as binders, working on the looseleaf principle, the binders being stored in racks. Once again we have complete flexibility; we can insert new entries at any point at any time, and of course remove them if necessary. However, slips are less convenient to handle than cards and for this reason filing is slightly slower—and therefore more costly. The binders are perhaps easier to consult than card drawers in that they are in the familiar book form, but the slips again are less convenient than cards to leaf through. Space requirements are less, and capital outlay is considerably less, though this is offset by the higher maintenance costs.

The question of producing multiple copies is important, for a variety of reasons. In the first place, we normally need more than one entry point to any given document and therefore need to be able to find the same description under a number of headings; so we need a number of entries in which the description will be the same but the headings will differ. In the second place, if we maintain only one copy of the catalogue, readers will have to come to that copy to be able to consult it; we shall be introducing one more hurdle for them to cross. It is therefore desirable to be able to maintain more than one copy; indeed, the ideal is to have as many copies available as there are individuals requiring them. If we look at the card catalogue from this point of view, it presents several disadvantages. If we want to produce more than one card we have either to type each one individually (and check to see that it is correct), or use some method of duplication. As has already been pointed out, to maintain two identical card catalogues involves twice as much work as maintaining one. Space is also a consideration. Sheaf slips are only marginally better; by using carbons, it is possible to produce up to six copies of an entry at one typing, but once we get beyond this limit the question of retyping arises. Space is still a consideration, though not so acutely as with cards, but filing is, if anything, more of a problem.

On the whole, the balance seems to be in favour of the card form, and this is strongly reinforced by the fact that cards are available from several central agencies, for example BNB and the Library of Congress. However, there seems to be little doubt that both forms are used with reluctance by the general public, and neither gives the user the opportunity to take the catalogue away and browse through it.

At one time, the printed catalogue in book form was the standard method used by public libraries, particularly those with closed access. The book form has several advantages: it is portable, it can be produced in multiple copies very easily, and it is convenient to use—the eye can scan a column of entries very easily instead of having to look at one at a time. It suffers however from one very important disadvantage: it is completely inflexible. The time taken to print it can mean that it is out of date when it is available, and though withdrawals can be shown by crossing out, additions cannot be shown at all. Supplements may be published, and from time to time a complete new edition, but this is not always a very satisfactory solution. The printed catalogue is then well suited to the situation where withdrawals are few, and additions are also a small proportion of the total stock. We find this situation in such large national libraries as the British Museum (though even here it seems likely that the last complete catalogue has been prepared), and the special library concentrating on a particular subject, for example the Library Association. In both cases, the catalogue is of value to a much wider audience than can actually visit the library, and the production of multiple copies is of more importance than absolute currency (though of course the library producing such a catalogue will often maintain an up to date version in some other physical form for its own use).

There has thus been a conflict in the past between the convenience of the printed book-form catalogue and its inflexibility; this conflict can now be resolved by the use of the computer, which makes possible the regular printing out of up to date copies.[8] The only problem now remaining is the one of cost; regular updating can become expensive, and so far figures on the relative costs of maintaining conventional catalogues and computer printout are difficult if not impossible to come by. However, in a library which uses a computer for its other operations, such as acquisitions and circulation control, the additional cost of manipulating the available information to produce a catalogue is likely to be outweighed by the convenience of having multiple copies available. The production of the catalogue can then take its rightful place as one of a series of interrelated library operations, and users can look forward to having a form of catalogue which suits them rather than the cataloguer! The economic situation is also affected by the number of service points where full catalogues are normally maintained; for example, in a county library or large borough, it may well prove feasible to provide a computer printout at every service point, whereas the task of maintaining complete card catalogues everywhere would be very costly if not completely impractical.

Very occasionally, other forms of catalogue are found. The British Museum uses a guard book, of which it maintains three copies. One of these is the master copy, while the other two are the copies for the reading room; while one is being brought up to date, the other is available for use. The method has an oldfashioned air, but appears to suit the peculiar circumstances of the BM. Another interesting experiment was carried out in the University of Malaya, in an attempt to produce a form more acceptable to the user than the card catalogue; this was the Stripdex,[9] a title-a-line set of strips of card fitted into metal holders. It appears that this was not the success that had been hoped, and it has now been abandoned.

The physical form of the catalogue does not affect its content; what it does affect is the ease with which it may be produced and consulted, and its cost. There is little doubt that librarians have been a great deal more impressed with the virtues of the card catalogue than have readers; with the possibility of a return to the more acceptable book form, we may well see a more intensive use of library catalogues than the few per cent of readers we have grown accustomed to.

BIBLIOGRAPHIES

Unlike library catalogues, bibliographies are normally printed and intended for wide distribution. Multiple entry is therefore almost unknown, because of its cost in a printed catalogue; instead we have a single main entry, which may range in detail from author, title and date to a full informative abstract, with various secondary indexes to give access through factors thought likely to be useful. We have exactly the same problems of arrangement and indexing as in library catalogues, but some other considerations also arise from the nature of bibliographies.

Bibliographies may be either current or retrospective. In the latter case, we select the entries to be included, and the list is then closed; we are thus in a position to be able to choose whatever method of primary arrangement we wish, and can opt for one which will reflect, as far as we can tell in advance, the needs of the potential users. Current bibliographies, on the other hand, are normally produced under some pressure of time; for example, one of the major reasons for the computerization of BTI and BNB has been to enable them to maintain a high degree of currency—in the case of BTI, published monthly, a maximum delay of seven weeks from the appearance of an article in print and its appearance in BTI. Under these circumstances, it may prove necessary to give up any pretence at helpful order in the main sequence, and use instead a chronological order of receipt. We find, for example, that in *US Government research and development reports* the main sequence is arranged by report number, *ie* order of receipt, while in other current bibliographies there is even less attempt to produce an order which is of some value in itself. (In the case of report literature, the report number is a significant identifying factor.) If the main order is an arbitrary one, the need for indexes becomes acute if we are to be able to conduct a search for a particular item or subject.

This need is related to the likely use to be made of a current bibliography. We have already pointed out in chapter 3 that there is a difference between bibliographies intended for current notification and those intended for retrospective searching; those intended for the latter purpose will normally have more, and more detailed, secondary sequences than those meant for temporary use only. The contrast is exemplified by *Chemical titles* and *Chemical abstracts;* the first covers some 700 journals, and consists of a basic list showing the contents of each issue indexed plus a KWIC index based on the titles, while the second covers some 12,000 journals, giving a detailed abstract for each item, the abstracts being arranged under eighty rather broad alphabetical headings. Each issue has always had an author index, but to supplement this a subject index generated by machine manipulation of keywords taken from the abstracts is now included. For each volume there are cumulated author and subject indexes, the subject approach being catered for by very detailed indexes of the articulated type described in chapter 5; these have now been cumulated in ten or five year blocks since the beginning of CA in 1907. The extra effort involved in the compilation of the abstracts and their indexes means that the cost is very much greater—$1,200 compared with $50—but there is no doubt that the extra cost is justified if any considerable number of retrospective searches is carried out.

Many of the techniques described in earlier chapters have in fact been developed for use in abstracting and indexing services and other bibliographies. In particular, those techniques which lend themselves to computer manipulation are likely to be found in this kind of tool rather than in library catalogues, even though many of the latter are now being produced by computer printout, and with the coming of MARC many more are likely to be in the future. It is not always realized that the arrangement of, and indexes to, bibliographical tools are in essence exactly the same as comparable features in conventional catalogues, and should be subjected to the same kind of evaluation.

BOOK INDEXES

The indexing of individual books is usually also regarded as something quite separate from other kinds of indexing, but this is not the case. We can employ the same kinds of approach as we would with any other classified sequence, since the book itself presents topics in a systematic way; in particular, it is possible to use chain procedure to give a full and detailed index which is nevertheless within economic bounds, as examples taken from the first edition of the present work will demonstrate.

If we consider a topic such as ' Dewey's use of notation ' we might, taking into account the overall structure of the book, expect to find information on this in two major places: the first is the chapter on notation (chapter 7), the second the chapter on Dewey's classification scheme (chapter 11). If we turn to these headings in the index, we find under Notation (selecting the relevant headings):

Notation ch 7 89+
    applied to books by Dewey 148
    DC 158+

These three entries tell us that chapter 7, beginning on page 89, deals with notation in general, and may well be worth reading through, and that in addition there are two other pages we should turn to, the first for information on a particular innovation, the second on the notation of DC generally. If we now turn to the name Dewey in the index we find:

Dewey, M 147+
    notation: allocation 92
    integrity of numbers 117
    see also DC

If we follow the instruction *see also* and turn to DC, we find:

DC ch 11 147+
    notation
        distorting order 97
        in *Sears list* 225
        instructions for cutting 109
        mnemonic features 94
        not always expressive 101

By following up the various references we have found we can discover everything in the book relating to Dewey's use of notation, but some of the searching may be indirect. Under Notation we are referred to chapter 7, but are not told exactly where in that chapter we should look for information on Dewey, while if we follow up the references under Dewey and DC we may find ourselves reading through the whole chapter, or at least looking for section headings. The only entries under Notation which are specific are those leading us to places *not* in the general chapter; similarly, the entries under DC which are specific are those *not* leading to chapter 11. This is not entirely satisfactory, but the alternative soon begins to look impracticable if we consider that under Notation we should have to list all the significant contents of the whole chapter on notation, and under DC the whole contents of that chapter, in addition to all the other entries which are there already. In order to gain an economic advantage we sacrifice a degree of specificity, giving us a result which is consistent (even in its imperfection!) and is of reasonable size in relation to the book.

As in the classified catalogue, chain procedure forces us to rely to some extent on the use of headings within chapters, and on the systematic presentation generally. Since the index leads us to pages, not to cards, the scanning which may be necessary is not intolerable, and may in fact be useful in drawing our attention to, for example, other features of notation mentioned in chapter 7 but not necessarily associated with Dewey. The systematic collocation of distributed relatives which is one result of applying chain procedure does at least make sure that we can find everything on notation indexed under that heading, and on Dewey indexed under his name, even though the information we want may be scattered throughout the book.

In compiling indexes to individual books we are faced with a problem that we can sometimes avoid when indexing whole documents. We are obliged to formulate some kind of subject description; we cannot rely on a title provided by the author, because we are actually trying to pinpoint ideas *within* the text. To set against this there is the fact that, since we are only dealing with the work of one author, we can usually rely on the terminology of the book rather than have to worry about using a controlled vocabulary.

Book indexes are usually of the alphabetico-direct kind. Since we are indexing a systematic presentation—the text of the book—we will gain little from using a systematic index, which would itself need a further guide in the form of some kind of alphabetical sequence; we do however sometimes find examples of the alphabetico-indirect kind of index, which may be said to be open to exactly the same kind of objection. It is desirable to avoid *see* references within the index, for the same reason that they should be avoided in the index to a classified catalogue: they send us to a place from which we shall be sent on once again. In the present work, the problem of long lists of entries under synonyms, which is the reason for the existence of *see* references, has been avoided to some extent by indexing only the preferred synonym in full, but giving entries under non-preferred synonyms which lead to the preferred synonym but also to the main section in the text. For example:

Optical coincidence cards (peek-a-boo) 232 +

leads us to the main chapter, but also points out that the user may find more entries if he turns to the preferred synonym peek-a-boo:

Peek-a-boo 232 +
    compared with Uniterm 236
    use of punched cards 251

Once again we have an economy measure intended to keep down costs while nevertheless providing the user with complete access at the cost of a little more effort on his part. Since publishers are in general anxious to keep costs as low as possible, the author is obliged to use economical methods; like hanging, indexing a book concentrates the mind wonderfully.[10]

SEARCH STRATEGY

So far we have looked at the theory and practice of the construction of pre-coordinate indexes, but we should also give some consideration to their use. How do we set about getting the best results from such an index? What procedure should we follow in conducting a search? We are faced with a question posed by a user, possibly not very well phrased, perhaps asking for something other than what is really wanted, but normally triggered off by some particular event or events. This question has to be resolved into an answer consisting primarily of a set of document descriptions identifying items which we think will provide the information wanted. The index or catalogue is the tool we use to perform this transformation, and, as in pantomime transformation scenes, the effectiveness with which it will do so depends on how well the machinery works and how carefully we have maintained it. (For some of our readers, no matter how we wave the magic wand of persuasion, the library catalogue remains obdurately a pumpkin.)

The first piece of advice may seem somewhat of a counsel of despair: it is that if we have some identifying factor, such as an author's name, it is easier to follow this up than to try to formulate a subject search. The whole success of such tools as *Science citation index* is linked to their avoidance of subject specification and their reliance on ' hard ' information such as bibliographical references. Similarly, if during the course of a subject search it appears that a few authors are major figures in the subject field concerned, it is often worth following their names up in a largescale indexing or abstracting service such as *Chemical abstracts* or the French *Bulletin signalétique,* or even a biographical reference work, since this will frequently reveal items which it would have been very difficult or even impossible to find through the subject approach.

If we do not have any identifying factors to go on, we have to pursue our search through the subject. The first point is to establish as closely as possible the exact nature of the subject we are interested in, and this can be quite difficult. Users often find it difficult to express themselves, and in many cases they are not quite sure what it is they are looking for; they will however always have some kind of springboard or trigger which has led to their question, and we can work forwards from this. The *reference interview* is an important part of any information retrieval process,[11] and from recent research on the performance of the MEDLARS service it would appear that such an interview is best carried out without reference to any particular indexing language; *ie* the enquirer should be encouraged to express himself freely and if necessary at length, so that we have as complete a statement as he is able to give of what he wants, in his own words.[12] We can then think about translating these into the indexing language of our catalogues and bibliographies, or rather languages, since the likelihood of their all using the same indexing method is remote.

If the search is for a single concept, it will be relatively simple. We have to determine which terms have been used to denote that particular concept in our indexing language; in an alphabetical system this will probably be straightforward, but in a classified arrangement we may well have to determine the context in which a concept is required, since this will dictate the notation we shall have to look for. We can then turn to the sequence of subject entries and find what is filed under the appropriate heading. If we find nothing, then we have to consider which other headings to consult; in an alphabetical sequence we should look for *see also* references, in a classified sequence try searching round about the place we have found. In both cases we shall be looking for related headings, but whereas in an alphabetical sequence these will be scattered, in a classified sequence many of them should be juxtaposed. By moving back in a classified catalogue, *ie* in the direction of earlier class numbers, we can, if the scheme used is in accordance with the principle of inversion, come to a broader heading; by moving forward, in the direction of later class numbers, we may come to useful material at more specific headings. For example, if we are looking for information on potato blight in a catalogue arranged by UDC, the class number representing the subject will be 633.491—24. If we find nothing at this point, we can move forward to the more specific subject, treatment of potato blight, at 633.491—24—293.4; alternatively, we may move back to the more general heading potatoes at 633.491. If neither of these moves gives any useful information, we can move further back to even more general headings: control of plant diseases 632.93, fungus diseases of plants 632.4, diseases of plants, injuries etc 632. We may find material on fungus diseases of other plants, but it must be pointed out that, because this is a distributed relative, it will be scattered; we shall however be able to locate it positively through the index to the classified arrangement, though this is of course not making use of the arrangement itself to help us.

As we have pointed out earlier, it is not usual to make upward references in an alphabetical catalogue; this means that we shall not find any references telling us where to look for a more general heading. If we find nothing at Potatoes, blight (or Potato blight) we can obviously look under Potatoes or Blight, but there will be no further guidance as to headings more general than these. We shall have to turn back to the authority list (*eg* Sears) to find what more general headings might be worth trying, *eg* Plant diseases. If we are using a tool such as BTI, for which the authority list is not published, we may find some difficulty in selecting a broader heading, and it will often be useful to consult a classification scheme to establish what concepts we ought to look for.

At all times the needs of the user have to be kept in mind. If he is satisfied with one document, then we can stop our search directly we have found one relevant answer; we do not need to worry about whether there are other answers, or even whether one of them might not be better. If the enquirer is satisfied, we have achieved our objective. This does not mean that we should not advise him if we think that we can easily find something better; he may still be quite happy for us to stop searching. There will be other occasions when we shall have to discover as much information as we can, by making our search as complete as possible. This will normally involve some knowledge of the subject area, as well as skill in the use of catalogues and bibliographies, as is shown by some of the examples quoted by Vickery.[13]

Much of the research described in chapter 23 is concerned with the evaluation of indexing techniques, and an interesting outcome from this research has been the idea of ranking documents according to their likely relevance; instead of dividing the collection of documents into relevant sheep and irrelevant goats, we rank every document, from 'most relevant' to 'least relevant'. We can then cut off the search at any point to suit the enquirer, from (in theory at least) one document to the entire collection. It will be interesting to see how the results of this research can be applied to the practical library search situation.

SUMMARY

THE VALUE OF PRE-COORDINATE SYSTEMS

Pre-coordinate systems are basically one-place systems, but problems arise here from the necessity for a fixed citation or significance order. Multiple entry adaptations of the basic single entry solve many of these problems, while often giving rise to problems of their own, mainly through loss of specificity, which leads in turn to sequential scanning of large numbers of entries: low relevance. Post-coordinate systems avoid the need for the citation or significance order, and thus avoid the inherent problems; why then should we bother with pre-coordinate systems at all? The answer is twofold.

In the first place, there are situations where one-place systems are a practical necessity; we do not want to scatter copies of a document throughout the library to ensure that one is found at every possible entry point, and the single sequence of entries in a bibliography, dictated by economic considerations, is most helpfully arranged by a one-place pre-coordinate system. In a general library, it is often the case that we can find an order which suits the vast majority of users; in such cases, it is cheaper to spend more time on searching for the occasional difficult enquiry than to make multiple entries for everything 'in case'. Single entry helps to keep down the bulk of the catalogue and thus makes it simpler to use and less costly to maintain.

Secondly, pre-coordinate systems, whether single or multiple entry, present certain advantages at the search stage. It is possible for a number of searches to be conducted simultaneously; for example, with a card catalogue hold-ups only occur if two or more people need to use the same drawer at the same time. This is not the case with post-coordinate systems, where the number of searches that can be conducted at the same time is normally very limited. Pre-coordinate systems also lend themselves to changes in search strategy; we can follow up a narrower, broader or related subject without starting again from scratch, as would be the case with a post-coordinate system. The long term answer lies with the computer, which can accept single entry as its input, but give us the kind of access that is normally associated with multiple entry. Indeed, many factors in the catalogue description which are now not even considered as access points can be found through computer searching. Pre-coordinate systems, which have been severely criticised in recent years by advocates of post-coordinate methods, may yet be restored to their previous importance by the computer revolution.

BIBLIOGRAPHY

1 Foskett, A C: 'Shelf classification—*or else.*' *Library journal*, 95 (15) September 1 1970, 2771-2773.

2 Vickery, B C: *Techniques of information retrieval*. In this work Vickery goes much further towards integrating 'information retrieval' and conventional subject bibliography than any previous author. There are large numbers of excellent examples illustrating the problems.

3 Horner, J L: *Cataloguing*. Chapters 8-17 are essential reading. Coates, E. J.: *Subject catalogues*. Chapters 7-13 are essential reading.

4 Shera, J H and Egan, M E: *The classified catalogue*. American Library Association, 1956.

Freeman, C B: 'Classified catalogue: a plea for its abolition in public libraries'. *Library Association record, 44* (10) 1942, 147-150.

Palmer, B I: 'Classified catalogue: a reply to Mr Freeman'. *Library Association record, 46* (4), 1946, 59-60.

Kennedy, R F: *Classified cataloguing*. Cape Town, Balkema, 1966.

5 Foskett, D J: 'Two notes on indexing techniques.' *Journal of documentation, 18* (4) December 1962, 188-192.

6 Sharp, J R: *Some fundamentals of information retrieval*. Deutsch, 1965.

7 Foskett, A C: 'SLIC indexing.' *The library world, 70* (817) July 1968, 17-19.

8 Maidment, W R: 'Computer catalogue in Camden.' *The library world, 67* (782) August 1965, 40.

Dolby, J L: *Computerized library catalogs: their growth, cost and utility*. Stechert-Hafner, 1969. A very useful summary of the advantages.

Hayes, R M and Shoffner, R M: *The economics of book catalog production*: a study prepared for Stanford University libraries and the Council on library resources, 1964. There have been a number of articles in periodicals in recent years on this subject, *eg* in *Library quarterly 34* January 1964; *Library trends*, July 1967; *Library resources and technical services, passim.*

9 Plumbe, W F: 'The "Stripdex" catalogue.' *Library Association record, 64* (4) April 1962, 128-131.

Stephen, P: 'The stripdex catalogue'. *Library review, 21* (3) Autumn 1967, 137-139.

Plumbe, W F: 'Another appraisal of the stripdex catalogue'. *Library review, 21* (5) Spring 1968, 234-236.

10 Langridge, D W: 'Classification and book indexing.' Chapter 15 in the *Sayers memorial volume*.

Langridge, D W: 'The use of classification in book indexing.' *The indexer, 2* (3) Spring 1961, 95-98. *The indexer* is the journal of the Society of Indexers, formed in 1958 with the aim of improving standards of book indexing. The pages of this journal are essential reading for anyone wishing to undertake this particular form of indexing.

Collison, R L W: *Indexing books: a manual of basic principles*. Benn, 1962. One of the very few books on the subject.

British Standards Institution: *Recommendations for the preparation of indexes for books, periodicals and other publications.* BS 3700: 1964. A brief but useful manual.

11 Grogan, D J: *Case studies in reference work.* Bingley, 1967. Chapters 1 and 2 indicate some of the problems.

12 Lancaster, F W: 'Evaluating the performance of a large computerized information service.' *Journal of the American Medical Association,* 207 (1) 1969, 114-120.

13 Vickery, B C: *Techniques of information retrieval.* p 140-145.

CHAPTER II

Introduction

So far we have studied the theoretical considerations which affect every system. In this section we shall be studying indexing languages that are widely used, to see how they measure up to the criteria we have established in part I. The schemes will be discussed in the following order:

1) The decimal classification of Melvil Dewey (DC). This was the first library classification in the modern sense, and in it we see foreshadowed many of the ideas we have been discussing.

2) The Universal Decimal Classification (UDC). Originally based on the fifth edition of DC, this was the second major scheme to appear. It is possible to conjecture that this is the scheme most likely to succeed in the new computer age. Like DC, UDC is basically enumerative, but has many synthetic devices grafted on to its main core, which give it a great deal of flexibility. The full schedules of UDC are probably the most detailed of any classification scheme.

3) The Bibliographic Classification of H E Bliss (BC). This was perhaps the last of the great enumerative schemes, and though Bliss did include many synthetic tables he does not seen to have appreciated the importance of the principles of analysis and synthesis he himself used. The main class order of BC is probably the most satisfactory of the major schemes. Until recently, it has lacked a satisfactory financial structure, though the efforts of a committee of devotees have helped to keep the scheme alive. It now seems possible that a solution to this problem has been found, and the second edition is to be published in the near future. This will mark a great advance on the first; in addition to the satisfactory main class order there is now a consistent use of facet analysis within main classes, and possibilities for synthesis will be found throughout the schedules. Despite this, one may still doubt whether libraries will feel sufficiently strongly attracted to the scheme to wish to change to it from one of the longer established schemes such as DC, though these may in theory be inferior.

4) The Colon Classification of S R Ranganathan (CC). This is the only completely synthetic general scheme and has many interesting and significant features, though from time to time one feels that the scheme is more of a testing ground for Ranganathan's theories than a practical means of arranging documents and catalogues.

5) The Library of Congress Classification (LC). This scheme is unique in that it is intended for use in one library only, yet because of the significance of that library it is used in very many others. Here we have a scheme in which the compiler and the classifier are one and the same; the published version is almost completely enumerative, and the external classifier has to accept the scheme as it is or not at all. Another aspect is that it is intended for shelf arrangement, and to be complemented by an alphabetical subject catalogue (in practice, usually a dictionary catalogue) arranged according to

6) Subject headings used in the dictionary catalogs of the Library of Congress (LCSH). This is the most important general list of subject headings, and it is valuable to see how it fits in with the LC classification, and also how it measures up to our criteria.

7) Sears' list of subject headings is a much smaller work intended for the medium sized library. It is quite widely used in Britain in libraries using dictionary catalogues, whereas in the USA LCSH is far more popular.

In each case the object of the discussion will be to highlight what appear to be the significant aspects, particularly those concerning the background which affect the nature of the scheme. Little attempt will be made to go into the fine details of each scheme; it must be stressed that familiarity with these can only come as the result of a firsthand study. Similarly, facility in use will only come as the result of practice. However, it is hoped that the student who works through the following chapters will then at least be in a position to make good use of such firsthand examination, and will be able to estimate the overall import- ance of the individual schemes, both in isolation and in relation to each other. All of the schemes are here subjected to considerable criticism (though perhaps less considerable than that levelled by Bliss at all schemes other than his own!), but we have as yet nothing better to replace them; they are used in libraries all over the world, and librarians have to learn to live with them. We shall however be in a much better position to overcome their defects if we are aware of them and know what countermeasures to take.

It may be argued that it is not fair to judge the older schemes by criteria which did not exist when they were compiled. This is a plausible point of view, but it will not stand up to close examination. Classification schemes, like issue systems, are tools, devised to carry out particular tasks in the overall organization of libraries; we have to judge them in the light of how well they perform their set task today, not yesterday, and we must also bear in mind how well they are likely to stand up to tomorrow's demands.

Some features of the schemes, for example main class order, have been discussed in some detail already, and as far as possible this will not be repeated. Occasionally it may be necessary to reiterate a point already made in order to put it into a different context, but the discussion of the practical schemes should not be divorced from the discussion of the theoretical framework into which they fit.

The Subject Classification of J D Brown (SC) is not considered here, though a few references to it occur in the first part of this book. It is no longer a practical scheme, and many of its features do not stand up to any sort of examination. Though it has been included in Library Association syllabuses for many years, it is now of historical interest only, and is therefore excluded from this text.

It should perhaps be stressed that the length of each chapter should not be treated as being a reflection of the relative importance of the scheme discussed. DC, as is to be expected of a pioneer, introduced many new ideas, which are described in that chapter, though they now apply to most schemes; UDC, with its synthetic devices, requires more explanation and examples than does LC, which has, in effect, none. The main feature of CC, analysis into facets and notational synthesis, has become so much a part of modern theory that it is covered in detail in part I, and does not therefore appear in the description of CC, except insofar as that scheme has certain unique methods of applying it.

The two lists of subject headings do not involve problems of order (except in a very minor fashion); they have no notation, or index. There is therefore much less to describe when writing about them than there is in a classification scheme, but in practical terms the two Library of Congress publications, LCSH and LC, are of equal importance.

It does however appear that three of the classification schemes are more likely to survive than the other two. DC is very widely used in public libraries throughout the world; LC is growing in popularity, and one estimate suggested that the 800 or so libraries using it might double by about 1975, as many university libraries abandon DC in its favour; UDC is the scheme most widely used in special libraries, particularly in Europe, though it is gaining a foothold in the USA. These schemes all have one feature in common: a powerful, adequately funded, central organization. It seems unlikely that any scheme which lacks this can survive, no matter how satisfactory it may be in theory.

BIBLIOGRAPHY

Readings for each scheme are given at the end of the text dealing with it. Students wishing to read further will find good accounts of the schemes in

Mills, J: *A modern outline of library classification*. Chapman & Hall, 1960. It should however be remembered that these accounts may now be out of date. A more recent text which does not go into so much detail is

Sayers, W C Berwick: *Manual of library classification*. Fourth edition edited by A Maltby. Deutsch, 1967. A brief account of each scheme will be found in

Needham, C D: *Organising knowledge in libraries*. Deutsch, 1971. An older work which contains trenchant criticisms of all of the schemes (except BC) is

Bliss, H E: *The organisation of knowedge in libraries*. H W Wilson, second edition, 1939.

CHAPTER 12

The Dewey decimal classification

Melvil Dewey was born in 1851, and at the age of five, we are told, he rearranged his mother's larder in a more systematic fashion; an early beginning for a career which was to transform librarianship! In 1872, at Amherst College, he obtained a post as a student library assistant, and in the following year put forward a plan for rearranging the library in a more systematic fashion. He was promoted in 1874 to Assistant College Librarian, and in 1876 published anonymously a work which was to have far-reaching effects: *A classification and subject index for cataloguing and arranging the books and pamphlets of a library.* When we consider that Dewey also became the first editor of the *Library journal* in 1876, was a founder member of the American Library Association in 1876 and became its first secretary, founded the first library school in the United States (Columbia University) in 1887, promoted the standard (12·5cm×7·5cm) catalogue card, and in the course of a long life (he died in 1931) took an active interest, not only in all aspects of librarianship, but also in related topics such as spelling reform, we may realise the full stature of the man and respect him, even though the classification scheme which bears his name and is the best known of his contributions to librarianship may in some ways look inadequate for today's needs.

Dewey's first edition consisted of twelve pages of introduction, twelve of tables and eighteen of index, and its novelty lay in three main areas: the first of these was the assignment of decimal numbers to books rather than shelves: the second was the specification of relatively detailed subjects; the third, the provision of a relative index. It is possible to argue that these three principles were in fact a greater contribution to the progress of library classification than the scheme itself, despite its wide acceptance throughout the world.

RELATIVE LOCATION

Dewey did not introduce subject arrangement into libraries; many libraries had previously been arranged by subject. What he *did* do was to introduce the idea of relative as opposed to fixed location. It was the practice to allocate certain areas of the library to various subjects, arranging the books within each area by accession number and giving them a *shelf mark* which identified their exact position: room, bay, tier, shelf, place on shelf. Once allocated, the shelf mark denoted the permanent home of a book in that library. New additions within any given subject area were invariably at the end of the sequence. Dewey introduced the idea of using notation for the subjects in his scheme, and *applying the notation to the books,* not the shelves. A new book on a given subject could be inserted into the middle of an existing sequence, in a position indicated by the notation; no longer was the end of the sequence the only place that new additions could be accommodated. The tool that enabled Dewey to do this was his decimal notation: the use of arabic numerals, arranged as decimals. As we have seen, there are certain problems arising out of the use of a pure notation, and Dewey did not foresee these; in places this inhibits synthesis in the scheme today, when subjects are far more complex than Dewey could possibly have envisaged a century ago. There is however no doubt that the simplicity of the notation has been an important factor in the widespread adoption of the scheme throughout the world.

DETAILED SPECIFICATION

Before Dewey introduced his idea of relative location, the number of subject groups into which the books in a library could be arranged was severely limited. It is not practical to leave large numbers of shelves empty so that books can be added at the end of a multiplicity of sequences. Once the idea of moving books at any particular point to accommodate additions is accepted, then it becomes far more feasible to specify more detailed subjects. Dewey listed nearly a thousand, and was criticized for giving unnecessary detail; the seventeenth edition, containing over 20,000 topics listed, is criticized for its lack of detail. Much of this change in attitude is due to Dewey himself, who made it practical for librarians to arrange their collections in a detailed fashion instead of in broad groups. The history of DC has, in general, been one of the provision of ever increasing amounts of detail to match the needs of documents which themselves treat of increasingly narrow areas of knowledge. By his adoption of the principle of detailed subject arrangement, Dewey made this progress possible.

One of the objections raised to detailed subject specification was that it would be impossible to find any given subject in the complex systematic arrangement. Dewey overcame this problem by the provision of a detailed relative index, showing exactly whereabouts in the scheme any given topic was to be found, and listing synonyms also in some instances. Indeed, it seems that Dewey was if anything inclined to favour the index over the classification; in the second edition we find the statement ' an essential part of the Subject Index is the table of classification ', and Dewey also wrote 'A clerk, if he only knows the subject of his book, by the use of the index can class just as the chief of the catalog department would class . . .'. While Dewey's enthusiasm for the index seems over-optimistic, there is no doubt that the detailed index was an important factor in the success of the scheme as a whole.

The three ' innovations ' described here are now taken for granted in library classification, and it is important to remember that it was not always so. In his scheme Dewey foreshadowed many of today's developments, even if he did not always recognize them explicitly.

DECIMAL NOTATION

Dewey's plan was to divide the whole of knowledge into ten main classes, then to divide each of these into ten divisions, then each of the divisions into ten sections. In the first edition he suggested that in a catalogue it would be possible to continue the division to a fourth or fifth place, though he did not recommend this for shelf arrangement; for example, *geology of Mexico* might be given the number 5578. The point was used to introduce the book number: 513.1 was the first book on *geometry* 513. Another method of division after point was by size; 421.3.7 was the seventh book on the *philology of the English language* 421, filed in the third (*ie* oversize) sequence. Dewey recognized that decimal division might lead to some anomalies, but claimed that it worked in practice; his devotion to practice as opposed to theory led him in fact to distort the hierarchical structure of the notation in places, as is shown by the second edition of 1885, in which a number of changes led to the scheme which is very largely the basis of the latest editions.

In the second edition, Dewey claims: ' we have not sacrificed utility in order to force subjects on the decimal Procrustean bed '. However, when there are less than nine subdivisions of a subject, the ' spare ' notation is used for further subdivision, while if there are more than nine some—the 'minor' subdivisions—are all accommodated at one number. In this edition we find the three figure minimum notation, with a point following the third figure if further notation is used; we also find many of the synthetic devices which characterize the scheme. For example, whereas in the first edition the form divisions (common facets) were enumerated at the main class headings and could only be used there, in the second we find a table of form divisions which may be used anywhere. There are instructions to 'divide like' various other numbers; *eg* 016 Bibliographies of subjects, divide like the classification. Division by period under a country is possible, using a zero to introduce the notation. What is even more interesting is that we find in some places, notably Class 400 Philology, a very clear facet structure. Dewey does not appear to have seen the real significance of this, and it was left to Ranganathan some fifty years later to make explicit and generalized the principle which is implicit and restricted in this example; nevertheless, in this as in many other points, Dewey showed the way ahead at a very early stage.

INTEGRITY OF NUMBERS

Just as the notational pattern was set in the second edition for all succeeding editions, so also was the systematic arrangement crystallized. Dewey realized that a scheme which changed substantially from edition to edition would not succeed, because librarians would not accept it; change means reclassification, altering notation on catalogue entries and books, reshelving, refiling—a great deal of work. In the second edition Dewey announced that the structure of the scheme would henceforth not be changed; expansions would be introduced as necessary, but the basic outline would remain constant. This has certainly been an important factor in the success of the scheme, but has led to severe problems in keeping pace with the growth and development of knowledge. Dewey wrote: 'Even if the decisions reacht were not the wisest possible, all practical purposes ar served'; H E Bliss named this attitude the *subject index illusion*—the idea that the overall order is relatively unimportant, provided that each subject has its own little pigeonhole where it can be found.

It is in this edition that we first find Dewey's simplified spelling. Dewey, who was keenly interested in reforming the spelling of the English language, lost no opportunity of pursuing this particular hobby; christened Melville, he soon dropped the final le, and even went to the extreme of spelling his final name Dui for a time. The classification scheme reflects this interest from the second edition to the fourteenth, so that we find headings such as Filosofy and Jeolojy used throughout the text. Unfortunately, Dewey's simplified spelling did not take account of all the problems of expressing forty two sounds using only twenty six letters, and in consequence some of his improved spellings were ambiguous. This feature was dropped after the fourteenth edition.

THE FIFTEENTH (STANDARD) EDITION: A NEW APPROACH

Up to and including the fourteenth edition, progress was mainly in the direction of ever increasing detail, without much change in the basic structure of the scheme. There was one interesting innovation in the thirteenth edition, where a completely new schedule for Psychology was included at 159.9, in parallel with the earlier schedules developed in 130 and 150. Evidently this choice was not widely accepted by DC users, for it did not appear in the fourteenth edition, and the only sign of its existence to be found now is in UDC. Much of the detail in the fourteenth edition was unbalanced, and reflects a haphazard approach to revision, unhampered by any considerations of literary warrant; Medicine was developed in great detail in a schedule running to eighty pages, while Chemical Technology, including such topics as Food technology, Fuel technology and Metallurgy, was hardly changed from the second edition, with many important subdivisions completely undeveloped. It was decided to make a determined effort in the fifteenth edition to bring the scheme up to date, and to base the amount of detail in the various sections on a more realistic assessment of need; this edition, published in 1951, therefore introduced several novel features.

There are basically two ways to even out varying amounts of detail in different schedules; the first is to increase the amount of detail where it is lacking, so that all the schedules are detailed, while the second is to cut down the amount of detail that is given until all the schedules are equally brief. It was the second of these alternatives that was adopted; from the 31,000 subjects enumerated in the fourteenth edition, we find a slashing reduction to 4,700 in the fifteenth. Chemical technology was increased, relatively speaking, but this was achieved more by cutting down subjects such as Medicine than by increasing greatly the hitherto neglected subjects. The form divisions (Dewey's common facets) were reduced to nine, though this number was increased in the revised version. In History, 942 stood for England, including Great Britain, Thames River; apart from the period divisions, the only subdivisions here were 942.1 London, 942.34 Channel Islands, and 942.89 Isle of Man, though Scotland and Wales each had its own number and Ireland had two. The criterion stated was that subdivisions were removed as being unjustified if no books were found to belong to them on the shelves of the Library of Congress, but evidently the reduction in the schedules went far beyond this. The objective seems to have been to have as few class numbers as possible longer than five digits; in view of Dewey's original allocation of notation, this decision was bound to bear hardest on the subjects such as Technology which had developed most since the original publication of the scheme.

In recognition of the changes that had occurred in the scientific and educational consensus since the second edition, many of the subjects found in the fifteenth edition were relocated from their place in the fourteenth edition schedules; in fact, of the 4,700 topics listed over 1,000 are in different relative positions. While the overall outline of the scheme remains the same, there are many changes in detail. In the tide of criticism which finally engulfed this edition, it was these relocations which were often blamed for its unpopularity, but one cannot help wondering if they would have caused so much dissension if they had not been associated with the overenthusiastic pruning mentioned above.

The index was also drastically pruned; so much so, in fact, that a revised index was published separately the following year, with one or two minor amendments to the scheme. The importance of the index to users of DC, shown by the need for this action, was evidently still not appreciated, for we find a similar state of affairs arising with the seventeenth edition, discussed at more length later.

On the debit side, then, lay several aspects of the fifteenth edition, but there were also some features on the credit side. The layout and typography was greatly improved, so that the structure of the schedules was clearly shown by a combination of indentation and typography; DC now compares favourably with any other general scheme in this respect. Dewey's spelling was dropped completely from both index and schedules, with the exception of the dozen words such as ' thru ' which are now part of standard (American) usage. The terminology was revised to bring it too into line with modern usage, and the examples quoted were changed in many instances. Scope notes were a noteworthy feature; these were of two kinds, those defining the coverage of a given heading and those reminding the user of other related headings. To sum up, in presentation, the fifteenth edition was a tremendous success, but what it presented was not, and the sixteenth saw a reversion in some respects to the mainstream, while retaining those aspects of the fifteenth which had met with a favourable response.

As a matter of policy, the period of seven years was set as the publication cycle, and the sixteenth edition duly appeared in 1958. It went back to the detailed enumeration of the fourteenth edition, and re-relocated some topics back to their places in that sequence, but retained the improvements of the fifteenth edition, particularly those of presentation. Changes from the fourteenth and fifteenth editions were clearly indicated, so that librarians with materials classified by these previous editions could see at once where changes might have to be made. The index was published as a separate volume, and was relatively more detailed than that of the fourteenth edition; whereas that had 65,000 index entries for its 31,000 subjects, the sixteenth had 63,000 for its 18,000—more than twice as many.

The sixteenth edition also contained the first of the 'phoenix' schedules. It was recognized that certain schedules were so out of date that the only satisfactory way to revise them was to replace them with entirely new classifications, and in DC16 we find that 546 and 547, Inorganic and Organic chemistry, are completely new and bear no relationship to the previous editions. This means of course that anyone wishing to adopt the new edition has to reclassify their collections at those two points, whereas at many other headings it is possible to transfer with little or no change at all, and this has led to cries of anguish from librarians faced with extra work. However, it is one of the penalties we have to pay if we want to keep our arrangement in line with current thinking, and the task of reclassifying is made easier in that the old schedules are usually printed somewhere in the new edition together with tables of equivalents. In DC17 a new schedule for 150 and 130 General and special psychology appeared, while DC18 contains two, one for 340 Law, the other for 510 Mathematics. All of these revisions are valuable, with that for Law being perhaps the least useful in that it does not recognize division by country as being the primary facet and thus leaves us with one of the major disadvantages of the previous schedule unchanged.

The sixteenth edition did not satisfy some critics, notably those connected with the BNB,[1] but it was adopted by a great many libraries as being the first valid postwar edition. The appearance of the seventeenth edition[2] in 1965 was awaited with more than usual interest to see whether the trend towards modernization evident in the sixteenth edition would be continued. When it was published it was greeted with very mixed feelings; it showed a modern trend in that there were more facilities for synthesis than ever before, but on the other hand it dropped some of the good features of the sixteenth such as the cross-references between related subjects in different main classes.

This edition represents a considerable effort on the part of the editorial staff, particularly in two major directions. The first of these is the attempt to introduce, within the limits of the existing notation, a great deal more synthesis than was previously possible, and at the same time to remove some anomalies which had crept into previous editions, notably in the confusion to be found in some classes between subject and common subdivisions caused by the use of the single o (normally used to serve as a facet indicator for the common facets) to introduce some divisions of the subject for which there were no other places available. Two examples of this are to be found in the Social sciences, where Sociology, given the number 301, precedes the common subdivisions, and Engineering, where Engineering materials at 620.1 precedes these divisions also. The effect of this can be seen very clearly in the five year BNB cumulation 1955-1959, where such headings as Engineering—Periodicals at 620.5 can only be found with some difficulty after looking through several pages of entries relating to Engineering materials. Anyone not familiar with this peculiarity, or having only a slight knowledge of the scheme (enough to tell him, for example, that common subdivisions are to be found immediately following the main heading) would probably miss these entries for the common subdivisions of Engineering. In the seventeenth edition, the common facets, or standard subdivisions as they are now called (in previous editions the term 'form divisions' was always used), are always introduced by as many o's as are necessary to distinguish them from subject subdivisions and to arrange them in their correct place, immediately following the heading to which they apply. In some cases this means as many as three o's (or even—very rarely—four), but it does achieve the objective, which is to return to the ' correct ' placing of these subdivisions.

215

The second major effort was also in the direction of a return to 'correct' classification. Dewey adhered to the scientific and educational consensus (of Amherst College) for his main class order; that is, he classified primarily by discipline. Thus a work on the economics of the steel industry is classified with other works on economics in the social sciences, not with other works on steel in technology. A classifier who did not find a particular subject enumerated was instructed to place it with the nearest broader heading until such time as a specific place was provided; so a work on the sociology of the Jews would be treated as a general work on sociology, failing a specific means of denoting ethnic groups. However, though this method works well in theory—one can always use verbal extensions until the notation is developed—in practice there is a considerable temptation for the classifier to ignore the discipline and find instead a pigeonhole where what seems to be the important aspect of the subject can be brought out: in this example, there is of course a place for the Jews in Religion, so everything on the Jews tended to be classified there, ignoring the correct approach by discipline. Classification by attraction, as this is called, saves the classifier mental effort in that he does not have to place a subject in its right place without guidance from the schedules, but need only scan the index for a catchword to lead him to a convenient pigeonhole. To set against this is the fact that the purpose of systematic arrangement, to provide a consistent means of grouping related subjects, is completely defeated by this practice. In the seventeenth edition, a return has been made to Dewey's original principle of classification by discipline, though one can still find occasional departures from this, *eg* in 320 Politics, where 324 is Suffrage, 324.24 Voting including voting machines.

This problem arose because classifiers prefer to be specific, and will look for what appears to be a specific heading, even if it is strictly speaking incorrect, rather than choose the correct, but non-specific, heading. If the use of verbal extensions had been recommended to give the possibility of achieving specificity where it was lacking in the schedules, we may speculate that the problem of classification by attraction might never have reached significant proportions.

Other changes were made to bring the scheme into line with modern thinking. As has been mentioned, a completely new schedule for Psychology was included; Women as a social group were transferred to Sociology instead of Dewey's own placing in Customs and folklore (habits that have become traditional). Facilities for synthesis were greatly increased, though many of these were clumsy because of the basically enumerative structure of the scheme and its notation. The Place facet was separated from the History schedules to give an 'area table' with the intention of making subdivision by this facet easier, and the common facets (Dewey's form divisions) were to some extent reorganized and retitled *standard subdivisions;* there was also a fairly detailed Time facet to replace the four divisions which seemed to have been included in earlier editions as an afterthought:

0901 Up to 500 AD

0902 500-1500

0903 1500-

0904 20th century.

A criticism which has been valid in the past is that DC is very much a Western-oriented scheme, with particular emphasis on the USA. Dewey seems to have assumed, as did Parson Thwackum, that Religion can only mean the Christian religion; other religions are, in past editions, largely neglected. In the sixteenth edition, about twice as many pages are devoted to the History of the United States as to the whole of Europe, including both world wars. In the seventeenth edition the editors have removed many of these examples of bias; non-Christian religions are developed in much more detail, and in many places it is possible for the user to treat his own country or religion as the preferred category and bring it to the beginning of the schedule.

THE EIGHTEENTH EDITION[3]

The publication of a new edition of DC is always an important event, and the eighteenth edition, published in 1971, is no exception. Perhaps the most significant point about it does not relate to the scheme itself, but to the use made of it; both BNB and LC have adopted it for their MARC records from the beginning of 1971, in the interests of international standardization. The scheme continues the developments seen in the sixteenth and seventeenth, with various changes intended to make the schedules easier to use. Instead of the 'divide like' device, we find instructions to 'add ... to the base number ...' followed by an example, *eg*

016 **Bibliographies and catalogs of specific disciplines and subjects**

> Add 001-999 to base number 016, e.g., bibliographies of astronomy **016.52**

The elimination of bias is carried a stage further by using a letter to permit the favoured category to be filed at the beginning of the sequence, *eg*

030   General encyclopedic works

.9   Historical and geographical treatment

Class encyclopedic works in specific languages in 031-039

▶   **031-039 In specific languages**

Class here specific encyclopedias and works about them

Arrange by language in which originally written as below; but if it is desired to give local emphasis and a shorter number to encyclopedias in a specific language, place them first by use of a letter or other symbol, e.g., Arabic-language encyclopedias 03A (preceding 031)

The notation for Christianity 220-289 may be used for a different ' home ' religion if preferred.

Perhaps the major development is the introduction of several more tables of common subdivisions. From the single table of form divisions in DC16, through the standard subdivisions and area table of DC17, we progress to seven tables in DC18, not all of which are applicable everywhere throughout the main schedules.

Table 1   Standard subdivisions

Table 2   Areas

Table 3   Subdivisions of individual literatures to be added to base numbers in 810-890

Table 4   Subdivisions of individual languages 420-490*

Table 5   Racial, Ethnic, National groups

Table 6   Languages

Table 7   Persons

There are nearly 400 relocations, about half as many as in DC17; as usual, these are all carefully indicated in the schedules. The new edition confirms the trend towards facet analysis and synthesis, though the strain of fitting this into the existing framework results in some problems and anomalies. On the whole, however, the editorial policy

218

is a satisfactory one, though whether the changes are keeping pace with needs is a moot point. Certainly the scheme remains a very practical one which will be used by a great many libraries.

THE SCHEME

The eighteenth edition is in three volumes, each of them substantial. After a tribute to Melvil Dewey by his son, and a historical outline forming the publisher's foreword, the first volume begins with the editor's introduction. This is an important part of the scheme, and must be studied carefully by anyone wishing to use DC, for it is here that the editor explains how the schedules and other features are to be used; it also contains much sound advice on how to classify in general terms. There follows a glossary, and an index to the preface, introduction and glossary. After this comes the introduction written by Dewey himself for the twelfth edition; this again is worthy of careful study, for it sets out at some length Dewey's own views on classification in general, and his own classification in particular, though one may have a minor struggle with Dewey's simplified spelling.

The two introductions are followed by the seven auxiliary tables of common subdivisions. These begin with a page of brief notes explaining how they are to be used; then come the standard subdivisions, shown in summary form here:

-01 Philosophy and theory
-02 Miscellany
-03 Dictionaries, encyclopedias, concordances
-04 General special
-05 Serial publications
-06 Organizations
-07 Study and teaching
-08 Collections and anthologies
-09 Historical and geographical treatment.

There is some confusion here between bibliographical forms -02, -03, -05, -08, and common subjects -01, -06, -07, though some progress has been made in this edition towards tidying up these subdivisions. Some provision is made for phase relationships *eg* -024 Works for specific types of users, *ie* bias phase. There is a schedule for Time, rather more detailed than was provided in earlier editions but still rather inflexible.

In DC 17, -04 was left unused, its previous meaning of *essays* having been relocated in -08 (it had proved very difficult to distinguish between *essays* and *collections*). It has been reintroduced into DC18 to accommodate concepts which are common to a particular class but not to the whole of knowledge:

'This subdivision is reserved for special concepts that have general application thruout the regular subdivisions of certain specific disciplines and subjects; it is to be used only when specifically set forth in the schedules.'

An example can be found in Engineering:

620   Engineering and allied operations

    .001-.003   Standard subdivisions

    .004   General concepts

    .0045   Quality and reliability

    .005-.009   Other standard subdivisions

The object of this use of -04 is to avoid extra zeroes in the standard subdivisions. In DC17, if it was desirable to introduce a 'general special' facet, this could only be done by increasing the number of zeroes used to introduce the standard subdivisions; as has been seen, this could mean as many as four zeroes, *eg* Dictionary of public administration 350.0003. However, in avoiding this problem, the use of -04 introduces the problem of order; it means that these 'general special' facets will be filed in the middle of the standard subdivisions. In other words, notational convenience is dictating order, which can never be satisfactory, even if it does represent an attempt to minimize complaints by users distressed by long notation.

The standard subdivisions are followed by the Area Table. This was a new feature in the seventeenth edition, and the intention is to make synthesis clearer; previously it was necessary to manipulate the notation from the History schedules in order to specify Place, and because of the many subjects in the schedules with special provision for place division this became rather complicated. In addition to simplifying its application, the new schedule for Place includes many subfacets not found in earlier editions, *eg* -17 Socioeconomic regions and groups. Where no special instructions are given for its use at a particular point in the schedules, the Area Table notation is introduced by the standard subdivision 09. For both standard subdivisions and other tables the notation is shown as beginning with a dash. This dash is merely to indicate that none of these tables can be used on its own; the notation must always be added to the notation for the main subject, and the dash is not used as part of the final class mark.

The Area Table includes one interesting example of a relocation. In order to make room for extraterrestrial worlds, Antarctica [*formerly* —99] has been transferred to —989, so that —99 can be used again, *eg* Venus —9922. Space in general is also included at —19.

Table 3 is for the subdivision of individual literatures. In DC17 the instructions in this class were difficult to follow, and the purpose of Table 3 is to make manipulation of the notation more simple and convenient. This table includes standard subdivisions in 01-07, collections in 08, and history, description and critical appraisal in 09, as well as specific forms in 1-8. However, for period divisions within any given literature it is necessary to turn back to the main schedules, where under English literature, for example, we find period subdivisions not just for English works from Great Britain but also for those written by authors in Asia, Australia, Ireland, New Zealand, South Africa (but not the American continent, which has a separate heading altogether). There is also in the main schedules a detailed table for Shakespeare at 822.33, which may be used to subdivide the works of any author, with appropriate modifications.

Table 4 is for the subdivision of those individual languages marked * in 420-490. Table 5 is for racial, ethnic and national groups, and Table 6 for languages. Table 7, Persons, is probably the most important of these new tables, and may be summarized:

01	Individual persons
02	Groups of persons
03	Persons by racial, ethnic, national background
04	Persons by sex and kinship characteristics
05	Persons by age
06	Persons by social and economic characteristics
08	Persons by mental and physical characteristics
1-9	Specialists

The latter heading is divided rather like the whole classification, *eg* persons occupied with psychology —15 corresponding to 150 Psychology.

There is a list of all numbers which have changed their meaning through relocations, those which have been discontinued, and the few three digit numbers which are not in use; in each case the classifier is given all the information he may require to adjust his own usage of the scheme.

The first volume concludes with the *Summaries*. The first summary lists the ten main classes:

000   Generalities
100   Philosophy & related disciplines
200   Religion
300   The social sciences
400   Language
500   Pure sciences
600   Technology (Applied sciences)
700   The arts
800   Literature (Belles-lettres)
900   General geography & history

The second summary lists the 100 divisions, *eg*

600   Technology (Applied sciences)
610   Medical sciences
620   Engineering & allied operations
630   Agriculture & related
640   Domestic arts & sciences
650   Managerial services
660   Chemical and related technologies
670   Manufactures
680   Miscellaneous manufactures
690   Buildings

The third summary lists the 1000 sections, *eg*

620   Engineering & allied operations
621   Applied physics
622   Mining engineering & related
623   Military & nautical engineering
624   Civil engineering
625   Railroads, roads, highways
626
627   Hydraulic engineering etc
628   Sanitary & municipal engineering
629   Other branches of engineering

These summaries are a valuable aid to classification, and their use will often prevent classification by attraction, by ensuring that the classifier finds the correct discipline rather than a catchword in the index.

The second volume consists entirely of the schedules, preceded by a page containing brief notes on their use, and explaining certain conventions, *eg* the use of square brackets.

The schedules are carefully set out to show the various hierarchies and to define headings or illustrate their use. Examples are given to illustrate notational synthesis. Instructions given at a broad heading apply to more specific headings within that hierarchy, and it is therefore necessary to study the schedules carefully to establish exactly how to deal with composite subjects. At times, the classifier is referred to another heading to find out how to synthesize a particular piece of notation. For reasons which have been discussed in chapter 8, it is sometimes the case that synthesis is only possible at some headings within a particular class; in such cases, the asterisk * is used to indicate the headings where synthesis is possible.

The following examples will show some of the more important features of the schedules. Each of course represents an extract only from the schedules at that particular point, and is selected to illustrate special features.

1) 000 **Generalities**
   001 **Knowledge and its extension**
                              SUMMARY
            001.2   Scholarship and learning
              .3   Humanities
              .4   Methodology and research
              .5   Information and communication
              .6   Data processing
              .9   Controversial and spurious
                    knowledge
      ·4   Methodology and research
      ·42   Methodology
2)   Derivation of basic principles, postulates, concepts
3)   Class surveys and appraisals [formerly 001.42] in 001.433
4)   Class methodology of a specific discipline or subject with the discipline or subject using " Standard Subdivisions " notation 018 from Table 1, e.g., methodology in linguistics 410.18; data processing and computerization in 001.6; mathematical methodology in 510

223

5)	·422	Statistical method [*formerly also* 311.2]
010		**Bibliographies and catalogs**
		Of books, other printed and written records, audio-visual records
6)		(It is optional to class here bibliographies and catalogs of reading for children and young adults; prefer 028.52)
7)		If preferred, class bibliographies and catalogs of motion picture films in 791.438
8) **350**		**Public administration Executive branch**
		Military art and science
9)		Use 350.0001-350.0009 for standard subdivisions of public administration, of executive branch

---

10) ▶   **350.001-350.009 The executive**

11)   Class comprehensive works in 350.003

▶   350.01-350.08 Specific executive departments and ministries of cabinet rank

---

▶   350.1-350.3 Government service [*formerly also* 350.4]

12) [·4]   Government service

               Class in 350.1-350.3

    354   Other central governments

13) ·3-·9   National, state, provincial

14)   Add "Areas " notation 3-9 from Table 2 to base number 354, e.g., government of Canada 354.71;

15)   except for Germany add further as follows:

16)   0001-0009   Standard subdivisions

               001-009   Government service, specific administrative activities, governmental malfunctioning

                       Add to 00 the numbers following 350 in 350.1-350.9, e.g., merit system 006

               01-05   Specific aspects of the executive

                       Add to 0 the numbers following 350.00 in 350.001-350.005, e.g., cabinet 05

	06	Specific executive departments and ministries
		Add to 06 the numbers following 350.0 in 350.01-350.08, e.g. ministry of foreign affairs 061
	09	Special commissions, corporations, agencies, quasi-administrative bodies
		Add to 09 the numbers following 350.009 in 350.0091-350.0093, e.g., government corporations 092
17)		Unless other instructions are given, class complex subjects with aspects in two or more subdivisions of this table in the number corresponding to the one that comes last in 350.001-350.996
551		**Physical and dynamic geology**
18)		Lithosphere, hydrosphere, atmosphere
19)		Class here geophysics
20)		*For astronomical geography* see 525; *geodesy, 526.1-526.7 mineralogy, 549; petrology, 552*
	·31	Glaciology
21)		Class here interdisciplinary works on ice
		Class a specific aspect of ice with the subject, e.g., ice manufacture 621.58

NOTES ON THE ABOVE EXCERPTS

1) A heading which is rather indefinite is often expanded by means of a summary giving an overall view which is difficult to get from the detailed schedules.

2) Where necessary, terms used in headings are defined.

3) Relocations are shown by means of the word *formerly* and the class number in square brackets, together with an instruction on the new practice to be followed. cf 12 below.

4) Instructions are given to class elsewhere if that is more appropriate.

5) Relocation from another number is shown by the words *formerly also* and the old class number in square brackets.

6) There are some alternatives in the scheme; the editor's preference is shown by the note in parentheses with instruction ' prefer '.

225

8

7) The converse of 6), showing a possible alternative for the classifier. The significance of the editor's preference is that it represents the number that will appear on Library of Congress cards, and in BNB.

8) The heading 350 includes in fact two quite separate classes, Public administration and Military art and science. The scope of the heading is shown to reflect the hierarchy (350 includes 351-354 *and* 355-359)

9) Because of the number of facets and lack of facet indicators, the common facets are here introduced by four zeroes, in order to make sure that they file in the right place.

10) Centred headings are used where there is no single number which represents a single concept. In this particular case, the number which would include 350.001-350.009 is 350.00, which is not used by DC.

11) For this reason, a specific number has to be singled out to replace the missing inclusive number, in order to have a place for comprehensive works.

12) A class number which is not used in this edition because its content has been relocated is indicated by enclosing it in square brackets. cf 3 above.

13) Unsought heading showing a step in division.

14) Use of the Areas table.

15) Germany does not fit into the given pattern and is therefore enumerated separately, an example of the care taken not to force subjects into arrangements or subdivisions which do not fit them.

16) The various facets by which this topic may be subdivided are set out, with instructions on notational synthesis for each. Here again the lack of facet indicators makes synthesis somewhat complicated and the instructions, though clearer than those in previous editions, are still hard work until they become familiar.

17) It is not possible to synthesize notation for a multi-faceted subject, but we are given a table of precedence, *ie* citation order, which in general follows the principle of inversion.

18) Scope note.

19) Instruction to include a topic not obviously comprehended by the heading.

20) Cross-references lead to other parts of the schedules to assist the classifier in defining his subject.

21) Interdisciplinary is used here in a rather different sense from comprehensive, to take account of the increasing number of works

which cross the artificial main class boundaries set up by any discipline-oriented classification scheme.

Because of Dewey's original allocation of the notation, this varies in length quite considerably. There is a three figure minimum, so that for the main classes and the 100 divisions the final o's are retained, *eg* 600, 510. In a few classes this is not exceeded, *eg* 160 Logic, where the schedule bears a very close resemblance to the original of 1876; in others, *eg* 621 Applied physics, six figure numbers are common and many ten figure numbers can be found, for this section includes ' Mechanical, electrical, electronic, electromagnetic, heat, light, nuclear engineering '. These are all subjects which have developed since 1876, when Mechanical engineering sufficed as the heading. On the other hand, 626 is now unused, for the subject to which it was originally allocated, Canal engineering, has so decreased in importance that it no longer justifies a separate heading. The use of 9 for ' other ' is well illustrated by 629 Other branches of engineering which includes:

629.1　Aerospace engineering
　　.2　Motor land vehicles and cycles
　　.3　Aircushion vehicles, Ground-effect machines, Hovercraft
　　.4　Astronautics
　　.8　Automatic control engineering.

While it has proved possible to accommodate all these subjects in 629, it cannot be argued that they are in the correct place in the schedules; they obviously are more closely related to Applied physics in 621 than to the subjects of Sanitary and municipal engineering in 628 with which they are in fact collocated.

In order to make the notation easier to use, a space is left after each three digits of a class number following the decimal point in both the schedules and index. This is purely for visual comfort, and is not an essential part of the class number; it is ignored in practice, *eg* by BNB, and has also been omitted from the examples given here.

INDEX
The final and not the least important part of the whole work is the *Relative index*. When the first and second editions of the scheme were published, Dewey stressed the importance of the index, as we have seen, and with the exception of the fifteenth edition, the indexes to the various editions have been well received. In the seventeenth edition an attempt was made to emphasize the importance of the schedules

for correct classifying by restricting the number of index entries; many ' minor ' subjects were not indexed directly but instead referred the user to a broader heading. This seems to have been the result of trying to graft an increased degree of synthesis on to a scheme which is basically enumerative; the editors were at great pains to point out that it was not possible to index all the composite subjects that might occur, and that it was therefore necessary to keep reminding users to consult the schedules. As we have seen, the index to a completely synthetic scheme makes no attempt to index any composite subjects; this is a reflection of the distinction between the index to the scheme and the index to the arrangement resulting from its application. In their efforts to stress this, the editors seem themselves to have missed the point at times. For example, Biophysics as an aspect of Biology had three index entries and a reminder:

Biophysics
  biology
    animals   **591.191**
    gen wks   **574.191**
    plants   **581.191**
    see also spec organisms.

These entries show that Biophysics is to be found in the Energy facet in Biology and its two main divisions Botany and Zoology, and that it may also form part of a composite subject with any individual animal or plant: *ie,* it is possible to combine the notation for foci from two facets. This is a useful reminder, but an adequate knowledge of the schedules and of the principles of synthesis make it superfluous. On the other hand, we have references such as

Hosea (O.T.) *see* Minor prophets

We turn to Minor in the index and find

Minor
  prophets (O.T.)
    gen wks   **224.9**

We turn to the schedules at 224.9, where we find

224.9   * Minor prophets
      For Hosea, see 224.6

Apart from the fact that this is apparently an example of special preceding general, there seems to be little point in making the user take this indirect route. The asterisk shows that some notational synthesis is possible, but this is shown also at the specific number for

Hosea. Similarly, if we are interested in the biophysical effects of gamma radiation, when we turn to Gamma we find

Gamma

rays

biophysics *see* **Biophysics**

rather than a direct lead to the specific number. The bold face type tells us that Biophysics is further divided in the schedule (a very neat convention for indicating that a particular topic is not the final link in its chain of division) but a direct entry would have told us this too.

The index was very strongly criticized, and in consequence the editorial policy committee decided to produce a new index, based on the sixteenth edition, but taking into account any changes in the schedules or in the terminology. This revised index was distributed free of charge to all purchasers of the seventeenth edition, at the end of 1967, in the form of a new second volume.

The revised index was, as is to be expected, very similar to that of the sixteenth edition. It contains, very approximately, three entries for each place in the schedules, but avoids repeating information that can be gained by studying the systematic arrangement. The conventional use of boldface type has already been mentioned. Synonyms are reasonably well covered, though a comparison of the entries under Railroad and Railway(s) seems to show that more could be done in this direction. Foci from the standard subdivisions or area table are labelled by the use of abbreviations s.s.- and area-. The lack of punctuation, intended to improve the layout, occasionally leads to ambiguity, as for example

Depravity Christian

doctrine 233.2

where Christian is meant to qualify doctrine rather than depravity.

In the eighteenth edition, the editorial policy has been to combine the good features of both kinds of index as far as is possible. There are many cross-references to enable the classifier to find a topic even if it is not specifically mentioned in the schedules, that is, if a specific piece of notation can only be obtained by synthesis. As is pointed out in the editor's introduction, there has never been a time when every composite subject that could be specified by using the schedules has been indexed, a point that has been discussed earlier in chapter 9. Classifiers will still therefore find it necessary to use the schedules to ensure that they have the correct class number, and one that is as specific as the scheme will allow; in general, they will find that the index to the eighteenth edition enables them to find the right place to start looking in the schedules more easily than either edition of the index to the seventeenth edition.

The index volume concludes with the obsolescent schedules for Law and Mathematics, showing the concordance between old and new schedules, so that the classifier can see very easily how to bring his own usage up to date.

ABRIDGED EDITIONS

The aim of the full editions of DC has always been to provide as much detail as is likely to be necessary in the largest library, but for many years there has been a parallel series of abridged editions intended for small libraries not requiring this degree of specificity. The first abridged edition was published in 1894, and the latest, the tenth, is published in 1971, shortly after the full edition to which it is related. It is about one tenth of the size of the full edition—2,331 topics enumerated compared with 26,141—but has a very full index with some 20,000 entries. In general, the notation rarely exceeds five digits, with a few exceptions in such areas as Electrical engineering. The layout and typography correspond closely to the eighteenth edition, but the facilities for synthesis introduced into that edition are omitted in the interests of simplicity. This edition is quite widely used in school libraries, where its lack of specificity is not a handicap. In addition to this 'official' edition, there is also an *Introduction to Dewey decimal classification for British schools*, compiled by M Chambers and published by the School Library Association in 1961.

ORGANIZATION

Dewey was nothing if not practical, and he devoted some of his tremendous energy to setting up the Lake Placid Club, a 'self-help' real estate development which turned out to be highly successful. Profits from this went to the Lake Placid Club Education Foundation, which has provided the funds for the continuation of the scheme, which has itself been highly successful; some 30,000 copies of the sixteenth edition were printed, which makes it a bestseller by any standard. The seventeenth edition has in fact already (1971) sold more copies than this, an indication of the continuing significance of the scheme, despite the many criticisms that have been made of it.

The Library of Congress started supplying catalogue cards to other libraries in 1901, and in the late 1920's discussions took place on the feasibility of including a DC number on these cards for the benefit of the many thousands of libraries using the scheme and buying the cards. In 1927 the Editorial Office was moved to the Library of Congress, and in 1930 a committee sponsored by the American Library Association started supplying DC numbers for LC cards. In 1933 the Library set up its own Decimal Classification Office to take over this function, and in 1953 was given the contract for the preparation of the sixteenth edition. In 1958 the Editorial Office and the Decimal Classification Office were merged, with the Editor given overall responsibility for both. With the backing of the Lake Placid Club Education Foundation and the Library of Congress, there is no danger that the scheme will collapse for lack of central organization.

Suggestions from users for revision are carefully considered, and in 1964 a Field Survey[4] was carried out to find out what changes users all over the world would like to see; though the recommendations came too late for the seventeenth edition, they have been taken into account in the preparation of the eighteenth. The fact that the editors are situated in the Library of Congress, and are hoping to extend the coverage of LC cards with DC numbers to most of that Library's accessions, means that they will be able to maintain the close contact with literary warrant which is an essential part of the development of any valid scheme.

REVISION
The main method of revision is by the publication of new editions at regular intervals, at present seven years. In additon to this, users are kept informed of new developments through *DC&: Decimal classification: additions, notes, and decisions,* now in its third volume. This originated in three series of *Notes and decisions on the application of the decimal classification* published by the Decimal classification office 1934-1955; the title was changed after the publication of the sixteenth edition, and the second volume began with the first issue, in Spring 1967, after publication of the seventeenth edition. The intention is to provide a regular service twice a year, but this seems not to be adhered to in practice. *DC&* provides a convenient method of publishing decisions likely to be controversial in advance of a new edition so that some sort of reaction can be obtained before they become irrevocable; for example, users were asked in the Spring 1967 issue to let the editors know if they had any views on the proposal to produce a completely new schedule for Law in the eighteenth edition. This issue also contains a list of corrections to the text of the seventeenth edition.

The lack of guidance on citation order in early editions of DC and other classifications, together with the lack of suitable textbooks, led the American Library Association to publish in mimeographed form in 1914 a *Code for classifiers*. This code was revised by W S Merrill and published in 1928, with a second edition in 1939, and for many years formed an essential part of the classifier's equipment. While it is not tied to DC, and gives many examples from LC, it is arranged by and large in accordance with DC, and endeavours to answer such practical questions as: where should a work on geophysical methods of prospecting, especially for oil, be classed? The questions and answers are illustrated by examples of books quoted by the various libraries contributing to the collection. Merrill's *Code* was essentially a pragmatic work, which did not try to give fundamental principles but instead treated each case on its own. We may see here a parallel with the Anglo-American cataloguing rules, 1908 edition. A clearer understanding of the problems of citation order, together with more notes and instructions in the text, has made such a work less necessary nowadays, but to aid users of the sixteenth edition the Forest Press published in 1962 a *Guide to the use of the Dewey decimal classification; based on the practice of the Decimal classification office at the Library of Congress*. This work in effect gathered together all the scope notes, cross-references and instructions in the sixteenth edition, but did not add to them significantly; it therefore left unanswered many of the questions raised by that edition, and was for this reason a disappointment to many users.

The more frequent and detailed instructions on synthesis in the eighteenth edition are likely to make such a publication superfluous in the future, and there seems to be little point in merely extracting rules from the scheme and publishing them separately if they have to be used with the scheme.

An interesting development in recent years has been the publication of three programmed texts,[5] for DC16, DC17 and now the eighteenth edition. These enable the students to work through the schemes under supervision, and to gain sufficient firsthand knowledge to give them a reasonable appreciation of the structure and mode of use.

THE BRITISH NATIONAL BIBLIOGRAPHY AND ITS USE OF DC

Soon after the outbreak of war in 1939, the Library Association, looking ahead to the coming postwar days, commissioned L R McColvin to conduct a study of the British public library service. In his report[6] —one of the few really inspiring documents to have come out of librarianship—McColvin castigated the standards of cataloguing and classification he found, and emphasized the great need for a centralized service comparable with that offered by the Library of Congress. When discussions began on the practicality of this recommendation after the war, the difficulties soon became apparent; the obvious centre for such a service, the British Museum, did not use a classification scheme, and had its own code of cataloguing rules. The solution was to set up a new body, the Council of the British National Bibliography, which would have access to the books deposited at the BM, but would be a separate organization; it was to publish a weekly list, as being the most economic and useful way of disseminating the information needed, and DC was chosen as the classification scheme to be used to arrange the main part of the list, a classified catalogue. DC was the obvious choice in that it was used by the great majority of libraries in Britain; UDC was considered as being more suitable for a bibliography, but it was felt that UDC numbers, while valid for arranging the bibliography, would be of no use at all as part of a central cataloguing service.

The edition of DC then current was the fourteenth, already some years out of date, but it was adopted in the hope that it could be superseded by the fifteenth edition then in preparation. The BNB began publication in January 1950, giving a catalogue entry according to the AA code and a DC class number; no subject index was included, as it was assumed that libraries would make use of the index to the scheme. By the end of the year it had become clear that changes would have to be made if the BNB was not to fail for lack of support, and some important decisions were made. The first of these was that the scheme would be extended wherever this proved necessary by means of verbal extensions, which would form part of a complete set of feature headings; the second, that a detailed subject index would be included in each monthly or larger cumulation. The effects of these two decisions have been demonstrated and will not be repeated here (page 176). The fifteenth edition proved unacceptable, with the exception of a few of the relocations, and BNB continued to use the fourteenth edition while awaiting the sixteenth. When the latter was published in 1958, it was carefully examined, but the conclusion was reached that it did not offer enough advantages over the fourteenth to justify its adoption; it still had most of the faults of overall organiza-

233

8*

tion of the fourteenth edition, and had introduced some of its own. BNB decided to continue with the fourteenth, but to start using its own notation to replace the [1] in those places where it had developed a complete new extension to the official schedules; this plan was put into effect with the beginning of a new five year cumulation in January 1960, and the schedules were published in 1963.[7]

They fall into two main parts: the common facets, and extensions to subject schedules. The common facets are a complete revision of those in DC, separating the form divisions into the four facets we have seen to be necessary: bibliographical forms, common subjects, time, including history, and place. The place facet develops many of the subfacets which have now appeared in the Area Table in DC17, but in addition brought Great Britain to the beginning of the political divisions as the favoured focus; a not unreasonable amendment in a national bibliography. BNB also makes provision for the four phase relationships: bias, which precedes the common facets, and influence, comparison and exposition, which follow them.

The subject schedules vary in size from a few minor amendments to existing schedules to complete new detailed schedules; a good example of the latter is that for nuclear science and engineering, in particular nuclear reactors; these do not appear at all in the fourteenth edition (the first nuclear reactor was built in great secrecy after DC14 was published) and are barely mentioned in the sixteenth.

In order not to conflict with official DC numbers and to avoid problems of copyright, BNB used lower case letters for their notation; this is used retroactively, so that composite subjects can be specified without the need for further facet indicators. For some time a conversion table was included in each issue to enable users to devise the standard DC number where this differed from BNB practice. The publication of the seventeenth edition did not make any fundamental difference to BNB practice, except for a few relocations, so that in effect BNB was using a mixture of DC15, DC16 and DC17 grafted on to the DC14 base; however, BNB did start to give a standard DC17 number in each entry as well as their own, which was used for the arrangement.

There has been a great deal of argument about the justification for BNB's usage of DC[8]. The editorial view has always been that DC on its own has proved to be inadequate for the arrangement of a national bibliography containing some 25,000 entries each year, and that all that BNB has done is to introduce detail and consistency, by applying the principles of analytico-synthetic classification. Critics claim

234

that DC is being distorted to satisfy the extreme views of an unrepresentative group, and that these distortions make BNB useless for one of its primary functions: the provision of centralized cataloguing copy. The editorial board of DC went so far as to advertise their dissociation from 'unauthorized' amendments, without actually saying where these were to be found. However, when we study the major changes introduced by the BNB's *Supplementary schedules* (more facilities for synthesis, revision of the common facets, provision of a more detailed place facet), we find an interesting parallel in the changes that were introduced in the seventeenth edition in 1965.

The introduction of the MARC project, with its emphasis on international standardization, has led BNB to abandon its own usage in favour of giving a straightforward DC18 class number, backed up by a detailed subject index using the PRECIS technique, from the beginning of January 1971. The Library of Congress has also started to use DC18, and there is now constant communication between BNB and the Decimal Classification Division with a view to achieving transatlantic consistency[9]. It is clear that many of the changes in recent editions of DC have been due to the work done by staff of BNB, and there is no doubt that many of the advances in classification theory during the past twenty years have resulted from the painstaking analysis of the problems presented by the detailed classification of over 300,000 non-fiction books.

THE FUTURE

Although DC continues to be the most widely used general classification scheme, it has been subjected to a great deal of criticism in recent years, and many libraries in the United States have decided to reclassify by LC. The reason appears to be that LC numbers appear on all LC cards, but DC numbers do not, so that libraries using the cards with DC may have to classify for themselves a proportion of their accessions. In 1967, DC numbers were available for some 25% of the titles (though these titles accounted for some 75% of the cards sold, since the editors have concentrated on English-language titles and others published in the USA).[10] There have been complaints about relocations, long class numbers and other features of DC, but since most of these criticisms apply with equal or greater force to LC (particularly the problem of relocations), it is difficult to accept them. It seems unfortunate that these libraries are changing, for the wrong reason, to a scheme which is in many respects no better than DC; although they may save some problems at the input stage, they will be faced with just as many problems at the output stage, when trying to *use* the class numbers to achieve a useful arrangement, and to find documents on topics about which the enquirer is not very sure—which is the major reason for systematic arrangement.

Nevertheless, DC is still used by a great many libraries all over the world, and will surely continue to be used. In Britain, BNB uses a DC18 number for each entry; in the United States, several bibliographical tools give DC class numbers, as well as LC cards. Editions are available in a number of languages other than English, and the 18th edition has made several provisions to help the non-American user, as we have pointed out. If in some respects DC has been overtaken by more recent developments, this is ever the fate of the pioneer. Much of the criticism of DC has come from users who are reluctant to change, as well as from those who consider that change has been too slow. No matter what the outcome, Melvil Dewey and his Decimal Classification are assured of one of the more significant places in the history of library classification and the systematic approach.

BIBLIOGRAPHY

1 Coates, E J: ' The Dewey decimal classification, edition 16.' *Library Association record, 61* (8) August 1959, 187-190.

Coates, E J: ' The decimal classification, edition 16: class 300.' *Library association record, 62* (3) March 1960, 84-90.

2 Custer, B A: ' Dewey lives.' *Library resources and technical services, 11* (1) Winter 1967, 51-60.

Metcalfe, J: *Dewey's decimal classification, seventeenth edition: an appraisal.* Bingley, 1965. 38p.

Several reviews of DC17 have appeared, *eg* Tait, J A: *Library review, 20* Winter 1965, 220-224.

3 Matthews, W E: ' Dewey 18: a preview and report to the profession.' *Library Association Record, 73* (2) February 1971, 28-30. (Also in *Wilson library bulletin, 45* (6) February 1971.)

4 Vann, Sarah K: ' Dewey abroad: the Field Survey of 1964.' *Library resources and technical services, 11* (1) Winter 1967, 61-71.

5 Batty, C D *Introduction to the Dewey decimal classification.* Bingley, 1965.

Batty, C D: *Introduction to the seventeenth edition of the Dewey decimal classification.* Bingley, 1967.

Batty, C D: *Introduction to the eighteenth edition of the Dewey decimal classification.* Bingley, 1971.

6 McColvin, L R: *The public library service of Great Britain*: a report on its present condition with proposals for postwar reorganization. Library Association, 1942.

7 British National Bibliography: *Supplementary classification schedules* prepared to augment the Dewey Decimal Classification for use in the British National Bibliography and first introduced in January 1960. Council of the British National Bibliography, 1963.

8 Davison, K: *Classification practice in Britain: report on a survey of classification opinion and practice in Great Britain, with particular reference to the Dewey Decimal Classification.* Library Association, 1966. This report was sponsored by the Dewey Decimal Classification Sub-Committee of the Library Association's Research and Development Committee; this body has done a great deal of work in keeping the editorial staff of DC aware of British opinion.

9 Bruin, J E: 'The practice of classification: a study towards standardization.' *Journal of librarianship, 3* (1) January 1971, 60-71.

10 In fiscal 1969 (*ie* July 1968-June 1969) and fiscal 1970 about 75,000 books were classified by DC in each year, including all those in English published in North America, Western Europe and Australia.

(*Thanks are due to the Forest Press, Mr Ben Custer, the Editor of* DC, *and* BNB, *for making it possible for me to gather information about* DC*18 in advance of publication.*)

CHAPTER 13

The universal decimal classification

In 1894 two Belgians, Paul Otlet and Henri LaFontaine, conceived the idea of a ' universal index to recorded knowledge ', to which people all over the world would contribute, and which would in its turn be available to all. An alphabetical arrangement was out of the question in so aggressively international an enterprise, and they turned their minds to systematic arrangement; what system could they use which would be acceptable on a worldwide basis?

Arabic numerals are used everywhere, and there existed a scheme already widely used in libraries in the USA which used arabic numerals as its only notation: the decimal classification of Melvil Dewey, then in its fifth edition. Otlet and LaFontaine wrote to Dewey and sought his permission to extend the detail in his scheme to make it suitable for arranging the kind of index they had in mind (although Dewey himself always stressed the importance of the classified catalogue, his scheme was then, as now, mainly used for shelf arrangement of books), and, having received this, settled down to classify several thousands of documents in time for the First International Conference on Bibliography, which they had arranged to be held in 1895. This conference welcomed the idea of an international index, and set up the Institut International de la Bibliographie (IIB) to act as the organization responsible. The development of the scheme went ahead, and in 1905 it was published as the *Manuel du répertoire universel bibliographique*, stressing its primary purpose. It already contained more detail than any edition of its parent scheme, and was adopted by many libraries and other organizations in Europe; indeed, it is still the most widely used classification on the Continent, where, in general, libraries have not seen the advantages of a common classification scheme and tend to use their own private schemes.

The Great War of 1914-1918 was a heavy blow for the Index, from which it never really recovered, and in the 1920's it gradually sank under its own weight, helped by a forced move from its previous quarters to make room for a trade fair. By this time, however, the scheme had become popular in special libraries all over the world, and a second edition was put in hand, with Otlet and LaFontaine to supervise the Humanities and Social sciences, and a newcomer, Frits Donker Duyvis, employed by the Dutch Patent Office, to supervise the Natural sciences. This second edition, published over the years 1927-1933, had the title *Classification décimale universelle,* an indication of the change of emphasis since the first edition. It was by far the most detailed classification scheme published up to that time, and its international nature was emphasized by the fact that the third edition, which started publication in 1934, was the German *Dezimal klassifikation;* this edition, interrupted by the war, was eventually completed in 1952, with an additional three volumes of index published 1951-1953.

Donker Duyvis became secretary of the IIB in 1929, and continued in that office until his enforced retirement (due to illhealth) in 1959; there is no doubt that UDC as we know it today owes a great deal to the tireless efforts of this one man (who incidentally continued to be paid by the Dutch Patent Office; either the Dutch are not very inventive, or their governments are more enlightened than most!). The IIB changed its name in 1931 to IID (Institut International de Documentation), and again in 1937 to FID (Fédération International de Documentation); neither of these changes altered its emphasis on the importance of the UDC (CDU or DK), but served rather to confirm and extend it. In Britain one of its most enthusiastic supporters was Dr S C Bradford, Librarian of the Science Museum Library; his book *Documentation*[1] is largely about UDC, he used it in the library, and he too started an index to recorded knowledge which eventually suffered the same fate as that of the IIB. (This is an interesting byway of British library history. Bradford built up a team of scientists to work on this index in a way that was unprecedented at the time, and the index quickly grew to considerable size; what it lacked was users. Too few people made their way to the library to make use of this invaluable resource; then, as now, information-seeking Mahomets want the mountain not merely to come to them but to be delivered to their desks packaged ready for use. By the time that the index had reached about two million cards it was no longer possible for the amount of effort spent on its compilation to be justified, and Bradford was obliged to abandon it. It is rumoured to be, at least in part, tucked away in one of the attics of the Science Library, a forgotten monument to a great but unsuccessful idea.) The first publication in English of any of the

UDC was the work of Bradford, who published the abridged schedules used in the Science Museum Library with the title *Classification for works on pure and applied science in the Science Museum Library,* the third edition appearing in 1936.

In due course, the British Standards Institution became the official British editorial body, and publication of the full English edition, the fourth, began in 1943; unfortunately, like FID itself, BSI has always suffered from a lack of funds to prosecute this work, and despite the enthusiasm and hard work of the national committee, this edition has not yet been completed. The situation changed radically in 1967, when OSTI made a grant to BSI to enable them to increase the scope and quantity of their documentation activities, including UDC; as a result of this, it now seems likely that the full edition will be available by the end of 1971, though some of the parts will by then be over twenty five years old and badly in need of revision.

Other full editions in preparation include revisions of the German and French editions, and new ventures in Spanish and Japanese. The complete schedules are, of course, available on cards at the headquarters of the FID, but to publish them may mean translating into the desired language, and since most work is done voluntarily in the national committees, there is little access to the master copy. The lack of full schedules has, however, been overcome to some extent by the publication of abridged editions, now available in some sixteen languages. The first British abridged edition was published in 1948 and was based on the Science Museum schedules; the second edition, published in 1957, was more detailed, as well as being more up to date, and had a far better index, with 20,000 entries compared with the 2,000 in the 1948 edition. The latest abridgement is the third, published in 1961, and this is the edition most likely to be found in use. It was hoped to set up a regular revision schedule for the abridged English edition, but this has had to be postponed in favour of publication of the full edition.

An interesting venture was the publication in 1958 of the tri-lingual edition, BS1000B. The text in this is in three columns, German, English and French, and there are three separate indexes; the notation in the text is in a fourth column at the left, and applies of course to each of the three texts. A supplement to this has been published covering the years 1958 to 1968; this is in effect a supplement to all of the abridged editions, and can be used to update the English abridgement of 1961.

Full English edition		Medium French edition		Abridged English edition	
631.542	Pruning and crown thinning	631.54	Soins aux plantes en cours de croissance	631.54	Tending and care of plants. Cf. 632
.1	Winter pruning	.542	Taille des arbres et des plantes	.542	Pruning. Thinning
.11	Theory of pruning	.1	Taille d'hiver		
.12	Methods of pruning	.2	Taille d'été		
.13	Heading back	.3	Taille des plantes dans des buts spéciaux, par exemple pour donner une forme à celles-ci, pour influencer la croissance		
.14	Thinning				
.15	Notching				
.17	Time of pruning				
.2	Summer pruning				
.21	Pinching				
.22	Nipping off buds				
.23	Clipping				
.24	Notching and ring barking				
.25	Defoliation				
.26	Suppression of flowers				
.27	Fruit thinning				
.3	Cutting of plants for particular purposes				
.32	For shaping				
.33	For influencing growth				
.335	For promoting branching				
.34	For removal of infected parts or for combating parasites				
.35	For increasing blossom or leaf production				
.36	For promoting development of fruit, e.g				
	Cutting of palm leaves				
.4	Desiccation before harvesting				
Full English edition		*Medium French edition*		*Abridged English edition*	

FIGURE 4: Comparison of Full, Medium and Abridged editions of UDC.

Two other methods of publication are used, both fairly recent innovations. The first of these is the ' medium ' edition, now available in German;[2] as is evident from its name, this falls between the full and abridged editions, containing about 30% of the full tables. The intention is to produce a scheme which is sufficiently detailed for all but the largest libraries, yet is more manageable than the full schedules. Medium editions are planned in French, Portuguese, Spanish and English; the English medium edition is likely to bear a considerable resemblance to the schedules used in the American Institute of Physics mechanization experiment, described later.

The second of these other methods of publication is the special subject editions; these give detailed schedules for the area of specialization and abridged background schedules for related sections, and are now available in several subject areas, *eg* nuclear science, mining and metallurgy, and building. These editions are usually based on the practice of a large library system, *eg* the UKAEA or the Iron and Steel Institute, and are thus of considerable value in that they give the user some assistance which is not available from the ordinary schedules, in the form of scope notes, cross-references and instructions.[3]

ORGANIZATION

The way in which UDC and its revision processes are organized is so much a part of the scheme that it deserves special study. As has been mentioned, the FID is the body having the overall responsibility, which it exercises through its international committee on universal classification, on which all national member committees are entitled to be represented. Day to day control is vested in the central classification committee, FID/CCC; for many years this consisted of the editors of the full editions and the FID Secretary General, but in May 1965 the constitution was amended to extend the membership. Each member nation of FID may also have its own national committee, which will then have the responsibility for editions in that language; in Britain, the national committee is a subcommittee of the documentation standards committee of the British Standards Institution, and has editorial control of all English language editions of UDC.

In addition to these administrative committees, there are international and national subject committees; the international committees report to the FID/CCC, while the national subject committees report to the appropriate national committee. Work for these committees is voluntary, and it can be seen that the combination of voluntary effort and a complex structure of committees is not a particularly efficient way of getting things done: committees do not meet very frequently, business has to be transacted through correspondence, and most of the work of revision has to be undertaken as a sparetime activity by librarians who are usually fully occupied with their daily work. Only in recent years has there been more money available to finance the organization, and much of the revision of UDC has been undertaken within organizations, such as the UKAEA, which have been using the scheme and have been able to devote a proportion of their official library effort to its maintenance.

REVISION

Suggestions for revision normally come from users who find that the schedules in a particular subject are inadequate for their needs, either through lack of detail or through obsolescence. A request forwarded to the national committee, and through them to the CCC, may well result in the original requester's being asked to prepare a draft for comment! The draft is circulated to interested parties by the appropriate national subject committee, and when agreement has been reached it is forwarded to the international subject committee. If they approve, the draft is sent to the CCC, who study it carefully to see that it does not clash with any existing or proposed schedules; if it is satisfactory in this respect, it is published as a *P-note*. These are provisional or proposed alterations, and lie on the table for four months, during which time any user of UDC may comment on them; if no substantive comment is received, the proposal is deemed accepted, and is entered into the master copy. Every six months P-notes which have been accepted are cumulated into the *Extensions and corrections to the UDC;* this is itself progressively cumulated into series covering periods of three years. The first five series of *Extensions,* together with the German *Ergänzungen* (supplements used to bring those portions of the German edition published before 1939 up to date when publication was resumed), have been cumulated in six volumes. Series six of the *Extensions* covers approved P-notes issued during 1965, 1966 and 1967, and series 7 will cover the following three years. It is thus necessary to look in several different places to make sure that the most recent schedules are being used. To add to the confusion, P-notes may be issued in English, French or German, and it is the exception rather than the rule for these to be translated; so to use the *Extensions* or the *P-notes* it is useful to be trilingual.

243

As with any scheme, there is the conflict between keeping pace with knowledge and maintaining integrity of numbers, but since UDC is used by many scientific and technical libraries, and devotes much of its schedules to those areas, the conflict is if anything more acute than usual. One means of overcoming it is the ' starvation ' policy. A piece of notation can be left unused for ten years, and at the end of this time can be reused with a different meaning; an example will show this. Prior to 1961 the schedule for Particle accelerators was found at 621.384.61 and 621.384.62; a new schedule was developed, using 621.384.63/.66 and leaving the previous numbers vacant. After ten years it will be possible to reuse 621.384.61 and .62, for example, to develop another new schedule for Particle accelerators. In science and technology the ' half life ' of literature is only a few years, and after ten years any documents still classified at a vacated number can be reclassified or discarded; the same is not true, of course, of the humanities or social sciences, where the method is less likely to be successful.

The revision process in UDC is both a source of strength and a weakness. New schedules are drawn up by users who need them and are working with the literature of the subject; they are closely scrutinized by other experts, with the CCC to ensure that proposals are sound from the classification point of view. On the other hand, the procedure is slow and clumsy; it took some ten years for a proposal for a new schedule for Space science and astronautics to gain acceptance, and two years is almost the minimum. In fast developing subjects, a schedule may be out of date before it becomes official.

MAJOR CHANGES

UDC was originally based on the fifth edition of DC, and though the two schemes tended to drift apart, there was for some time an attempt to bring them into line again, at least as far as the first three figures of the notation. In 1961, two studies of UDC commissioned by UNESCO[4] were published, which were highly critical of the scheme; much of the criticism arose from the unsatisfactory outline, still tied to a large extent to the outdated outline of DC. As a result of these studies, a decision was taken to try to carry out a large scale revision of the outline,[5] while still maintaining momentum on regular revisions of detail. The first move has been made: Language has been moved from its place between the Social sciences and the Natural sciences to Literature, where it occupies a place at the beginning of the schedule. This means that it will be possible to reuse the notation 4 in due course, and several suggestions have been made; the most useful of these seems to be to develop here those sciences, such as Communication, which may be described as bridges between the social and the natural sciences. This kind of large scale recasting will have to be done slowly if the scheme is not to lose its popularity with librarians who have large collections already classified, but it does offer an opportunity for the scheme to go forward rather than stagnate until it is completely overtaken by events.

THE SCHEME

In the absence of the whole of the full English edition, it is the abridged edition which is most widely used. The full edition is British Standard BS1000, while the abridged is BS1000A; BS1000B is the trilingual German-English-French edition published in 1958. The third abridged edition, BS1000A:1961 is the one which will be considered here.

The scheme begins with a contents table which serves the dual purpose of indicating the contents and of showing the more important changes since the 1957 edition. After the foreword there is a brief note comparing DC and UDC; this is followed by the general introduction, which includes a brief historical outline and then describes the scheme as it is today. The ' auxiliaries ', which will be described in detail, appear next, followed by an outline of the main divisions (corresponding to Dewey's second summary), and the schedules.

The overall outline of the schedules is similar to that of DC, but the notation is slightly different and the layout is rather less satisfactory. There is no three figure minimum in UDC, so Science is 5, Mathematics 51; in order to break up the notation, which tends to be rather long, a point is used every three digits, eg 621.039.532.5, if no other notational device is applicable. In general the notation is expressive and reflects the structure of the schedules, shown by choice of type face and indentation. The main outline is as follows:

0   GENERALITIES

1   PHILOSOPHY. METAPHYSICS. PSYCHOLOGY. LOGIC. ETHICS AND
     MORALS.

2   RELIGION. THEOLOGY

3   SOCIAL SCIENCES. ECONOMICS. LAW. GOVERNMENT. EDUCATION.

5   MATHEMATICS AND NATURAL SCIENCES.

6   APPLIED SCIENCES. MEDICINE. TECHNOLOGY

7   THE ARTS. RECREATION. SPORT, ETC.

8 LITERATURE. BELLES LETTRES. PHILOLOGY. LINGUISTICS. LAN-
   GUAGES

9 GEOGRAPHY. BIOGRAPHY. HISTORY

(NB This outline takes into account the transfer of Linguistics etc to 8, which took place *after* the publication of the 1961 edition.)

Because the final o is not used to give the three figure minimum, it can be used with some meaning, *eg*

8   Literature, etc
82   Western literature in general
820   English

Many of the schedules are short because they use synthesis for composite subjects; for example, the Literature schedule occupies less than a page. There are occasional cross-references, *eg*

523.78   Eclipses of the sun. *Cf* 521.8

and instructions, *eg*

632.4   Fungus and mould diseases. *By A/Z or as*
           582.28

Scope notes are rare, but are found in a few places. Terminology is good; the 1957 edition was thoroughly revised from this aspect and the terms used are up to date and represent correct usage.

However, if we had to judge UDC solely on its main schedules, we should have to admit that it compared unfavourably with DC; it is in the auxiliaries, which provide UDC with its means of synthesis, that the difference lies. There are several of these, which may be divided into two groups: the common auxiliaries, which may be used at any point in the main schedules, and the special auxiliaries, which have different meanings according to their context. The auxiliaries are, in fact, a set of common facets and facet indicators which enable us to synthesize freely where the more restricted notation of DC does not. Some of them are of fairly restricted application while others may be used frequently. They appear in the scheme in the following order:

a) Addition and consecutive extension signs + and /. The plus sign + may be used to join the notation for two subjects which are commonly associated but are separated by the scheme. Its use is not recommended, as it is difficult to index such combinations satisfactorily and because they file before the first number on its own they may easily be overlooked.

246

Example: 539.1 + 621.039 Nuclear science and technology.
In filing, the plus sign may be ignored if an entry is made under each of the elements.

The stroke / (slash in USA) is used to join consecutive UDC numbers to indicate a broader heading for which no single piece of notation exists. As the basis for UDC left out some quite important steps of division, the / can be very useful; it too files before the first number on its own.

Example: 22/28   The Christian Religion.

b) Relation signs: [ ]   : :

The colon is the most widely used of the synthetic devices, but is an imprecise weapon which may have several different meanings. It may be used for phase relations:

Example: 635.965:697.38   Effect of hot-air central heating on indoor plants

or it may be used to combine foci from different facets of the same basic class:

Example: 635.965:632.38 Virus diseases of indoor plants

or it may be used to enumerate the foci within a facet by using the schedule from another class (as DC uses the divide like device):

Example: 635.965:582.675   Indoor anemones

The colon enables the classifier to make multiple entries very simply by cycling, and is popular for that reason; however, it is so generally used that it lacks precision, and it seems probable that if UDC is to be used in mechanized systems, the colon will have to be replaced by a set of more precise indicators.

In the introduction to the abridged English edition, square brackets are suggested as a means of 'intercalating', ie changing the facet order when the normal means of subdivision would be by means of the colon. If we wanted to gather everything on particular plants together under the general heading Horticulture, we might change the above example to 635.9[582.675]65 to make the main facet the in-dividual plant (in this case anemones), with environment (indoor . . .) a secondary feature. This use of square brackets has never had the official seal of approval of the FID, but this has now been given to another use, that is as a form of algebraic grouping device. If we join two UDC numbers by means of a + or :, and then follow this by, say, a form division, it may be difficult to arrive at an unambiguous subject statement. By using square brackets, the ambiguity can be eliminated:

247

Example: 01 +655(05)   Bibliography, and, Periodicals about printing
[01 +655](05) Periodicals about Bibliography and Printing
22/28:294.3(540) Christianity in relation to (Buddhism
in India)
[22/28:294.3](540) (Christianity in relation to Buddhism) in India

(Note that the stroke already performs a similar function; in the
above example, we read 22/28 as a unit before considering the relationship implied by the colon).

As mentioned above, the colon is widely used as a ' pivoting ' device
for generating additional entries by reversing or cycling. Once the
indexer has generated the original class number, cycling is a purely
mechanical task which can be done by a clerical worker or a machine.
There will, however, be occasions when we do not want to reverse
because the second part of a class number is very clearly subsidiary.
The use of the double colon is now suggested as a means of indicating
this situation. If for example we did not think it necessary to make
entries in the Botany section for individual plants specified in Horticulture, we could use the double colon thus:

Example: 635.965::582.675

This would *not* lead to an additional entry under 582.675.

c) Common auxiliaries of language =

The schedule for Linguistics may be used to give the notation for
this common facet, which applies rather as part of the description of a
particular book than as part of the subject.

Example: 678(038)=82=20   Russian-English dictionary of rubbers and plastics.

d) Common auxiliaries of form (0. . .)

The bibliographical forms are listed in some detail in this facet, which is
generally satisfactory, though the use of (091) for Historical presentation
may lead to a separation between general histories (091) and works dealing with specific periods in which the dates are used without the (091).

Example: 678(038)   Dictionary of rubbers and plastics.

e) Common auxiliaries of place (1/9)

This is well worked out, containing not only the usual political divisions
but also several other subfacets of place. It may be used as a primary
facet, though there is the possibility here of separating entries which
should be together if both the auxiliary numbers and the geography

numbers are used. Relationships between countries may be shown by the use of the colon within the brackets.

Example: 327(42:44) International relations between Britain and France.

622.33(73) Coal mining in the USA.

Because the facet indicator shows the end of the notational element it may be intercalated, *ie* inserted into the middle of an existing piece of notation to change the facet order.

Example: 329.14 Socialist parties

329(42)14 The Labour party.

f) Common auxiliaries of race and nationality (=...)

These are based on the common auxiliaries of language and may be developed from the main linguistics schedule in the same way. This facet is obviously of rather more limited application than the others.

Example: 301.185(=924) The sociological importance of kinship among the Jews.

g) Common auxiliaries of time "..."

Dates may be specified in detail, and in addition many other aspects of time are listed, though their use will be rare. The complete flexibility of the time facet in UDC is very useful, and is superior to any other scheme.

Examples: " 1969.12.25 " Christmas day 1969.

820"19" Twentieth century English literature

05"53" Weekly periodicals.

h) Alphabetical and (non-decimal) numerical subdivision

There are occasions when it is useful to be able to name individuals, or to list items denoted by a number. This can be done, though care must be taken to distinguish such numbers from the ordinary subdivisions.

Example: 025.45 DC17 Seventeenth edition of Dewey

Names of individuals can be inserted in the middle of a piece of notation if this is appropriate; this is convenient in such subjects as Literature, where it permits the systematic arrangement of the works of an author.

Example: 820-2"15" Shakespeare 7 Hamlet 03=30 of which a complete restatement is: literature-English-drama-16th century - Shakespeare - individual works-Hamlet-transla-tions-into German

Names may be abbreviated if this is preferred, *eg* Shakespeare might be denoted by his full name, or by Shak, or by SHA.

i) Common auxiliaries of point of view .oo...

These may be used straightforwardly by adding them to the main number.

Example: 621.039.577.003.3 Nuclear reactors for power production, from the accountancy point of view.

A more sophisticated use is described in the introduction; this is to add precision to the colon by using the point of view numbers with it to give, in effect, an extended facet indicator. By this means the 'blunderbuss' effect of the use of the colon for a wide variety of purposes can be countered, and a more satisfactory arrangement results. The three different uses of the colon exemplified earlier might be expanded thus:

635.965:697.38 → 635.965.004:697.38
635.965:632.38 → 635.965.004.6:632.38
635.965:582.675 → 635.965.002.3:582.675

This device can introduce an element of order into what could become an unhelpful arrangement if the colon is used indiscriminately to introduce a large number of different kinds of subdivision.

A recent addition to the point of view numbers, not included in the 1961 abridged edition, is the use of .000.0/.9 to indicate the author's point of view. This is a rather different kind of approach, but one which could be useful.

Example: 162.6.000.335.5 Dialectics from the Marxist point of view

k) Another recent addition to the common auxiliaries is the use of —0, of which the only example so far is —05 Persons. In the 1961 abridgement, this facet was enumerated under 3 Social sciences, and instructions were given in a few other places permitting its use; since then, it has been transferred to the common auxiliaries, and may thus be used at any point where it is appropriate.

Example: 02-055.1 Male librarians.

The common auxiliaries may be added to any main number, and always have the same meaning; there are in addition three other facet indicators which form the Special (auxiliary) subdivisions, and which have different meanings depending on their context. These are the hyphen -, the .0. . ., and the apostrophe '. The - and .0 are used to introduce facets peculiar to a given basic class; in Engineering the - is the indicator for the parts facet, in Literature it introduces the Literary form facet, while the .0 is used in Electrical Engineering to introduce various facets, and in Chemical Engineering to introduce the Operations facet.

Examples: 62-31   Reciprocating valve gear parts
          820-31   English novels
          621.3.066 Electrical switch mechanisms
          66.066   Clarification etc: chemical engineering

These indicators can only be used within the class in which they are enumerated. The apostrophe is at present used with a rather different meaning, in Chemistry and similar subjects, where it is used to indicate synthesis of material elements as well as notational.

Example: 546.33   Sodium (chemistry)
         546.13   Chlorine
         546.33'13 Sodium chloride (*ie* common salt)

However, the apostrophe is a useful symbol, and its use may be extended in the future. All of the symbols used to introduce the auxiliaries are available on a standard typewriter keyboard, but there are not many left now, and those that are available will need to be exploited as fully as possible.

NOTATIONAL PROBLEMS

It should be clear from the examples given and from a study of the schedules that the notation of UDC tends to be clumsy. The scheme is most detailed in science and technology, to which Dewey allocated insufficient notation in his original outline; in the third edition (the full edition in German, which is the latest to be published *in toto*), science accounts for 20%, technology for 52%, of the schedules, but of course they only have 20% of the notational base. In consequence the notation in these subjects is frequently long, even without the addition of any of the auxiliaries. Another source of undue length is the need to repeat the notation for the basic class when using the colon to combine foci within it, *eg*

621.384.6:621.318.3:621.311.6 Power supplies for the electro-
                              magnets of particle accelerators

in which 621.3 is repeated twice. This seems to be inevitable when synthesis is used with an enumerative base. For private purposes, *eg* within a library, base numbers can be replaced by a letter; the UKAEA use N instead of 621.039, for example. Since such devices do not have universally accepted meanings, they cannot be used outside the organization, but must be replaced by the full official notation. The complete revision of the outline which is under consideration might lead to a reduction in the length of the notation, as would a more consistent approach to synthesis within basic classes; however, UDC

251

is intended to give detailed specification of detailed subjects, and it is not possible to do this without long notation.

INDEX
The index to the abridged edition is, in general, very satisfactory; various examples have been quoted from it already, and will not be repeated. The terminology is good, synonyms are covered, there are cross-references; there are about 20,000 entries all told, for about 12,000 estimated topics in the schedules. Occasionally, however, the index can be confusing; in some cases it gives a number more detailed than can be found in the schedules (*eg* Ku-Klux-Klan is 363.2(73) in the index, 363 in the schedules), while in other cases the reverse is true. These are minor problems which will no doubt be removed in the next edition.

AIDS FOR THE USER
A very useful *Guide to the Universal Decimal Classification* (*UDC*) has been published by the BSI as BS1000C: 1963; compiled by J Mills, this is not merely a practical tool for users of UDC, but contains also much on classification that is of quite general interest. Similar works exist in other languages, and further works are planned in English. There is also a new programmed text,[6] similar to those for DC.

An additional help is that UDC is used by many bodies which publish, such as the UKAEA; these bodies often include a UDC number in their publications which can be of considerable assistance in libraries where the subject matter is covered is unfamiliar. Many abstracting services include UDC numbers with each abstract, *eg Electrical engineering abstracts* (part B of *Science abstracts*).

The main problem from the user's point of view, the lack of rules within the scheme, is only reduced to some extent by these aids. This flexibility has been cited as an advantage, in that the user can select for himself the way in which he will use the scheme in any given basic class (page 148), but there is no doubt that it is at the same time a source of danger. No classification scheme can work without rules; if these are not included in the scheme, they must be added by the classifier, otherwise inconsistency will be the result. This is also possible because of inconsistencies in the scheme itself; for example, fractional distillation appears in the operations facet in Chemical engineering as .048.3, so that fractional distillation of petroleum can be denoted 665.5.048.3—but it is also enumerated as

665.52. The classifier has to build up a set of rules for himself to avoid this kind of difficulty. The ' Code of practice ' drawn up by the UKAEA for its own purposes later became the basis for the special subject edition in nuclear science and engineering; these editions often give the user more help than the standard abridged or full editions.

THE FUTURE

At one time it looked as though the future held little for UDC, but recent developments have changed the picture considerably. The editorial decision to try to revise the outline to bring it up to date over the next few years was a big step forward, though we have still to see the implementation of this beyond the transfer of Linguistics. However, of possibly greater significance is the research programme which has been carried out in the USA under the auspices of the American Institute of Physics[7] to examine the feasibility of using UDC in computer-based information retrieval systems. The results of this work have shown clearly that UDC will function very well in this situation, though some changes will have to be made if it is to be wholly successful. Most of the changes are concerned with making the colon more precise; in the experiments it was found necessary to replace it by a series of devices, each with a definite meaning. UDC has been used by a great many libraries for a number of years; the fact that these libraries do not need to change to another system if they want to mechanize is obviously very important, both for the libraries and for UDC.

Many of the complaints about UDC that have arisen in the past stem from the unsatisfactory methods used to publish the scheme and keep it up to date. the use of computers could transform this situation almost overnight; again, the AIP Project has shown that UDC schedules can be revised and printed out by computer with a greatly reduced amount of editorial work. Because the notation is still largely expressive, it is even possible to program the machine to select the correct type face, according to the length of the notation.

A further important use may be seen for UDC in the future, arising from its international nature. Many information retrieval systems now use words, often in post-coordinate techniques, rather than classification schemes, but words apply only in their language of origin. The possibility of using UDC as an international concordance to IR systems is being explored; for example, a Japanese wishing to know the meaning of an English term used in a thesaurus would find the

UDC number, then look this up in the Japanese edition to find the equivalent term.

To sum up, although the scheme has its faults, both in construction and in publication methods, it does seem at present that these can be overcome and that UDC will continue to be the most important international scheme. The fact that its use is now widespread in the USSR, and that valuable research has been carried out in the USA, indicates that far greater resources will be available in the future to overcome the problems arising from its historical background, and to maintain it as an invaluable tool for the librarian.

BIBLIOGRAPHY

1 Bradford, S C: *Documentation*. Second edition edited by J H Shera. Crosby Lockwood, 1953.

2 Dezimalklassifikation DK-Handausgabe: *Internationale mittlere ausgabe der Universellen Dezimalklassifikation* (FID 396). Band 1, Systematische Tafeln. Deutscher Normenauschuss (DNA) 1967.

3 For an indication of the wide range of editions available, and the various associated publications, *see* 'Keep up to date with your UDC'. FID *News bulletin, 17* (12) December 1967, 137-138.

4 Kyle, B: 'The Universal Decimal Classification: a study of the present position and future developments with particular reference to those schedules which deal with the humanities, arts and social sciences'. UNESCO *Bulletin, 15* (2) 1961, 53-69.

Vickery, B C: 'The UDC and technical information indexing'. UNESCO *Bulletin, 15* (3) 1961, 126-138, 147.

5 See the articles by G A Lloyd (science and technology) and R Dubuc (Human sciences) in *Revue internationale de la documentation, 30* (4) 1963, 131-140.

6 Perreault, J: *Introduction to the UDC*. Bingley, 1969. Not everybody found Perreault's programmed text to their liking and an alternative is available.

Wellisch, H: *The Universal Decimal Classification: a programmed instruction course*. University of Maryland, School of Library and Information Services, 1970.

7 Freeman, R R: 'Computers and classification systems'. *Journal of documentation, 20* (3) 1964, 137-145.

Freeman, R R: 'The management of a classification scheme: modern approaches exemplified by the UDC project of the American

Institute of Physics'. *Journal of documentation, 23* (4) December, 1967, 304-320. For another similar piece of research see

Rigby, M: 'Experiments in mechanised control of meterological and geoastrophysical literature and the UDC schedules in those fields'. *Revue internationale de la documentation, 31* (3) 1964, 103-106.

8 A useful account of the scheme is to be found in Mills, J: *The Universal Decimal Classification*. Rutgers, the State University School of Library Science, 1964. 132 pp. (Rutgers series on systems for the intellectual organisation of information, edited by Susan Artandi. Vol 1.)

CHAPTER 14

The bibliographic classification

Henry Evelyn Bliss devoted his life's work to the study of classification, and BC is the results of his efforts, tested over a number of years in the library of the College of the City of New York, where he was librarian. In addition to a number of articles in periodicals, he published two major works on classification: *The organisation of knowledge and the system of the sciences*, 1929, and *The organisation of knowledge in libraries*, second edition 1939. Yet despite his great erudition and powerful writings, his scheme has had little success in establishing itself as a major competitor to such schemes as DC, UDC and LC, which Bliss himself held in some contempt; in the fifteen years since it was finally published, BC has been adopted by about eighty libraries, some of which have since changed to other schemes, and in many ways it is no longer adequate for today's literature.

Bliss considered that the most important part of a classification scheme was its order of basic classes, and BC demonstrates this emphasis very clearly. The three major principles on which Bliss based his order of classes: collocation of related subjects, subordination of special to general, and gradation by speciality, together forming the scientific and educational consensus: have already been discussed in part 1. While in theory these ideas are sound, and are in accordance with the philosophical systems of such writers as Comte, in practice their application is not so simple, and in BC sometimes leads to unsatisfactory results, for example the separation of science (including some technology) from useful arts (the rest of technology) by the whole of the social sciences.

Although he recognized the need for some forms of synthesis (composite specification), Bliss was hostile to the idea of complete analysis and synthesis put forward by Ranganathan; his scheme may thus be regarded as the last of the great enumerative classifications, despite its provision of systematic schedules.

It seems unlikely in the light of today's needs that an enumerative scheme can hope to succeed, be it never so good, but BC has been hampered still further by its past lack of a powerful central organization. However, in 1967 the British committee for the Bliss classification, a group of librarians who had adopted BC in their libraries, was reconstituted as the Bliss Classification Association, and took over responsibility for the future development of the scheme. The positive attitude of this association under its chairman, Jack Mills, has led to a considerable change in the outlook for BC, though it is perhaps too early as yet to be too optimistic.

HISTORY

The scheme was first tried in outline before 1908, and first published in this form in *Library journal* in 1910. In 1935, in *A system of bibliographic classification*, Bliss published the scheme in much more detail; the reception of this venture led him to begin publication of the full schedules, which took him the rest of his life. Volume I, containing the common facets and classes A to G, appeared in 1940, volume II containing classes H to K, in 1946; these two volumes were revised and published in one in a second edition, 1951. Volume III, containing the remainder of the schedules (classes L to Z), appeared in 1953, as did the index, volume IV. Bliss died not long afterwards, leaving the scheme as his memorial.

THE SCHEME

Volume I-II begins with a long (188 page) introduction, falling, in effect, into two parts; the first is a general introduction to problems of bibliographic classification, including such matters as ' the dictionary catalogue versus the classified ', while in the second Bliss discusses the problems arising in the Natural sciences, which form the area covered by this volume. (NB The introduction is divided in the contents list into two parts, corresponding to the separate volumes rather than the theory/practice separation given here.) These discussions are valuable contributions to classification thought, and may be read with profit by any potential classifier, not merely those intending to use BC. The schedules section begins with two synopses, one concise, the other general; in these, Bliss sets out as a two dimensional matrix the ' order of sciences and studies '. It is the conversion of this synopsis into linear order that gives Bliss his order of classes, which is the next table; this is followed by tables of systematic and auxiliary schedules, alternatives, and literal mnemonics.

The systematic schedules are an important feature of the scheme. Bliss recognized that composite specification was necessary, and that there were two kinds; the first is the provision of common facets which may be applied anywhere, the second is the provision of facets appropriate to particular subjects. Schedule 1 includes bibliographical forms, some common subjects, *eg* Biography and History (separated here from period subdivisions, as in UDC), and one division for ' antiquated or superseded books '. Schedule 2 is for place division; there are two versions, one condensed, the other detailed. Schedule 3 is for division by language or nationality, while schedule 4 is for division by period. Other schedules numbered 4a, 4b and 4c, are found in the History schedules; 4a is for division of any country, 4b for division of any state, county or smaller unit, and 4c for division of wars, but there does not seem to be any good reason for not allocating them a separate set of numbers as they bear little or no resemblance to the common facet. The other systematic schedules, 38 in number, relate to particular classes or persons, *eg* 13 for subclassification under any disease or disorder, 7 for special subjects relative to any personage. However, despite this provision Bliss found it necessary to enumerate many composite subjects which could have been adequately designated by synthesis, and in some cases allocated notation which was not in accordance with the systematic schedule. For example, we find in Religion P a systematic schedule, 16, ' for specification under any religion, sect, church or religious community ' in which c is used to indicate Founder; but Buddha and Mohammed are enumerated, as PJC and PKC respectively, while Christ is also enumerated, but at PNB. This kind of redundancy is found in nearly every case where a systematic schedule is given; Bliss does not seem to have been convinced of the efficacy of his own devices.

Alternatives are of two kinds, alternative locations and alternative treatments. Though Bliss laid such stress on the educational and scientific consensus, on the grounds that it provided a universally acceptable order, he realized that for some situations it would be more helpful to give some other arrangement. For example, aviation and aeronautics can be treated as branches of science in Physics, or as branches of useful arts in Engineering and shipbuilding; international law may be placed in Law or in Political science following international relations; Religion in P and Sociology in K may be interchanged. Within a given class, it may be necessary to suit the arrangement to the users, and Bliss gives a number of alternative treatments; for example, biography of individuals may be scattered by subject, or gathered in one place; law may be similarly treated; the fine arts may be treated in a variety of ways; literature may be arranged in any one of four modes. This flexibility is valuable, though as usual once a decision has been made as to which method is to be adopted, the others must be deleted from the scheme; this is not as simple as it sounds, for in literature, for example, the different modes are largely enumerated as well, and it is not just a question of making a decision on synthesis. In some cases, for example the systematic schedule 1, there are so many possibilities that the classifier may feel that he has the task of constructing the scheme from scratch!

Following systematic schedules 1 to 4 we find the anterior numeral classes; these correspond to some extent with the common subdivisions in schedule 1, *eg* 6 is Periodicals in both. The intention is to provide for those books which for some reason or other are not primarily classified by subject, *eg* reading room collections, segregated books and historic books. Many classification schemes do not allocate any of their notation for this purpose, and using DC, for example, it is necessary to introduce some symbol to indicate that a book is in the stack rather than in the main sequence.

The schedules themselves are variable, both in their validity and in the amount of detail given. The biological sciences have been found acceptable, though they do not include any of the recent startling developments in those fields, but the librarian of a College of Art[1] found it necessary practically to rewrite the schedules to produce an arrangement acceptable to his readers. In physical science and technology, some of the schedules have an old-fashioned air; under illumination, we find incandescent mantles—a term long since disused—but we will look in vain for any trace of nuclear engineering (though atomic bombs find a place). Radio communication has a halfpage schedule (including a mention of television, which existed as a public service[2] some years before the publication of the first edition of these schedules), but when we find that this includes geiger counters as radio receiving apparatus, we may begin to lose confidence.

Classes M to O cover both history and geography of the various nations; there is not the separation that we find in DC between these two aspects of a country. The social sciences in general are probably the best worked out in the scheme, though the schedules for language and literature are also quite detailed. Bibliography and Library science reflect the changes that have taken place in recent years; almost as an afterthought we find a mention of mechanical devices for sorting and resorting index cards.

There are some cross-references, *eg* under Libraries—relations to the public—special services, we find a note: see also Adult education. Some scope notes are given, *eg* under Documentation we find: for the definition of documentation and discussion of the distinction between documentation and bibliography see the introduction . . ., while in some cases extended headings serve this purpose, *eg* under Industrial insurance we find: Casualty, accidents, health, illness, death; compensation; pensions; social security. Instructions for the use of the systematic schedules are given with each of these, but in addition special instructions appear at some headings, *eg* at United States—history—Civil war, we find: Schedule 4c is adaptable in part, but the numeral subdivisions should not repeat those for the period . . .

NOTATION

Bliss had strong views on notation, and criticized schemes such as UDC and CC for the complexity of theirs. He believed that brevity was an important quality, and set out to allocate his notation in such a way that most items would not need more than three digits. For the main schedules he chose capital letters, giving him a base of 26; to this he added the numbers 1 to 9 for the anterior numeral classes. Numerals are also used for the common subdivisions of schedule 1, while place subdivisions are shown by lower case letters. Thus although the main enumeration uses a pure letter notation, if synthesis is used the notation becomes rather mixed; furthermore, Bliss uses the comma , as an indicator to introduce the language and period divisions, both of which use capital letters, and mentions the possibility of using the hyphen - to show phase relationships (though only in a footnote). Some of the examples of composite notation provided are far from simple, *eg* TSQ,Bbsvu; JTNbd,o6,L; admittedly, Bliss seems to have chosen some peculiar topics to demonstrate notational synthesis, but this kind of symbol can arise if the systematic schedules are used in almost any class.

Bliss does not seem to have appreciated some of the problems arising from synthesis. As we have just seen, the comma is used to introduce both language and period divisions, both of which have the same notation and are thus indistinguishable. As an afterthought, Bliss does suggest using 4 from schedule 1 to introduce the language

260

divisions, and 3 to introduce period divisions, but this does not give a very satisfactory order.

The notation is not always expressive, and Bliss makes good use of this to achieve short notation for topics with considerable literary warrant, *eg* in the Place facet:

d   Europe, Eurasia, Eastern hemisphere
dw   western Europe
e   British Isles

and another example:

AK   Science in general
AZ   Physical science in general
AZD   Physics and Chemistry
B   Physics
C   Chemistry

However, we sometimes find examples where Bliss has allowed his wish for short notation for an important subject to outweigh considerations of correct order:

YE   Elizabethan, Jacobean and Caroline periods of English literature
YEN   Drama—Shakespeare's contemporaries
YEW   Caroline period
YF   Shakespeare

Here, in order to obtain a two letter base notation for the subject likely to have most literature, Shakespeare, Bliss has distorted the order. General works on the history of the Caroline period (1625-1649) will be separated from individual authors of the period, who will be found in YEI (Poets), YEP (Dramatists); between Shakespeare and his contemporaries there is a great gulf fixed; and altogether the schedule does not give any sort of logical order.

Though Bliss stressed that literal mnemonics are not important, he thought them significant enough to justify tabulation in the preliminary pages. Examples given above include dw for western Europe, YE Elizabethan literature; in the preliminary table we find NA North America, NB British America. These mnemonics are not so helpful as the consistent use of the same piece of notation which is found in UDC and to a lesser extent in DC.

Some phase relationships are enumerated; for others, Bliss recommends the use of Y (special subjects) or the comma. The first of these transfers these relationships to a place after the subject subdivisions instead of before them, while the second leads to even more confusion.

The use of the hyphen, suggested in the introduction as a possible substitute for the comma, is recommended by Mills to avoid at least some of the problems.[3]

Bliss occasionally used other symbols such as &, *eg* MN& Finland; he also uses lower case letters for some subdivisions in Chemistry, *eg* cIg Hydrogen peroxide. We also find the apostrophe in places, *eg* v' Africa, R'5 1905. Altogether, the notation can be quite complex; more serious is the fact that no guidance is given on the filing order of all these different symbols. For example, cIg is evidently (from the schedule) meant to file immediately after CIG and before CIH, but if the lower case letter denoted the place subdivision, as it usually does, this would not be true; for example, HYe Dentistry in England files before HYA, not between HYE and HYF. We are not told where HYe files in relation to HY,E Dentistry in the sixteenth century. In the article referred to already, Mills has suggested the filing order:

$1/9; a/z; - ; , ; A/z$

with the use of 3 and 4 to distinguish time and language.

To sum up, the notation of BC is good, provided that only the basic symbols shown for enumerated subjects are used (though even here one has to enter the proviso that brevity is often simply a reflection of lack of detail). However, when any of the synthetic devices are used, the notation tends to become less satisfactory and the mixture of different kinds of notation is unhelpful. It is also clear that the allocation was poor to begin with; far too much of the base is given to History, far too little to Science and Technology. If the scheme is developed, before very long notation in the latter areas will certainly exceed Bliss's economic limit of three to four digits by a considerable margin.

OUTLINE OF THE SCHEME

1	Reading-room collections
2	Alternative for z (NB similarity of symbol)
3	Select or special collection, or segregated books
4	Departmental or special collections
5	Documents or archives of governments, institutions, etc
6	Periodicals
7	Miscellanea
8	Collection of local, historic or institutional interest
9	Antiquated books, or historic collection

A	Philosophy and general science
AK	Natural science in general
AM/AY	Mathematics
AZ	Physical sciences in general
B	Physics (including some technologies)
C	Chemistry (including chemical technology)
D	Astronomy
DG	Geology
DQ	Geography
DU	Natural history
E	Biology
F	Botany
G	Zoology
H/HL	Anthropology (including human body, hygiene, physical education)
HM/HZ	Medicine
I	Psychology
J	Education
K	Sociology, Social science
L	Historiology, Ancillary studies, General history, Ancient history (including L9 Collective biography)
LY	Modern history (general)
M/O	Modern history (particular places) (including travel, etc)
P	Religion
Q	Social welfare, Amelioration, Women, Socialism and Internationalism
R	Political science
S	Jurisprudence and law
T	Economics
U	Arts in general, and useful and industrial arts
V	Aesthetic arts
W	General and comparative philology, Linguistics, and Languages not Indo-European
X	Indo-European languages and literatures, except English
YA	English language
YB/YN	History of English literature
YO/YT	English literature, collections
YU/YY	Literature in General and Comparative literature
Z	Bibliology, Bibliography, Documentation, and Libraries.

263

Bliss did not prepare all the schedules himself. In some cases he acknowledges assistance, for example in U, 'compiled with the assistance of J Albani' and T, revised by F W Weiler and J Mills; while in others it appears to have been Bliss who did the revising, for example P, where the schedule is based on one submitted to Bliss by J Ormerod.

Y, which is devoted by Bliss to English literature, may be used in other countries for the 'home' literature by changing round the basic notation and redeveloping the schedule. This would still leave Literature in general at the end of the sequence, of course. Q Social welfare is separated by the whole of History and Religion from Sociology in K; hardly the collocation of related subjects, though Bliss does permit us to interchange K and P to bring the two together.

INDEX

Some 45,000 entries appear in the index to BC; Bliss's own estimate was that only 5,000 of these represented synonyms, and that there were therefore some 40,000 topics enumerated in the schedules. However, we have seen from DC that thorough indexing can give as many as three times the number of index entries as topics enumerated. The index to BC must also be criticized on the grounds that it is not a 'correct' relative index; in many entries it repeats, in alphabetical order, some of the subdivisions found in the systematic arrangement, a practice which is both wasteful and misleading. For example, under the term Chemistry we find first a useful reference to see terms such as Agriculture for Agricultural Chemistry; useful, because we do not find an index entry for Chemistry, Agricultural. We then have an entry for Chemistry itself, leading us to C-CA in the schedules, and immediately followed by a reference, see also Biochemistry, which simply repeats the reference already given. We then have some ninety entries, of which only one does not direct us to a subdivision of C; we find an entry Chemistry—calculations in—Electrochemistry, but we do not find a similar entry Chemistry—Experiments in—Electrochemistry, though the two are side by side in the schedule, and there is an index entry for Chemistry—Experiments.

There are some odd omissions; for example, we search in vain for Sermons, but have to turn instead to Preachers, Preaching, which leads us to PXP, where we find sermons. There are also some errors, as for example the entry *Pearl, The,* Middle English poem, XBV, which should be YBV (XBV is Czech literature). These would almost certainly have been corrected for a second edition. However, to be an adequate tool the index would probably have to be completely revised and recast; at present it is too erratic to be reliable.

ORGANIZATION
As has already been indicated, BC was very much the work of one man, and this has had a number of effects. The first of these is the fact that Bliss himself typed out the whole of the schedules, which are reproduced from his typescript. The layout and typography leave a lot to be desired, particularly if it is compared with a scheme such as DC; Bliss had a very limited range of type faces and sizes available to him, and on some pages we find a slightly larger than usual type used for main headings, normal size for intermediate and slightly smaller than normal for subordinate divisions, together with italic for scope notes and reverse italic for cross-references. Some use is made of indentation to show subordination, but this too is limited. The overall effect is unpleasant to look at and difficult to use; this is accentuated by the fact that the schedules are not paginated (a convenient means of showing serial order which DC ignored till its fifteenth edition!), and the systematic schedules are only located by their relative place in the schedules, *eg* schedule 4a follows MC in volume III. The practising classifier is almost obliged to thumb index the volumes to make their use less time-consuming.

The large number of alternatives has also to be considered. Though these give the scheme a good deal of flexibility, they are usually set out rather clumsily from the point of view of the classifier wishing to select one, and only one, method, and the schedules often need considerable annotation to eliminate all the unwanted possibilities; such annotation, added to the already confusing typography, makes the scheme unwieldy to use. While none of these points affects the validity of the systematic arrangement, it must be remembered that classification schemes have to be used, and poor presentation and layout can actively hinder this.

The scheme was published by the H W Wilson Company, as were Bliss's other books, and they continued for some years to publish the Bliss Classification Bulletin as a service to the profession. However, at the end of 1966 they decided to withdraw and to hand over the rights to the British committee, which was then reconstituted as the official supporting organization. Enough funds were gathered together to make

it possible to appoint a research assistant at the North-Western Polytechnic School of Librarianship to revise the scheme under the editorial direction of Mills, and work began in the middle of 1969. Before
the change, some progress had already been made. We have already
noted Mills's rationalization of filing order in BC; in September 1964[4],
he proposed a method of keeping at least some of the schedules up to
date, which was to use the *BNB supplementary schedules* wherever
appropriate, by simply changing the lowercase notation to uppercase.
This has provided several new schedules for the revised edition, and
substantial progress has been made in working out others along the
same lines.[5]

The aim is to provide approximately the same degree of detail as is
found in DC or LC, but not as much as the very full expansions in UDC.
Facet analysis is used consistently in every class, both within the
enumeration and also in the systematic schedules; synthesis will be
used throughout, with the enumeration of composite subjects kept to
the minimum. The multitude of alternatives provided by Bliss will be
simplified and removed from the main schedules, which will show
only the editor's preference; they will however still be available for
anyone wishing to use them. Phase relations will be included, and the
common facets will be tidied up, both of these on the basis of the
BNB's expansions.

The anterior numeral classes have been little used in the past,
which has given scope for an ingenious idea. This is to redevelop
these classes along the lines of the CRG and PRECIS analysis into
entities and attributes. The objective is to provide a definite place for
comprehensive works on entities, which are normally scattered by
discipline, and attributes, which are normally overlooked altogether.

The revised edition is expected to be published in the near future,
with early 1973 as a possibility. It is expected to fill two large volumes,
and in order to keep down costs will be prepared on electric type-
writers for printing by offset lithography. The *Bulletin* will continue to
serve as a medium for updating, though it is hoped that the consistent
application of facet analysis will make this task easier in the future.

ABRIDGED EDITION

Because of its close adherence to the educational and scientific consensus, BC has found most favour with educational establishment
libraries, and for some years an edition for schools was mooted. This
project finally came to fruition in 1967, when the School Library

Association published the *Abridged Bliss classification*. Schools are less likely to be affected by the need for revision in science and technology, and more likely to find the overall order suited to their needs, than are most other institutions, and this edition could well be a success, though here again the need for revision will eventually arise.

THE FUTURE

At one time it was difficult to see any future for BC at all, but the situation has been radically changed by the efforts of the Bliss Classification Association, whose proclaimed objective is to produce a classification scheme superior to any other available today. The scheme is at present used by a rather limited number of libraries, and has never been as successful as, say, LC in winning converts from DC. With the coming of MARC, DC and LC have a further edge over other schemes, and though there is no reason why BC class numbers should not form part of the MARC record, this does imply a continuing effort to generate them. An interesting possibility that is being explored is the use of the PRECIS statement as a basis for classification by BC, or indeed any scheme which is consistent throughout its schedules; this is still at the research stage, but it might prove to be the solution to this particular problem.

The ideas which Bliss developed on the theory of systematic arrangement, notation, and other aspects of classification have influenced every writer since; we are told, for example, that Ranganathan read both of the works on the *Organisation of knowledge* in a single sitting, and was inspired to write his own *Prolegomena* as a result. It would be a pity if the scheme were to join such others as Cutter's *Expansive classification* in the limbo of the unsuccessful; a monument to its author's scholarship, but no longer a practical tool. This seems less likely than before but only the future can reveal whether the efforts now being made will result in success.

BIBLIOGRAPHY

1 Many of the comments on BC in this chapter reflect the views of the staff of the Library of Loughborough Colleges of Art and Further Education, where the scheme has been in use for some fifteen years.

2 The first public TV service was provided by the British Broadcasting Corporation in 1936; by the time the second edition appeared in 1951, television and its equipment were well established, but this is not reflected in the schedules.

3 Mills, J: ' Number building and filing order in BC.' *Bliss classification bulletin, II* (1) March, 1957.

4 *Bliss classification bulletin, III* (1) September, 1964.

5 The *Bulletin* contains information about the revision in general in the 1969 and 1970 issues, the latter including also a detailed discussion of the problems that have been resolved in the revision of the schedules for Class Q, Social welfare.

CHAPTER 15

The colon classification

Shiyali Ramamrita Ranganathan, the 'onlie begetter' of CC, began his academic career as a mathematician, until in 1924 he was appointed Librarian of the University of Madras. One of the conditions of his appointment was that he should spend some time in England studying library science, and it was while attending a series of lectures by W C Berwick Sayers[1] on classification at the University College School of Librarianship that he began to formulate his own ideas on the subject, spurred by his dissatisfaction with DC and UDC.

Undeterred by the warnings of Sayers as to the task he was setting himself, Ranganathan determined to compile his own classification scheme; the basic essentials were in fact worked out during his passage home to India. After some years of experimentation in the Madras university library, he published the first edition in 1933; subsequent editions appeared in 1939, 1950, 1952, 1957 and 1960. The latest edition, the sixth, was reprinted in 1963 with some important amendments, and the seventh is in preparation. This is a rate of publication which has only been equalled by DC, but, unlike Dewey, Ranganathan has never accepted the idea of integrity of numbers, and has in fact from time to time introduced major changes. Few libraries have adopted the scheme (a not unexpected result of its continual state of flux), yet it has been one of the most influential classifications ever published, and the ideas incorporated in it have affected the whole of classification theory. As we have seen, Dewey included some synthetic elements in his scheme, but only in certain places; Ranganathan developed the theory of facet analysis, demonstrating that analysis and synthesis apply in every basic class and could be systematized. He also developed his own terminology in a correct scientific fashion; much of this is now widely used (for example in the present work), though some of it has excited the contempt of unsympathetic critics unwilling to accept the often flowery metaphors of the East.

As stated above, there have from time to time been major changes in the scheme. One such change was the decision after the fifth edition to develop two parallel editions, the basic classification (Stage 1) and the depth classification of microthought (Stage 2); in effect, an abridged and a full edition comparable with UDC. A further similarity to UDC lies in the fact that the abridged edition is published as a whole, whereas the full schedules (which are still being developed) are to be published in parts; some have appeared in *Annals of library science, Revue internationale de la documentation,* and *Library science with a slant to documentation,* while another important vehicle is the *Proceedings of the DRTC Annual Seminars.* Because of these changes, the following remarks are to be understood as applying only to the 1963 reprint of the sixth edition, unless otherwise stated.

In the first edition we find each basic class analysed into its facets, but with only one notational device for synthesis, the colon; in the beginning, the use of this symbol was so much a part of the scheme that it gave it its name, just as Dewey's notation did to his scheme. However, we have seen the problems that may arise in notational synthesis if the devices used are inadequate, and his struggles with these problems led Ranganathan to develop one of his most important theories: the citation order of decreasing concreteness, PMEST. This new idea was first introduced in the fourth edition, and led to a complete reconstruction of the scheme.

PMEST

In the first three editions Ranganathan had used the kind of *ad hoc* analysis described in the earlier chapters of this work, but in this, as in all aspects of library science, he was continually seeking the underlying principles which had led him to select one method rather than another. By studying carefully the kind of facet to be found in different basic classes, he was able to establish that despite their apparent surface differences they could be accommodated in five large groups. Time and place, as we have seen, can apply to any topic: they are common facets, but important nevertheless, and Ranganathan included them as Time [T] and Space [S] in his *fundamental categories.* He isolated the concept of Energy [E] as being the common factor appearing in such apparently disparate topics as Exports in Economics, Curriculum in Education, Grammar in Linguistics, and Physiology in Biology. Matter [M] is straightforward; we find such examples as Gold as a material of Money (Economics), various instruments in Music, Ivory in Painting, and Periodicals in Library Science; however, though we have earlier referred to Metals in Metallurgy as the materials facet, they do not appear as [M] in CC but rather as the final, somewhat elusive, category of Personality. Personality [P] is hard to define, but easier to understand; it corresponds to what we have called the primary facet, and usually includes Things, Kinds of things or Kinds of action. We find as examples Persons in Sociology and Psychology, Christianity in Religion, Electronics in Engineering, and Periodicals in Bibliography. The last of these examples indicates that the same isolate (in this case Periodicals) does not always fall into the same fundamental category; we find other examples of this, *eg* in Fine arts, where Personality is a combination of Space and Time.

The same fundamental category may occur more than once in the same basic class; it would in fact restrict us to not more than three major facets if this were not the case. For example, in an Energy facet we normally list kinds of operation or problem; this listing is thus a combined Energy plus Personality (kinds of thing) facet, denoted by Ranganathan [E] [2P]. This second *round* of Personality may itself be followed by another round of [M] and [E]; for example, in Medicine we find the first round of [P] is the organs of the body; there is no [M], the first round of [E] including problems such as Physiology and Disease; for Disease there is a second round of [P], kinds of disease; again no [M] in the second round, but [E] is represented by Treatment, with a third round of [P] to indicate kinds of treatment; for Injections, we may have a manifestation of [M] to show the substance injected. The citation order (facet formula in CC) is thus [P]:[E] [2P]:[2E] [3P] ; [3M].

There may be more than one occurrence of a fundamental category, particularly [P], within the same round; these are then denoted by the term *levels*. We have already seen that the Personality facet in Fine arts is a combination of [S] and [T], these two form the first two levels, but there are in addition others; *eg* in Architecture we find the third level [P3] is Kinds of building, and the fourth level [P4] is Parts of buildings. In Literature there are four facets: Language, Literary form, Author and Work; these are respectively first, second, third and fourth level [P]. (Authors are arranged chronologically; the arrangement is in fact the same as in DC.)

There are now no *ad hoc* facets in CC; every basic class is given a facet formula in terms of [P] [M] and [E]. ([S] and [T] are not normally quoted because they may be used anywhere that they apply.) Analysis into Ranganathan's fundamental categories is often useful in establishing the correct citation order for subjects in other schemes, but we must be cautious about accepting them uncritically. For example, as we have seen, Periodicals fall into the Matter facet in Library science, but are in the Personality facet in Bibliography; when we ask why they are [P] in the second case, the answer seems to be that in Bibliography, materials are the primary facet, and the primary facet is Personality. If we ask why all the four facets of Literature are Personality (it could be argued that Literary form is Energy), the answer seems to be that that is the way Ranganathan decided. In fact, PMEST does not solve the problems of citation order; it simply removes them to a different stage of the process of analysis, though it does give us a framework which may help in guiding our decisions. However, the fact that it is possible to disagree with the use of PMEST does *not* mean that the citation orders found in CC are incorrect; in the vast majority of cases they are both clear and helpful, and this is the only scheme in which we find this situation. One disadvantage is the lack of flexibility; we cannot select a facet order which suits our particular group of users if this conflicts with PMEST. However, to get over this rigidity Ranganathan has introduced the idea of ' Special Collection ', in which the user can adapt the schedules to his own needs.

SELF PERPETUATING CLASSIFICATION

One of the basic ideas behind CC is that of 'autonomy for the classifier '. We have seen that in an enumerative scheme we have to wait for the decision of the compiler before we know where to classify a composite subject that is not already listed, and in an analytico-synthetic scheme we may find ourselves in the same position if the foci we require are missing—though we can cater for composite subjects if the individual foci are enumerated. Ranganathan has tried to go one stage further: to give the individual classifier the means to construct class numbers for new foci which will be in accordance with those that the central organization will allot, by means of a set of devices or rules of universal applicability. In this way, the need for a strong central organization is reduced, though it still exists. In CC there are a number of such devices, which may apply to the formation of modified basic classes or to the enumeration of new isolates.

SYSTEMS AND SPECIALS

An existing basic class may be modified in two ways. The first of these is the situation when there is more than one mode of approach to the whole basic class; for example, in Physics, relativity theory and quantum theory have led to a new approach to the whole of the subject. These new approaches are called *Systems;* the favoured system is the one into which the majority of the literature falls—in this example, classical physics—while the other systems have to be catered for separately. The second way in which a basic class may be modified occurs when part of it can be considered in a special context; for example, in Medicine, Space medicine is a *Special* of this kind.

DEVICES FOR THE ENUMERATION OF NEW FOCI

Within a basic class we may from time to time have to make provision for new foci, and CC gives five ways in which this may be done. The first of these is the Chronological device; we specify a new focus by means of its date of origin. CC uses this device in Literature, where authors are specified by their date of birth (though Ranganathan has a rather tetchy note about the difficulty of establishing this in some cases). This device is often used to specify systems also. The second is the Geographical device, which simply means the use of the place facet other than in its normal way. We have already seen the use of a combination of Time and Space, *ie* (CD) and (GD), to form the first two levels of [P] in the Fine arts.

The third is the Subject device. This is the use of a schedule from elsewhere in the overall order, *eg* in Education, where any subject may form part of the curriculum; in DC, this is called ' divide like ', and is used in similar circumstances, though CC carries it rather further. The fifth is Alphabetical device, which is simply the use of names as a method of arrangement; this is not recommended unless no other device gives a more helpful order.

The fourth is rather more interesting, though, as with PMEST, we may view it with caution. Ranganathan's study of the schedules that he drew up in the early editions led him to believe that he had unconsciously followed certain principles in allocating the notation; these principles, extracted from practice, form the Mnemonic device, or, to use the term coined by Palmer and Wells[2], ' seminal mnemonics '. For example, the digit 1 is used for unity, one dimension, solid state, the first, etc; 2 is used for two dimensions, second, constitution, etc. So far, the device does not seem to stretch probability too far; but when we come to 5, which is intended to represent ' instability ', we may begin to wonder when we find energy, water, emotion, controlled plan, women, sex, crime, all lumped together. The real objection to seminal mnemonics appears to be that this is a case of notation dictating order, but Ranganathan himself sounds a note of caution when he warns that, because the use of this device requires an uncommon degree of 'spiritual insight', any notation suggested by it should be discussed widely before being finalized.

A sixth device, the Superimposition device is used to specify composite topics arising from the combination of foci which fall into the same facet. For example, in the Libraries (*ie* [P]) facet of Library science, we can consider libraries from several points of view, giving us several subfacets or *arrays* within the same facet; we may need to combine foci from these subfacets, and the superimposition device permits us to do this. Note that if we treat these subfacets as facets in their own right we shall have to devise a notation that will permit us to combine them anyway; the need for the superimposition device arises from the rationalization of *ad hoc* facets into the PMEST frame work.

The sixth edition of CC consists of three parts: part 1, the rules; part 2, the schedules of classification; part 3, schedules of classics and sacred books with special names. In previous editions, part 3 consisted of some 4,000 examples of CC class numbers, but it is now felt that there are enough textbooks and bibliographies demonstrating the use of the scheme for these to be superfluous.

Parts 1 and 2 have to be considered together, as it is not possible to use the schedules without the rules. A more satisfactory arrangement would in fact be to merge the two parts so that the rules for a particular class were found with the schedules to which they apply. As an example, let us consider Literature, Class O. The complete schedule for this is as follows:

CHAPTER O

LITERATURE

O [P], [P2] [P3], [P4]

Foci in[P]

as the Language divisions in Chapter 5

Foci in [P2]

1	Poetry
2	Drama
3	Fiction, including short stories
4	Letters (literature written in the form of letters)

5	Oration
6	Other forms of prose
7	Campu

Foci in [P3]

| 1 | To be got by (CD) |
| 2 | For authors born later than 1800, if year of birth cannot be found out at all, (CD) to be worked only to one digit. Thereafter, (AD) may be used. |

Foci in [P4]

See Rules in Chapter O of Part 1.

On the other hand, we find that the rules for this basic class occupy some six pages of close type in part 1. In contrast, there are rather more than five pages of schedules for Engineering, but only one page of rules. Reference from one part to the other is facilitated by the use of parallel chapter numbering (each chapter of the rules has the same notation as the class to which it refers), but even so the arrangement is not convenient.

Ranganathan distinguishes between the class number, denoting the subject of a work, and the book number, which identifies a particular document once the subject has been determined; the two together form the call number, which shows the exact place on the shelves or in the catalogue that the item is to be found. Book number includes Language, Form of exposition (not specified for prose), Year, Accession number, Copy number, etc, *ie* those factors which do not affect the subject matter. The first four chapters of the rules cover the construction of the call number, including the Collection number, *eg* reference, junior, etc. Chapter 05 is a useful exposition of the essentials of analytico-synthetic classification theory as it appears in CC; this is followed by various minor sections, *eg* a list of contractions.

Chapter 1 of both rules and schedules is concerned with Main classes, including the partially comprehensive groups. In the 1960 printing several greek letters are used, but these have been dropped from the 1963 reprint with the exception of Mysticism Δ. The problems created by the use of greek letters have been discussed, and it is perhaps surprising that Ranganathan introduced them at all. The table of main classes is followed by the common facets, which are of two kinds, anteriorizing and posteriorizing. Anteriorizing common isolates include the bibliographical form divisions, and are so named because they precede the subject on its own; thus a Dictionary of physics ck files before a general work on Physics c. Posteriorizing common isolates include many of the common subject subdivisions, and file after the subject number; thus a learned society in the field of physics c,g files after c.

OUTLINE OF THE SCHEME

z	Generalia
I	Universe of knowledge★
2	Library Science
3	Book Science†
4	Journalism†
A	Natural sciences★
AZ	Mathematical sciences★
B	Mathematics (including Astronomy)
BZ	Physical sciences★
C	Physics
D	Engineering
E	Chemistry
F	Technology (*ie* Chemical technology)
G	Biology
H	Geology
HX	Mining (misprinted as HZ in the schedules)
I	Botany
J	Agriculture
K	Zoology
KX	Animal husbandry (misprinted as KZ in the schedules)
L	Medicine
LX	Pharmacognosy (misprinted as KZ in the schedules)
M	Useful Arts
Δ	Spiritual experience and Mysticism
MZ	Humanities and Social Sciences★
MZA	Humanities★
N	Fine Arts
NZ	Literature and Language★
O	Literature
P	Linguistics
Q	Religion
R	Philosophy
S	Psychology
Σ	Social Sciences★

276

T	Education
U	Geography
V	History
W	Political Science
X	Economics
Y	Sociology
YX	Social Work†
Z	Law

There are certain peculiarities about the outline which are worth noting. The Generalia class consists of the common isolates (shown by lowercase letters) applied to the whole of knowledge, and though it is shown by z in the outline, in fact the z is dropped in use, so that the generalia class is shown by the whole lowercase alphabet used for common isolates. z itself is used for generalia materials on a specific area, *eg* z7 Americana; or a specific person not assigned to a particular subject, *eg* zG Ghandiana.

There are no schedules for the partially comprehensive main classes (marked ⋆ in the above list); the reason for this is that the main subdivisions are the main classes, *eg* the divisions of A are B to M, and therefore the only pieces of notation to be added are those for the common facets. This was set out explicitly in earlier editions under A, but in the current edition A only appears in the Outline; this is an example of Ranganathan's ' canon of parsimony '—there is no need to repeat something explicitly if it is clearly implicit—but it is somewhat puzzling at first.

There are also no schedules for some of the basic classes (those marked † in the above list); the reason for this would appear to be that the schedules have not as yet been developed. In the 1963 reprint most of the greek letters have been removed and replaced by the use of the ' empty ' digit z to signify partially comprehensive classes.

For each main class, the rules show the facets, what they represent and how the foci are obtained; for example under NR Music we find

Facet	Term	
[P], [P2]	Style	(IN) by
[P3]	Music	(GD) and (CD)
[M]	Instrument	Enumeration
[E], [2P]	Technique	Enumeration
		(To be worked out)

In addition, there are comments on the kinds of classification problem likely to be met, and on the subject where it is thought necessary; in some cases useful reference books are noted, *eg* in Literature. The rules for each class conclude with a set of examples showing how the notation for specific examples is worked out. The parallel chapter in the schedules begins with the facet formula, then enumerates the foci in the various facets as appropriate (cf the outline for Literature previously given). Rules and schedules must be used together; the rules are of no use without the schedules, and the schedules are not usually selfsufficient enough to be used without the rules.

Most of the general schemes have been criticised for their Western bias; it is probably true to say that CC reveals an Eastern bias. While the schedules for such topics as Hindu sacred books are worked out in detail, major classes such as Engineering are not; the lack of detail here is one of the more important factors militating against the widespread adoption of the scheme.

NOTATION

It will have become clear already that the notation of CC is very mixed. The main classes are denoted by capital letters or, in a few cases, arabic numerals. Division within a facet is usually by arabic numerals, but in some cases capitals are introduced to increase the base available; lower case letters are used for the common bibliographical forms and subject divisions, numerals for the place facet and capitals for time. In addition to these symbols denoting classes or the foci within them, there are several connecting symbols (facet indicators): [P] is introduced by a comma, (not needed for first level personality); [M] by the semicolon ;; [E] by the colon :; [S] by a point .; and [T] by an apostrophe. Notation obtained by the use of the subject device is enclosed in curves ( ). The zero o (not to be confused with the capital O) is used to show phase relations, which in CC are well worked out. The filing order of these connecting symbols is the reverse of the citation order PMEST, so that the principle of inversion is followed. Unless this filing order is borne in mind, some confusion may arise, for in the schedules it is the Personality facet which is listed first, though it files last.

The notation of CC has been criticised on the grounds of its length and complexity. Ranganathan has always endeavoured to make his notation an ' artificial language of ordinal numbers ' into which the subject of a document can be completely translated; specificity and synthesis combined are bound to give lengthy notation for complex subjects. However, the schemes with which CC is contrasted frequently avoid long notation by avoiding specificity; for simple subjects CC frequently gives notation which is comparable in length with, or shorter than, such schemes as DC and LC, though it cannot be denied that many class numbers are confusing because of the variety of symbols used.

INDEX

It is not strictly correct to write of the index to CC, for there are in fact four; in addition to the general index there are indexes to the place facet and to the natural groups in Botany I and Zoology K. Like the separation of rules and schedules, this is perhaps a good idea in theory, but not in practice. The general index is of the kind we should expect in an analytico-synthetic scheme; it does not list any composite subjects, but shows the places in the schedules where a particular isolate is to be found, as does any relative index. Until the method is understood, the index entries may well be puzzling, especially to someone accustomed to the straightforward nature of the index entries in, say, DC. For example, if we turn to Fire in the index we find the following:

Fire   E [E], 2131. J, KZ, L, [E], 4 [2P], 91. Y [E], 4351, 831
——   clay H2 [P], 3311
——   damp HZ [E], 41
——   insurance X [P], 8191
——   place NA [P3], 2 to 9 [P4], 94

These somewhat cryptic entries can be deciphered quite easily once the method is learnt, but it would obviously be unwise to attempt to classify from this index without referring to the schedules! The interpretation of the above entries is as follows:

Fire appears in the Energy facet of Chemistry with the notation 2131; this turns out to be part of Physical chemistry, and the correct class number is E: 2131.

It appears as a cause of disease in Agriculture, Animal husbandry and Medicine, where it is found in the second round personality facet following disease; the correct notation is (in Medicine) L: 491, in Agriculture J: 491, in Animal husbandry KZ: 491.

In sociology, fire appears twice in the energy facet; Y: 4351 denotes fire as a cause of destitution, while Y: 831 denotes fire as an item of social equipment, used for cooking, etc.

Fire clay appears in the Personality facet of Petrology as a form of rock; notation, H23311.

Fire damp is a hazard in the Energy facet in Mining; notation, HZ:41.

Fire insurance is a branch of Insurance in Economics; notation, X8191.

Fireplace is a part, appearing in the fourth level of Personality in Architecture, where it may be subordinate to any of the kinds of Building enumerated in the third level, *eg* fireplaces in domestic dwellings NA,3,94 (NB the first comma is necessary because we have not specified either of the first two levels).

The index is set out in this way to emphasize the synthetic qualities of the scheme, but there does not seem to be any very good reason for not casting it in a more conventional form. This would certainly make it easier to use, without any loss of its special qualities.

CLASSICS AND SACRED BOOKS

The third part of CC is a long and detailed list of Indian classics, with a few exceptions such as the *Bible*. There is a separate index, but in any case the Western classifier will have only rare occasion to turn to this section, which does not form an essential part of the scheme as a whole.

ORGANIZATION

CC began as the work of one man, and most of the work on the early editions was carried out by Ranganathan himself. In recent years a band of disciples (the word hardly seems too strong) has grown up in India, and has contributed to the revision and expansion of the schedules. An organization now exists, endowed by Ranganathan, and charged with the maintenance of the scheme now that he himself has retired. Whether this will prove strong enough to perpetuate the scheme indefinitely has still to be seen.

REVISION

New editions of the scheme are published at intervals, but in the past each new edition has differed in some quite important features from its predecessors. In some cases the changes have been discussed in print in advance, for example the change in the facet indicator for Time from a point to an apostrophe, which was first published in *Annals of library science*[3]. Development of the scheme is still grossly inadequate in some sectors.

The scheme itself gives the user rather more help than do most, by including the detailed rules for each class. It has been the subject of one of the Rutgers seminars on systems for the intellectual organization of information[4], and a programmed text exists to help students to gain familiarity with it[5]. Ranganathan has written several textbooks setting out his ideas on classification, notably the *Elements of library classification* and the more advanced *Prolegomena to library classification*; an understanding of these is a considerable help in using the scheme, particularly in respect of some of the terminology[6].

It must however be pointed out that as a practical tool for the working librarian, CC has many defects of production. It is poorly printed; mistakes abound, and while the 1963 reprint corrected some of these, it introduced others of its own. In many cases, revision from one edition to the next has been inadequate; some of the examples are incorrect according to the present schedules, but are found to have been correct at some point in the past. Some topics have disappeared between editions; for example, a search in the schedule of common isolates or the index for Instruments is fruitless, but one may come across a schedule in Electrical engineering which shows that the correct notation is e, and reference back to the second edition confirms this. In the index, Mustard appears between Multiphase and Multiple. It is possible to feel that if a new edition were produced which measured up to the high standards of DC, it would create a rather better impression of the scheme than can be obtained from the present format.

THE SEVENTH EDITION

Work has been in progress over the past ten years at the Documentation Research Training Centre at Bangalore in preparation for the new edition of CC, to be published in 1971. There will again be a number of changes from the previous edition, but Ranganathan expresses in a detailed explanation of these[7] the hope that the revision will enable the scheme to last for a considerable time into the future. Changes are apparent in definitions of terms, in the schedules, in the notation and in the index, and examples are given here, though we have yet to see the complete edition.

The scheme is now said to be a ' freely faceted ' classification, the term facet being defined :

a generic term used to denote any component—be it a basic subject or an isolate—of a compound subject.

A basic subject (single concept) on its own cannot have facets; they are essentially a reflection of the structure of composite subjects. This appears to be a tightening up of the definition rather than a new approach, but some of the examples would appear to be more than this; for example, ' bones ' and ' leg ' are said to be subfacets in the compound isolate facet ' bones of the leg '. Another statement may give rise to some surprise :

A facet formula is in a sense meaningless; it is indeed an anachronism.

However, for the benefit of the weaker brethren the scheme will continue to give facet formulae for the main classes. The objective of the whole exercise seems to be to make it possible to combine concepts quite freely, without any restrictions imposed by a pre-conceived pattern; for depth classification, *ie* the close classification of periodical articles and similar documents, any predetermined rules are likely to prove more of a hindrance than a help.

In the schedules, there are several new ideas as well as some rearrangement. From the forty six main classes of the sixth edition we find no less than one hundred and five : eighty two main classes and twenty three partially comprehensive classes. Among the former we find a new group of ' distilled ' classes, including Cybernetics, Management and Research methodology; among the latter another new group of ' fused ' main classes, arising from the fusion of previously distinct subject areas, for example Chemical engineering and Biophysics. Although these topics were represented in the sixth edition it is only in the seventh that they are recognized as main classes. Another kind of main class for which provision is being made, particularly in the natural sciences, is the ' subject bundle ', for example Space sciences. These may be described perhaps as agglomerations of subjects for which there is literary warrant; indeed, they formed a part of Wyndham Hulme's argument for literary warrant. To some extent they may be regarded as the first signs of a new fused subject in the making, though Ranganathan suggests (as did Wyndham Hulme) that they are the result of the way books are produced rather than intrinsic to subjects.

Another major change has been the recognition of properties as a manifestation of matter rather than energy. In the original PMEST analysis in the fourth edition, (E) was taken to include (correctly) isolates representing actions, but also (incorrectly) any other isolates listed in energy schedules. Sceptics might adduce this as another example of the unreliability of PMEST as a basis of analysis, along with the elusive personality.[8] Be that as it may, in CC7 we find that (M) is divided into two categories, (M-M) Matter-Material and (M-P) Matter-Property, with many concepts previously treated as (E) being transferred to the latter (including incidentally Curriculum, Grammar and Physiology, quoted earlier in this chapter as typical manifestations of (E)!) This rather large stone in the pond casts quite widespread ripples, as not only do many (E) and (E) cum (2P) facets become (M-P), but this means that many (2E) and (2E) cum (3P) facets become (E). The effect of the change is to alter the facet indicator from : to ; for the Property isolates, and to alter the facet formulae for a number of classes, eg Medicine, in which L [P] : [E] [2P] : [2E] [3P] becomes L, [P] ; [M-P] : [E], [2P].

Systems and Specials are now regarded as forming part of compound basic subjects, as are such concepts as Style in Fine Arts, so that the facet formula for, eg, Architecture changes from NA [P], [2P] [3P] , [4P] : [E] to NA, [P] , [2P] ; [M-P], with the primary division of NA not forming part of the facet formula.

In the past, there have been common fundamental category isolates (ie common facets in the terminology we have used earlier) for [S] and [T]; in CC7 there are additional tables for [P], [M-P] and [E]; these correspond to some extent with the BNB table of common subject subdivisions.

In the notational plane, there are some changes in addition to those already mentioned. In previous editions lower case roman letters were used for common subdivisions, with anteriorizing value; in order that they should be generally available, their anteriorizing value has disappeared, and the symbol ↑ is used to denote this instead, so that a Dictionary of physics now becomes c ↑ k. Instead of being introduced by a zero o, phase relations are now shown by the ampersand &, releasing o for its normal purpose in the sequence of arabic numerals. The uppercase letters T to Z are used as empty digits, with Z frequently used for partially comprehensive main classes, thus eliminating greek letters altogether, with the exception of Δ. All levels of [P] are now introduced by the comma, where previously first level personality was taken not to require a facet indicator; in addition, second level personality on its own is introduced by a zero, to ensure that it files in the right place.

TABLE 9: Outline of CC7
Partially comprehensive classes are in italics
Fused main classes are in bold
*New classes are marked with an asterisk**
Relocations are shown by a dagger†

z   *Generalia*
1   Universe of subjects; structure and development
2   Library science
3   Book science
3V   Note-taking*
3X   Note-taking*
4   Journalism
5   Exhibition technique*
6   Museology*
7T   Systemology*
7X   Cybernetics*
8   Management science† (previously (x))
9b   Career*
9c   Metrology*
9d   Standardization*
9f   Research methodology*
9g   Evaluation technique† (previously an energy common isolate)
9p   Conference technique† (previously a common isolate)
9s   Seminar technique*
9t   Commission technique*
9P   Communication† (previously (P))
9Q   Symbolism*
9ZZ   *Natural and social sciences**
A   *Natural sciences*
AZ   *Mathematical sciences*
B   Mathematics
BT   Statistical analysis† (previously B28)
BTT   Operations research*
BUZ   *Astronomy and astrophysics**
BV   Astronomy† (previously B9)
BX   Astrophysics† (previously B9 : 6)
BZ   Physical sciences
C   Physics
CV   Space physics*

284

TABLE 9 : Outline of CC7 *continued*
Symbols shown on facing page

CZ	*Engineering and technology**
D	Engineering
DV	Draughtsmanship*
DZ	*Chemical sciences**
E	Chemistry
EYD	**Chemical engineering**† (previously D9E)
F	Technology
FZ	*Biological sciences**
G	Biology
GT	Microbiology† (previously G91)
GUA	*Molecular biology**
GUB	**Biomechanics**† (previously G : (B7))
GUC	**Biophysics**† (previously G : (C))
GUE	**Biochemistry**† (previously E9G)
GZ	*Geological sciences**
H	Geology
HUB	**Geodesy**† (previously B9182)
HV	**Geophysics**† (previously H : (C))
HVT	**Geochemistry**† (previously H : (E))
HX	Mining
HZ	*Plant sciences**
I	Botany
IZ	*Agriculture and animal husbandry*
J	Agriculture
JX	Forestry† (previously JB)
JZ	*Animal sciences**
K	Zoology
KX	Animal husbandry
KZ	*Medical sciences**
L	Medicine
LT	Medical technology*
LU5	Public health† (previously L : 5)
LU5Z	Hospital and Sanitorium*
LU6	Hospital† (previously L : 14)
LU7	Sanitorium† (previously L : 15)
LV	Pharmacognosy† (previously LZ)
LX	Nursing† (previously L : 4 : 1)

TABLE 9 : Outline of CC7 *continued*
Partially comprehensive classes are in italics
Fused main classes are in bold
*New classes are marked with an asterisk**
Relocations are shown by a dagger†

LYZ	**Medical jurisprudence**† (previously L : (Z))
M	Useful arts
MZ	*Humanities and social sciences*
MZZ	*Humanities*
Δ	Mysticism and spiritual experience
N	Fine arts
NZ	*Language and literature*
O	Literature
P	Linguistics
PU1	Calligraphy† (previously P(1))
PU6	Typewriting† (previously P(6))
PU7	Shorthand† (previously P(3))
PZ	*Religion and philosophy**
PZZ	*Religion and ethics**
Q	Religion
QZ	*Philosophy and psychology**
R	Philosophy
RZ	*Psychology and education**
S	Psychology
SX	Applied psychology*
SZ	*Social sciences*† (previously Σ)
T	Education
TZ	*Geography and history**
U	Geography
UZ	*History and economics**
V	History
VT	Historical source (as a pure discipline)*
W	Political science
WUU	**Geopolitics**† (previously WOGU)
X	Economics
XX	Economics of industries† (previously XB(A))
Y	Sociology
YZ	Social work
Z	Law

For example, in cc6 Drama is O,2 filing before English literature O111 and English drama O111,2. In cc7 English literature becomes O,111 with English drama O,111,2 and in order that Drama should file in its correct place a zero has to precede it, giving O,02 instead of O,2 (which would file *after* O,111). The reason for this is to break up long class numbers for basic subjects with one level of personality, which may exceed six digits; the point serves the same purpose in UDC.

Where compound basic subjects are involved, the hyphen - is used to link the various items of notation. Examples of this occur in Fine Arts, where Elizabethan architecture, NA56,J in cc6, becomes NA(56-J); the parenthesis is needed because otherwise the filing position would be wrong.

Most of the changes in the notational structure have been introduced to make it possible to combine notational elements for any desired combination of concepts; as was demonstrated in chapter 8, this is only possible if each concept has a clearly demarcated individualizing piece of notation. In fact, we owe this demonstration to Ranganathan, and it is a little surprising that only now is his own classification scheme beginning to reflect the idea.

There will be only one index in cc7. The idea of having several indexes, tried out as an experiment in cc6, has not proved to be a success and has been dropped, with the four indexes merged into one for the new edition. The index is still compiled along the same lines, but again it must be stressed that this is an index for the classifier, not for the user of the catalogue; the latter will have a detailed index to all the topics in the catalogue, as should be the case with any classified catalogue.

THE FUTURE

The DRTC is now well established and will continue to function after Ranganathan himself has withdrawn from all active work, and it thus seems that CC has at last found the kind of institutional backing which is necessary for survival. Over the past few years a great deal of work has been done, both in the preparation of the seventh edition and in the expansion of the schedules for depth classification. The latter work could be particularly significant in that it has been specifically related to the computer with a view to the mechanization of information retrieval. However, CC itself has caused barely a ripple on the surface of Western libraries, though it is used in a number of libraries in India; on the other hand, Ranganathan's ideas on classification theory have formed the basis of most of the progress made in the past thirty years, though in recent years he seems to have been following a rather different path from many of his Western admirers. It is to CC that we owe the consistent development of such ideas as facet analysis and phase relationships, which certainly appeared in such schemes as DC, but haphazardly and without any underlying plan. No matter what becomes of the scheme, Ranganathan's contributions to librarianship must rank in breadth and significance with those of Dewey, and we certainly cannot afford to ignore them.

BIBLIOGRAPHY

1 Ranganathan has given an interesting account of this in his chapter 'Library classification on the march' in the *Sayers memorial volume*.

2 Palmer, B I and Wells, A J: *The fundamentals of library classification*. Allen & Unwin, 1951. Although this text is now rather out of date, it does give a very clear introduction to many of Ranganathan's ideas.

3 Ranganathan, S R: 'Connecting symbols for time and space in CC.' *Annals of library science, 8* (1), 1961, 1-11.

Ranganathan, S R: 'Connecting symbols for space and time in CC.' *Annals of library science, 8* (3) 1961, 69-79.

4 Ranganathan, S R: *The colon classification*. Rutgers, the State University, Graduate School of Library Science, 1965. 298pp. (Rutgers series on systems for the intellectual organization of information, edited by Susan Artandi, vol. 4.)

5 Batty, C D: *Introduction to colon classification*. Bingley, 1966.

6 Ranganathan's own writings are of course an important source of information about CC. In particular, the *Elements of library classification*, second edition 1959 or third edition, 1962, and the *Prolegomena to library classification*, third edition 1967 (both published by Asia Publishing House) may be consulted; the former is a good elementary textbook, while the latter is rather more advanced.

7 Ranganathan, S R: 'Colon classification edition 7 (1971): a preview'. *Library science with a slant to documentation, 6* (3) September 1969, 193-242.

8 Moss, R: 'Categories and relations: origins of two classification theories'. *American documentation, 15* (4) 1964, 296-301.

Roberts, N: 'An examination of the personality concept and its relevance to the Colon classification scheme. *Journal of librarianship, 1* (3) July 1969, 131-148.

CHAPTER 16

The Library of Congress classification

In 1814, the Capitol of the United States, together with its library of 3,000 books, was burned to the ground by British soldiers. Thomas Jefferson, third President of the US, offered his own library to Congress to replace the books lost, and with this library of 6,000 books came a classification scheme, devised by Jefferson himself, which was to be the basis of the library's arrangement until the end of the century. The range of Jefferson's library was also wider than that of the previous Library of Congress, and formed the basis of an increasing breadth of coverage, which was greatly accelerated when Ainsworth Spofford became Librarian in 1864. Spofford set out to make the library, in fact if not in name, the national library of the United States, and to this end increased the rate and scope of accessions to such an extent that towards the end of his tenure of thirty three years as Librarian a new building had to be provided. When the move took place in 1897, shortly after Spofford's retirement, it was found that some threequarters of a million books needed reclassification or re-cataloguing, and that there was a backlog of some thirty years of uncatalogued and unbound material.[1]

Jefferson's classification, though it had been modified and extended, was no longer adequate for a library of the size to which this had grown, and the decision was made to reclassify the whole collection —but by what scheme? Three possibilities were considered carefully : Dewey's *Decimal classification,* the *Expansive classification* of C A Cutter,[2] and the Halle *Schema,* used in the library of the German University of Halle. None of these commended itself for the particular situation of the library, and in 1900 Herbert Putnam, Librarian from 1899 to 1939, decided that the staff should proceed to devise a new scheme, intended to fit the library's collections and services as precisely as possible, without reference to outside needs or influences. The classification which has resulted, LC, reflects this situation very clearly, and some of its special features can only be understood in this context.

The first part of the new scheme to be developed took shape before the decision had been made to develop a new scheme at all. The urgent

289

need to be able to make use of the uncatalogued material led logically to the recognition of the bibliographical collections as the key to this, and the first outline of class z Bibliography was drawn up in 1898, drawing on Cutter's unpublished seventh expansion. Since then, the various classes have been drawn up over the years and published separately, with no apparent overall plan. American history was the first of the new schedules to be published, in 1901, and Russian language and literature the last, in 1948, but many of the schedules have now been revised several times, eg Q Science, now in its fifth edition.

One surprising gap remains: the schedules for class K Law have not all appeared. Though the decision to allot K to this subject was taken when the outline of the scheme was first drawn up, and some progress seems to have been made in the first few years of the century, works dealing with the law of a subject were arranged with the subject, and no progress was made on a schedule for Law as a whole. However, in 1949 it was decided to end the classification of law as a common subject subdivision and to concentrate all legal works, and not merely those dealing with law in the strict sense of the term, in the Law library, bringing together well over a million volumes. Work on the schedules began and that for law of the United States, KF, was completed in 1967, and the schedules were published in 1969. The final draft for KE, British law, is now complete, and a draft outline for the whole class was published in 1970.

THE SCHEME

The outline of the classification most closely resembles that of Cutter's Expansive Classification, but is dictated by the organization of the library, rather than by theoretical considerations. Because the scheme is primarily an internal one, in which the schedules are matched to the needs of the collections—ie compiler and classifier are one and the same—there is no need for synthetic devices, and the scheme is very largely enumerative. In some classes there are tables, eg for division of the works of individual authors in Literature, but these are not synthetic in the usual sense, and there are no common facets such as we have found in other schemes. In consequence, the schedules are very bulky; in all, the twenty one classes occupy some 6,000 pages, with Literature and Language accounting for about a third of this.

The notation is mixed, but the different symbols used fall into a clear pattern, so that no problems arise. Main classes are denoted by a capital letter, and in most of them a second capital is used to denote the major sections, *eg* Q Science, QD Chemistry. Arabic numerals are then used to denote the divisions; they are used integrally, from 1 to 9999 if necessary, with gaps left liberally to accommodate new topics as they arise. However, there is no question of notation dictating order; if a new topic has to be inserted where no gap exists, a decimal point is used for further subdivision. Further arrangement is often alphabetical, using Cutter numbers after a point; these consist of a capital followed by one or two figures, to give a shorter arranging symbol than the name of the topic. Alphabetical arrangement is in fact used very frequently, even in places where its use would seem to be unhelpful, *eg* in Science. In some cases, no facet analysis has been carried out, which gives the possibility of cross-classification; for example, at TK6565, Other radio apparatus, we find arranged alphabetically

.A55 Amplifiers (circuit)
.C65 Condensers (part) (NB outdated terminology)
.R4 · Recording apparatus.

Condensers (capacitors) may be used in amplifiers, and amplifiers may be used in recording apparatus, but we are given no guidance as to which of these is the primary facet. In other cases, straightforward alphabetical arrangement scatters topics within the same facet which could be arranged more helpfully; *eg* in Psychology we find

BF575   Special forms of emotion
   eg .A5   Anger
         .A9   Awe
         .B3   Bashfulness
         .F2   Fear
         .H3   Hate
         .L8   Love
         .S4   Selfconsciousness

(among others) where some grouping would have been more useful. At some points an indication of facet order is given; for example, at the above number BF575 there is an instruction: Prefer BF723 for emotions of children. Such instructions are the exception rather than the rule, and the external user finds little help in the scheme from this point of view; within the library, of course, procedure is well established, and the answers to questions of facet order are found by reference to previous practice.

Gaps are left in the notation to accommodate the tables referred to above, which are inserted rather than added; for example, in Literature, we find within English literature, 19th century, individual authors:

PR5400-5448   Shelley, Percy Bysshe (II)

This shows that the numbers allocated to this author are to be defined by using Table II from the set at the end of the schedules; turning to this, we find that 3 or 53 is the number for Selections, 24 or 74 the number for Parodies. Inserting these numbers in the gap, we have

PR5403   Selections from Shelley

PR5424   Parodies of Shelley.

Had we instead been looking at Wordsworth, PR5850-5898, we should have used the second set, thus:

PR5853   Selections from Wordsworth

PR5874   Parodies of Wordsworth.

There are thirteen such tables in Literature; the one to use depends on the importance of the writer, and is shown in the schedules. Class H Social sciences also includes a number of tables, particularly for division by place.

ORGANIZATION

The way in which the schedules are compiled is again unique to LC among the general schemes. Literary warrant is very important; there are no provisions for subjects not represented in the library. The original technique of compilation was to arrange the books in what seemed to be a helpful order; this order was written down and studied carefully to remove anomalies, and the arrangement of the books was revised to take account of any changes. There was thus a constant interaction between the collections and the scheme, with the latter matched as closely as possible to the needs of the former. In the case of Law, this technique has had to be slightly modified—it is not practical to experiment with the arrangement of over a million volumes —but there is still the very close interaction.

REVISION

Each main class is revised on its own, without reference to the publication schedule for other classes, though cross-references are included where they will be useful, *eg*

HM Sociology

HM (31) relation to Religion, see BL60

HM (32) relation to Education, see LC189-191

The class numbers in parentheses are not used by LC but are included in case any other libraries prefer the alternative. The process is continuous; as new books are received, new places are made to accommodate them in the schedules if this is necessary. When it seems appropriate, a new edition of the class is published; in recent years, the normal method has been to reprint the previous edition, but to insert a supplementary table and index listing additions and changes. This means of course that the user has always to look in two places to make sure that he has the latest schedule. All the changes are published as soon as they occur in *LC Classification— additions and changes,* quarterly; in addition, the publication of revised editions of main classes is noted in the Library of Congress *Information bulletin,* published weekly. The number of new class numbers generated in a year can exceed three thousand, a point which is not always realized by those advocating a change from DC on account of the reclassification involved with each edition.

LC class numbers are of course included in LC cards, which are the major source of cataloguing copy in the USA; libraries using the cards have therefore to check carefully to see that class numbers have not been changed, and to decide whether to take account of changes as they occur or to retain their past practice.

INDEX

Each class has its own index, with the exception of A and some parts of P, but there is no overall index to the scheme. The lack of schedules for law has in the past been considered an insuperable barrier to the production of such an index, but consideration is now being given to the use of data processing techniques to produce an index to all the rest of the schedules, with of course the intention of incorporating K as it is completed. Users must therefore select the correct main class before they can consult the index, though in some cases the index to one main class does contain cross-references to another; for example, if we look in Religion for Freemasons, the index will direct us to HS397 in Social sciences. To some extent the Subject headings list acts as a general index, as it gives LC numbers for many of the headings listed; there is also the *Outline* of the scheme, which is available free and which shows the overall arrangement, though not in much detail.

The indexes to the individual classes are reasonably full, but somewhat wasteful, in that they tend to repeat much of the detail of the schedules; for example, in Religion there is an index entry Bible: BS, which is followed by two columns of entries, of which only 25 (out of nearly a hundred) lead to other parts of the schedules; on the other hand, many of the topics within BS are *not* indexed in this way, *eg* Astronomy, for which one has to turn to Astronomy in the index. The haphazard approach to indexing illustrated here renders the indexes less reliable than they should be.

THE FUTURE

LC would appear to be very well established, but there are two factors which may influence it in the long run.[4] The first of these is the transfer of the library's bibliographical records to computer operation, which will render the shelf arrangement far less important; in the system envisaged, consoles would replace the conventional catalogues, and would provide the facility for browsing now afforded by the open stacks (though it must be remembered that a catalogue entry, whether automated or not, is not a substitute for the book it represents!). The second factor is the need to economize on space in order to accommodate new accessions over the years; one way in which it has been suggested that this might be done is to abandon classified arrangement in the stacks in favour of a more economical method, involving primary arrangement by size. Here again the need for the classification as a means of shelf arrangement disappears.

To set against these two factors are two on the other side. In the first place, even if the stacks are closed, there will still be an open access browsing collection, substantial in relation to most libraries, and this will need to be systematically arranged. Secondly, progress towards automation is slow within the library, and is likely to be a great deal slower outside; there will for many years to come be a demand for the schedules to be maintained, and the library seems to be willing to accept this responsibility.

That a degree of confidence in the future of the scheme exists is shown clearly by the number of libraries which have decided to adopt it in recent years.[5, 6] In 1964 it was estimated that 800 to 1,000 libraries had adopted it, and that this number might double in eight years. The fact that LC cards give a ready made class number certainly appeals to librarians hard pressed for staff, and in the USA its use for shelf arrangement is normally complemented by a dictionary catalogue using LCSH, so that its failings are often overlooked. It will be interesting to see how well it matches up to the challenge of the computer.

OUTLINE. 2nd ed 1970. This revised edition gives more detail than the first, particularly for Science and Technology.

A   GENERALIA. 1911, 3rd ed 1947. Some literal mnemonics, *eg* AE Encyclopedias. AZ is now used for History of the sciences in general, Scholarship, Learning.

B-BJ   PHILOSOPHY. 1910. 2nd ed 1950 (1960s). Includes Psychology, Ethics, Etiquette.

BL-BX   RELIGION. 1927. 2nd ed 1962.

C   AUXILIARY SCIENCES OF HISTORY. 1915 (except Epigraphy, 1942). 2nd ed 1948 (1961S). Includes Archeology CC and Numismatics CJ. Collective biography CT, but normally biography is classified with the subject.

D   HISTORY: GENERAL AND OLD WORLD. 1916. 2nd ed 1959 (1966s). DA is Great Britain (Favoured category); other European countries in approximately alphabetical order, with DE Greco-Roman world between Germany and Greece. DX Gypsies.

E-F   HISTORY: AMERICA. 1901. 3rd ed 1958 (1965s). The first of the main schedules to be published, this does not use a second letter in its notation. There are special tables for Jefferson and Washington.

G   GEOGRAPHY. 1910. 3rd ed 1954. Includes maps and atlases. Most branches of Geography are in this schedule, also related topics such as Anthropology GN, Folklore GR, Recreation GV.

H   SOCIAL SCIENCES. 1910 (except Social groups, 1915). 3rd ed 1950 (1959s). Economics occupies HB-HJ, but Socialism, Communism, Marxism in HX follow Criminology in HV.

J   POLITICAL SCIENCE. 1910. 2nd ed 1924 (1966s). Place is the primary facet in many of the basic classes in this group, *eg* Local government JS, where the schedule under United States consists largely of a long list of individual towns etc arranged alphabetically. JX International law.

K   LAW. The schedules for American law KF were published in 1969. British law KE will be next to be published. An outline of the whole schedule was published in 1970. The classification for Law compiled by E Moys[7] has been suggested as an alternative.

L   EDUCATION. 1911. 3rd ed 1950 (1966s). Curriculum is subordinate to grade of school. Much of the schedule is simply a listing of educational establishments under country.

M   MUSIC. 1904. 2nd ed 1917 (1968s). M used for scores, ML History and criticism, MT Instruction. Ballet music appears to be a form of vocal music (M1520).

N   FINE ARTS. 1910. 4th ed 1970. The latest edition has been completely revised, and in addition introduces a publishing innovation; it is printed on one side of the paper only, to facilitate looseleaf filing and consequent updating.

P   LANGUAGE AND LITERATURE. 1909-1948 in parts, each of which is revised as a unit, *eg* PB-PH Modern European languages, 1933 (1966s). For ' minor ' languages, literature and language are treated together; for major languages, the two are treated quite separately. The very detailed enumeration includes provision for particular editions of the more important works, but twentieth century literature is poorly treated in comparison with earlier periods. Literary form is usually ignored (an exception is the Elizabethan period of English literature, where drama is an important factor). Fiction and Juvenile literature go in PZ, which has led to problems of cross-classification with juvenile non-fiction and novels which may claim to be ' literature '.

Q   SCIENCE. 1905. 5th ed 1950 (1963s). There is no synthesis in this class at all, and though science might be expected to lend itself to systematic arrangement, the schedules are notable for their use of alphabetical order. The 6th completely revised edition is to be published in 1971.

R   MEDICINE. 1910. 3rd ed 1952 (1960s). Primary division is by medical discipline, *eg* RD Surgery.

S   AGRICULTURE. 1911. 3rd ed 1948 (1965s). Crop subordinate to pest at SB608. SB975 ends with SB987 General Works; there is no provision for the treatment of a particular pest by a particular method.

T   TECHNOLOGY. 1910. 4th ed 1948. Supplement (published separately) 1965. The 4th edition differed little from the 3rd of 1937. Alphabetical arrangement widely used, little provision for composite subjects. The 5th edition, to be published in 1971, will retain the existing structure, but incorporate all the amendments which have been found necessary since the 4th edition.

U MILITARY SCIENCE. 1910. 3rd ed 1952 (1966s).

V NAVAL SCIENCE. 1910. 2nd ed 1953.

Z BIBLIOGRAPHY. 1902 (but prepared earlier). 4th ed 1959 (1965s). Includes Book industry and trade, Library science. Copyright has not been developed since 1949, as it will in due course be transferred to a new schedule in K. Basic arrangement of bibliographies is by subject, arranged alphabetically; a parallel arrangement to the whole classification would now be considered more useful, but the schedule was the first to be prepared and a decision had to be made quickly and on the basis of very little experience.

All the schedules were in print in mid-1971, and since the process of revision is a continuous one some of the dates given here as the latest printing will have been superseded. (The dates given in curves with an s indicate that the latest *edition* was reprinted at that date with supplementary pages.)

BIBLIOGRAPHY

1 By far the best account of the development of the scheme is to be found in

LaMontagne, L E: *American library classification, with special reference to the Library of Congress.* Shoestring Press, 1961. Although this began as a work specifically on LC, it is in fact much broader in scope, and presents a valuable outline of the history of library classification.

2 Cutter, C A: *Expansive classification.* The idea of this scheme was to enable librarians to select a classification detailed enough for their needs, but not too detailed; it was intended to have seven expansions, the first having only seven classes, the seventh being large and detailed enough for the largest collection. The seventh expansion was never completed, but the first six were published together by Cutter in 1891-1893.

3 Symposium in *Law library journal,* 57 (4) November 1964, 353-374.

4 Angell, R: 'On the future of the Library of Congress classification'. (*In* International study conference on classification research, 2nd, Elsinore, 1964. *Proceedings* p 101-112). See also the annual report of the Librarian of Congress for current progress.

5 American Library Association: *The use of the Library of Congress classification*: report of a seminar held in New York, July 1966. ALA, 1968. Edited by R H Schimmelpflug and C D Cook.

6 Immroth, J P: *A guide to Library of Congress classification.* Rochester, NY, Libraries Unlimited Inc, 1968.

7 Moys, E: *A classification scheme for law books.* Butterworths, 1968.

CHAPTER 17

Subject headings used in the dictionary catalogs of the Library of Congress

When the Library of Congress moved to its new building in 1897, two problems had to be faced: the selection of a more satisfactory classification scheme, and the choice of the kind of catalogue to be compiled. In the nineteenth century several classified catalogues of the library's holdings had been published, but the practice was discontinued by Spofford, who was not in favour of classification. However, it was decided to conform to the majority practice in US libraries at the turn of the century, and a dictionary catalogue was chosen to be the main information retrieval tool. Work began on the compilation of a list of subject headings in 1897, and the first edition was published in two volumes, 1910-1914. Since then the list has grown enormously, and the latest edition, the seventh, is a large volume of 1,432 pages weighing several pounds. Published in 1966, it includes headings used in the library from 1897 to June 1964, and it is kept up to date by the issue of quarterly supplements, which have been cumulated so far to cover July 1964-December 1965, and each year to 1970. Production is by computer controlled typesetting, which means that once the machine readable record is prepared, it can be used any number of times—for the quarterly list, the annual cumulation, and eventually the eighth edition.

The LCSH contains the complete entry vocabulary of the LC catalogues with certain exceptions mentioned below; terms in the index vocabulary, *ie* headings which are used, are in bold type, while those in the entry vocabulary only, *eg* synonyms, are in light type. In some cases LC class numbers are given to help define the subject area, in others scope notes and cross-references, *eg*

Canteens (Wartime, emergency, etc.)

> Here are entered works on temporary establishments which provide members of the Armed Forces and, in emergencies, civilians with food and recreation . . .

Works dealing with employee lunch rooms, sometimes called canteens, are entered under the heading Restaurants, lunch rooms, etc.

Links with related subjects are shown conventionally, *eg*

1) **Cant** (*English PE3726*)
2)   sa Shelta
      Slang
      Swearing
3)   x Argot
      Crime and criminals—language
4)   xx English Language—dialects
      Slang

1) Heading used, in bold type. LC class number given.

2) Related headings, which should be considered in case they are more precise for the book in hand.

3) Make *see* references from these unused headings.

4) Make *see also* references from these related headings to Cant.

It should be noted that sa and xx are in effect two sides of the same coin; under **Slang** we will find a reference sa Cant and another xx Cant. However, this is not always true, since the principle of making only downward references applies; a sa reference under a broad term will be reflected by an xx reference under the narrower term, but there will not be comparable references in the other direction. For example, under **Sun** we will find a reference sa Eclipses, Solar, reflected by a reference under **Eclipses, solar,** xx Sun; but there will not be references under **Sun** xx Eclipses, Solar or under Eclipses, Solar sa Sun. There are also inconsistencies which are less easy to explain, as for example is shown above, where the link **Cant** sa Shelta is not reflected by a reference **Cant** xx Shelta, although the two headings would appear to be of equal rank.

Certain categories of heading are not included; these include persons, family names, corporate bodies, structures such as castles, ships, religious bodies, mythological characters—in fact, any individuals of a species bearing a distinctive name. They may however appear in the list if they are used as examples under other headings, and five names—those of Lincoln, Napoleon, Shakespeare, Richard Wagner and Washington—are included to demonstrate the range of subdivisions that may be used in similar cases, and various other headings, *eg* Harvard University, Jesuits, are also worked out in detail to serve as examples.

Division by place may be used where appropriate; in general, direct subdivision is used, *eg* Art—Paris, not Art—France—Paris. Some headings have an instruction that they are to be subdivided indirectly, *eg* Music—Austria—Vienna, but even at these headings certain countries are subdivided directly, and a list of these is given in the Introduction. The use of indirect subdivision is gradually dying out; the only objection to direct subdivision—the problem of finding all the material on a broad area which includes many places used as direct subheadings—can be overcome in the same way as all the similar scatterings of related subjects, *ie* by the use of references.

Other subdivisions which may be used throughout include the bibliographical forms, *eg* Dictionaries, Bibliography, Periodicals. Period subdivisions may be used quite widely, but are not given everywhere for reasons of space.

Natural language is used almost without exception, with the result that some headings are not at all obvious, and the filing order requires some study. For example, the following headings are found if we look under Wood :

Wood
Wood—Preservation
Wood, compressed
Wood-alcohol
Wood as fuel
Wood waste
Woodburytype

Other examples have already been given in chapter 5 to illustrate the problems of filing order.

The heading Thrift shops and rummage sales has a reference to it from Rummage sales and thrift shops, but none from Sales or Shops. Suites (2 bagpipes) precedes Suites (balalaika); helpful, but not alphabetical.

It is sometimes very difficult to see any sort of consistency among sets of similar headings; for example, if we turn to Libraries we find

	Libraries, naval
but	Libraries, military *see* military libraries
	Libraries, Catholic
but	Libraries, Hebrew *see* Jewish libraries
	Libraries, nursing school
but	Libraries, school *see* School libraries
	Libraries, children's

but   Libraries, Negroes' *see* Libraries and Negroes
We will also find
      Library administration   (*not* Libraries—administration)
but   Acquisitions (libraries)
      Literature and science
but   Literature and religion *see* Religion and literature.
      Cataloging of moving-pictures
but   Classification—Moving-pictures
the latter two actually occurring on the same Library of Congress card! (LC 67-12056)

The use of both singular and plural forms of nouns can lead to unsatisfactory separations, *eg*
      Plastic films
      Plastic sculpture
      Plastic surgery
      Plasticity
      Plasticizers
      Plastics
      Plastics—research
      Plastics, Effects of radiation on
      Plastics in building
      Plastics industry
where Plastic films should clearly be with the other items on plastics if it is not to be overlooked. It is quite true that the liberal use of cross-references can overcome these problems, but this does not seem to be a good argument for abandoning the attempt to help the reader by giving him immediate direct entry, which is the main justification for the use of alphabetical headings.

Sometimes the noun form is used, sometimes the adjectival, *eg*
      Abdomen—diseases
but   Abdominal pain
      Thorax *see* Chest
but   Thoracic duct
Many of the sets of cross-references linking related subjects seem to be compiled by chance rather than by design. There are in effect two such sorts of reference, those showing genus-species relationships, and those linking subjects from different hierarchies or even different basic classes. For example, we find a reference
      Insects, Fossil *see also* Thrips, Fossil

but not	Insects *see also* **Thrips**
	Thrips *see also* **Onion thrips**
but not	Thrips *see also* **Sugar-cane thrips**
	Education *see also* Libraries
	see also General semantics
but not	*see also* Museums

though this may well be as relevant as the first and is probably more so than the second. J Daily investigated the cross-references that could be followed up started from the heading Hunting; after finding about 2,000, including one trail that led to Pimps, the search had to be abandoned for lack of time.[4]

Another rather more serious fault found by Daily was that of the 36,468 main headings, no less than 7,033 are ' orphans ': that is, they have no references to or from them, and can therefore only be found by chance if they are not known in advance.

We would expect to find a fairly close relationship between the classification scheme used for shelf arrangement and the alphabetical headings used in the catalogue, but in practice this does not seem to be the case. The two systems are treated quite separately, and indeed it is often argued that there need be no connection because they serve different purposes. Even the structure of *see also* references does not appear to be based on the LC scheme; Coates suggests that the scheme to which it bears most affinity is DC!

It can be argued that a list of subject headings should not be tied to any classification scheme, since the freedom to make cross-references in an alphabetical sequence would be hampered by too close an adherence to a classified structure. However, unless the task of making cross-references is approached systematically the resulting network is likely to be less helpful than it might be. This does not mean that subject headings should reflect one and only one systematic approach; BTI, for example, uses a number of classification schemes to help in the generation of its cross-reference network. LCSH, however, does not seem to reflect any kind of plan at all; cross-references seem to be inserted by chance, without reflecting any kind of systematic overview. The main objection to this is the lack of predictability; users do not know whether the cross-references they find are all that might be worth following up, or whether they have to cast about for additional headings under which relevant material might be filed.

It is clear that LCSH and its companion classification are by no means perfect tools. Both suffer from inconsistencies and from lack of specificity, and the user outside the Library of Congress needs to view them with caution rather than the uncritical acceptance with which they are sometimes hailed as being the solution to the problems posed by DC. It is only fair to point out, however, that both show in a very acute form the conflict we have already discussed between keeping pace with knowledge and ' integrity of numbers '. Whereas DC and similar schemes are not tied to any particular collection, LC and LCSH represent the arrangement of some millions of items on the shelves and in the card catalogues of the Library of Congress; though the subject cataloguers are well aware of inconsistencies and errors, the amount of effort that would be needed to remedy these is simply not available. Indeed, one of the reasons given for changing to LC from DC is that the former *is* tied to the collections and will therefore not be subject to large scale changes. There is no easy solution to this dilemma, as we have pointed out; however, the extent to which we can make good use of LC and LCSH depends on our awareness of the problems involved in the maintenance of such large scale tools. Uncritical acceptance of Library of Congress cards, complete with call numbers and subject headings, will lighten the work of the cataloguer, but we should be aware of the possible pitfalls for the reference librarian.

The start of the MARC project prompted a suggestion that the main catalogue of the library, which now contains over 15,000,000 cards, should be closed and a new sequence begun using a completely revised list of subject headings. LCSH would have remained as the authority file for the old catalogue, with a new list on similar lines, but avoiding the inconsistencies of the old, being used for the new catalogue. However, the proposal was given a rather mixed reception and it was decided not to take such a drastic step. At least the use of computers will make changes much easier in the future.

BIBLIOGRAPHY

1 Coates, E J: *Subject catalogues*. Chapter VII.

2 Haykin, D J: *Subject headings: a practical guide*. Washington, Library of Congress, 1951.

3 Horner, J L: *Cataloguing*. Chapters 9 and 13.

4 Daily, J: *LC and Sears: their adequacy for today's library needs*. ALA Pre-Conference Institute on Subject Analysis, Atlantic City, June 19-21, 1969.

CHAPTER 18

Sears list of subject headings

The LCSH has always been very detailed, and a demand arose for a list which should be less comprehensive and more suited to the needs of small libraries—though as we have seen, LCSH is itself frequently not specific. The argument advanced in the preface to Sears ninth edition is that 'specificity is relative and depends on the size of a library, its function, and its patrons . . . Practicality rather than theory should determine the degree of specificity'. It is not clear that these two statements can be reconciled, but in any case this represents a very different approach to specificity than the one put forward in this text.

The first edition was prepared by Minnie Earl Sears, and was based on the practice found in 'nine small libraries known to be well cataloged'. The headings adopted were edited to conform with LCSH practice, so that libraries using LC cards or wishing to add headings from the larger list would find it possible to do so. This edition contained *see* references with their corresponding refer froms, but not see also references; these were added in the very much enlarged second edition. In the third edition, Miss Sears included the 'Practical suggestions for the beginner in subject heading work' which for many years served as one of the few textbooks on the subject, and still forms a significant part of the work. In the fourth edition the scope was enlarged, and DC numbers were added to the headings; common subdivisions, *eg Bibliography,* were indicated by the use of italic type.

The sixth edition was retitled *Sears list of subject headings* as a recognition of Miss Sears' contribution, and the qualification *for small libraries* was dropped; in order to bring the list more into the line with LCSH practice, x and xx were introduced in place of the more explicit 'refer from' used in earlier editions. The latest edition, the ninth, edited by Barbara M Westby, continues the by now traditional format, with the exception of the omission of DC numbers from the headings; it is very largely in line with LCSH seventh edition, with a few modifications, largely in the direction of popular terminology.

The work begins with the preface, in which the policies followed in bringing the list up to date are outlined, with examples of some of the headings which have been changed, *eg* Spinsters, altered to Single women. Over 300 new headings have been added, and the revision process is to continue in subsequent editions. The preface to the eighth edition follows, giving the historical outline, and explaining the layout and typography used, which is the same as that in LCSH; there are also lists of classes of headings included, *eg* names of the most common animals, and excluded, *eg* names of persons and places.

In total, the ninth edition contains about 4,000 headings, compared with over 36,000 in LCSH. However, it would appear that the pruning has at times been somewhat uneven; there are three headings for varieties of pig (Pigs, Hogs, Swine—some nice distinctions here!) and four for cattle (Cattle, Cows, Bulls, and Calves).

The ' Suggestions for the beginner in subject heading work ' are now attributed to Bertha M Frick, who edited the sixth, seventh and eighth editions. These notes must be studied by anyone wishing to use the list, but they also form a useful introduction to the subject generally, though in many ways they are not in agreement with the principles outlined in the present work. They are followed by a brief bibliography of 'Aids to subject cataloging ' and by a two page spread showing how the list is to be used. The preliminaries end with a list of subdivisions which may be used, *eg Laws and regulations*, and a list of headings to be supplied by the cataloguer, *eg* proper names.

The list itself is in double column format, but only one column is used; the vacant parallel column is for the cataloguer to add any amendments, so that the list may serve as an authority file without the necessity to compile a separate record. The headings used are, in general, current terminology, and recent techniques, such as Finger painting, are included; however, the list reflects (reasonably enough) its American origin, and some of the terms would need to be altered in British libraries. As well as the obvious differences, such as Railroads, we find such terms as Showers (Parties), and Commencements (meaning a kind of university graduation ceremony). Natural language is used with its attendant problems; we find such headings as Cookery for the sick, First aid in illness and injury. ' Compound ' headings are used; by these are meant such pairs of terms as Pilgrims and pilgrimages, Pilots and pilotage, Voyages and travels, as well as phase relationships such as Science and state. Many of the headings are not specific, and double entry is recommended as being frequently necessary. The example of a work on Medieval church architecture, which has to be entered under Church architecture and Architecture, Medieval, has already been quoted; a book on Multivariate statistical analysis for biologists would presumably have to take its chance at the general heading Statistics. At one time, books were not written about such specific subjects; now, they are—but subject headings do not seem to keep pace with the tendency. We find the same inconsistencies with Sears as with LCSH; for example, the excerpts quoted from the LCSH heading Libraries could equally well be quoted from Sears, though the latter contains fewer of them.

Despite its American origin, Sears is probably more widely used proportionately in British libraries than in American, where LCSH is more popular. Its helpful presentation and relative simplicity may appeal to the librarian anxious to speed up the processing of his accessions, but it is doubtful if it is adequate to carry the burden of an intensive exploitation of today's literature.

BIBLIOGRAPHY

1 The four readings given for LCSH also apply to Sears.

2 Corrigan, P R D: *Introduction to Sears list of subject headings.* Bingley, 1967. (Programmed text).

CHAPTER 19

Term entry systems

The systems we have been discussing so far have been pre-coordinate systems in which the headings used—the index language—have included composite subjects. Many of the problems with such systems arise from the fact that in a heading representing a composite subject, some of the elements cannot be found directly, but must be sought indirectly, through additional entries (multiple entry systems), or through indexes or cross-references. Furthermore, the existence of a fixed significance or citation order may separate some elements of a composite subject that would, if brought together, be of interest to a user; again, it is necessary to follow through this kind of searching by indirect means, or make multiple entries by such techniques as SLIC. The problems that arise in the construction of adequate means of finding the headings which will answer a particular enquiry—a satisfactory entry vocabulary—and the drawbacks to the various multiple entry methods, have been considered in earlier chapters. If we could use single concepts instead of composite subjects as our headings, many of these problems would be removed immediately. Post-coordinate systems enable us to transfer the act of coordination— the bringing together of the elements which together make up a composite subject—from the input, or indexing, stage to the output, or searching, stage. By doing this, they eliminate all the problems associated with significance or citation order, and their proponents have often claimed that there are no others; however, we have already seen that there are numerous problems relating to selections of terms, genus-species relationships and so on, which are quite separate from those of order of elements, and we may expect to find these problems in post-coordinate systems just as we do in pre-coordinate.

A post-coordinate system thus consists of an input in which the headings used are (normally) single concepts, and an output which enables us to compare the entries under a number of these headings in such a way that we can select the ones which are common to them. Take, for example, the composite subject for which we established a heading in accordance with the principles of Coates (p. 60): manufacture of multiwall kraft paper sacks for the packaging of cement. Without having to make any decisions as to relative importance, we simply enter this under the relevant terms: manufacture, multiwall, kraft, paper, sacks, packaging and cement. Note that these are exactly the same terms as we used earlier, but instead of making one entry we have made seven. There are some points which need to be considered here. Firstly, none of these entries is a specific entry; there will be a relatively large number of entries under each heading, of which the majority will relate to documents which deal with much more specific subjects than the heading. In our example, everything we have in the system to do with *paper* will be entered under that heading. If we have to rely on these headings as they stand, we may find it necessary to do a certain amount of unnecessary sequential scanning. Secondly, the number of entries in the system will be much larger than if we were using a single entry pre-coordinate system; it will be the same as the number arising if we use multiple entry consistently. Thus far we are in the same position as with any of the multiple entry systems already studied; in these we also found the need for sequential scanning and a large number of entries. However, the third point is a vital one, and it is here that we see the first major difference: the number of different headings will be relatively small.

We have already seen that one advantage of a synthetic scheme is that it can be far smaller than an enumerative scheme of the same specificity, simply because it lists only individual foci, whereas the enumerative scheme lists many composite subjects as well. A post-coordinate system is exactly the same as a synthetic classification; it lists only single foci. However, in use the synthetic scheme is employed to build up a catalogue in which composite subjects do appear, so the number of headings which may appear in such a catalogue is very large, but in a post-coordinate system the number of potential headings remains simply the sum of the foci available. A simple example will demonstrate the difference very clearly. In the schedule compiled earlier for library science (figure 3), we found seven facets (excluding common facets) containing between them about forty five foci; if we used these headings in a post-coordinate system, there would be a maximum of 45 headings, but in a pre-coordinate system we might have many thousands of different headings arising, for the number of different combinations of facets is 127 $(2^7 - 1)$, and this has to be multiplied by the number of foci in the different facets involved in each combination.

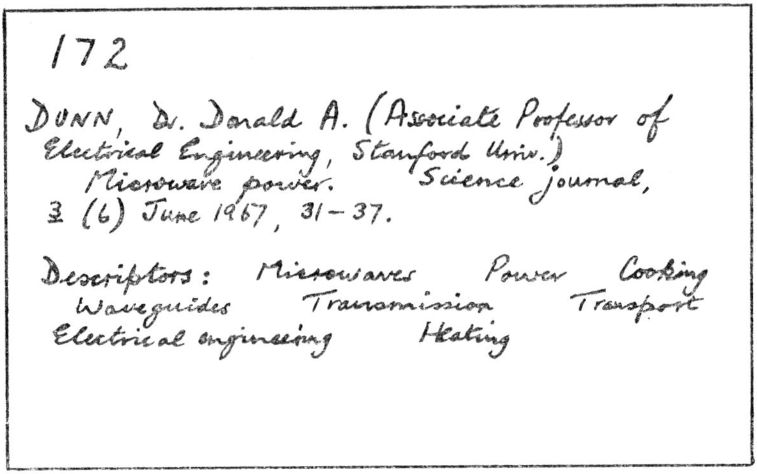

172

DUNN, Dr. Donald A. (Associate Professor of Electrical Engineering, Stanford Univ.) Microwave power. Science journal, 3 (6) June 1967, 31 – 37.

Descriptors: Microwaves Power Cooking
Waveguides Transmission Transport
Electrical engineering Heating

FIGURE 5: A typical accessions card

A post-coordinate system is thus characterized by a relatively small number of different headings, each with a relatively large number of entries under it. At the output stage, we have to be able to select the headings in which we are interested and compare the entries under them; what we do is coordinate single concepts to build up a composite subject, but we do this at the output stage instead of the input. If we think in terms of a conventional card catalogue, it becomes rather difficult to carry out this process of coordination; we cannot conveniently scan two sets of entries, let alone more than this, especially since, as we have seen above, there is likely to be a large number of entries under each heading. The use of a post-coordinate system implies the use of some kind of new physical medium which lends itself to this new kind of searching. Basically, of course, entries remain the same in that they consist of a combination of a heading and a document description, just as do entries in any pre-coordinate system. However, to facilitate searching, document descriptions are usually reduced to a number, which identifies but does not describe; to obtain the description, it is necessary to turn to a subsidiary file kept in number order. Such a file is an essential part of most post-coordinate systems, and a search through the subject file will yield, not a series of document descriptions, but a series of numbers, which we then have to look up in the subsidiary file. Browsing is clearly not helped by this procedure, and whereas in a conventional card catalogue we can skim through a number of entries quickly, discarding those which do not suit our purpose, we cannot do this with a post-coordinate index, but must instead go to each of the entries in the subsidiary file in turn to establish its relevance. If none of the items found are relevant, or if a change of search strategy is needed to find additional items, we have to begin the new search from scratch; it is difficult to make the kind of alteration of strategy in mid-search which is possible with pre-coordinate systems.

UNITERM

The simplest form of post-coordinate index is the Uniterm index, introduced by Mortimer Taube in 1953. The name is a portmanteau word, from unit and term, and is intended to emphasize the system's use of single terms as opposed to composite headings. A Uniterm card has a space at the top for the headings, the rest of the card being divided up into ten columns. When the terms which are to be used as headings for a given document have been decided, the cards for those headings are removed from the index (or new cards are made out if necessary), and the document number is entered on them, using *terminal digit posting*. This simply means that it is the final digit which determines the filing column: 795 is entered in column 5, not column 7. The method helps to spread entries over the card at random instead of filling it up a column at a time. The cards are refiled in the alphabetical sequence when the number has been entered on them all. Searching is equally simple; once the search terms have been decided, the cards for those terms are removed from the index and compared to see which numbers appear on them all; the card with the fewest numbers on it is taken as the basis of comparison, and first checked against the card with the next fewest, corresponding numbers being jotted down. These numbers can then be checked on any other cards, until we end up with a few numbers which have appeared on all of the cards. We now turn to the subsidiary accessions file to obtain details of the documents.

OPTICAL COINCIDENCE CARDS

Searching a Uniterm file is unsatisfactory in that it relies on our ability to notice matching numbers on the cards we are scanning; it is easy to miss a number, which might of course be a particularly important document. One way of making searching easier is to translate numbers into positions, indicating the presence of a number on a

TRAINING

111 681	52	83 743B	374 584	5A 25 845	66 176 746	37	728	89	100 490 750

STUDENTS

11 81 141 371 711 801	62 92 102	13 73 113 233 483 523 643 743B 703	34 144 414	25 375 805	36 66 136 206 316 526	57A 127 457 547 667	88 478 498 518 638 748 818	119 329 489 689 779	210 240

SCHOOLS

91 621	52	23 383 743B	424 744	5A 375 745		27 387B	148	659	120 570

LIBRARIES

71 231 241	232	23 233 743AB 783	234	235	86 236 826	237	88 128 238A	9 239	240

BUILDINGS

71		23 743A	345 825			89 389B

FIGURE 6: A set of Uniterm cards showing the use of links

card by punching out a hole at its position; now when we wish to search, all we have to do is to hold the relevant cards up to the light, which will shine through those positions which are punched out on all the cards we are holding. Such cards are known by a variety of names: Batten cards, optical coincidence cards, peek-a-boo cards, feature cards, peephole cards; of these, optical coincidence is probably the best description, but peek-a-boo and feature cards the most widely used.

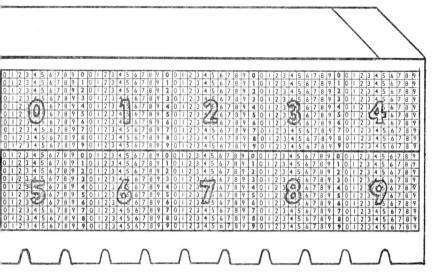

FIGURE 7: Diagram of a 1,000 position peek-a-boo card

A peek-a-boo card contains a space at the top for the heading, like a Uniterm card, but the body of the card is divided up into numbered squares. A small card will probably contain 500 or 1,000 positions, while a large one will contain up to 10,000. To enter information into the system, we select the terms we require to describe a document, and remove these cards from the file; then, using a punch of some kind, we drill out a hole in the position corresponding to the document number, and refile the cards. The punch may be a simple hand drill or it may be a much more elaborate electrically operated model; the difference lies in the cost and in the accuracy with which the holes

313

may be made, and the user will normally purchase the cheapest model which gives the required accuracy. When large cards are used, with small holes to give the maximum number of positions, accuracy is important, for inaccurate punching will introduce an element of error. For this reason, large punches will normally go through a number of cards at a time, so that the holes will all be in the same position provided that the cards are properly aligned at the time of punching; this is much more difficult to achieve with a hand punch which will only go through one or two thicknesses at the same time.

Another useful piece of equipment is the light box. This simply consists of a box containing a diffuse source of light, with one side of the box translucent; instead of holding the cards we are searching up to the light, we place them on the box, and the light shines through from below or behind, which is more convenient than holding the cards up above eye level. There is an additional advantage, relating to search strategy. If we wish to coordinate, say, four terms, but find that when we hold the appropriate cards up to the light that no holes coincide in all of them, we can broaden the search by reducing the number of cards to three; since there are four to start with, we can reduce the number to three in four different ways, by removing each of the cards in turn, scanning the remaining three, then replacing it. With a light box, we can do the same thing in one operation, by stepping up the light power so that light shines through one thickness of card. Some manufacturers are making their cards of translucent material to facilitate this process.

Peek-a-boo cards may have certain refinements to make their use easier. For example, a series of notches along the bottom edge fit on to a corresponding set of rods in the bottom of the card tray; these rods enable each card to be stepped in relation to its immediate neighbours. At the top right hand corner, each card has a space for the heading; if a card is removed from the stepped sequence, instead of a heading we see the word OUT, or a row or dots, or some similar symbol to indicate that a card is missing from the sequence. We can refile cards very quickly, without having to search through a set of cards in which we can only see one at the time, as would be the case if the cards were not stepped. There may be room on the card to note items of useful information such as related headings. These refinements do not in any way affect the principle of operation.

Although the basic principle is the same, these two methods differ in their ease of use and in their cost. Uniterm is very cheap and easy to establish; it requires no special apparatus at all. A peek-a-boo system may involve considerable capital outlay; not only does it require such apparatus as punches, but the cards themselves must be accurately printed on good quality card stock, so they too are not cheap. On the other hand, scanning a large Uniterm index is a very tedious process, and the probability of error is high through the likelihood of numbers being missed; peek-a-boo indexes are easy to use. An interesting compromise is to use a Uniterm system to start with, transferring to peek-a-boo when some experience has been gained in the choice of vocabulary, exhaustivity required and similar factors—or, to use an inelegant but expressive phrase, when the ' bugs ' have been ironed out.

Another point of comparison which becomes significant when peek-a-boo is considered is the problem of correcting input errors which are detected. With any system, errors may arise at the input stage; in an alphabetical file, words may be misspelt, while in a systematic file notation may be incorrectly typed or copied. If undetected, such errors, together with any that arise in filing correctly headed entries, will result in loss of recall, and can only be rectified if they are discovered, which will normally be by chance. Highly complicated notational symbols accentuate the possibility of undetected errors through misfiling, but they may arise in any system. What happens to errors that are detected before they become irretrievable? In a card catalogue or Uniterm catalogue, errors can be altered to the correct form without much difficulty, but a hole punched in the wrong place is not so easy to correct!

Withdrawals can also present something of a problem. It is of course possible to stamp Withdrawn on the accessions card, but it would be better not to lead the reader up this blind alley if it can be avoided. One ingenious solution is to have a coloured translucent sheet which is punched out in the appropriate place *when an item is withdrawn;* this sheet is included in the pack of peek-a-boo cards for every search. If a hole shows through all the subject cards but is coloured, the item is potentially relevant and still in stock; if however the hole is clear, it means that the item was potentially relevant but has been withdrawn. If the accessions card is kept, it may be possible to obtain another copy of the item, for example from the NLL.

In any system, part of the work involved will be intellectual and part will be clerical. Deciding which headings a document should be entered under is an intellectual operation, but the actual mechanics of placing an entry in a file is not. Similarly, in searching, we need to make an intellectual decision as to which headings are likely to reveal the answers to an enquiry, but the task of displaying the entries under those headings does not involve intellectual effort. Conventional forms of catalogue, which give document descriptions, tend to blur these distinctions; although filing is a routine operation, it is usual for it to be checked before cards are finally accepted into the catalogue (a junior assistant files ' on the rods '), and at the search stage we tend to perform a subsearch at any given heading by looking at the document descriptions and estimating relevance from these. Because of their physical form, Uniterm and peek-a-boo make the distinction between clerical and intellectual effort much clearer and, indeed, emphasize it. Posting numbers on to Uniterm cards, and comparing the lists of numbers so generated, is very obviously a clerical operation!

The distinction becomes important when we are considering the use of computers. Computers can perform clerical operations very well: they are more accurate, and much faster, than their human counterparts, provided that they are given the correct instructions. At present, however, we do not know nearly enough about the way in which the human mind works to be able to give computers the right instructions to enable them to perform intellectual operations; these must still be done by human effort. In a mechanized retrieval system, it becomes essential to distinguish the two sides of the operation, and post-coordinate systems using document numbers enable us to do this very easily; it is equally possible to do it with pre-coordinate systems, but it means taking a very close look at the way in which we operate the systems, and often we have to revise our approach as a result. This kind of analysis can be very valuable in enabling us to see more clearly what actually happens in any given system, and how we can operate it more efficiently, and from this point of view post-coordinate systems are probably more amenable than pre-coordinate; this does not mean that it is not possible to gain valuable information about our use of pre-coordinate systems through operational analysis, but that the answers we find may require us to adopt new methods rather than try a piecemeal attack on the old.

This brief discussion of the physical format of Uniterm and peek-a-boo cards has assumed that we knew which terms we wished to use as headings in indexing and searching. As has been shown in the first part of this book, it is precisely this choice which often leaves us in doubt. Early proponents of post-coordinate indexing claimed that to select the correct keywords it was sufficient to read through the document to be indexed and underline the words which appeared to be significant. This procedure is clearly open to several objections; it takes no account of synonyms, and cannot demonstrate any kind of relationship. Though relevance may be high, recall is likely to be low, and the only kind of situation where the results are likely to be tolerable is in a clearly defined subject area with well established terminology, and with readers who can state precisely what they want. If we are to achieve good results under normal conditions, we must use as closely controlled a vocabulary with post- as with pre-coordinate indexing.

The problems associated with the use of words have already been discussed, and there is no need to go into detail again. We have to select a preferred term and refer to it from *synonyms*; we have to distinguish *homographs*; we have to be aware of *genus-species relationships*. These requirements imply the necessity of some sort of authority to show usage, just as with a pre-coordinate file; however, to distinguish lists intended for post-coordinate systems, they are usually referred to as *thesauri* (singular, thesaurus). The only difference between a thesaurus and a list of subject headings is that the former normally excludes headings for composite subjects; with some examples, even this is not true, and one is forced to the conclusion that the name is intended to signify a distinction which does not exist. Many lists of subject headings have left much to be desired, and thesaurus constructors have perhaps endeavoured to persuade us (and themselves) that their lists were free from fault. It is certainly true that thesauri in general are more precise in listing relationships to broader and coordinate terms than are most subject headings lists, which have tended to follow Cutter in relying mainly on downward references.

Whereas lists such as the Library of Congress *Subject headings* and *Sears list of subject headings* normally give only downward references, but in any case do not distinguish between different kinds of reference (the same symbols xx and sa are used for all kinds), thesauri have usually made clear the kind of relationship. For example, the EJC Thesaurus[1] uses the conventions shown below, here compared with standard subject headings practice.

Once the meaning of the abbreviations is understood, they are quite unambiguous, whereas the older method leaves at least the new user in some doubt as to how to use these cross-references (as is shown by the difficulties experienced by students coming to them for the first time).

	EJC	LCSH
Preferred	Thorax	Chest
Instruction	UF Chest (*ie* Use For)	x Thorax
Synonym	Chest use Thorax	Thorax see Chest
(NB choice of scientific term by EJC)		
Preferred	Forging	Forging
Instructions	UF Cold forging	x Drop forging
(broader term)	BT Metal working	xx Blacksmithing
(narrower term)	NT Drop forging	sa Ironwork
(related terms)	RT Cold working	sa Blacksmithing
	Heat treatment	xx Explosive forming

SYNTAX

The choice of terms and the establishment of genus-species relationships together provide us with an indexing vocabulary, but we must also consider the other aspect of an indexing language, its syntax. It is possible to use a completely unstructured vocabulary; this may give good recall but is likely to result in low relevance. For example, consider the two subjects: *electrolytic extraction of aluminium from bauxite* and *welding of aluminium beer cans*. In the first, aluminium is the end product, whereas in the second it is the raw material from which another end product is made. A classification scheme would clearly distinguish these two aspects of aluminium by their context; the first would be found in metallurgy, the second in container manufacture. It is possible to introduce a similar differentiation into postcoordinate indexing systems by using *roles*; thus in the present example we would have two cards for aluminium rather than one, the first headed Aluminium 1, the second Aluminium 2, where 1=raw material, 2=end product. By so doing we can improve specificity, while still leaving ourselves the possibility of high recall by considering both entries in our search rather than just one. We can also introduce an element of direction into the relationships shown by bringing together two terms; to quote an example mentioned earlier, if we merely collate Albums and Photographs, we may mean albums of photographs or photographs of albums. By specifying ' end product ' or ' raw material ' we can make the direction clear. An often quoted but unlikely example is the ambiguous concatenation of blind and Venetian, but the problem is likely to be rather more acute when we are indexing materials in such subject areas as Chemistry, where the direction of a particular reaction is likely to be important. For example, a paper on *the observation of solar eclipses using artificial satellites* would be recalled if we were searching for information on *the observation of artificial satellites* if we did not use roles. If, however, we have more than one card for satellites, according to whether they are end product (manufacture of . . .), or agent (observations by . . .) we can eliminate this source of low relevance. The EJC Thesaurus has a detailed set of roles which may serve as a model,[2] or of course we could use a systematic approach to show the different contexts in which a particular topic might appear, so that we could draw up a set of roles for each term for which it proved necessary.

Another tool which has proved valuable is the use of *links*. Suppose that we have a document dealing with two separate subjects, *eg* a description of a piece of research which also describes in some detail a particular method. In a pre-coordinate system we should make two entries, which would be quite separate, but an unsophisticated approach to post-coordinate indexing could lead to errors which may be described as *false drops*. For example, a document which dealt with new library buildings, but included a discussion of the needs arising out of the practical training of library school students, might be indexed under the headings Libraries, Buildings, Training, Schools, Students; if we search for library school buildings, this document will be retrieved, although it does not deal with this subject and is therefore not relevant. If we link the elements of each of the two subjects, this kind of false drop can be eliminated. In a Uniterm index this can be done by adding a letter to the document number when it is entered on the cards; in the example above, if we denote the subject of library buildings A, and practical training of library school students B, the document will be entered on the cards as follows (assuming this is document 743) in Figure 6. Now if we search for library school buildings, we shall be warned not to retrieve this document, for Buildings is 743A while Schools is 743B. In a peek-a-boo index, this kind of differentiation is not possible (a hole is a hole!) but it is possible to give a document two or more accession numbers, to cater for as many different subjects as appear in it.

A second example will illustrate the use of links to avoid false drops in a slightly different situation. It is sometimes necessary to split the subject dealt with by a document into two or more parts, even though the document does not itself do this so definitely. Take for example a document dealing with ' The testing of magnesium and aluminium alloys '. This will be indexed under Testing, Magnesium, Aluminium and Alloys, and will be retrieved if we search for magnesium-aluminium alloys, although it may have nothing on alloys containing both of these metals. We have to distinguish *two* subjects here: the testing of magnesium alloys and the testing of aluminium alloys; once we have done this, we can use links to prevent the incorrect association of magnesium and aluminium. Note that in a pre-coordinate index we should have had to make two entries in both this and the previous example; the two composite headings would have performed the work done here by links, by showing which concepts were associated and which were not.

A further use of links is possible within a single subject, but must be viewed with caution, since it may exclude associations incorrectly. Consider the subject ' Plastic coatings for tinplate containers '. If this is indexed without any controls, it will be retrieved when we search for documents on plastic containers, or tinplate coatings. Straightforward indexing of ' Manufacture of multiwall kraft paper sacks for the packaging of cement ' means that this document will be retrieved when we search for items on the manufacture of cement, though it may well have nothing on this subject in it. If we link Plastics and Coatings, and Tinplate and Containers, then we shall avoid the false drop of plastic containers, but we shall also at the same time exclude the legitimate associations of Tinplate and Coatings, and Containers and Coatings. If we introduce additional links to show these, eventually we end up by linking every index term to every other—but this is where we started, with simple, unlinked, numbers! It is probably better to avoid this use of links, and employ roles instead in this kind of situation; in addition to the problem just described, the use of a link between Tinplate and Coatings does not give any indication of whether we are dealing with coatings *on* tinplate, or tinplate *as a* coating, whereas the use of roles does.[3]

As yet the use of weights in any kind of indexing is in an elementary stage. In conventional catalogues, of course, it has always been possible to make *added entries* for subsidiary subjects; the fact that they are added entries in itself indicates that they are not as important as the main entry, but no kind of quantitative indication of importance is normally given, except perhaps for the number of pages covered by the subject of an analytical entry. In recent years attempts have been made to introduce quantitative weightings, for example those shown below,[4] but it seems likely that their application is likely to be too subjective to be of value in a retrieval system.

Weight	Description	When used
8/8	Major subject	The term is highly specific, and covers an entire major subject of the document
7/8	Major subject	The term is specific and covers most of the major subject of the document
6/8	More generic subject	The term is too broad and covers a major subject
5/8	Other important terms	Terms that would be used in binary indexing but not a major subject
4/8	Less generic subject	The term relates to but is too narrow to cover a major subject
3/8	Minor subject	Includes such terms as relate to results of experiments, intermediate methods, possible uses etc
2/8	Other subjects	Other relevant tags
1/8	Barely relevant	Subjects classifier would not want to use, but feels that some users might consider relevant

A rather simpler system uses only the numbers 1 to 3:

Weight	When used
3	The concept is central to the theme of the document
2	The concept is important, but not central to the theme of the document
1	The concept is worth indexing but is not important nor is it central to the theme of the document

Uniterm systems lend themselves to devices such as weighting, since it is simple to add a designation of this kind to the document number; using a peek-a-boo, it is necessary to list the descriptors and their weights on the accessions card if this technique is to be used— it is not possible to weight a hole! Most weighting systems have been intended for use with computer retrieval of information.

ELIMINATING THE ACCESSIONS FILE

The need to refer from the subject file to a separate accessions file is a disadvantage of post-coordinate systems; it makes searching much more tedious than, say, flicking through the cards in a card catalogue or scanning the entries in a book catalogue. Two methods of overcoming this problem have been suggested. The first of these is to have a master matrix with a micro-image of an abstract of each document at the appropriate position; peek-a-boo cards are superimposed on this, and those images where the presence of holes in all the cards permits it are projected one at a time on to a screen. In view of the very high degree of reduction necessary in the images, and the accuracy with which the holes must be aligned, this technique is likely to remain expensive, and though the development of PCMI (photochromic micro-images) may make it technically feasible, it seems probable that other techniques will prove more practical.

The second method is a development of the *dual dictionary*. Using a computer, it is simple to print out the contents of a post-coordinate index in the form of a series of headings under which are listed the document numbers to which they apply; in effect, the contents of a set of Uniterm cards are transferred to a printed sheet. If two such printouts are made and bound up side by side, it becomes easy to compare the entries under two headings; the first is found in one printout, the second in the other, and they can be viewed side by side. A dual dictionary has two advantages over the usual form of index; the first lies in the ease with which it may be scanned, while the second lies in the fact that it is printed and can therefore be multiplied, so that copies are available in a number of places. An additional advantage is found if brief details of each document are printed out in one of the lists by the side of each accession number; now, comparison of the two lists will show not only the co-occurring numbers but also details of the relevant documents.[6]

BIBLIOGRAPHY

1 Engineers Joint Council: *Thesaurus of engineering and scientific*

terms: a list of engineering and related scientific terms and their relationships for use as a vocabulary reference in indexing and retrieving technical information. New York, EJC, 1967. This, named ' First edition ' on the title page, is actually a major revision of the earlier *Thesaurus of engineering terms,* 1964.

2 Problems in use led the EJC to omit these from the revised thesaurus. See, for example:

Lancaster, F W: ' Some observations on the performance of EJC role indicators in a mechanised retrieval system '. *Special libraries,* 55 (10) 1964, 696-701.

Lancaster, F W: ' On the need for role indicators in post-coordinate retrieval systems '. *American documentation, 19* (1) January 1968, 42-46.

3 Taube, M: ' Notes on the use of roles and links in coordinate indexing '. *American documentation, 12* (2) 1961, 98-100.

Artandi, S and Hines, T C: ' Roles and links—or, forward to Cutter '. *American documentation, 14* (1) 1963, 74-77.

4 Maron, M E, Kuhns, J L and Ray, L C: *Probabilistic indexing.* Los Angeles, Ramo-Wooldridge, 1959.

5 There are a number of general works on coordinate indexing, including

Foskett, A C: *A guide to personal indexes.* Bingley, second edition 1970.

Costello, J C Jr: *Coordinate indexing.* Rutgers, State University Graduate School of Library Science, 1966. (Rutgers series on systems for the intellectual organization of information, edited by Susan Artandi. Vol. 7.)

Documentation, Inc: *The state of the art of coordinate indexing :* report prepared for the National Science Foundation, Office of Science Information Services. Washington, NSF, 1962.

Reichman, J: *The state of the library art, volume 4.* Rutgers, State University, Graduate School of Library Science, 1961.

Bourne, C P: *Methods of information handling.* Wiley, 1963.

Sharp, J: *Some fundamentals of information retrieval.* Deutsch, 1965.

Lancaster, F W: *Information retrieval systems :* characteristics, testing and evaluation. Wiley, 1968.

6 Cherry, J W: ' Computer-produced indexes in a double-dictionary format '. *Special libraries,* 57 (2) 1966, 107-110.

CHAPTER 20

Item entry systems

TERM ENTRY AND ITEM ENTRY: All the systems we have considered so far have been *term entry* systems; that is, in searching we select the terms in which we are interested and turn to them, to see which documents are entered under these headings. This is true whether the terms used are referring only to single concepts, as is usual in post-coordinate systems, or to both single and composite concepts, as is usual in pre-coordinate systems. We have to make as many entries for an item as we select terms to describe it. Another way of describing this kind of system is ' item-on-term ', which emphasizes this aspect.

A rather different approach is to make only one entry for each item, but to do this in such a way that access can be gained to it through as many terms as we wish. This is known as *item entry* or term-on-item, and it implies once again a new kind of physical format to make it possible; neither the conventional catalogue, nor the Uniterm or peek-a-boo form will permit multiple access to a single record. There is some confusion in the literature over this distinction; Uniterm and peek-a-boo are frequently contrasted, as term entry systems, with conventional catalogues as item entry systems, and it is not uncommon to find them described as ' inverted indexes ' to emphasize the difference. Though a difference exists, it lies in the use of single concepts which are coordinated at the search stage, rather than being stored as composite headings, not in the use of term as opposed to item entry.

EDGE-NOTCHED CARDS

The simplest example of item entry is the edge-notched or edge punched card, which consists basically of a card with a series of holes punched round the edges. To enter information on to the card, holes are converted into notches by means of a wedge shaped punch, so that they are open to the edge of the card. If a needle is passed through that hole in a pack of cards, only the cards which are not notched will remain on it; the others will fall. We thus have a simple method of selecting those cards on to which we have entered a particular piece of information.

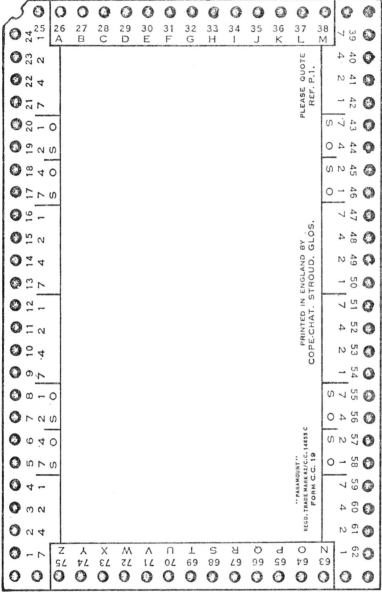

FIGURE 8: A typical edge-notched card (illustration by courtesy of Copeland-Chatterson Co)

325

The body of the card can be used for a written entry which may be in any convenient form; there is usually enough room to include an abstract if this is thought desirable. The description should include the terms or other factors which we wish to use for indexing; these terms have now to be converted into notches, a process known as *coding*. If we only have as many terms to code as there are holes on the card, we can use *direct* coding; each hole represents one particular term and no other. However, the number of holes on a card is limited; one standard card available in the UK has 75 holes, another 128, and if we are thinking in terms of subjects this is a very small number. We therefore have to use combinations of holes rather than single holes, in what is known as *indirect* coding. There are various ways of doing this.

7-4-2-1

In this method, four holes are selected to give a *field;* the holes are labelled 7, 4, 2, and 1, and it is now possible to code any number up to 9 with one or two holes:

0	no holes punched out	5	4 and 1
1	1	6	4 and 2
2	2	7	7
3	2 and 1	8	7 and 1
4	4	9	7 and 2

This gives us a convenient way of coding numbers of any length, by using one field of four holes for each digit; *eg* for numbers from 0 to 999 we shall need three fields, one for the hundreds, one for the tens, one for the units. However, in any of the fields we are liable to get *false drops;* for example, if we select 4, we shall get cards coded 4, but also those coded 5 and 6, while if we select 1, we shall get cards coded 1, 3, 5 and 8.

7-4-2-1-S-0

By using an extra two holes in each field we can eliminate these false drops; coding is now as follows:

0	0	5	4 and 1
1	1 and S	6	4 and 2
2	2 and S	7	7 and S
3	2 and 1	8	7 and 1
4	4 and S	9	7 and 2

In order to avoid false drops we use 50% more holes, and we have to needle twice every time instead of only half the time. It is probably the first of these which is the more serious; on a 75 hole card there is room for eighteen four hole fields, but only twelve if we use six holes.

PYRAMID

By using a 'pyramid' as in figure 9d we can avoid false drops using only five holes; we have to needle twice for every number, including 0, but this is a small price to pay for the lower number of holes needed for the field. Pyramid coding is a special case of two hole coding, discussed later. On a base of five holes, a pyramid is constructed by drawing lines at an angle from the midpoint between each pair of holes, and inserting the numbers 0 to 9 in the diamonds formed by the intersecting lines. Each diamond is formed by the intersection of two pairs of lines; if each pair is followed out to the edge, it will be found to lead to one of the five holes. The number in the diamond is encoded by notching the two holes; for example, in the diagram, to encode 6 we should need to punch out the first and last holes in the base of five forming the field.

BINARY CODING

A little used method is binary coding, in which each hole in a field represents a power of 2; thus the first hole represents 2^0 (ie 1), the second 2^1 (ie 2) etc. We shall need as many holes as is necessary to accommodate the highest number we wish to code in each field; for example, to code up to 999 we shall need 10 holes, since 2^9 is 512. (The sum of all the powers from 2^0 to 2^9 is $2^{10} - 1$, ie 1,023). However, the potential for false drops is very high, so although this method becomes economical in terms of the number of holes needed as the numbers to be coded grows, it is not generally used.

SORTING

Edge-notched cards do not need to be kept in order, since a card will fall at the appropriate time no matter whereabouts in the pack it is. However, it is sometimes useful to be able to sort the pack of cards into order; this can be done very easily provided that the fields are coded in the way shown in figure 9. All that has to be done is to needle the righthand hole, placing the cards which drop in order at the back of the pack. The next hole is then needled and the procedure repeated until the complete set of holes has been dealt with; the cards will then be in numerical order. It is possible to compile a table to convert names to numbers; using such a conversion table, we can sort into alphabetical order if necessary.

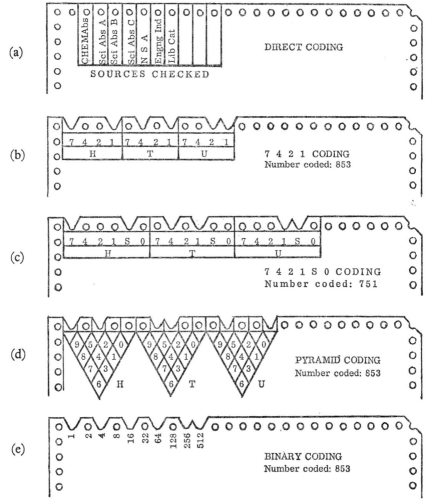

FIGURE 9: Various methods of coding

PROBLEMS OF FIXED FIELD CODING

Using the methods described so far, we can only make one code entry in each field. The reason for this will be seen very clearly if we consider what would happen if we were using three 7-4-2-1 fields to code numbers up to 999, and coded the numbers 742, 421, 217 and 174 in the same three field group. We cannot superimpose codes in the same field or groups of fields. Suppose that we have a table of subject terms, each with a number equivalent, we shall need a separate group of fields for every term that we wish to use to describe any given document. If our set of terms is restricted to a few hundred, as is often the case with collections covering a limited subject field, we may need three four hole fields for each entry; on a 75 hole card, this restricts us to no more than six entry terms. Further, we shall have to search every field every time, for we shall not know which field has been used to code any particular descriptor, and this will in fact vary from card to card. Clearly this is not satisfactory, and some other means must be found if we are to be able to code subjects.

SUPERIMPOSED RANDOM CODING

If we take the whole card as one field, and notch out two holes for each code, we have a potential maximum of $\frac{n(n-1)}{2}$ different codes, where n is the number of holes available. In a 75 hole card, this gives us 75 × 74 ÷ 2 or 2,775 codes. (We can choose the first hole in 75 different ways, which leaves us 74 different ways of choosing the second; but the combination of, eg, 24 and 37 is the same as that of 37 and 24, so we divide by 2). If we only need a few hundred, a possible maximum of 2,775 is ample. Suppose that we notch more than one code into the same field, eg 24 and 37, and 15 and 62; we have introduced the possibility of false drops, for we have now in effect coded not only the two pairs we meant to, but also 15 and 24, 15 and 37, 24 and 62, 37 and 62; however, if we choose our code pairs at random, and limit the number of codes that we enter in any given field, we can limit the number of false drops to an acceptable proportion of the total number of cards which fall when we conduct a search. The mathematics involved is quite complex, but the resulting limit is that we should not notch out more than about 45% of the available holes; thus in a 75 hole field, using two hole coding, we should not code more than 17 headings for any given card.

CHOICE OF TERMS

There are no special considerations relating to the terms that we may use with edge notched cards. It is usual to prefer post-coordinate techniques, since these involve only the coding of single concepts;

329

composite concepts can be coded, but this may lead to problems if we wish to search for one of the single concepts involved. It is necessary to have a separate authority file; unlike Uniterm or peek-a-boo systems, it is not possible to use the cards as their own authority list. We can use roles by giving a term qualified by roles as many codes as there are roles; it is not however possible to use links.

Edge notched cards are of value for small files, where their use has been described by the present author; because of the physical problems of sorting a large pack, they are of very limited value if more than a few hundred cards are involved. They do however illustrate very clearly the item entry approach, which will recur in our study of computer retrieval systems.

MACHINE SORTED PUNCHED CARDS

Standard 80-column punched cards have been used in information retrieval systems, though they have now in most cases been superseded by the use of computers. Most card sorting machinery works on the fixed field principle (though more sophisticated machines do exist which can overcome this limitation, they are not common) and is thus subject to the same sort of limitation as we have seen with edge-notched cards; there is a further limitation in that it is not possible to use superimposed coding, since the existence of more than one hole in the same column can lead to missorting. One mode of use is the item-term card; in this method, one card is made out for each combination of item and term. Thus for an item which we need to describe by ten different headings we shall require ten different cards. This leads to a big increase in the total number of cards, and the system is no longer an item entry system in the normal sense of the word. As the number of cards increases, so the time taken to search the pack increases; one way of overcoming this problem is to presort the pack to bring related terms together, so that a search need only be carried out on a section of the total set of cards. So we find the idea of classification brought in to solve the problems caused by the uncontrolled use of machinery!

80-column cards have also been used as peek-a-boo cards; there are twelve positions in each column, giving a maximum of 960 positions, enough for a fairly small collection. The cards are used manually in the same way as conventional peek-a-boo cards, but have the advantage that they are a great deal cheaper than the latter!

An interesting use of these cards is the system developed by the British Patent Office to index British patents in the field of alloys. The number of terms required in such a field is limited, but their combination permits highly specific subjects to be represented. The first sixteen columns of the card are used for bibliographic information: patent number, country of origin, and manual search field to which the specification is allotted in the Patent Office. Columns 17 to 22 are not used, and the remaining columns are used for the subject specification. Each punching position is given a particular meaning; for example, in column 77 we find the positions allocated as follows:

Y Controlled cooling
X Quenching in oil
0   ,,   ,, water
I   ,,   ,, air
2   ,,   ,, solution
3 Cooling by liquid spray
4   ,,   ,, molten metal bath
5   ,,   ,, salt bath
6 Isothermal treatment
7 Cooling by unclassified methods.

To make the system more powerful, there are two files, one for what are largely ferrous alloys, the other for alloys in which the base (*ie* the metal present in the greatest proportion) is not one of the metals specified for the first group. Patents are allocated to one or both of these groups depending on the variety of alloys they specify. This division means that columns 23 to 70 may be used with different meanings in the two packs; for example, in Pack A columns 23 and 24 are used to show the proportion of Cobalt present, while in Pack B they are used to show the proportion of Silver. The following excerpt from the table for Pack A shows how the positions are allocated:

Element	Co	
Column	23	24
Y	Pres.	
X	Base	4·5
0	50	
I	36	3·5
2		
3	26	2·5
4		
5	16	1·5

6

7   11   0·5

8

9   7·5   0

Thus a patent for an alloy in which Cobalt was present in the proportion of 30% would have positions Y and 1 punched in column 23; one in which cobalt formed more than 50% would have positions Y and X punched in column 23; while one in which the proportion of cobalt might vary from 0% to 5% would have positions Y and 9 punched in column 23 and position 9 in column 24. Thus a wide variety of compositions can be specified for any particular alloy. Searching is carried out by a similar process of deciding the limits for each required constituent and setting a sorter to select the desired combination of codes. With the simplest kind of sorter, it is possible to search for only one position in one column at a time; with the booklet explaining the coding system the Patent Office supply a frequency table so that the characteristic wanted which occurs least often can be the one to be searched for first. More sophisticated machines can sort on a number of columns at a time so that it is possible to search for all the wanted characteristics simultaneously. The complete set of cards, manual, frequency table and updating service are available from the Patent Office, an interesting example of a practical system using machine sorted cards.

The problems involved in the choice of terms for use with such a system do not differ from those inherent in any system. Machinery for sorting and printing out the cards is widely available, as it is used for accounting purposes in many offices. However, the main use of these cards now is as computer input, for which purpose they have advantages over many other forms; the Patent Office system described above must be regarded as the exception rather than the rule, and the cards included in it could of course be used as input to a computer for searching purposes if desired.

BIBLIOGRAPHY

References for this chapter are the same as those for Chapter 19. The Patent Office system referred to is described in detail in:

GREAT BRITAIN. *Patent Office*. Alloys: manual for punched-card retrieval system. London, Patent Office, 1965.

CHAPTER 21

Science and technology

Of the indexing languages prepared specifically for post-coordinate indexing, those in science and technology were first in the field, and still preponderate, both in areas covered and in number. There is however, no equivalent of the general classification scheme covering the whole of knowledge; even those lists which cover substantial areas are all within one subject field such as science and technology, education, and economic development. There is also no equivalent to the widespread use of DC, UDC or LCSH; the most widely used post-coordinate scheme is probably the EJC Thesaurus and its near relations, but this is still used as it stands by only a limited number of libraries. Most libraries using post-coordinate indexing methods have tended to generate their own lists, perhaps using one of the major lists as a model. This situation may change in the future, but for the present these two chapters will set out to present some basic information about some of the more important lists now available.

These lists are usually called *thesauri,* though as we have pointed out in chapter 19 they are in fact lists of subject headings. The term thesaurus will be used here to denote such lists, with the proviso that this is strictly speaking a misuse of the term. The only one which fits into the conventional meaning of the word is the English Electric *Thesaurofacet,* for which a new term had to be coined. It is only recently that much guidance has become available for the indexer wishing to construct his own thesaurus, but there are now two publications available from Aslib[1] which should fill this gap very satisfactorily.

EJC THESAURUS

This thesaurus is the most significant work to come out of the US in this subject area, and it is worth tracing its history in some detail. One of the major information handling agencies in the United States is the Defense Documentation Center (DDC), formerly the Armed Services Technical Information Agency (ASTIA). As part of its work ASTIA compiled a list of subject headings, which developed through four editions, the last being published in 1959 as the *ASTIA subject headings list.* By this time the agency was exploring the possibilities of using mechanized methods for information retrieval, and a new vocabulary was drawn up for this purpose, the *Thesaurus of ASTIA descriptors,* the first edition being published in 1960, with a second following shortly afterwards in December 1962. The thesaurus was used for the indexing of the *Technical abstract bulletin,* as well as the internal searching within the agency. With the development of interagency abstracting and indexing services, in particular *US Government research and development reports,* the need for a vocabulary common to the four major government agencies became obvious, and led to *Project LEX.* (The four agencies included DDC, NASA—the National Aeronautics and Space Agency, USAEC—the Atomic Energy Commission, and OTS—Office of Technical Services; the latter was later redesignated the Clearinghouse for Federal Scientific and Technical Information—CFSTI, and has recently changed its name yet once more to National Technical Information Service—NTIS, and is now the main source of supply for unclassified (in the military sense!) US government information in the technical and scientific fields.)

At the same time as the US government was beginning to show interest in the development of vocabularies for post-coordinate indexing, the scientific and engineering societies were also becoming concerned. A significant proportion of the world's scientific and technical literature is published by these societies, and they became aware that —for a variety of reasons—much of this information was not reaching its goal. They therefore set about raising the standards of technical writing, paying particular attention to indexing problems; one of the results of this effort was the improvement in titles, making them more suitable for KWIC indexing, while another was the compilation of the EJC *Thesaurus of engineering terms,* published in 1964. This was based on a rather rigorous selection from about 120,000 terms submitted by a number of societies as well as DDC and other government agencies, resulting in a list of nearly 8,000 preferred terms and over 2,000 non-preferred synonyms or near-synonyms. It is not clear how the reduction was achieved, though a preliminary selection seems to have been made by rejecting terms which were suggested by only one of the contributing bodies—though some of these were later restored in order to maintain a balance within each discipline.

The terms were very largely single concept terms, but did include a fairly high proportion of composite headings, *eg* Oil circuit breakers; Ionizing radiation scattering; Salt spray tests. No attempt appears to have been made to introduce consistency of form, so we find Salaries, but also Salary administration; Electrical measurements, Electrically powered instruments, Electric devices and Electricity. Some phrases appear, *eg* Modulus of rupture in torsion; center of gravity; these correspond to normal usage, and would be difficult to eliminate. The problem with this kind of usage is predictability; the user does not know with any certainty where to look for a particular concept, and it is very difficult to insert new terms with any confidence. Some of the terms have scope notes, though this does not apply to very many; example,

NOISE (SPURIOUS SIGNALS)
(LIMITED TO INTERFERENCE GENERATED
INTERNALLY WITHIN A SYSTEM OR
EQUIPMENT)

Others have a note advising against their use, because of their lack of specificity:

ELECTRIC POWER
(USE MORE SPECIFIC TERM IF POSSIBLE)

The symbol # is used to denote a term for which two or more broader terms may be substituted, the converse of this being &; the net result of this convention is rather confusing, especially at a heading such as Electric motors:

ELECTRIC MOTORS &
NT A-C MOTORS &
AMPLIDYNES #
CAPACITOR MOTORS #
D-C MOTORS &
POLYPHASE MOTORS *etc*

Relationships between terms are shown rather more precisely than is usual in subject headings lists, as has already been pointed out in chapter 19. Synonyms are linked by means of USE and UF (*ie* Use For)

BURSTS (MINES)
(EXCLUDES EXPLOSIONS)
UF GAS OUTBURSTS
ROCK BURSTS
GAS OUTBURSTS
USE BURSTS (MINES)

Generic terms are indicated by BT (Broader term), with specific terms NT (Narrower term); related terms, which may be linked in a variety of ways, are indicated by RT:

COLD WORKING &
UF COLD BENDING
    COLD DRAWING
    ...
NT DIE DRAWING
    METAL POINTING
    PLANISHING
BT METAL WORKING &
RT BULGING
    CLADDING
    DEEP DRAWING #
    etc

The list is produced by photoreduction from computer printout, and is not particularly elegant, though it is certainly usable; preferred terms are emphasized by printing twice to give a bold effect. There are two appendices; the first of these is a short note on information retrieval thesauri, the second a brief account of the Engineers Joint Council action plan mentioned earlier. Following this appendix is a table showing the EJC set of roles, of which the following is an excerpt:

8   The primary topic of consideration is; there is a description of

1   Input; raw material; a material being corroded; energy input

2   Output; product, by-product, co-product; device shaped or formed

3   Undesirable component; waste; scrap; rejects; unnecessary material present

4   Indicated, possible, intended present or later uses or applications

5   Environment; solvent; host

6   Cause; independent or controlled variable

7   Effect; dependent variable

9   Passively receiving an operation or process with no change in identity, composition, configuration ... or physical form

10 Means to accomplish the primary topic of consideration

0   Bibliographic data, personal names of authors ... adjectives

These seem to bear some relationship to Ranganathan's seminal mnemonics, though their purpose is of course rather different. In practice, some problems were found with their use and they are not now recommended.

There were a number of critical reviews, particularly by British librarians, who found the list inadequate for a variety of reasons.[2] In the first place, it made no attempt to cover English as opposed to American terminology, or British technical developments; for example, though several types of nuclear reactor are mentioned, gas-cooled reactors are not, though Britain had had several such reactors producing quantities of electricity for several years. Secondly, and more significantly, the complete disregard of any kind of systematic basis for the network of BT-NT and RT-RT relationships meant that these were quite haphazard, and did not in many cases bear close examination. In 1965, a large-scale revision was set in motion, with the intention of enlarging the vocabulary, tightening up the network of relationships, and resolving any differences between this thesaurus and that being prepared by the DDC in Project LEX. The joint result of both projects was the second edition of the EJC thesaurus, now entitled *Thesaurus of scientific and engineering terms*, published in December 1967.

One of the first steps was to formulate rules and conventions governing the selection of terms and the construction of cross-references; these rules are printed as Appendix 1 of the thesaurus, and are a useful guide, with, for example, one of the few tables of guidelines on when to use the singular or plural form of a term that has appeared. Many of these rules are refinements or restatements of rules that have been used by subject headings lists since Cutter, but it is convenient to have them in this concise form.

The terms used were drawn from a total of some 150,000 taken from about 150 major sources and a further 200 lists which were used for reference purposes. From these the final list of 17,810 descriptors —preferred terms—and 5,554 USE references was selected by a team of over 300 scientists and engineers, with a final review by an editorial panel. The resulting thesaurus is a complex and useful tool, though it is still open to criticism, particularly from the point of view of British users—for whom of course it was not intended. There are several improvements over the first edition, notably in the organization of relationships between terms. The printing, carried out by computer controlled typesetting, is also of a much higher standard, though the small type face used for cross-references could be something of a hindrance.

The main list consists of preferred and non-preferred terms in one sequence; both are printed in bold, but non-preferred terms are in italics. In some cases, a single non-preferred term is replaced by more than one preferred term, *eg*

Artificial sea water

USE Sea water

and Simulation

This is indicated under the preferred terms by a dagger, thus

Sea water

UF †Artificial sea water

Broader terms, narrower terms and related terms are shown in the same way as in the first edition, with one additional convention. A dash preceding a NT reference indicates that the narrower term has itself further narrower terms; a useful indication, corresponding to the use of bold type in the relative index to DC to show that a topic is subdivided in the schedules. An example:

Personnel

NT—Craftsmen

though when we turn to Craftsmen it is something of a disappointment to find only two subdivisions:

Craftsmen

NT   Electricians

Electronic technicians

Scope notes appear, as they did in the first edition; there are also a few occasions where a context note is shown in parentheses:

Microorganism control (sewage)

Microorganism control (water)

Control of organisms such as bacteria, viruses, plankton, algae,
and protozoa

There are two other important new features, which represent in effect a recognition of the importance of the classified approach in linking related subjects. The first of these is a tabulation of single terms showing every heading in which they appear in the main sequence; this is called the Permuted index, though it is not very clear why, as none of the terms in it are permuted. A rather confusing difference from the main sequence is found in the type face; terms which are used on their own in the main sequence are printed there in bold, but in the permuted index they are printed in bold italic. Terms printed in bold in the permuted index are those which are *not* used on their own in the main sequence. An example will demonstrate the use that might be made of this index; suppose that we wish to find all the headings in which the term *membrane* appears, we turn to that heading in the permuted index and find:

Membrane
Hyaline membrane disease
Ion exchange membrane electrolytes
Membrane filters

Membranes
Webs (membranes)

Membrane is in bold type; this tells us that it does not appear on its own, but only as a component of the headings Hyaline membrane disease and Ion exchange membrane electrolytes. Under Membrane filters we shall find a USE reference, which turns out to be

Membrane filters
USE Fluid filters
and Membranes

Membranes is used as a preferred term, but there is a reference from Webs (Membranes) USE Membranes. In effect, the permuted index serves the same purpose as the chain index to a classified sequence or the cross-references in BTI, by enabling us to get from a particular term to those places in the main sequence where it will appear.

The second is the Subject Category Index. This is in effect a broad subject classification with 22 major subject fields, each of which is subdivided into groups; the largest group is Biological and medical sciences, with 21 headings, the smallest Atmospheric sciences and Mathematical sciences, each with two. The classification was originally devised by COSATI, the Committee on Scientific and Technical Information, which is part of the organization which exists to advise the US President on matters scientific; it has been modified slightly for use in the EJC Thesaurus. It is discipline-oriented, so it suffers from all of the problems that we have already noted with conventional classification schemes; for example, nuclear propulsion is under Propulsion, nuclear explosions under Nuclear science and technology, nuclear warfare under Military sciences, explosions under Ordnance, nuclear reactions under Physics, and so on. One is tempted to wonder why an existing scheme such as UDC was not used, since there is no basic difference, and not even very much difference in detail. Each category has a two-figure number, and each group has a further two-figure number; thus Computers is group 02 in Category 09, Electronics and electrical engineering. If we turn to 0902 in the classified tabulation we find about 100 terms falling into that category and group. Preferred terms in the main sequence have their group number, giving a second method of finding related headings, *eg*

The third method is the Hierarchical Index. Any term in the main sequence which has no BT references, but has at least two levels of NT references, is tabulated in this index, showing all the terms related to it directly or at one or more remove by an NT reference. The level is shown by indentation, *eg*

Addition resins
.Vinyl resins
..Styrene resins
...Styrene copolymers
....Styrene butadiene resins

A heading may appear in more than one hierarchy, not necessarily at the same level. We can get to the last heading in the above example through another hierarchy leading to the same level:

Addition resins
.Vinyl resins
..Vinyl copolymers
...Styrene copolymers
....Styrene butadiene resins

Another example shows how the same term may appear at two different levels, though both within the same generic heading:

Vertebrates
.Domestic animals
..Livestock
...Cattle
....Beef cattle
.Mammals
..Eutheria
...Ungulata
....Artiodactyla
.....Ruminants
......Cattle
.......Beef cattle

A third example shows a concept which occurs at different levels under different generic headings:

Addition resins
.Olefin resins
..Ethylene resins
...Polyethylene

Thermoplastic resins
 .Polyethylene

These three indexes certainly add to the value of the thesaurus by enabling the indexer or user to find related terms in a systematic way, but they call into question exactly what is meant by the term ' concept '. The guide lines inform us that ' a descriptor represents a concept ', so it would appear that Radioisotope thermoelectric devices; Target drone aircraft; Marine biological noise; and Microorganism control (sewage) are all ' concepts '. This is clearly not what we have been considering as a ' concept ' when referring to facet analysis, for example.

The subject coverage of the thesaurus is reasonable, including some fringe subjects which might be thought to be outside the scope of such a list. Information retrieval is well represented, and there are headings for Religions and Religious buildings, Literature, Musical instruments and Drama, among others. There are problems with American terminology, *eg* Pavements and Sidewalks, just as there are with Sears List and LCSH, but in general the terms used in science and technology are more standardized than those used in the social sciences or humanities.

The revised EJC Thesaurus is clearly a very important tool, and is likely to continue as such for some time to come. One wonders what would have been the result if the same amount of effort had been devoted to the revision and updating of UDC, and the Thesaurofacet, described later, shows what can be done with very much smaller resources if a more systematic approach is used.

BUREAU OF SHIPS THESAURUS OF DESCRIPTIVE TERMS
This thesaurus was compiled within the US Navy Bureau of Ships as part of Project SHARP (SHips Analysis and Retrieval Project), and the first edition was published in 1963. The second edition, a revision and updating of the first, was published in 1965, some sixteen months later, after implementation of a plan to computerize the production. There are some interesting points of comparison with the EJC Thesaurus, though generally speaking the BuShips Thesaurus is not on the same scale.

The printout is by computer line printer, which has meant certain limitations: uppercase letters only, no aspostrophes, hyphens inserted by hand where absolutely necessary! Each term is limited to 36 characters, which means that occasionally terms have to be abbreviated, *eg*

NUCLEAR POWERED BALLISTIC MSL. SUBS.

Non-preferred terms are shown by a USE REFERENCE, but the converse of this is not UF but INCLUDES:

NUCLEAR REACTIONS
    INCLUDES:
        REACTIONS (NUCLEAR)

REACTIONS (NUCLEAR)
    USE:
        NUCLEAR REACTIONS

BROADER TERMS, NARROWER TERMS and RELATED TERMS are all spelled out instead of abbreviated. Definitions and scope notes are very similar to the EJC pattern.

The unique feature of this thesaurus is that it gives a list of codes for the descriptors, suitable for use in a computerized retrieval system; these codes have a maximum length of seven digits, though for words which are shorter than this no attempt is made to bulk out the code to give a standard length. Examples:

ACTINSR	ACTINIDE SERIES
ACTSCOM	ACTINIDE SERIES COMPOUNDS
ACUITY	ACUITY
ACIDS	ACIDS

There is one tabulation alphabetically by descriptor, and another alphabetically by code.

This thesaurus and its use in Project SHARP was the subject of an investigation by Lancaster[3], the major result of which was the recommendation that roles should be discontinued as an indexing device. The roles used had been those from the first edition of the EJC Thesaurus, and their use was shown to give only a few per cent improvement in relevance for an increase in both searching and indexing costs of about 100%.

AMERICAN PETROLEUM INSTITUTE

This list is not called a thesaurus, but has the title *Information retrieval system subject authority list,* and the latest edition was published in 1970. In appearance, the list is rather like the first EJC Thesaurus, being produced by computer printout, with preferred terms emphasized by double printing. The terms included are of course rather more specialized, including many chemical terms, *eg* 2-AMINOETHANOL, (filed by ignoring the 2-) but also names of important firms, *eg* AMERICAN CYANAMID, used for indexing patents only, and place names, *eg* GREECE, GREAT LAKES. There are several different kinds of scope note, *eg*

342

INTERSTATE
SCOPE NOTES
ADDED IN APRIL 1968
NOT FOR INTERNATIONAL, FOR WHICH
USE WORLD WIDE

IONIZATION DETECTOR
SCOPE NOTES
ADDED IN 1968. IN 1966 AND 1967
SEARCH RADIATION DETECTOR

INTERFEROMETER
SCOPE NOTES
WHEN CITED ONLY TO INDICATE THAT
THE EQUIPMENT IS USED, INDEX THE
PROCESS INSTEAD

INTERMEDIATE, REACTION
INDEX THE MATERIAL PRODUCED
AND REACTING, WITH ROLE I.
SEARCH THE MATERIAL WITH ROLES P
AND A

MULTIPHASE
SCOPE NOTES
INDEX IF IMPORTANT OR DISCUSSED.
CATALYSTS OR TREATING AGENTS ARE
NOT COUNTED AS PHASES.

MULTIPLE
SCOPE NOTES
MODIFIER. LINK TO WORD MODIFIED

These scope notes are aimed at both indexer and searcher, and are a valuable feature.

Relationships between terms are shown, though not quite in the usual way. Non-preferred terms are indicated by USE references:

MONO
USE
ONE
MOSSBAUER EFFECT
USE
GAMMA RAY
PLUS RESONANCE

The converse of this USED FOR:

RESONANCE
 USED FOR
  MOSSBAUER EFFECT
  PLUS GAMMA RAY

BROADER TERMS are autoposted; that is, in the API usage, they are indexed whenever one of the narrower terms is used. RELATED TERMS and CHEMICAL ASPECTS are also autoposted; NARROWER TERMS are not, and in addition to these and related terms we find SEE ALSO references:

MORTAR
 BROADER TERMS (AUTOPOSTED)
  CONSTRUCTION MATERIAL
 NARROWER TERMS
  GUNITE
 SEE ALSO
  CEMENT

VARNISH
 BROADER TERMS (AUTOPOSTED)
  PAINT
 RELATED TERMS (AUTOPOSTED)
  COATING MATERIAL
 SEE ALSO
  GUM DEPOSIT

FLUOROETHYLENE HOMOPOLYMER
 CHEMICAL ASPECTS (AUTOPOSTED)
  C2 MONOMER
  SINGLE STRUCTURE TYPE
  UNSATURATED CHAIN MONOMER
  HALOHYDROCARBON
  FLUOROHYDROCARBON
  MONOOLEFINIC MONOMER
  TERMINAL OLEFINIC MONOMER
  HOMOPOLYMER
 USED FOR
  POLYFLUOROETHYLENE

The list of terms is followed by several smaller sections. The first of these is a list of descriptors added in 1970, with a very short list of four terms dropped during that year. The second is a list of Chemical aspects, with scope notes showing how each is to be understood; it is, for example, possible to use the descriptor **IDE** for anions and compounds ending in ide, *eg* chloride, cyanide, etc. There is a short list of document descriptors, *eg* Glossary; theoretical study; a list of major chemical companies, used for indexing patents; and a very brief list of descriptors for illustrations and data. These descriptors all appear in the main list, but it is useful to have them tabulated separately also. The next page is concerned with links and roles. The indexer is told to use links in five situations:

Chemical descriptors—assign a link so that autoposted broader and related terms will be linked

Chemical aspects—assign a link to all aspects of a chemical compound

Common attributes—link to the descriptor they modify

Materials—link terms from different facets used to index the same materials, *eg* Function and Composition, to the materials

Structure—link descriptors from the Structure facet to the materials they relate to.

Many of these situations are in fact noted in the thesaurus under the appropriate descriptors. There are five roles:

Role A (agent/reactant)=raw material

Role B (reaction product)=end product

Role I (intermediate) is used when a material is both a product of a reaction and the starting point for a further reaction. When the index entries are transferred to computer tape and the dual dictionary printout, this role is converted to $A+B$

Role T (prior treatment) is used to particularize a material which has been produced as the end product of a process, *eg* for Frozen food one would index Freezing with Role T and Food

Role X (substance determined) is used to index documents relating to the detection or determination of a specific material in a mixture.

The final section of the thesaurus is headed Hierarchy, and consists of a systematic tabulation of terms in the list based on the broader term—narrower term relationships, with a supporting alphabetical index leading to the appropriate column. The tabulation includes Place and Common attributes as well as the expected Materials and Processes, etc.

The API Subject authority list is a good example of a thesaurus tied to a particular indexing situation. Like the special subject editions of UDC, it gives a lot more help to the indexer than the more general lists, which are developed out of contact with any particular collection of literature.

NASA THESAURUS

As might be expected, a considerable effort was made to ensure that this thesaurus, of which the preliminary edition, published December 1967, replaced the previous *Guide to the subject indexes for scientific and technical aerospace reports*, was made compatible as far as possible with the DDC and EJC compilations. The points noted here will therefore be those points of difference which appear to be interesting or significant. The main alphabetical list occupies two volumes, with a third volume containing four appendices: Hierarchical display, Category term listing, Permuted index, and Postable terms.

The main list of terms is very similar to the EJG list, with four exceptions. The first of these is that acronyms and abbreviations, of which there are great numbers in the aerospace industry, are used as preferred terms, with USE cross-references from the full form. This again represents a difference between a thesaurus intended to be of general utility and one tailor-made for a specific purpose. Secondly, names of specific models or items are used as descriptors and fitted into the BT-NT-RT structure; one might include an entry:

BOEING 747 AIRCRAFT
   UF JUMBO JET
   BT PASSENGER AIRCRAFT
      BOEING AIRCRAFT
 # JET AIRCRAFT
    etc

Thirdly, the # symbol is used to indicate those terms which are generic headings in the Hierarchical display; these terms can only be found in the EJC Thesaurus by trial and error. Fourthly, there is a note on alphabetization, though it may be thought to be rather less helpful than one might expect. Most of the list described so far have used letter by letter filing, but the NASA list has a note:

'The ordering of subject terms into an alphabetical arrangement can be accomplished in several ways. The most commonly used methods are the letter-by-letter, word-by-word, and the computer sorting order. In the absence of any universal agreement on a standardized approach, the last-named technique has been adopted in this *Thesaurus* as the most useful and economic for this purpose.'

346

It is useful to have such a note, but as one reviewer has pointed out,[4] there are at least a dozen computer sorting orders! We are left to assume that NASA's own computer sorting order is used; the overall effect is to give word by word filing, as opposed to the letter by letter filing in EJC.

The appendices differ again to some extent from the EJC parallels. The hierarchical listing corresponds, though the layout is perhaps a little clearer, and the permuted index is also similar. However, the 34 categories and 217 subcategories in the Category term listing are devised by NASA rather than the COSATI categories used by EJC. The Postable terms index is simply a listing of preferred terms without any of the cross-reference structure of non-preferred terms; it does not give any information not available rather easily from the main sequence, and it is a little difficult to see its purpose. One final point worth mentioning is that, like many US Government publications, this is very good value for money at $8.50 for the three volumes!

THESAUROFACET

A number of libraries in Britain have compiled thesauri, but none on the large scale of the EJC or Project LEX, with the exception of the English Electric Company. The EE *Classification for engineering,* which we have already mentioned in chapters 8 and 10, was the first large faceted classification devised by a member of the CRG, and reached its third edition in 1961. In the course of the next few years it became clear that a detailed revision was becoming essential, but at the same time the company's libraries were investigating the possibilities of using computer techniques and post-coordinate indexing, and the decision was therefore taken to develop the new edition of the classification scheme in conjunction with a thesaurus. The result, given the rather ugly name *Thesaurofacet,* was published in 1970 (the date 1969 in the scheme proved to be a little optimistic), and is an important contribution to subject indexing theory and practice. The full title: *Thesaurofacet: a thesaurus and faceted classification for engineering and related subjects,* shows that there are in fact two tools here, a classification and a thesaurus, but it is necessary to emphasize that the two have to be used together if the best results are to be obtained; the two are complementary rather than parallel.

The work begins with a detailed introduction in which the construction and use of the list are outlined, and these have also been described by Jean Aitchison, the chief editor, in *Journal of documentation.*[5]

There are several points of interest here. The classification is no longer entirely synthetic, for reasons which are relevant to analytico-synthetic classification generally. There will, in any given situation, be a number of composite subjects which arise regularly, and of which the individual concepts rarely appear on their own in the literature; in such a case it is better to enumerate the composite rather than give the classifier the trouble of constructing a piece of notation each time. As we have pointed out, synthesized notation tends to be longer than non-expressive notation allocated to enumerated topics; the notation used in Thesaurofacet is largely non-expressive, and can thus be used economically in this way. However, there are advantages in synthesis, particularly in providing for the composite subjects which have not yet appeared but which may do so in the future, so provision is made for this in the notation, and instructions are given in the introduction as to when this is to be used. An attempt has been made to strike a practical balance between the advantages of synthesis and those of enumeration, in a way which emphasizes that this is a practical working tool, not just a theoretical exercise.

A classification scheme can only display one set of genus-species divisions; in *Thesaurofacet*, others are shown in the thesaurus, using BT-NT-RT cross-references, and others by cross-references in the schedules, denoted by an asterisk. To use the scheme, the indexer or user looks up a term in the thesaurus; this will give him a class number, but may also give him some related terms. These related terms may come from the hierarchy to be found at the given class number, but they may also be from other parts of the schedules, in which case they are marked as *additional, eg* BT(A). Class numbers derived by synthesis are shown by the use of *synth* and an *S* preceding the constituent terms.

The notation is mixed, using uppercase letters and numerals, and the stroke / to indicate synthesis. Where synthesis occurs, instructions are given, with examples showing the kind of notation that results. The filing order is stroke, number, letter, *eg*

TM	**Cutting (flame)**
TM/TA2	Cutting machine tools
TM2	Arc cutting
TMB	Flame deseaming.

Alphabetization in the thesaurus is letter by letter, so that Lawrencium precedes Law reports. This is in accordance with EJC practice, which has been followed to a large extent.

348

Some examples will demonstrate the use of the two halves of the system. Suppose we are asked for information on 'thinners'. When we look this up in the thesaurus, we find:

Thinners *use*
Solvents

We turn to Solvents, and find:

Solvents		HXG
UF	Thinners	
RT	Dispersants	
	Dissolving	
	Plasticisers	
	Solutes	
	Solutions	
	Solvent extraction	
NT(A)	Paint thinners	
	Turpentine	

If we turn to HXG in the classified schedules, we find:

HX	**MATERIALS BY PURPOSE**
HX2	Additives
HXG	Solvents

However, the terms mentioned in the thesaurus may have caused us to realize that what is actually wanted is information on *paint* thinners, so we turn to this, and find that the class number is VGD; by turning to this class number, we find that VGD is a subdivision of VG Paint constituents within VF Paint technology.

In contrast to the NASA list, abbreviations are normally spelled out, so if we look up α,n reactions we are referred to alpha particle neutron reaction; at this heading we find:

Alpha Particle Neutron Reaction
$$E8C/E5V/E8E/E5N$$

Synth

UF	α,n reaction
S RT	Alpha particle projectiles
S BT(A)	Neutron product reaction

When we turn to the classification we find that the notation for this topic is synthesized from E8C, Projectile particles in E8 Nuclear reactions; E5V alpha particles; E8E product particles; and E5N neutrons. The complete notation is enumerated under a heading which tells us:

Classify specific reactions by combining the notation above, in the order Projectile/Type of reaction

Some terms appear in the thesaurus with a class number only, *eg*

Butter   VMO

this indicates that the only relationships with other topics to be found are those at the class number; if we turn to this we find:

VM	**FOOD TECHNOLOGY**	
	*Food industries ZKCB	
	By products	
VM	Food	
VMM	Dairy Products	
VMN	Milk	
VMO	Butter	
VMP	Cheese	

From this display we see that Butter falls into the BT Dairy products, along with Cheese and Milk; Dairy products itself is a subdivision (*ie* NT) of Food; and that if we are interested in the industry we should turn to ZKCB. If we do this, we find that ZK Industries and its subdivisions are to be used only for economic aspects, not technological.

The whole system depends on the interaction of classification schedules and thesaurus; once this point is grasped, the scheme becomes easy to use and helpful to both indexer and user. Because of the systematic approach, relationships are displayed more clearly and precisely than in the subject category lists provided by EJC and similar bodies. In coverage, the scheme is, not unnaturally, biased towards subjects of particular concern to English Electric, but a serious attempt has been made to avoid undue imbalance. In size, it compares with the EJC Thesaurus, with about 16,000 preferred terms and another 7,000 non-preferred. It is likely to prove a very useful tool, especially in British libraries, where the US bias of the EJC Thesaurus could be a hindrance in its use.

MeSH

This list is called by the old-fashioned name: *Medical Subject Headings,* and is published as Part 2 of *Index Medicus* in January each year. It is, however, a thesaurus in the sense in which the term is being used here, that is, a list of headings for use in a post-coordinate indexing system. MeSH is in fact used in two different situations; it is used in *Index Medicus,* and also in the computerized MEDLARS. In the first, articles appear under an average of four terms; the headings are not precoordinated, and in consequence one may have to endure a fair amount of sequential scanning in the search for information on a specific composite subject. For example, if one were interested in allergy to penicillin in children, it would be possible to scan the entries under Penicillin, or those under Hypersensitivity (the preferred term for allergy), or those under Child, but there would be no composite heading specific to this topic. In MEDLARS, the same articles are indexed by, on average, ten terms, and it is possible to perform coordinate searches using the computer; the additional terms tend to increase recall, but the ability to coordinate terms enables us to counterbalance this with a gain in relevance.

The cross-reference network between related headings is worked out in some detail, but uses rather different symbols from those we have seen so far. A non-preferred term may lead to more than one preferred term:

CARPUS see WRIST (A1, A2)

CARPUS see WRIST JOINT (A2)

The converse of SEE is X, as in conventional subject cataloguing:

WRIST (A1, A2)
  X CARPUS (A1, A2)

WRIST JOINT (A2)
  X CARPUS (A1, A2)

The notation in curves after each heading indicates the subject category or categories where it will be found in the second part of the list. Some non-preferred terms lead to broader terms, rather than direct synonyms; in this case, the reference is see under, with XU as the converse:

CARPUS, ANIMAL see under FORELIMB (A13)

FORELIMB (A13)
  XU CARPUS, ANIMAL (A13)

Headings are all in bold, whether preferred or non-preferred, but preferred terms are in large capitals; the overall effect on the page is a little daunting. Related terms are linked by means of two kinds of see also references, see also related and see also specific; some obvious cross-references, *eg* those from organs to their diseases, are omitted. See also related cross-references link terms from different categories, and are reflected by XR notes under the heading referred to:

OCCUPATIONAL THERAPY (E2, G2)
see also related
ART (K)
MUSIC (K)
ART (K)
XR OCCUPATIONAL THERAPY

See also specific cross-references are rare; they serve to link a heading to a specific heading in another category, *eg*:
TEA (B6, J)
see also specific
THEOPHYLLINE (D2, D6)
THEOPHYLLINE (D2, D6)
XS TEA (B6, J)

Theophylline is an organic chemical forming a constituent of tea leaves; tea appears in Class B6 as a member of the plant kingdom, and in J as a food, whereas theophylline appears in D2 as an organic chemical and in D6 as a drug acting on the central nervous system.

As in Sears and LCSH, there is a list of subheadings which can be added to any heading within the stated categories as appropriate, *eg*

Pathology (A, C, F)—Used for tissue or cellular structure in disease states; includes biopsy and post-mortem examination.

Categories A, C and F are Anatomical terms, Diseases, and Psychiatry and Psychology, respectively. In addition, if MESH is used for book cataloguing, there are form subheadings which may be added, and certain headings may also be divided geographically or by language.

Headings which have been added during the previous year are listed together with the headings they replace or expand; this may reflect a more detailed approach within a given topic, *eg*

GROOMING (F) (new)   BEHAVIOUR, ANIMAL (F) (previous heading)

or a change in emphasis leading to classification in a different category, *eg*

HOSPITALS, GENERAL (N2)   HOSPITALS (G3)
HOSPITALS, SPECIAL (N2)   HOSPITALS (G3)
HOSPITALS, TEACHING (N2) HOSPITALS (G3)

where G3 is Environmental health, hygiene and preventive medicine within G Biological sciences, whereas N2 is Health facilities, manpower and services within N Health care.

The Categorized lists which form the last part of MESH are in effect a rather simple classification of Medicine, with fourteen groups and sixty two subgroups. As well as the expected groups, some of which have already been discussed, there are groups for Communication, library science and documentation (L) and Named groups of persons (M); the latter includes those groups ' for which no satisfactory activity name is available ' or in which primary emphasis is on the individual, eg

HOSPITAL VOLUNTEERS

TISSUE DONORS

TWINS

WOMEN

(Men do not appear in the list at all).

A far more detailed arrangement in classified order is available in *Medical subject headings: tree structures*, published separately; this gives not only the headings which are in MeSH but others which form a necessary part of the classification structure but are not used for indexing.

In both lists, a subject may appear in more than one category, as has been seen, and both give the additional class numbers in these cases, but the notation in the tree structures is much more detailed. For example, Blood appears in three subgroups in Category A Anatomical terms; in MeSH it appears in the *alphabetical* sequence in A7 Cardiovascular system twice, once in its own right, so to speak, and once as a subdivision of Cardiovascular system. In the Tree structure for A7, however, it appears in the *classified* sequence in its own right at A7.15, but also as a subdivision of Hematopoietic system at A7.60.21; in both cases there is a cross-reference to the other placing, as well as detailed cross-references to A10.66.16 and A12.13.18 instead of the broad cross-references to A10 and A12 in the categorized list. The Tree structures list also has a place facet, Z1, which consists of an alphabetical list of major areas, *eg* Asia, New Zealand, North America, with alphabetically arranged subdivisions. This seems, like some of the features we have seen in other thesauri, to be somewhat pointless; it would have been as easy to use DC or UDC and probably more satisfactory.

Investigation of MEDLARS has shown that in general MeSH functions reasonably well; failures have arisen from inadequacies in MeSH, but more appear to have resulted from inadequate use of what was available by the indexers. In recent years there has been a much more systematic approach to revision, and the list is likely to go on improving with each annual revision.

BIBLIOGRAPHY

1 Gilchrist, A: *The thesaurus in retrieval*. Aslib, 1971.

Gilchrist, A, and Aitchison, J: *Manual of thesaurus construction*. Aslib, 1971.

See also Blagden, J F: 'Thesaurus compilation methods: a literature review'. *Aslib proceedings 20* (8) August 1968, 345-359.

2 See for example the review by D J Campbell in *Journal of documentation, 21* (2) June 1965, 136.

3 Lancaster, F W: 'Some observations on the performance of EJC role indicators in a mechanised retrieval system'. *Special libraries, 55* (10) 1964, 696-701.

4 *American documentation, 19* (2) 1968, 208-209.

5 Aitchison, J: 'The thesaurofacet: a multipurpose retrieval language tool'. *Journal of documentation, 26* (3) September 1970, 187-203.

CHAPTER 22

Social sciences

Thesauri in the social sciences have tended to be even more specialized than those in science and technology; there have also been rather fewer so far, with nothing on the scale of Project LEX; the largest single effort supported by the US Government in this field has been in the field of education.

ERIC

The Educational Resources Information Center Clearinghouses network was set up in 1966 to disseminate information in the field of educational research; one of its key publications is the monthly abstract journal *Research in education*, and the Office of Education Panel on Educational Terminology decided to sponsor a thesaurus for the indexing of this bibliography. The first, preliminary, edition was published in January 1967; this contained just over 3,000 descriptors, and was issued in revised form in 1968 as the *Thesaurus of ERIC descriptors* (first edition). The first edition proved somewhat inadequate for indexing, and a second edition was published in 1969, replacing the first edition, dated 1967, and the supplement dated March 1968. This edition contained over 6,000 descriptors, twice as many as in the preliminary edition and over 2,000 more than in the first edition. It also contained other new features such as the descriptor group display.

After a brief foreword, there is an introduction setting out the purpose of the thesaurus and the way it functions. One of the important features in this is the *descriptor justification form*, which must be used by anyone wishing to submit a term for consideration as a new indexing descriptor. There is a description of the method of linking related headings, which is the same as that used by EJC: USE, UF, BT, NT, RT; some descriptors have qualifiers to distinguish homographs, *eg* PATTERN DRILLS (LANGUAGE), while others have scope notes, either because they have a rather broad meaning or because they have an unusual meaning in educational terminology. For example:

CORRESPONDENCE STUDY
   SN METHOD OF INSTRUCTION WITH TEACHER
      STUDENT INTERACTION BY MAIL

though it is not found necessary to define CORRESPONDENCE COURSES or CORRESPONDENCE SCHOOLS. Some of these scope notes hardly add to the descriptor, *eg*

MAN DAYS
    SN UNIT CONSISTING OF ONE HYPOTHETICAL
        AVERAGE MAN DAY

which rather leaves us where we started. An important part of the introduction is the section justifying the use of compound terms, which are used quite frequently; this is not only a reflection of normal usage within the subject area, but also avoids the use of large numbers of links. For example, if we index the subject ' student attitudes to teachers ' under the three concepts involved, it will be retrieved by someone searching for information on teacher attitudes to students; by using a composite heading Student attitudes we can prevent this. However, the use of links would also achieve the same objective, and give us in addition the possibility of widening the search; after all, teachers' attitudes to students and students' attitudes to teachers are certainly related. The use of large numbers of composite headings means that in fact the thesaurus is very similar indeed to a list such as Sears or LCSH. Another difference from the thesauri we have considered so far is that the adjectival form is permitted in some cases, though this is restricted to terms in which the additional term ' people ' can be understood, *eg* HANDICAPPED.

As composite headings are used, it is necessary to provide an index to reveal those terms which are hidden by their position *after* the filing word; this index, called the Rotated descriptor display, is a KWIC listing of all the descriptors in the list. If, for example, we were looking for information on Addiction, we should not find that term listed in the main sequence, but by turning to the Rotated descriptor display we can quickly find that it is used only in the heading DRUG ADDICTION.

Related subjects are brought together in the Descriptor groups display. This feature, which appears for the first time in the second edition, begins with an alphabetical tabulation of 52 groups; this is followed by a second tabulation in alphabetical order, this time with scope notes, *eg*

080 COMMUNICATION
    Methods and characteristics of communication,
    e.g., Oral Expression, Verbal Communication,
    etc. For types of communication equipment, *see*
    also EQUIPMENT

The third section consists of yet another alphabetical tabulation, this time with terms within each group displayed, also in alphabetical order. This section can only be welcomed on the grounds that *any* systematic approach is better than none.

The main sequence, like the rotated index and the group display, is produced from computer printout, and is poor in quality; headings, consisting of the descriptor and its group number, are in large bold capitals, with subheadings showing related terms in small capitals, *eg*

PARKING AREAS   **210**

   SN SURFACE AREAS DESIGNATED FOR VEHICLE
        STORAGE ALONG CURBS OR IN SPECIFIC
        DELINEATED AREAS
   UF PARKING LOTS
        STREET PARKING AREAS
   BT FACILITIES
   RT DRIVEWAYS
        PARKING CONTROLS
        PARKING METERS *etc*

The first edition was criticized in a review in *American documentation;*[1] some of the points made there have been amended in the second edition, but not all. There is still no clear statement of how or why one descriptor is accepted and another omitted (or rejected); the bibliography at the end omits one or two items that might have been thought particularly relevant, such as the *Information retrieval thesaurus of education terms* reviewed below, or the *London education classification* referred to in chapter 8. A programmed text was devised and published by the University of Maryland School of Library and Information Services in 1967,[2] but is also not mentioned in the bibliography to the second edition. All in all, one feels that this is a tool which means well but which shows very clearly the problems which arise if a thesaurus is constructed on a non-systematic basis for use in a co-operative indexing project, where consistency is of the essence.

INFORMATION RETRIEVAL THESAURUS OF EDUCATION TERMS
As part of the preparatory work for the ERIC project, the School of Library Science at Case Western Reserve University developed a thesaurus of terms; this list was not the one finally used, though it is not clear why, as it appears to be much better than the ERIC Thesaurus as it now stands. Compiled by G C Barhydt and C T

Schmidt, with assistance from K T Chang, the *Information retrieval thesaurus of education terms* was published by the University in 1968. After a brief foreword, there is a very useful introduction preceding the three sections of the list: alphabetical array, faceted array, and permuted list of descriptors. The introduction is more than just an introduction to this thesaurus, it is a very good albeit brief summary of the kind of problems that are likely to be found in indexing or searching for material in a subject field such as education, and the steps taken in the construction to deal with these problems. The original development arose from the indexing of some 7,500 documents and the compilation of a *Semantic code dictionary of education* containing nearly 11,000 terms. (The WRU experiments with semantic coding are described briefly in chapter 23 below). This list was reduced to a working list of about 5,000 terms by eliminating abbreviations, different spellings and identifiers, *ie* terms which denote specific institutions, etc. Although further terms were added during the development of the thesaurus, rigorous editing and selecting of terms has meant that the final list contains just over 2,000 preferred terms, with cross-references from additional non-preferred terms. However, the compilers point out that because the vocabulary is clearly structured it is relatively simple to add new terms if this is thought appropriate in any given situation.

In addition to straightforward synonyms, which are relatively few, five classes of USE reference are defined, most of which are already familiar:

1 prefer the appropriate grammatical form, dictated in many cases by the facet analysis, *eg* Interviewing rather than Interview, since this falls into the activities facet

2 prefer general terms to trade names

3 prefer normal word order to inversion

4 use one term for a concept and its opposite, *eg* Attendance for Non-attendance

5 use a general term rather than specific terms for subjects of fringe interest.

Scope notes are of six kinds. The first of these is the qualifier added in parenthesis, which could usually be replaced by an ordinary scope note, *eg* Sampling (statistical). Second and third are positive and negative limitation; the former is a kind of definition, the latter serves to exclude concepts which might otherwise fall into the scope of the heading but which in fact have separate headings of their own. Fourth is a straightforward definition, or definition with positive limitation. Fifth is a kind of positive limitation, but applies to terms of rather general meaning which are used in particular sense in the field of education, or where only one meaning of several is of interest in the subject. The sixth kind of scope note is unusual, consisting of an asterisk, *eg* Facilities SN *. These are terms which are unlikely to be used for indexing because of their generality, but which are given because they form a potential link in genus-species division or because the compilers felt that they would, *in a given indexing situation*, become more meaningful.

Broader term - narrower term relationships are shown by use of BT-NT entries in the usual way. Related terms are however given more elaborate treatment. Each descriptor has at least one RT reference leading to the subfacet in which it is to be found in the faceted array, but in many cases this is the only RT reference, since there are no related terms in other hierarchies. Where other RT references appear they fall into two groups: reciprocal and non-reciprocal. Reciprocal RT references work both ways and are marked with a kind of blob in the shape of a distorted inverted comma; non-reciprocal references work only the way shown, and are not marked. For example:

PRESCHOOL EDUCATION
   SN *
   RT   2012
       CULTURAL DEPRIVATION
       EARLY CHILDHOOD
       PRESCHOOL LEVEL ☓

This means that we should first of all consider very carefully whether we wish to use this term (SN *); we shall find it in subfacet 2012; and there will be an RT reference to it from PRESCHOOL LEVEL but not from the other two related terms mentioned.

Related terms are hard to define and isolate once we go outside a particular facet; the introduction discusses the semantic aspects, and in addition to whole-part and near-synonymous relationships lists sixteen different kinds of other relationships. Some of these are difficult to distinguish, resting as they do on distinctions so nice as to be almost invisible; on the other hand, in some cases the compilers have taken a pragmatic view and eliminated RT links between terms which file close together in the alphabetical sequence. This useful summary of the problems emphasizes the fact that we are still only at the beginning of the solution to this particular problem.

The faceted array is broken down into 17 facets, with 133 subfacets. Within each subfacet there may be several groups, which are not given any notation because, it appears, of the lack of a suitable computer program; there would of course be no objection to notation for these, but as it stands, order within groups is alphabetical rather than systematic. This is not a hindrance in practice, as the groups are rarely longer than about ten terms and can be scanned easily. Guide lines for thesaurus use, immediately preceding the thesaurus, stress the importance of the interaction between alphabetical and faceted displays, just as in *Thesaurofacet*.

The permuted index is a KWIC index, necessitated by the use of composite headings. These are used because so many of the terms in this subject field are rather general, and to use single terms would require a massive use of links in indexing practice; it was felt to be more helpful to give ready-linked, *ie* precoordinated, terms in a good proportion of cases.

The significant point about this thesaurus in contrast to the ERIC thesaurus is of course the systematic approach. This permits later additions and amendments to be consistent with the original structure in a way that is not possible with a more haphazard first construction. It seems a pity that so many thesauri have adopted the *ad hoc* approach exemplified by LCSH, rather than the more systematic approach shown in this example.

OECD ALIGNED LIST OF DESCRIPTORS

When a number of organizations are concerned with the same subject area, it seems sensible to try to arrive at some common indexing language; this was of course the justification for the EJC *Thesaurus*, as we have seen. This holds good even if the organizations are in different countries, but clearly the work involved in rationalizing lists in different *languages* is considerable. Nevertheless, the Organization for Economic Cooperation and Development (OECD) felt that the effort would be worth while, particularly in the subject areas related to economic and social development, and the thesaurus under discussion was the result.

The list includes all the terms in three existing thesauri: the International Labour Office *List of descriptors*, 1966 and later amendments; the Food and Agriculture Organization *List of descriptors*, 1967, supplemented by the French edition of 1968; and the German Foundation for Developing Countries *Thesaurus*, 1968. In addition, use was made of the indexes to the *International bibliography of social sciences,* though these had to be modified rather more than the other lists. English is used as the major language, since two of the existing lists were in that form, with French and German as ' translating ' languages. In order to recognize related descriptors, the list was grouped into semantic fields, though there appears to have been a considerable reluctance to adopt ' hierarchical ' classification, and in consequence arrangement within the groups is alphabetical. It is not clear whether facet analysis is considered to be ' hierarchical ' classification; however, as composite terms are included, it would seem probable that it is what we have called enumerative classification that was rejected. It would appear that a more systematic approach would not in fact have been a handicap; it would have avoided such sequences as:

ALFALFA
ANNUAL PLANT
AQUATIC PLANT
AQUATIC WEED
ARTICHOKE
BAMBOO
BEAN
BEET
BIENNIAL PLANT
BLACK PEPPER
BROADLEAVED SPECIES

It is however claimed in the introduction that this pragmatic approach is advantageous in not tying the thesaurus to any particular structure; it will be possible to modify it in the future without too much trouble.

French and German terms are scattered as a result of the primary arrangement by English terms, and therefore require indexes; in addition, there is an index for the English terms to reveal those which form part of a composite heading. These three indexes are in separate volumes, in the by now familiar KWIC form; reference to the main list is by page and line number; the lines are not actually numbered in the main list, but as there are sixty lines to a page it is not difficult to estimate the position of a given line, and the system works satisfactorily.

A fifth volume contains lists of geographical terms and of named institutions. Difficulties had been found in integrating these into the main list, and indeed the list of institutions is still not integrated; there are four lists of names, one each in English, French and German, and a fourth arranged by abbreviations which are put forward as potential international designations.

Though it is possible to criticize this thesaurus on some points, there is no doubt that it represents a very significant step forward in the development of international standards. If indexers in these three languages can be reasonably sure of using terms which can be directly equated with terms in the other two, it will make international cooperation in documentation very much simpler.

BIBLIOGRAPHY

1 *American documentation, 19* (4) October 1968, 418-419. For an account of the background to the ERIC thesaurus, see:
Eller, J L and Ranek, R L: ' Thesaurus development for a decentralized information network '. *American documentation, 19* (3) July 1968, 213-220.

2 *Indexing for ERIC : a programmed course.* 3 vols. University of Maryland, School of Library and Information Services, 1967.

NB The items listed under item 1 of the bibliography to chapter 21 are, of course, also relevant to this chapter.

CHAPTER 23

Research in information retrieval

For many years the little research that was carried out on classification and indexing was largely the work of individuals engaged in compiling schemes or teaching. In the first category we may place H E Bliss, in the second W C Berwick Sayers, whose ' Canons of classification ' formed one of the earliest attempts to present students with a complete rationale. As has already been mentioned in the chapter on CC, one of Sayers' brightest students was S R Ranganathan, who returned to India determined to devise a new kind of classification scheme, in which ideas present in existing schemes such as DC and UDC in embryo would be brought to fruition. For some years this work went largely unnoticed in the West, until after the second world war it was discovered by a new generation of librarians, notably through the efforts of B I Palmer, who had met Ranganathan in India during the war.

At the same time that Ranganathan's ideas were beginning to make an impression in Britain, another important event took place; this was the Royal Society's Scientific Information Conference, held in London in 1948. One of the topics discussed was classification, and a committee was set up, with Professor J D Bernal as secretary, to examine the situation and suggest ways in which improvements might be made in existing methods of subject organization. Little progress was made, and in 1951 B C Vickery was invited to form a group to take over the work of the committee. The result of this invitation was the formation of the Classification Research Group (CRG) in 1952— probably the first opportunity that librarians and others interested in the organization of knowledge had had to get together and discuss problems as a team over an extended period of time. Since its formation the CRG has met regularly at monthly intervals, though in true British fashion it has always remained an amateur organization— amateur in the sense that it does not dispose of large funds, and its members are actuated by enthusiasm for the subject rather than by the hope of wealth.[1]

During the 1950's the CRG was mainly concerned with the application of the principles of facet analysis and synthesis to the development of classification schemes for special subjects. Probably the largest of these was the English Electric Company's classification for engineering, which has now reached its fourth edition, but many other schemes were produced. Among these may be mentioned the Kyle classification for the social sciences, J E L Farradane's scheme for diamond technology, D J Foskett's scheme for occupational safety and health, and the classification of aeronautics drawn up for the Cranfield Project by Vickery and Farradane. The most recent special classification has been the one for library science which was mentioned in chapter 6.

In recent years the CRG has devoted more of its efforts to the formulation of principles for class order in a general scheme. Special schemes have the advantage that subjects not forming part of the core, but still of interest to libraries concerned with the core (fringe subjects), can be treated in a fairly cavalier fashion, since their importance is likely to be far less than that of core material. In a general classification there are, of course, no fringe subjects: all are of equal weight, and must be given their due place in the overall order. In 1955 the CRG published a memorandum[2] on the need for a faceted classification as the basis of all methods of information retrieval, and this was followed up at the 'Dorking conference', at which speakers from a number of countries were able to meet to discuss, and agree upon, this basic point. In their sixth *Bulletin,* the CRG report on some of the problems that they had been discussing in relation to a new general scheme; following a grant from NATO to the Library Association, a conference was held in 1963 to discuss the problems at some length and to report on the progress that had been made.[3] Since that time, some practical work has been done towards the compilation of the new scheme, and further progress is reported in the ninth *Bulletin.*

The work done so far is summarized under the heading 'Recent trends', pages 121-125 of chapter 7. The most detailed statement of progress is contained in the pamphlet *Classification and information control,* which gives samples of the proposed schedules. However, at the moment more progress is being made on the development of PRECIS, which is very largely the verbal equivalent of the classification scheme. As PRECIS is used in BNB, research into its implementation can be carried out by that organization, and work is currently in progress, with support from OSTI, on the construction of the PRECIS thesaurus. In view of the amount of progress that has been made on the classification so far, it is to be hoped that it does not founder now through lack of funds.

It is worth noting at this point the fact that the CRG has always been concerned with practical results, and has based its theorising on practical problems. The special schemes that have been compiled are in daily use, and many of the members of the group have been connected with bibliographical tools such as BNB and BTI. It is in the development of such large-scale services that problems are seen most acutely, and the solutions proposed have to stand up to detailed scrutiny by users. Much of the impetus for the development of a new general scheme has arisen from the dissatisfaction of BNB subject cataloguers with DC, and a new scheme could be used to arrange the bibliography in a more satisfactory way; existing users of DC could be helped by the provision of DC numbers, as is done at present, but these numbers would no longer be used for the arrangement.

There is no doubt that the CRG has been the most potent influence in the development of classification theory over the past decade. Starting with the theories of analytico-synthetic classification developed by Ranganathan, the group has moved forward in a rather different direction from Ranganathan himself; for a variety of reasons, it seems probable that future developments are likely to be along the lines indicated by the CRG rather than those used in CC. The present work is largely concerned with the exposition of CRG ideas, while if imitation is the sincerest form of flattery, the formation of a similar group in the USA, the Classification Research Study Group, must have given the members of the CRG some pleasure. The work of the group is best studied through the series of bulletins published in the *Journal of documentation*, while students should also try to examine as many of the special classifications compiled by members of the CRG as possible. The CRG is also interested in postcoordinate indexing, as is clearly shown by the publication of *Thesaurofacet*. The technique of facet analysis is of quite general application in the construction of index languages, and the work done by the CRG on the development of both special and general classification schemes has helped greatly in clarifying problems which beset indexing languages generally.

THE ASLIB CRANFIELD RESEARCH PROJECT[4]
One of the earliest tests to establish the comparative efficiency of various indexing systems was carried out in the early 1950's by ASTIA (Armed Services Technical Information Agency: now DDC—Defense Documentation Center), to try to establish whether the set of subject headings it had developed were more useful than the Uniterm system

proposed by Mortimer Taube. The results of the investigations were inconclusive, though ASTIA did adopt the post-coordinate system; the difficulty lay in the fact that the two sides were unable to agree on what were the 'correct' answers to the test questions. As has been pointed out in the early pages of this work, relevance is a subjective judgement, depending on the background of experience which the user brings to the collection of documents being tested. The ASTIA test did little to show which system was more efficient, but it did show that there was a need for a more objective test. A great deal of money is invested in different methods of information retrieval, and the amount increases each year; if one method can be shown to be clearly superior to all the others, then that method should be adopted, and its rivals allowed to fall into disuse.

With this mind, Aslib set up in 1957 what has come to be known as the Cranfield Project, under the direction of the librarian of the College of Aeronautics at Cranfield, C W Cleverdon. Under the title 'An investigation into the comparative efficiency of indexing systems' the project set out to try to establish a methodology which would make possible the objective comparison of four systems: a faceted classification; UDC; alphabetical subject headings; and Uniterms. Several variables were taken into account in addition to the four schemes. Three indexers were employed, one with experience of indexing and subject knowledge of aeronautics, the field chosen for the experiments; one with experience of indexing, but little relevant subject knowledge; and one straight from library school, with neither indexing experience nor subject knowledge. Different times were used: 2 minutes, 4, 8, 12 and 16 minutes (though the time was only controlled for one of the indexing methods, each report being indexed by the other three methods without the operation being timed). The whole experiment was run through three times, to see whether the indexers improved their performance as they gained more experience. The material indexed consisted of batches of 100 technical reports and articles on various aspects of aeronautics; thus with three indexers, four systems, five time periods, and three runs, a total of 18,000 items were indexed.

The next problem was to arrive at a method of testing which would eliminate the subjective element. The method chosen was to ask a number of people in different organizations to select documents from the collection and in each case phrase a question to which that document would be an answer. From the 1,400 questions suggested, four

366

hundred were selected by a screening panel of three experts in aeronautical information. These questions were then put to the four indexes, and a search was counted as successful if the ' source document ' was revealed. Rearrangement of the subject elements in a search did not count as a new search, but dropping or changing one element did, except in the case of the Uniterm index, where an additional term could be dropped without being counted as a failure if the source document was found.

Both the indexing and searching situations are clearly artificial and do not bear much relationship to real life situations. There was no feedback during indexing, and the indexers were not able to concentrate on one particular system as they would normally. To count a search as a success if one particular document is found but a failure if it is not is to alter completely the nature of searching by subject, converting it to the yes/no situation valid for the factors which identify. There was no feedback at the search stage; a question once framed was permanent, though in real life we would normally expect to modify a question if our first search did not reveal the answer. Despite these criticisms, the results of the experiment are very interesting, and their influence has been considerable.

The first important finding was that all of the systems were of approximately equal effectiveness; to begin with, the Uniterm index was found to give best results, with the faceted classification giving the worst, but a subexperiment run with the latter showed that it could give slightly better results than Uniterm. The main problem with the faceted classification was in fact the fixed citation order coupled with a chain index; as has been shown in chapter 10, this can lead to problems if the users' approach is not a standardized one, and in the Cranfield experiment this was the case. Using the faceted classification as the basis of a multiple entry system, with a simplified alphabetical index, improved the test results—but we are speaking of an improvement of some 10% only. (It is also necessary to remember that this test was not conducted under the same experimental conditions as the main comparison, so the results obtained cannot be strictly compared with those obtained to begin with.)

No significant difference was found between the indexers or the three runs; since we normally find that indexers improve as they gain in knowledge and experience, these findings are unexpected. The other findings were perhaps equally unexpected. There was, it appeared, little point in spending more than four minutes indexing a particular document, for the additional time gave no improvement in results, though to spend only two minutes was inadequate and gave rise to a high proportion of the failures. However, the largest single factor leading to failure was human error: failure to use the systems correctly, or to search correctly, was the cause of about half the total number of errors.

Though the results of the experiment were very interesting, perhaps more important were the developments in thinking to which the project as a whole was to lead. These developments form in fact a significant part of the approach in this text. The concept of two related factors, recall and relevance, was the result of studying the documents revealed by the Cranfield searches, and the quest for factors which might influence recall and relevance led to the formulation of the criteria of specificity and exhaustivity. The isolation of these basic factors has enabled experimental work in the comparison of indexing systems to go forward on a far more satisfactory basis, and has also indicated practical ways in which we can improve the results we obtain in using information retrieval systems in our libraries. It is probably true to say that none of these ideas was completely novel; writers on classification have been discussing the merits of close and broad classification for many years now, for example. However, it has been very valuable to see them isolated and defined, just as it was valuable for Ranganathan to isolate and define ideas which were implicit in schemes such as DC.

A further test of the Cranfield ideas came with a comparison of the index to metallurgical literature compiled at Case Western Reserve University using semantic factoring, with an index to a selection of this literature compiled using the English Electric faceted classification. The major criterion for success or failure was again the performance of the two systems in revealing answers to questions based on documents within the systems, but this time the response was measured on searches of the complete collection, not merely on predetermined documents as in Cranfield I. Although the WRU workers were able to obtain slightly better recall, the Cranfield workers consistently obtained better results as far as relevance was concerned.

SEMANTIC FACTORING

It is legitimate at this point to digress slightly to discuss the WRU technique,[5] to which we referred in passing in chapter 5. Kaiser was concerned to avoid the use of Processes as filing terms in his system, and therefore analysed many concepts which may be regarded as unitary processes into a combination of a concrete and a process. During the 1950's a team at WRU worked on a development of this kind of analysis, which was to break down every concept into a set of fundamental concepts called semantic factors. Because of their fundamental nature, there would be only a limited number of these factors, and concepts would be specified by coding them to show the semantic factors involved and also the specific concept. For example, the generalized concept metals is coded M TL; metal is coded MATL; and aluminium, a particular metal, is coded MATL.I.☐AQL, where I is a role indicator and the ☐ Q is a special code into which can be fitted the chemical symbol, in this case AL for aluminium. Thermometer is coded MACH.MUSR.RWHT.4X.002, where MACH=device, MUSR= measurement, RWHT.4X=heat, and .002 is a role indicator. By the use of a complex set of roles and links, codes for the concepts involved in a document can be strung together to form a ' telegraphic abstract '—a detailed subject specification which forms the input to the computer-based system.

The method is clearly a powerful one, but is open to some doubts and objections. Exactly how far does one carry such an analysis? Heat and temperature, for example, could be specified as *movement* of *molecules*. Again, is it possible to specify a concept by using only some of its attributes; or perhaps more significantly, is it ever possible to specify *all* the attributes for a given concept? For example, thermometer may be specified as above, instrument: measuring: temperature; and barometer may be specified as instrument: measuring: pressure. Neither reveals the fact that both of these may have other factors in common, for example the fact that they may be mercury-in-glass devices. Certainly for most purposes a mercury barometer has more in common with an aneroid barometer than it does with a thermometer, but this may not be the case if we are thinking of the instrument maker. If we think of a particular individual, we may have no difficulty in putting a name to the object of our thoughts; we may find it impossible in practical terms to think of all the possible terms that might be needed to denote that individual without naming him or her. Sex, age, nationality, family status, marital status, height, weight, occupation, language, —the list is almost endless. Furthermore, we may find ourselves in the position of not knowing all of the information we require; we have to remember that we are dealing with the information in our collection of documents, and this will often be incomplete. The problem has no easy solution, as can be seen from the fact that it is still being actively discussed by the CRG: to what extent is it permissible to 'telescope' concepts from different facets when their combination is itself a wellknown isolate? When is it legitimate to decide that one will carry one's analysis no further? We still have some way to go in terms of linguistic and semantic analysis before we can have any confidence in our answers to these questions.

Despite these doubts, it is a little surprising that the WRU system did not show up very well in the test, and a number of reasons were advanced by its protagonists to explain their relative failure.[6] The chief of these was the nature of the questions, which were largely framed on the basis of document titles. The WRU system involved lengthy analysis of the subject content of each document, whereas the Cranfield workers tended to take the overall subject as being the most significant factor—indeed, it is possible to do little else if the time needed for indexing is measured in intervals of four minutes—and were thus more likely to match the questions. Whatever the reasons, the failure of the WRU system led to its abandonment by the American Society for Metals, who had been one of its most important backers.

CRANFIELD II

Most of the criticisms levelled at the original Cranfield project and the English Electric-WRU test stemmed from the fact that the real-life situations involved led to the existence of too many uncontrolled—and uncontrollable!—variables. It was therefore decided to make the second project a purely experimental one in which indexes could be manipulated under 'laboratory' conditions, and the effects of changing one variable at the time judged. To avoid the problems that had arisen in previous tests from the use of the subjective term relevance, it was decided to use the term *precision* instead. In addition, to avoid problems of bias introduced by searching for particular predetermined documents as in Cranfield I, the whole collection of documents is scanned with reference to every question, and the set of relevant documents is established in advance for each case; the results of each search are then compared with this predetermined norm. There is thus much less likelihood that the answer will be biased by the question, and the results are not tied to the finding of one particular document, as they were in the original tests. The result of a search is to divide the collection into two sets: those retrieved and those not retrieved. Each of these sets may be further divided into those documents which are relevant and those which are not, to give a small matrix:

	Retrieved	Not retrieved	Total
relevant	a	c	a+c
not relevant	b	d	b+d
	a+b	c+d	a+b+c+d=N

We can produce a graph showing the relationship between the recall ratio, $\frac{a}{a+c} \times 100\%$, and the precision ratio, $\frac{a}{a+b} \times 100\%$ to give a measure of the performance of the system.

Thirty three different index languages were tested, ranging from simple terms taken from the documents being indexed to highly controlled vocabularies with built-in relationships. In some of the index languages terms were grouped together to form hierarchical groups, in others paradigms (*ie* words having the same stem but different forms) were classed together. Each question was translated into the vocabulary of each indexing language, and a series of searches were performed. Let us suppose that we have a question containing four significant natural language terms, and we wish to use the natural language single term index. A search is performed coordinating all four terms, and will reveal a certain number of documents; of these, a proportion will be among those previously judged relevant to this question. A further four searches are now performed, using any three of the terms only; once again, a certain number of documents will be revealed, of which a proportion will be relevant. Further searches are made using only two of the terms, and finally each of the terms is used on its own. For this question there will be four ' levels of coordination ' depending on how many terms are coordinated together for each search. The main problem was to find a performance measure which would make possible the comparison of results between systems, but also of results obtained by changing one variable within a system, for example the coordination level.

Such a measure had been developed by G Salton, whose work on the SMART project is described in the next chapter. It is known as *normalized recall ratio,* and it depends in the first instance on the establishment of a method of ' ranking ' the relevant documents discovered. This rank is given by a formula which links the number of

371

relevant and non-relevant documents revealed at each level of co-ordination:

$$^cR_n = x_0 + (n - y_0)\left(\frac{x_0 + 1}{y_0 + 1}\right)$$

Let us assume that in carrying out the search used as an example in the last paragraph we have found 4 relevant and 58 non-relevant documents by the time we reach the second level of coordination (*ie* taking two terms together); in taking the final step to the first level of coordination (*ie* single terms) we reveal another 2 relevant and 34 non-relevant documents. We wish to find the rank ^cR_n of the sixth relevant document, found at level 1, so $c=1$ and $n=6$. The total number of documents found before we searched at level 1, x_1, is 62 $(4+58)$, while the total number of *relevant* documents we found before we searched at this level, y_1, is 4. The total number of documents retrieved at the level 1, x_1, is 36, of which 2 are relevant, y_1. The formula thus gives us the result for this particular example:

$$^1R_6 = 62 + (6-4)\left(\frac{36+1}{2+1}\right) = 62 + 2(12\tfrac{1}{3}) = 87$$

The ranks obtained in this way were grouped into seventeen ranges; at the lower levels, from 1 to 5, each range contains only the equivalent rank, but ranks from 51 to 200 were grouped into six ranges, each containing 25. In our example, the sixth relevant document found, with rank 87, will fall into the range 76-100. If we tabulate for each index language the number of the question showing which ranges the relevant documents found fall into, we can build up a cumulative recall pattern for the language as a whole. The normalized recall ratio is obtained by totalling the steps of this cumulation and dividing by the number of steps, 17. For example, we may find the following results with one particular language:

Range (ranks)	1	2	3	4	5	6-7	8-10	11-15	16-20	21-30	31-50	51-75	76-100	101-125	126-150	151-175	176-200
No. of relevant answers	21	24	18	17	13	16	14	14	13	10	10	8	7	7	4	3	1
Cumulative recall %	10	22	31	40	46	54	61	68	75	80	85	89	92	96	98	99	100

This gives us a cumulative sum of the recall ratios of 1146, and this divided by 17, the number of ranges, gives us a normalized recall ratio 67.4%, which may be compared with the similar figure found for other index languages.

It will be seen that the rank is a measure of how quickly a given index language reveals the relevant documents; the more we have to broaden our search strategy, the higher the ranking of the relevant documents found at each level. When the ranks are tabulated for all questions, the more results there are in the lower ranks, the more quickly our cumulative recall ratio will approach 100%, and the higher will be the normalized recall ratio. If all our relevant documents were revealed at the first search, with no unwanted documents at all, we should very quickly reach 100% cumulative recall ratio, giving us a normalized recall ratio also near 100%. It should be noted that even with this perfect result, it is not possible to reach 100% normalized recall, as only the first document found can have rank 1; if there are five, they will be ranked 1, 2, 3, 4 and 5, according to the formula.

It is perhaps worth emphasizing that the normalized recall ratio does act as a measure of relevance (precision), not merely recall. Its main advantage is that it gives a single figure of merit, rather than the recall-precision graph, and it is thus easier to handle. Another advantage is that it serves to rank *all* documents in response to a given question, rather than just those thought to be relevant; the user can in fact set his own cut-off point to give him the number of documents that he feels he can conveniently handle.

The results of the experiments were somewhat surprising. The use of natural language single terms gave results which were bettered only if synonyms were eliminated or paradigms confounded, while the worst results were shown by the use of natural language to express simple concepts. Controlled vocabularies gave results rather worse than single terms, but in general much better than simple concepts. It is important here to know what is meant by 'simple concept'; for example, 'axial flow compressor' is quoted as being a simple concept, but this is clearly not what we have referred to in this book as a simple concept. The question is obviously allied to the depth of analysis discussed earlier in this chapter, but it is also related to what we have called pre-coordination; in fact, it appears to be pre-coordination which led to a number of the failures.

Other tests were carried out to study the effects of, for example, weighting and relevance judgements. At the time of indexing, documents were weighted for each index term according to the simple scale:

1   main concepts
2   less important concepts
3   minor concepts

Relevance decisions were also weighted on a similar scale:

1   complete answers to the question
2   high degree of relevance
3   useful as background, or for certain aspects
4   minimum interest, *eg* historical

These tests do not appear to have affected the main results significantly.

The conclusion that may be drawn from Cranfield II is that terms taken from documents may be used successfully with the minimum of control in a post-coordinate index; it is helpful to eliminate synonyms and paradigms, but apart from this any measures taken to control the vocabulary are likely to decrease its efficiency. This is a rather unexpected conclusion, and is of course contrary to most of what has been stated in this text; it is also contrary to the experience of large numbers of librarians, who have found that controlled vocabularies are helpful in practice. There is a need for further research to reconcile these differing points of view, in particular to establish the relationship between the artificial experimental set-up at Cranfield and the kind of situation met in real life.

The two factors which seem to have had most effect on the Cranfield results were specificity and exhaustivity. The use of complex concepts, *eg* axial flow compressor, in the indexing language, means that the vocabulary will be a large one, as we have seen in the discussions earlier; on the other hand, we can reduce the vocabulary to a minimum if we group simple concepts hierarchically. It appears that there is a happy medium; in the project, language I.3, containing single terms only and merging paradigms, used 2,541 terms and gave a normalized recall ratio of 65.82%, the highest recorded. This was better than language I.9 with 306 terms representing the third level of hierarchical grouping, which gave a ratio of 61.17%, and much better than II.1, simple concepts expressed in natural language, which used a vocabulary estimated at some 10,000 terms and gave a ratio of 44.64%. (Note that the description ' simple concepts ' here refers to what we have called complex concepts, *ie* composite subjects used in a pre-coordinate manner.)

374

The effect of exhaustivity is shown by comparing the results obtained by the use of titles (average number of terms 7), various indexing languages, and abstracts (average number of terms about 60). Within a particular language, different levels of exhaustivity may be compared by studying the results given by terms with weight 1 only, terms with weights 1 and 2, and terms with weights 1, 2, and 3. In the project, it was found that the best results were obtained with a language using an average of 33 terms per document.

These results were confirmed by a rather similar test carried out on the MEDLARS (MEDical Literature Analysis and Retrieval System) service.[7] Part of MEDLARS is the compilation of bibliographies in response to requests, using the file of entries in the system, which at the time of the test totalled 800,000. 299 searches were analysed, and showed that the system as a whole worked at an average recall of 57.7% and precision of 50.4%. Failures due to the indexing language were shown to be the result of lack of specificity, false coordinations and incorrect term relationships; the vocabulary used, MeSH, (Medical Subject Headings)[8] appears to need both revision and expansion. Failures due to the level of exhaustivity were of two kinds, those in which the indexing was too exhaustive, and those in which it was not exhaustive enough. This is to a certain extent a reflection of the fact that articles from periodicals thought to be of primary importance were given an average of ten terms, while others were only given an average of four terms; increasing the level of the latter to ten would have given a significant increase of some 30-40% recall, but to improve the performance beyond this would have required a rather large increase in the number of terms used, from ten to, say, twenty. A high proportion of the failures were due to human error, as was found in Cranfield I. While mistakes in indexing accounted for only 1% of the failures, omissions contributed to 10% of the recall failures; in many of these cases, a better vocabulary would have prevented the error. A much higher proportion of the failures were due to unsatisfactory search procedures; either the searcher failed to cover all the reasonable approaches, or the search was conducted at the wrong level of generality.

Another very interesting result, and one that was quite unexpected, was that the best results were obtained in response to requests stated in natural language narrative by the person needing the information; it seems that discussion with an intermediary—a librarian or search analyst—may lead to poor results, perhaps because the original question gets distorted into the pattern imposed by the respondent or by MeSH. This may also be a reflection of the present-day limitations of searches conducted in computer-based systems, discussed in more detail in the following chapter.

The results of these tests on a largescale operational system will, it is hoped, lead to continued improvement in the services offered. This is the first example of such a system being subjected to a continuous process of 'quality control' and the results will certainly influence practice in similar systems as they are set up.

COLLEGE OF LIBRARIANSHIP WALES[11]

A further laboratory comparison of index languages has been carried out at the College of Librarianship Wales. Using a collection of eight hundred documents in the field of library and information science, the complete collection was examined for relevance in relation to the questions by independent judges, who were neither project indexers nor enquirers. Most of the sixty three requests used represented real information requirements which were posed directly at the time of the test, or had previously been submitted to Aslib or the Library Association. The main tests were of three different postcoordinate indexing languages:

Compressed term: a 'minimum vocabulary' based on a list compiled by the Research department of Aslib. This had fewer than 300 terms, and a structure of related terms was added for the test.

Uncontrolled natural language: single words derived from the documents by the indexers. Some 1,200 words were used, and no related word structure or even synonym control was provided.

Hierarchically structured: based on the CRG Classification of library science. Some 800 facet terms were used, without synthesis at the indexing stage and thus without a fixed citation order; the notation and the hierarchical linkage were retained.

Since the exhaustivity and specificity of indexing in the different languages was kept at the same level, the number of terms used in each gives a very rough indication of language specificity. More accurate measurements of specificity were attempted by means of searches in which the exhaustivity and specificity of searching were held constant, and these showed that the Hierarchically structured was somewhat less specific than Uncontrolled, but considerably more specific than Compressed term. Measurement of the cross-reference structure or hierarchical linkage formally provided in the schedules of each language showed that Hierarchically structured and Compressed term both had nearly five cross-references per term, while Uncontrolled had less than one, derived from the accidentally helpful collocation of terms in the alphabetical list.[12] These attempts to measure specificity and linkage were seen to be an essential preliminary to the main test in order both to advance the understanding of what constitutes the essential differences between languages, and to increase the capability of generalizing research findings by relating performance merit to measures of index language properties.

Test searches simulated real world searching as closely as possible, and searches for each request in each system were designed to give the equivalent of four searches, to cover variants of recall target. For example, a minimum recall target of only one highly relevant document per request satisfied represented the needs of one type of 'high precision' user, whereas a maximum recall target of all the highly or partially relevant documents in the file represented the needs of one kind of 'high recall' user. A time limit was imposed on searches, which were terminated when either the time limit was exceeded or the searchers reached the predetermined recall target.

All three languages easily attained the two variants of low recall target set for the high precision need, but in terms of non relevant documents retrieved Compressed term always performed worst, with Hierarchically structured and Uncontrolled very similar, the latter being slightly worse in individual request differences. However, none of the differences between the three languages was statistically significant. In the high recall cases, Compressed term was best, with Hierarchically structured worst—by 7% recall in one test, a statistically significant result. Uncontrolled lay midway between these two. If, however, we consider the non-retrieval of non-relevant documents in the high recall situation, Hierarchically structured was best, with Compressed term worst. These effectiveness measures were complemented by efficiency measures based on search time and the number of separate sub-programs used in the searches; Compressed term was best here with Hierarchically structured worst, but the differences were small.

Two of the many conclusions arising from the tests of these three languages were that Compressed term was not specific enough, and that lack of structure in Uncontrolled showed no significant disadvantage. The failure analysis in the final report to be published will give some further explanation of these results, and will include comparisons of variations in indexing exhaustivity and specificity.

Limited tests were also conducted on two more index languages. One of these was the Hierarchically structured faceted classification, used in a precoordinate file with a fixed citation order, synthesized class marks and a chain index. Full comparison of this with the postcoordinate version were limited to measures of recall and efficiency; for high recall, the performance was significantly worse (by 11% in one case) in the precoordinate version. This was due at least in part to the longer search time needed; some 35% of the searches were terminated by the time limit, compared with 10% in the postcoordinate system.

In order to determine whether precoordination prevented many false drops which might occur with postcoordination, a controlled test was carried out. This showed virtually no difference at all, with only 10% of the searches affected, and an average 1% loss of recall with precoordination for a gain of 0.1 fewer non relevant documents retrieved. A further comparison was made of the effect of providing a fully rotated chain index. The searchers used this to select and reject the entries they found, as would be the case in many operational situations, and this nearly halved the average number of non relevant documents retrieved for a loss of 14% recall when compared with searching all matching entries.

The second limited test was of Farradane's relational indexing, described in chapter 5. Because of the limited use that had been made of this system previously, some new rules and conventions had to be developed for the subject area of the test. A subset of rather less than 250 of the documents were indexed, and a comparison test using 60 of the questions was completed, by measuring the performance of the system with and without the operators. These would be expected to act as a precision device, improving precision at the expense of recall, but in the event their effect was very slight. Only 13% of the searches were affected at all; of these, 10% were improved in precision, 3% worsened in recall, but the improvement in the suppression of non relevant documents was very small—about 0.2 on average, with a drop of 2% in recall. Although no realistic tests of efficiency were possible, it became very clear that in terms of indexing time the differences between Relational indexing and Uncontrolled were very considerable.

It is as yet too early to make any estimate of the significance of this work for the indexer in general. It is, however, clear that we shall have to pay more attention in future to questions of overall efficiency. In chapter 2 we discussed the balance between effort devoted to the

378

input stage and that expended at the output stage; it is fairly obvious that the more complex the indexing language we use, the more indexing time it will require. If, as these tests seem to indicate, any gains from the use of complex index languages are slight, it will be difficult to justify the extra time involved in their use. Perhaps the next stage is to attempt to assess the extent to which the test results can be extrapolated to the wider situation in general.

SYNTOL

The Cranfield Project showed that all information retrieval systems were aggregates of various devices affecting recall and precision and were thus fundamentally similar. This suggested that it might be feasible to develop a ' meta-language ' which would form a common ground between various other systems. This would be particularly useful in computer-based systems, which tend to use specially designed indexing languages. A contract was awarded by EURATOM in 1960 to a team headed by J C Gardin, Director of the Section on Automatic Documentation of the CRNS (the French national centre for scientific research). Certain assumptions formed the basis of the project: that there *is* an information explosion requiring new methods to solve new problems; that indexing is still a valid method of storing and retrieving information, as opposed to searching of natural language texts; that intellectual effort is involved in indexing; and that a computer-based system should be the objective, even though other mechanized forms of information are available and widely used (*eg* peek-a-boo).

The most significant feature of SYNTOL,[9] the SYNTagmatic organization Language developed by the team, is its explicit differentiation between *a priori* relationships, *ie* those that are known in advance of scanning any particular document, and *a posteriori* relationships, *ie* those which are found only by scanning a particular document. As has already been mentioned, Gardin coined the terms paradigmatic and syntagmatic to denote these two kinds of relationship, but he emphasizes that the distinction he has in mind is an operational one; the relationship between two concepts may be either, depending on how we build it into the system. It is for this reason that the term genus-species is used in this text rather than paradigmatic, to emphasize the distinction between semantic and syntactic relationships.

Any meta-language must be simple if it is to be able to accept a wide variety of inputs. In SYNTOL, this simplification has led to a

379

basic unit consisting of two terms plus a relationship: a 'dyadic string' in the form (R, a, b), in which a and b are the terms and the relationship R is directional a→b. Where R is a syntactical relationship the expression (R, a, b) is called a *syntagma*; in one format, there are four such relationships, which are thus even more generalized than Farradane's relational operators. The four are:

R_1 predicative, usually exemplified by an adjective plus a noun, *eg* close, classification

R_2 associative, often shown by noun plus noun, *eg* information, retrieval

R_3 consecutive, involving the concept of dependence or sequence, *eg* economic crises (due to) wars

R_4 co-ordinative, involving the idea of comparison, *eg* treatments using drugs (or) surgery

It is admitted that these relationships are ill-defined, but to offset this it is claimed that in practice the context shows exactly what significance we should read into the syntagma.

Vocabulary control is achieved through a 'lexicon' or thesaurus. Since the system is intended to permit the use of a variety of inputs, the lexicon must also be very flexible, and it is suggested that the system might contain not one but a number of thesauri, taken from the different inputs. In addition, the system will accept a wide variety of syntactical relationships, the group of four shown above being but one example; another example might be the facet indicators from a synthetic scheme. At the output stage it is possible to search at different levels by ignoring some or all of these relationships. The flexibility of the input could lead to difficulties in a manual system, and requires complex programs in a computer-based system.

So far experimental work and use of the system has been confined to some of the social sciences, in particular physiology and psychology, sociology, and cultural anthropology. The team felt that if the problems could be solved for these fields, where terminology tends to be ill defined, it would almost certainly prove successful if the system were applied to other fields where terminology is used more precisely, *eg* the physical sciences.

For the student, perhaps the main value of the SYNTOL project is the emphasis it places on the fundamental similarity of all information retrieval systems, and its formalization of syntactical relations. If Farradane is correct, it is in this direction that most progress is to be made, and SYNTOL may be regarded as one step in this direction.

SPECIAL CLASSIFICATIONS AND THESAURI
Strictly speaking the compilation of schemes for particular subjects must count as development rather than research, but it is perhaps worth mentioning that in recent years a large number of subjects have been covered either by special classifications or by thesauri; we have already mentioned the English Electric scheme, which combines both. Some of these special schemes have been mentioned in the text to illustrate particular points, but this does not of course mean that others are not worthy of study. The Bibliographic Systems Center of Case Western Reserve University maintains a collection (originally the Special Libraries Association collection) and publishes a list from time to time;[10] the CRG bulletins usually contain a bibliography of members' publications. Students should not concentrate on the major general schemes to the exclusion of these special schemes, for it is often in the smaller scale ventures that fundamental principles can most clearly be seen.

BIBLIOGRAPHY
1 For the history of the CRG, see
    Foskett, D J: 'The Classification Research Group, 1952-1962'. *Libri*, *12*(2)1962, 127-138.
    Crossley, C A: 'New schemes of classification: principles and practice'. *Library Association record*, *65* (2) 1963, 51-59.
    The work of the CRG is reported in its bulletins. The first three of these were published as separates and are now out of print; since no. 4, the bulletins have appeared in the *Journal of documentation*, in the following issues:
    12 (4) 1956, 227-230 (Bibliography of publications by members)
    14 (3) 1958, 136-143 (Bulletin 4: BCM classification)
    15 (1) 1959, 39-57 (Bulletin 5: Cranfield)
    17 (3) 1961, 156-168 (Bulletin 6: new general classification)
    17 (3) 1961, 169-172 (Bibliography of publications)
    18 (2) 1962, 65-88 (Bulletin 7: special classifications)
    20 (3) 1964, 146-165 (Bulletin 8: integrative levels)
    20 (3) 1964, 166-169 (Bibliography of publications)
    24 (4) 1968, 273-291 (Bulletin 9: new general classification)
    The main topic in each bulletin is indicated, but many other matters are also discussed.
2 'The need for a faceted classification as the basis of all methods of information retrieval'. *Library Association record*, *57* (7) 1955, 262-268.

3 Library Association: *Some problems of a general classification scheme: report of a conference held in London, June, 1963.* Library Association, 1964.

See also the references listed in item 8 of the bibliography in chapter 7.

4 A comprehensive bibliography of the project for the years 1961-1965 will be found in the ' Classification ' chapter in *Five years work in librarianship, 1961-1965.* The basic reports are as follows:

Cleverdon, C W: *Aslib Cranfield Research Project: report on the testing and analysis of an investigation into the comparative efficiency of indexing systems.* Cranfield, College of Aeronautics, 1962.

Aitchison, J and Cleverdon, C W: *A report on a test of the index of metallurgical literature of Western Reserve University.* Cranfield, College of Aeronautics, 1963.

Cleverdon, C W, Mills, J and Keen, E M: *Factors determining the performance of indexing systems.* Cranfield, Aslib-Cranfield Research Project, 1966. 2 v in 3. Briefer summaries of the work will be found in several articles and reviews, of which the following is a selection:

Cleverdon, C W and Mills, J: ' The testing of index language devices '. *Aslib proceedings, 15* (4) 1963, 106-130.

Swanson, D: ' The evidence underlying the Cranfield results '. *Library quarterly, 35* (1) 1965, 1-20.

Cleverdon, C W: ' The Cranfield tests on index language devices '. *Aslib proceedings, 19* (6) 1967, 173-194.

5 Perry, J W and Kent, A: *Tools for machine literature searching : semantic code dictionary: equipment: procedures.* New York, Interscience Publishers Inc, 1958. 972 p.

6 Rees, A M: *Review of a report of the Aslib-Cranfield test of the index of metallurgical literature of Western Reserve University.* Cleveland, Ohio, Western Reserve University School of Library Science, 1963. 32p.

Rees, A M: ' Semantic factors, role indicators et alia: eight years of information retrieval at Western Reserve University '. *Aslib proceedings, 15* (12) 1963, 350-363.

7 Lancaster, F W: *Evaluation of the MEDLARS Demand Search Service.* Bethesda, Maryland, National Library of Medicine, 1968. (Full report.)

Lancaster, F W: ' Evaluating the performance of a large computerized information service '. *Journal of the American Medical Association, 207* (1) 1969, 114-120.

8 MeSH is published annually as a supplement to *Index medicus*.
9 Gardin, J C: *SYNTOL*. Rutgers, The State University School of Library Science, 1965. 106p. (Rutgers series on systems for the intellectual organization of information, ed Susan Artandi, Vol 4.)
10 Denison, B: *Selected materials in classification*. Special Libraries Association, 1968.
11 I am indebted to E M Keen for the information on this project. A full report will be published by OSTI: Keen, E M and Digger, J A: *Report on an information science index languages test* (to be issued in 1971).
12 Kochen, M and Tagliacozzo, R: 'A study of cross-referencing'. *Journal of documentation*, 24 (3) September 1968, 173-191.

It should be evident that it is not possible to turn to one convenient source for the results of current research. To keep in touch with what is going on now it is necessary to go to primary sources such as reports or periodical articles. A selection of these is given here for the benefit of the student who wishes to pursue these matters further; others may be found through *Library and information science abstracts* or *Library literature,* and by scanning current issues of such periodicals as *Aslib proceedings* and the *Journal of documentation.* The student taking an elementary course should find the references given here adequate.

CHAPTER 24

The computer

As we have indicated in chapter 1, the quantity of information that we have to handle nowadays is one of the main reasons why we have had to develop new techniques of information handling. One other reason is that the tempo of life generally is faster, and techniques which were adequate in a more leisurely age are so no longer. Computers offer a means of processing large quantities of data at very high speeds, and it is therefore obvious that we have to consider their relevance to information retrieval; we should however be on our guard against the assumption that the use of these machines will solve all our problems without any further intellectual effort on our part. This is not the case; a great deal of work has still to be done in such fundamental areas as linguistic analysis before we can devise programs that will enable us to process texts in natural language in such a way as to obtain satisfactory retrieval results without any human intellectual intervention. That is for the future, but it does not mean that computers cannot usefully be employed now to facilitate the non-intellectual aspects of information retrieval systems. As we have seen, any system is a mixture of intellectual and clerical operations, and if we can clearly distinguish the two we may well be able to use a computer for the latter. Indeed, the computer's high speed may enable us to undertake operations which we *can* perform manually, but usually do not for lack of time.[1]

Costs are an important factor in any library operation. In the past, costs of using computers have been such as to prohibit their use in libraries on a large scale, but new developments in computer technology have reduced costs to the level where they are competitive with clerical effort, at least in highly developed countries. However, it seems likely that the advantage in turning to computers does not lie in a reduction of costs, but in the fact that for about the same cost we can get a great deal more output; in other words, we spend no less but we get more for our money.

It is not necessary for librarians to know the technical details of how computers work, but it is helpful to have some overall understanding of computer processing if we are to be able to judge what is required of us before we can use the machine, and what the machine can give us in return. For this purpose it is helpful to regard the computer as a set of ' black boxes '; we can then consider the functions of these without having to know how they perform them. The heart of the computer is the core store; this is where information in the form of electrical signals is kept while it is actually being processed. Core stores are expensive units, and in older computers they were usually quite small. The amount of information that the computer can process depends on the size of the core store, so older computers (first generation, using electronic valves (tubes) and second generation, using transistors and similar devices) were best suited to the handling of relatively small amounts of information, on which they could perform very speedily a large number of operations. Information retrieval systems involve the handling of large amounts of information, on which basically only one operation is performed, that of matching. With the development of third generation computers, using integrated circuits, we now have machines which can handle much larger quantities of information at much higher speeds than before. In addition to making the computer more suitable for the kind of requirement found in library operations, this has other consequences of value which will be discussed later under the heading Time-sharing and multi-programming.

The core store may receive information from several sources. First of these is the input; this may take a variety of physical forms, but they must all have one thing in common. They must all present the information to the core store in the form of electrical impulses, and in the vast majority of cases at present this involves some form of conversion of the original text. The most commonly used form of input is 80-column punched cards, which have to be prepared by a key-punch operator. Another common form is punched paper tape, which may be prepared specially or may arise as a by-product of some other operation, for example typing on a tape typewriter. Magnetic tape may be used, in fact large scale computers normally convert all forms of input to magnetic tape as an intermediate step; its advantage is that it can be ' read ' into the machine at very high speeds, much higher than those possible with cards or tape. Magnetic tape may also be available as a by-product of some forms of typesetting, for example using the Photon filmsetting machine; thus the production of the text in conventional book form may at the same time make it possible to process the text in a computer without any additional input effort.

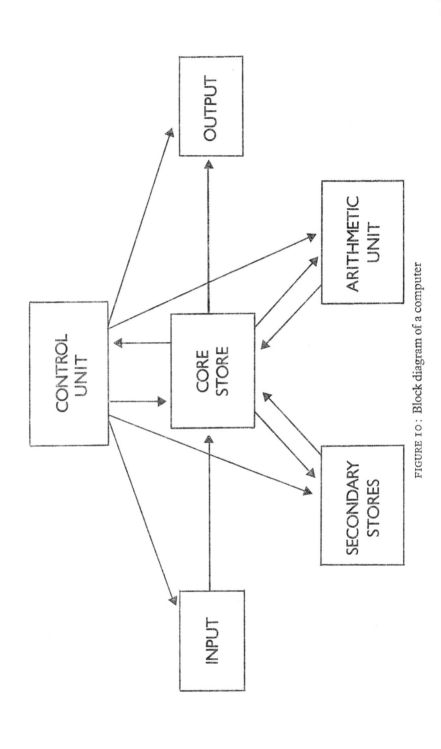

FIGURE 10 : Block diagram of a computer

It would be very convenient if we could simply use normal text and some sort of reading device. Such *optical scanners,* as they are known, do indeed exist, but as yet they can read only certain varieties of type face; the stylized figures found along the bottom edges of cheques can be read by machine, and IBM have developed a typewriter type face which can be used as input to a scanner. We are a long way from a device that can interpret the many varieties of type face found in even a modest library, while the ability of the human eye to read handwriting is well beyond the capability of any existing machine even in the laboratory. Such machines will come eventually, but in the meantime we shall have to make do with other forms of input!

An electric typewriter works by means of electrical signals; it is therefore possible to link an electric typewriter directly to a computer. It can also serve as the output device; such an input/output device is known as a *terminal* and will be discussed in more detail later. It seems that this kind of device may have particular value for some library operations.

An important factor which must be taken into account in considering computer input: field length. The simplest mode of operation is to use fixed fields; on a punched card, for example, we might always use the first six columns for accession number, the next twelve for author's name, then four ten-column fields for subjects. We can then instruct the computer that the information it finds in those positions will always be that particular kind of information, and this simplifies programming. However, suppose that we want to include titles or abstracts? We have no idea how long to make the field (one field may occupy more than one 80-column card), and if we make it long enough to cover the worst possible case, most of that field will be unused for most of the time.

The solution is to use variable fields: to make each field as long as we need it for the particular document we are dealing with. What we must do if we adopt this procedure is to instruct the computer how to recognize a new field; we have to label each field with its own identifying tag (facet indicator!) and include in our program the information that tells the computer that when it meets the tag for 'title' it goes to the next line and indents four spaces. It is of course possible to use a combination of fixed and variable fields, provided the instructions take account of this. Most modern computer-based information systems use variable fields, but this does mean that programming is made more complicated.

The core store may also obtain information from other sources. As it is limited in size, even in the largest computers, it has to be supplemented by secondary stores; these are usually in the form of magnetic disks, drums or cards, but magnetic tape may also be used. These secondary or back-up stores are limited in size only by questions of cost; although they are a great deal cheaper than core stores, they still cost quite a lot! Magnetic tapes have to be attached to the computer as required, since each tape can only hold a limited amount of information; the others may be left permanently connected to the core store. The advantage of this is of course that we can call on the computer at any time without having to perform any external physical action such as mounting a tape.

Another important factor, particularly with regard to secondary stores, is the question of random as opposed to serial access. Information on a magnetic tape can only be utilized by passing the tape through a reader until the required section is reached; we have serial access only—sequential scanning. In contrast, we may utilize information stored on a magnetic drum or disk almost instantaneously; we have random access to any part of the storage. A parallel may be found in the fact that we can select any band on a record simply by moving the pickup to the required spot before setting it down, whereas with a tape recording we have to run the tape through the deck until we find what we want, often by trial and error. (A similar parallel may be seen between the book and the papyrus roll.) The significance of this for libraries is considerable. With information stored on tape, we may have to search the whole tape to find what we want, and if we want to add further items we can do so only at the end unless we are prepared to 'rewrite' the whole tape. With random access storage we can go at once to those items likely to be of value, and updating the file presents no problems.

The core store will also transmit information to the processing or arithmetic unit, where it will be operated upon before being sent back to the core.

This leads us on to a discussion of the output. In effect, the same considerations apply here as to the input; any device that can be operated by electrical signals can be operated by a computer. Again, in practice certain kinds of output are more commonly found than others, the most common being the line printer. This is a device which prints a line at a time at high speeds, present limits being of the order of 1,200 lines per minute. Quality is not particularly high,

388

and is usually restricted to a limited range of characters; most line printers can only give upper case letters, for example. The output may also be in the form of punched cards or punched tape, but these are of limited interest for library purposes. Magnetic tape may however be useful, as it is a convenient means of storing information we want to re-use at some later date; it is also significant in that it can be used to control a filmsetting machine, as has already been mentioned, and thus makes possible computer controlled typesetting. Though this is outside the scope of our discussions here, it is a very important development in printing technology which should not be overlooked.

A television screen is operated by electrical signals, and it is possible to connect a cathode ray tube to a computer and display the output in this form. When a CRT display for the output is combined with an electrical typewriter terminal, the combination is known as a console, and this kind of device may well have some importance in information retrieval, as will be explained later.

Brooding over the whole assembly is the control unit, which is the part of the computer which controls all the rest. The control unit switches on the input and output, it initiates the transfer of information to the arithmetic unit and its return, and it governs the transfer of information from and to the secondary stores. However, like all the rest of the computer, it is simply a set of electronic circuits, and it functions as it does because it is in its turn controlled by a set of instructions which we feed into it via the core store. This set of instructions is the program.

PROGRAMS

So far we have been considering the physical units which together form the computer; these are known as the hardware. The core store, the arithmetic unit and the control unit together are known as the central processing unit, while the rest of the equipment is known as the peripherals. We now have to consider programs, usually known as software. Computers can only respond to electrical signals; we have to make sure that we feed in the right set of signals for them to respond to, that is, we must feed in the correct data; but we must also feed into them instructions which cause the control unit to operate in the right way. It has to switch on the input at the right time, to recognize the information we are feeding in, to see that the correct transformations are performed by the arithmetic unit, and that the output reaches us in the form that we want. Since the computer does not ' know ' anything that we have not told it, we have to make quite sure that our instructions are complete down to the last detail. For example, if we tell somebody to look something up in a book, we do not normally find it necessary to tell him to open the book first; we assume that he will do this without having to be told. No such assumptions can be made with computer programs; in effect, we have to tell the machine to fetch the book, open it and turn to the required page, then read what is on the page and record it in some form.

To write such a set of instructions we have to have a very clear idea of what we are trying to do; the first stage of writing a program is thus the analysis of the operation that we wish to transfer to the computer. This kind of rigorous analysis can often have a beneficial effect in itself, for it leads us to question the established routines that have grown up over the years. Indeed, it has in some instances led to such an improvement in the library's functioning that it has not proved necessary to take the next step and computerize the operations! Programming is a skill which is not normally part of a librarian's training; we should however be able to analyse the operations performed in our libraries sufficiently accurately for a programmer to be able to use our analysis to compile a program that will achieve the desired objective.

TIME SHARING AND MULTIPROGRAMMING

First and second generation computers only had room in the core store for one program, together with the information it was processing. They could also only accept one input at the time. The new models have much larger core stores and can thus find room for more than one program *and* the input information for them. To make it possible for the computer to work on more than one program at the time, a sort of super-program, known as director or supervisor, is necessary, to control the way in which the computer handles all the different sets of information. It would not do if the input intended to be processed according to one program were in fact processed according to another! This method of operating a computer is called multiprogramming, and is usually associated with another development found with third generation machines, time-sharing.

Electrical signals travel with the speed of light, and their transit from one part of a computer to another is very nearly instantaneous, particularly in recent models using integrated circuits which enable the whole machine to be built on a much smaller scale than was possible with circuits using conventional components. Operating speeds have thus increased as the size of computer units has diminished so that we now have computers which can complete one operation in a matter of a fraction of a micro-second, *ie* less than one millionth of a second. To perform some meaningful process may take several or perhaps even hundreds, of operations, but even so it is obvious that the machine is working at a very high speed. Compare this with a typist working at a rate of 600 characters a minute (100 words, average length 6 characters); this is not a bad speed for a typist, yet it only represents 10 operations a second—each operation takes 100,000 microseconds! In fact, only a tape typewriter could keep up this speed for any length of time, yet between each keystroke a computer could perform tens of thousands of operations. This difference between input speeds and computing speeds is the basis of time sharing, which consists of connecting up several separate input devices to the same computer at the same time.

ON-LINE OPERATION (REAL-TIME OPERATION)
Older computers could only accept one input at a time, and in consequence a particular job had to wait its turn in the queue to be fed into the machine. Time sharing means that a terminal or console can be left permanently connected and used whenever the need arises. Multiprogramming means that the terminals do not all have to use the same program, though they will always need to identify the program they wish to use. This kind of flexible, direct access, use is known as on-line operation, and is one of the most significant developments as far as library needs are concerned. No longer do we have to wait until it is convenient to run our program; we can use the computer at any time we want to. On-line access is an essential part of the pattern of library computer use predicted for the future, though at present (1971) it is still available to relatively few computer users.

LIBRARY APPLICATIONS
Computers have been used in libraries for two rather different purposes.[2] The first of these, and the more straightforward, is the mechanization of clerical and accounting operations such as book ordering and circulation. We are not concerned here with this side of library science, but with the second, which is information retrieval. Here computers have been used in a variety of ways. Some of these are now accepted practice, while others are still highly experimental; we may divide them into three groups:

computerization of existing services (by far the largest group)
automatic indexing and abstracting
natural language searching of complete texts.

EXISTING SERVICES

We have already discussed in chapter 10 the relative advantages of
different physical forms of catalogue; the conclusion reached was that
the use of computers to print out catalogues in book form may lead
to the re-emergence of this as the most popular form.[3] Up to now,
any library wishing to produce its catalogue in this form has had
to prepare the input itself (though it is important to remember that
if the catalogue is produced as one of a series of integrated operations,
the additional work involved here may be small—most of it will have
been done at the ordering stage). However, an important project is
now under way, Project MARC,[4] the object of which is to make available
machine-readable cataloguing copy to any librarian who wants it. The
project was originally put forward by the Library of Congress, but
a much wider scope than one library or even one country was always
the aim, and the ultimate objective is to make machine readable cataloguing copy available for any library that wants it and for any book
published throughout the world. Obviously this is a hope for the
future, but progress so far has been very promising. After some years
of experimenting with MARC I, the MARC II format was developed;
perhaps the most significant factor here was the realization that the
original ideas were inadequate, and that a new approach to bibliographic records and computer processing was required. (One might
even argue that the contribution made by the MARC studies to our
understanding of what is involved in complete bibliographic records
has been just as important as the actual development of the computer
programs to handle these records.) After a year of full scale experimentation, BNB went over to complete MARC processing on January 1
1971; there is complete interchange of copy with the Library of
Congress, so that between them the two services cover a very substantial proportion of all English-language publishing without unnecessary duplication.

From the subject point of view, MARC is significant in that it permits
a variety of subject designations to be used. There are places for not
only DC and LC class numbers, but for UDC and BC as well; in addition
to LCSH, PRECIS entries are made—in fact, it will be possible to put
in as many subject designations as is economically feasible. From the

same MARC record, it will be possible to generate BNB weekly issues and also the regular cumulations; BNB cards (in a different layout more suitable for this purpose); LC cards; and entries for any particular library catalogue, whether on cards, computer printout, or computer output microfilm (COM). It will of course also be possible to use the tapes as input to a computer, and thus perform searches through any of the subject designations. We are only beginning to see the full potential of this very important project, which is certain to transform library cataloguing.

Computer-produced catalogues are usually thought of as being associated with pre-coordinate systems, but an interesting example of their use with post-coordinate systems is the dual dictionary described in chapter 19. Production in this printed form makes it possible to distribute a post-coordinate index to whoever wants it; physical forms such as Uniterm or peek-a-boo are of course essentially single-copy methods.

MEDLARS

The possibility of producing a library catalogue by using a computer applies of course to published abstracting and indexing services also. Many such services are experimenting with computers, for example Chemical Abstracts and Science Abstracts, but the most highly developed is Index Medicus, linked to MEDLARS.[5] Incoming journals are indexed in the usual way, using MeSH as the source of terms, but from that point the whole operation is computerized. Bibliographical details and indexing terms are fed in, and the computer then sorts the material, making an entry under each heading allotted to an article, and controls the filmsetting operation which leads to the printed index. The information on the magnetic tapes generated for this operation also serves as the store which is searched for bibliographies and enquiries; the whole system is integrated, and represents a very suitable way to make use of the computer's potential. As with any machine system, it is the regular re-use of the basic records which is the basis of success.

MEDLARS is also interesting in that it is the first large scale service which has been subjected to detailed 'quality control'. The tests carried out on a selection of the searches were described in chapter 23, but it is worth going into more detail here on one particular aspect, that of conducting searches in a computerized system.[6] In a conventional system, it is possible to perform heuristic searches, a point which has been discussed in chapter 2. With a computer based information retrieval system using batch processing, searches must necessarily be iterative, and this may be a less effective way of conducting searches, particularly in situations where the user is not very sure of what he wants. The use of on-line systems, with the user in direct contact with the computer through a terminal, restores the possibility of heuristic searching and thus gives the advantages of both methods: the ability to modify one's search as it progresses plus the ability to handle very large amounts of information and still find quickly what one wants. A typewriter terminal may still be relatively slow, even at 900 characters per minute, if one wishes to look at a large number of references, so the future would appear to lie with the visual display. Using the same kind of technique as is used to generate a television picture, it is possible to display information on a screen at very high presentation speeds; if a reference looks useful, a signal can be sent to the computer to print out that particular item while the user is looking at other items, and discarding those which do not look useful.

Searches in a computerized system such as MEDLARS exclude this kind of interaction. The computer is not used in an on-line fashion, and for economic reasons it is normal to gather several searches together to form a batch rather than process them one by one. Since the searches are carried out at the limited number of centres which have copies of the magnetic tapes, the user may well be many miles away at the time of the search, and indeed may never have any closer contact with the search than is afforded by correspondence. This kind of situation can obviously lead to poor results in terms of relevance unless we adopt new strategies when planning searches. One method is to set up, on the basis of the original request, a set of searches rather than a single search, in an attempt to cover all possible approaches. This is not likely to improve relevance, since—as we have seen—in normal practice we frequently find the final search bearing only a limited relationship to the original. There is however another very simple method, which we may sometimes use with conventional searches; this is to explore the background to the enquiry. We often find that an enquiry has been triggered off by a document which the enquirer has read; possibly he can give us details of more than one document. If so, we have in effect reached the first stage of an iterative search and can use this information in formulating our search strategy.

Another point which should be taken into account is the purpose for which the enquirer needs information. A flexible system such as MEDLARS can work at different levels of recall; we can work at a high recall level to ensure that we find as much material as possible, or we can aim for low recall and obtain only a few documents. In the first case we shall of course have low precision, and as well as the relevant documents we shall have a large number of unwanted items; in the second case we shall retrieve only a small proportion of the relevant documents, but most of those we do retrieve will be useful.

The MEDLARS search request form is being modified to take account of these and other factors. However, by 1972 it is hoped that the National Library of Medicine will have an on-line system in operation, using consoles; in this situation it should be possible to return to the search modes used in conventional systems and conduct heuristic and iterative searches as well as the present all-or-nothing type. The difference will lie in the fact that the computerized system will give the user access to a very large amount of information in a very short time; it should be possible to perform in minutes searches which would take hours using manual methods. It is however likely to be some time before all users have this kind of access, and in the meantime searches have to be planned with the limitations of batch processing in mind.

As was mentioned briefly, the success of a computerized system depends on the re-use of the basic records. Magnetic tapes can very easily be duplicated and distributed to other centres, and this has been done very successfully with MEDLARS. The tapes are prepared at the US National Library of Medicine and are made available to a number of centres in the USA and other parts of the world. In Britain, the NLL acts as the centre, in collaboration with the University of Newcastle Computing Laboratory; other centres are found in Europe and other parts of the world. Though it is not the only service of its kind, there is no doubt that in many ways it can serve as a model of what will be possible in the future; particularly important is the fact that computerization has not been allowed to set aside the importance of intellectual organization. The system has been shown to fit into the same pattern as any other system, and recognition of this fact has led to substantial improvements in the service.

BRITISH TECHNOLOGY INDEX

As has been mentioned, BTI has now started using a computer[7] to carry out the clerical work associated with the production of the monthly index and annual cumulation. The major problem was to devise a program that would generate *see* references in accordance with BTI practice, given the original heading. The difficulties have now been overcome by using differential punctuation to indicate to the computer how it should treat a particular chain of terms. BTI's practice differs from straight-forward chain procedure, which would have been relatively simple to mechanize; indeed far from making the intellectual work involved in indexing easier, computerization has imposed new stringencies. It is essential that the indexers consider carefully the function of each term they include in the chain when these functions have to be shown by indicators.

The existing authority file of synonym cross-references has been put into machine readable form, so that the machine will automatically generate any that are necessary in a given monthly issue, without this having to be entered. (New synonyms have of course to be entered into the authority file as they arise.) The computer will also print out the authority file regularly and thus relieve the staff of the maintenance of this file on cards.

Now that this computer based system has been fully implemented, it will have many advantages. Perhaps the most important is that it will permit the staff to devote more of their time to the intellectual effort of indexing, and conversely will make the prompt indexing of any particular periodical issue less dependent on hazards such as ill-health. It will also speed up considerably the production of the annual volume, which will no longer have to be sorted manually. However, it would be shortsighted not to see the further possibilities presented by a computerized operation. The production of an author index, which previously would have required considerable clerical effort, can be a desirable by-product, as can a listing by journal; this latter would provide convenient indexes to the periodicals held by a library until such time as the official indexes were available (or even beyond this, when one considers the standard of many published journal indexes!) The programs should also lend themselves to the production of similar periodicals; the only major constraint appears to be that the complete heading should be a meaningful statement of the subject.

Like MEDLARS, BTI will continue to rely on intellectual rather than computer indexing. The object of computerization is to enable the staff to concentrate on these intellectual tasks, freed from the heavy clerical burdens involved in the actual production of the printed issues.

MULTIPLE ENTRY SYSTEMS

These have already been discussed in part I of this work, and it is not necessary to go into detail again here. It is important to remember that computers are well suited to the manipulation of a standard entry, *eg* a title or synthetic class number, to generate a number of additional entries according to a set pattern. It is possible to compile KWIC, KWOC or SLIC indexes manually, but the amount of work involved is considerable; using a computer such indexes can be produced quickly and cheaply.

Chemical Abstracts is one of the services most concerned to take advantage of computer processing, and some interesting work has been done recently on the derivation of subject indexes automatically. This work has been discussed in chapter 5, but the major significance again lies more in subsequent use of the machine readable records than in the original production of a ' conventional ' service. Many of the Chemical Abstracts services are now available on magnetic tape, and the United Kingdom Chemical Information Service (UKCIS) based on Nottingham University uses these tapes to give both an SDI service and some retrospective searching.[8]

PRECIS is of course another method of generating multiple entries from a single original statement, and was developed specifically for computer manipulation. It gives a very flexible subject statement, which can be used either as an alphabetical subject heading or, as in BNB, as an index to a classified sequence, and the fact that it will form part of the MARC record will mean that PRECIS strings will be available to anyone who wants to use them.

At one time the English Electric Company library used an interesting variant of the KWOC method. We have seen that cycling and rotating are kinds of KWIC indexing; in the EE library, a reports bulletin, arranged in classified order, was indexed by using a KWOC program applied to the chain of division for each class number. For example, the chain of division for fatigue in steel bearings would be Bearings: steel: fatigue. This would give rise to index entries as follows:

Fatigue: steel: bearings (usual chain index entry)

Steel: fatigue: steel: bearings

Bearings: fatigue: steel: bearings

The significance of this is that each index entry is specific, unlike normal chain index entries, where only the first is specific. The method has now been abandoned in favour of post-coordinate techniques in order to fit in with the rest of the library's operations, but it remains an interesting variant which might well be used more widely.

Computerization has usually implied the abandonment of existing classification schemes, which gives added significance to a research project carried out for the American Institute of Physics[9] to find out whether UDC could be used in a computer-based system. The first problem faced was the lack of schedules for anything fuller than the abridged edition in English. The text of the German medium edition was made available, and much of this was translated; the results were fed into a computer, together with the text of the abridged edition and those parts of the full edition that were available, and from these a printout was obtained. It was shown that the computer provides a practical means of updating and printing out UDC schedules; it even proved possible to introduce typographical distinctions based on the length of the UDC number (though this has to be treated with caution, as the rather haphazard development of UDC has meant that the relative importance of subjects is not reflected by the notation). It also proved possible to produce alphabetical indexes to the schedules, though these could not always be used exactly as they stood.

Once a usable set of schedules was available, it was possible to get to the main point of the project, ie to see whether they could be manipulated in a computer file. It was found that in general the schedules could be fitted without much expenditure of time or money into an already existing system, the Combined File Search System, a set of programs developed by IBM and used by a number of information centres in the USA. The system was intended for use with a thesaurus of alphabetical headings, but this did not prove to be an obstacle. One problem was that UDC notation is in some ways not suitable for computer processing. The basic decimal notation presents no difficulties, but the arbitrary symbols used for the auxiliaries are a different matter. The colon is too ambiguous to be used conveniently (as has been pointed out earlier), and some of the other symbols have different meanings in different situations. For example, the equals sign = means one thing on its own, something rather different when enclosed by a parenthesis (= . . .); the point . is normally used for visual convenience only, without any significance, but when it is followed by o or oo this is not the case. A new set of indicators was worked out using letters to overcome this problem.

Experiments were carried out using both batch processing and on-line operation. In both cases UDC performed quite adequately, and demonstrated that it could be used in such systems. The overall conclusions reached were on the whole favourable. Because it was not designed with computer manipulation in mind, it is probably not as satisfactory as a scheme devised specifically with this objective could be; on the other hand, there are some situations where UDC would have particular advantages, for example in a library with large amounts of material already classified by the scheme, or in a situation where documents were being processed for international use. The fundamental problem is the one which bears no particular relationship to computer processing, ie the difficulty of obtaining the complete schedules in up to date form. This is basically a problem of finance; if UDC were to become the international concordance suggested in chapter 13, more support would be forthcoming and this problem could be solved.

Other organizations have also been interested in applying computer techniques to UDC files, among them the UKAEA[10] and the American Meteorological Society.[11] A seminar was held in Copenhagen in September 1968 on UDC in a mechanized retrieval system, and while it is probably too soon to foresee exactly what progress will be made, it is possible to strike a note of cautious optimism. UDC has a unique place among classification systems, and it would be a pity to waste all the efforts that have gone into its development over the years; further, the pressure of adapting it to the machine age may well lead to important improvements in the scheme, such as the replacement of the present set of indicators by a completely new and more precise set more suited to modern needs.

SELECTIVE DISSEMINATION OF INFORMATION

For many years now libraries have been concerned to see that readers were kept informed of new materials in their fields of interest. In the public library, this might be on a haphazard, ' old boy ', basis, but in the special library it has always been regarded as an important part of the library's function. There are, however, certain difficulties in the way of running such a service successfully, some intellectual, some clerical. The use of a computer can solve many of these problems and enable us to give a more complete and accurate service to our readers.[12]

A system for computer operation was developed by H P Luhn of IBM and is still valid today, though it has been modified in some respects. In effect, it involves each reader in stating his requirements in the same method of subject description as is used in indexing the library's holdings. If the library uses a thesaurus, then terms will be chosen from this; if a classification scheme, this will be used. These reader 'profiles' are fed into the computer together with the similar profiles for new accessions; when the computer finds a match between the two, it prints out a notification.

Clerical problems are thus fairly easily solved. The intellectual problems are rather more intractable. A research project begun by the National Electronics Research Council and later taken over by the Institution of Electrical Engineers with support from OSTI showed that perhaps the most pressing difficulty in setting up a viable SDI system was to obtain a valid statement of readers' needs. Users were asked to state their interest profiles, and were sent a selection of articles on the strength of this. At the end of the month they were asked to state which of the articles had been of use, and which article they had read during the month had proved most interesting to them. While the majority of the references notified by the SDI systems were of some value, the 'most interesting articles' were often found to bear little relation to the reader's profile! By asking readers to return the notification form, indicating whether the reference had been of interest or not, a degree of feedback can be obtained which can be used to modify their profiles, but there will never be any means of foretelling the wayout' article which may prove of interest.

Despite the difficulties, the IEE has developed this work into a satisfactory integrated system, INSPEC, in which all the operations involved in the SDI service and the production of the various parts of *Science abstracts* and *Current papers* are integrated.[13]

While SDI systems may not be able to achieve the impossible, they can function very effectively within a particular organization, and computer processing enables us to extend the benefits to a larger audience. The IEE project, and that in the field of plasma physics originating in the UKAEA Culham Laboratories, have shown that provided the users do their part by stating their needs precisely, a very effective service can be given on a nation wide scale.

ISI

The Institute for Scientific Information has already been mentioned in connection with *Science citation index* in chapter 3. It is worth pointing out here that ISI in fact uses the SCI data base for several different services. As journals are received, entries are keypunched for each item in them; the information noted is 'manifest', *ie* it is there already and does not need any intellectual effort to define it. The items noted include author, author's affiliation, title, citations and bibliographical reference. By suitable programming it is possible to produce SCI and also provide an SDI service, ASCA (Automatic Subject Citation Alert). SCI contains not only the citation index but also an author index and the 'Permuterm' index, in which items are indexed under pairs of significant terms; judged by the criteria of manual production, the latter is a very inefficient method of indexing, but when it is realized that it can be generated quite automatically from the existing data base, conventional economics are seen to be irrelevant. The ASCA service again uses exactly the same data base, and a user profile may include not only keywords but also authors' names, institutions (ie, authors' affiliations), and previous references which have been found useful. The service is not cheap, but then it does provide access to information through a number of channels which do not usually feature at all in indexing services. The more such a service is used, the cheaper it is likely to become for each individual user, since the cost of the input remains constant.

AUTOMATIC INDEXING AND ABSTRACTING
The first attempts at computer indexing were based on word counts. It was assumed that a word which occurred frequently in a document (excluding of course common words) would bear a significant relationship to its subject content, and—vice versa—that the most significant words would be those which occurred most frequently. This is too much of a simplification, and it was soon realized that purely statistical techniques were inadequate for this particular task. More useful results were obtained when the co-occurrence of terms was measured; if two words were frequently found together, the significance of their joint occurrence was likely to be a great deal higher than that of their occurrences measured in isolation. A technique for automatic abstracting was developed, which involved selecting and printing out those sentences of the original which contained the most significant word pairs, but this proved to be inadequate and was abandoned.[15]

Recent work has been in the direction of refining the criteria for selection of sentences. Instead of a simple statistical criterion, one may introduce four measures of significance, and give each sentence a weight according to these. Sentences with the highest weights are likely to be those which best summarized the content of the document, and it is possible to program the computer to extract all sentences with weights above a predetermined level, which will

401

depend on the subject matter, kind of literature and so on. The four measures proposed are based on 1) keywords determined statistically; 2) clue words, *eg* significant, important, which indicate that the author wishes to emphasize a statement; 3) title and heading words, which may be assumed to have particular weight; and 4) position of the sentence in the overall structure—for example, the first sentence in a paragraph is often a ' topic ' sentence and would thus be useful as an indication of the content of the paragraph. The overall result compares reasonably well with an abstract prepared by a skilled abstracter, who will of course be basing his own summary on a similar analysis. The preferred term for this technique is now ' autoextracting ' rather than ' autoabstracting ', to emphasize the fact that it is essentially based on the existing content of the document and can only extract from it.

KEYWORDS AND CLUMPS

Another promising line of approach has been developed at the Cambridge Language Research Unit (CLRU).[16] As we have seen in part I, to develop a classification scheme we need to study the documents in our collection, list the concepts found in them, and organize these in a helpful way. We do this by intellectual effort, and the result is thus coloured by our prior knowledge; we tend to add to the structure found within the document our own *a priori* understanding of the structure of the subject. This is in fact the basic difference between Gardin's paradigmatic and syntagmatic relationships: the former are those which we are aware of outside any particular context, and the latter those which we find only in a particular context: the document collection we are analysing.

The CLRU work has used the co-occurrence techniques already mentioned to build up matrices of related concepts: related, that is, in the sense that they occur together, in the document collection being analysed, to a significant extent. The resulting ' clumps ' form a kind of classification, based strictly on the document collection; the computer cannot, of course, add anything of its own prior knowledge, for it has none. The results may resemble a conventional classification, for example:

> grammar, paradigm, parts of speech, adjective, preposition, phrase, phrase marker, tense, ending, stem, syntax, diacritic

where the main difference from the kind of grouping that we are accustomed to lies in the fact that many foci are missing (noun, verb, clause) simply because they do not occur in the document collection.

Other clumps appear less conventional:
> style, text, paragraph, chunking, interlingua, post-editor, source language, thesaurus head, Roget, Pask machine, Latin, technical language.

Such clumps do however reflect the nature of the collection.

In a particular document collection there will be a number of terms which, though important, do not occur frequently enough to form part of a clump; some experiments were therefore tried using a combination of clumps and non-clumped keywords. These seemed to give good results, whereas retrieval using clumps alone (and thus excluding non-clumped but possibly important terms) was poor. Several different retrieval techniques were in fact tried, using the Cranfield methods. One interesting suggestion to arise is the use of classes as a precision device rather than recall. Normally, by substituting a more inclusive heading for the one we have been using, we would expect to increase recall at the expense of precision. It is, however, possible to use a combination of keywords and classes to improve precision without too much loss of recall. Suppose that we have a request which involves six terms; we begin our search at the most specific point, *ie* by coordinating all six terms. We broaden the search by dropping one term at a time, first searching at a coordination level of five, then four and so on. If we consider the documents recalled at a coordination level of four, we can grade them in likely order of relevance:

> terms 1 to 4 plus term related to 5 plus term related to 6
>
> terms 1 to 4 plus term related to 5 or term related to 6
>
> terms 1 to 4 only

Grouping related terms has here permitted us to select from the four possible groups of documents here those which are most likely to be what we require.

One of the main objectives of the CLRU work is to make retrieval easier by concentrating more effort on the input. There is a balance of effort between input and output, as we have shown in chapter 2; by using more sophisticated indexing and classifying procedures, we may be able to transfer much of the effort to the input side and thus lighten the output effort. A set of documents needs to be indexed but once, but we shall try to retrieve information from it many times, and effort spent on indexing will thus be amply repaid later. This philosophy is directly contrary to that of the IBM retrieval system described below, but has advantages for the librarian who does not have access to computer time for elaborate searches.

This work has been continued in the Cambridge University Mathematical Laboratory, the main direction being the refining of the techniques used to generate the automatic classifications. Four types of connection structure are now recognized: strings, in which the connection runs from the first concept to the second, thence to the third, and so on; stars, in which one concept is connected to a number of others; cliques, in which each element is connected to every other element; and clumps, in which each element is connected to at least one other, but in an irregular structure. Results seem to be promising, indicating that classifications of this kind can give better results than similar but unclassified vocabularies. Since this result is in contrast to those obtained by the CLW research project described in the previous chapter, it is evident that more work needs to be done before we can reach any firm conclusions. There is however no doubt that this work is very valuable in clarifying our ideas about classification.

COMPLETE TEXT SEARCHING

The CLRU method is to use a classification which stems directly from the documents being indexed to help in the searching procedure. It does, however, rely on the selection of key words from the texts. Is it possible to dispense with this basic operation and use the complete text (or, more commonly, an abstract) as the basis of our retrieval system? Obviously, if this is the case we can save a great deal of time and effort at the input stage; if at the same time we can use a computer to do the searching at the output stage, we may be able to speed up this process sufficiently for it to be acceptable. Such systems are already in existence, and appear to give satisfactory results.

IBM

As befits the library of the largest manufacturer of computers in the world, IBM information services are very largely computer-based. The whole library is taken as a system, so that the primary machine-readable record is generated when the documents are first received, and serves a multiplicity of purposes: cataloguing, circulation control, stock control, use studies, and information retrieval, including an SDI service.[17]

The core of the collections is formed by IBM technical reports. Each author is asked to prepare an abstract at the same time as he writes the report; these abstracts are written with the advice of technical information staff, to ensure that they adequately represent the subject of the document. Although no thesaurus is now used, the vocabulary may still be said to be controlled to a certain extent, in that all the authors concerned are working on similar subjects, within the same organization. The abstracts are fed into the computer, together with the usual bibliographical details, to give the data base on which the information retrieval system works. Some periodical articles are also included, and this coverage is likely to increase steadily in the future.

To answer a request for information, a member of the technical information staff collaborates with the enquirer in framing his request in the same form, *ie* a natural language abstract. This is fed into the computer, which matches it against the stored abstracts and prints out the results (or possibly a statement to the effect that the enquiry as phrased would yield an undue number of references). This answer is studied to see whether it is what the enquirer wants, or whether it is necessary to restate the search. In the USA, the search may be conducted on-line, so that the iterative process does not cause any significant delay; this is not the case in Britain at present, for enquiries are batch processed overnight at the major IBM centre in France. Extra care has to be taken to ensure that the question put to the system is a valid one in these circumstances.

The SDI system works on a similar basis, except that users are asked to give their profiles in keyboard form, as described earlier. Additional refinements that are possible include setting the level of coordination which must be reached before the user wishes to be notified. For example, a user may give Computers, Information, Retrieval, among the keywords in his profile; if at the same time he sets the level of coordination at three, he will be notified of new items on the use of computers for information retrieval, but not of articles on information retrieval or computers generally.

Computer searching of natural language texts does open up some extended possibilities for varying search strategies. For example, one can search for COMPUTERS, but one can also search for COMPUT*, in which case the machine will find not only comput*ers* but also comput*ing,* comput*ors,* comput*ability,* comput*ation,* and any other words based on the same stem. Boolean logic—the use of AND, OR, NOT—can be used to give a measure of precoordination, though with much more flexibility than is found in the conventional precoordinate index, or postcoordinate index using links.[21]

The development of a large number of different retrieval systems could be wasteful if it could be shown that one, or a few, systems were superior to the rest. This is of course the objective of the Cranfield Project; the SMART system is the equivalent for computer-based systems.[18] Natural language texts in the form of abstracts are the input (though there is no reason why full texts should not be used other than the economic one). These can be analysed according to a very wide variety of methods, including the following:

a system for reducing paradigms to their stem

a thesaurus for the elimination of synonyms

a hierarchical arrangement of the terms in the thesaurus

statistical association

syntactic analysis

statistical phrase recognition

Three collections of documents have been used, covering computer science, documentation and aeronautics respectively. (The aeronautics collection was part of that used for the Cranfield tests.) Various methods of evaluating the results have been used, the overall conclusions being much the same as for the Cranfield II tests: keywords give the best results on the whole, the only improvements in results being obtained by eliminating synonyms, and the use of hierarchical expansions does not in general improve performance. Abstracts are found to give better results than titles, and full texts better than abstracts—but not so much better that we can be sure that full texts will always give better results. On the basis of the comparison with the Cranfield results, the cautious conclusion is reached that computer processing of abstracts, with thesaurus control of synonyms, can give results comparable with indexing carried out by human indexers. Further work is in progress on the problems raised by larger collections of documents; the three tested so far contained 780 abstracts, 82 short papers, and 200 abstracts respectively. In addition, problems of search strategy are being studied, particularly those related to on-line systems where the user can react quickly to the output from a particular search. Questions of cost are outside the scope of the investigation; though they are obviously highly important, they are too closely tied to the local circumstances of an information retrieval system for generalized conclusions to be valid.

For some years MIT has been experimenting with Project MAC, an on-line system which permits up to thirty users to be in contact with a large central computer at the same time through a network of consoles. The success of this experiment led to the much wider concept of a nation-wide library and information service of the future in which the number of potential users would be unlimited. This project was given the name INTREX (INformation TRansfer EXperiments),[19] and a planning conference was held in 1965 to discuss the scope and aims of such a concept. The major problem is seen as the gradual breakdown through overloading of conventional library services, in particular those intended for the scholar and research worker. The planning conference did not suggest any solutions, but rather served to define the problems. Two main methods of approach were seen: the application of computers and other technological developments (*eg* those in photocopying) to conventional library operations, and the development of a completely new information network based on computer stored information, with new documents being entered at source, by the authors, thus by-passing conventional publication procedures.

The logical conclusion of such developments has been outlined by one of the participants, J C R Licklider,[20] who foresees the disappearance of the book—that inefficient means of conveying information—and its replacement by the console, connected on-line to a vast central computer network, with information displayed on a screen in response to the user's requests, and with facilities for immediate interaction between user and computer.

CONCLUSIONS

The library of the future, as foreseen by the computer expert, may seem very strange to the librarian of today. Librarians tend to be conservative, since for many years their task was indeed seen as that of conservation rather than exploitation. In this chapter we have discussed very briefly some of the significant developments that are taking place in the application of computers to information retrieval; there are others, but those mentioned here form a representative selection. In some ways the picture seems to be perhaps a little depressing; if computers can perform all the operations necessary to the functioning of a library, where is the need for skilled librarians? However, we should not take too gloomy a view. As yet, it seems that skilled indexers do have a slight edge on the computer; the MEDLARS project has shown that users need the help of skilled searchers to formulate the right questions; and since the pace of actual change is usually very much slower than the pace of potential change, libraries in their present form are likely to continue in existence for many years to come. The computer can help to lighten the burden of clerical effort in libraries and enable librarians to devote more of their time to the worthwhile ends of serving readers. We should welcome the opportunities it presents for us to devote more of our efforts to the productive side of librarianship—enabling our users to find the information that they want, when they want it. Perhaps we may take some comfort from Vickery's description of the MARLIS: the Multi-Aspect Relevance Linkage Information System which could solve all our information retrieval problems in the future.[22]

BIBLIOGRAPHY

As was the case with the previous chapter, most of the books and articles available in this area are not suitable for the beginner. The following list is intended to provide further information on the points covered in the text; those marked* are suggested as being elementary texts.

1 *Artandi, S: *Computers in information science.* Metuchen, New Jersey, Scarecrow Press, 1968.

*Cox, N S M, Dews, J D and Dolby, J L: *The computer and the library.* Newcastle, University Library, 1966.

*Henley, J P: *Computer based library and information systems.* McDonald, 1970.

*Houghton, B, ed: *Computer based information retrieval systems.* Bingley, 1968.

Kent, A: *Textbook of mechanized information retrieval.* Interscience Publishers, 1962.

*Kimber, R T: *Automation in libraries.* Pergamon, 1968.

*Library Association. *North Midland Branch.* The library and the machine; edited by C D Batty. Scunthorpe, NMBLA, 1966.

*———. Libraries and machines today; edited by C D Batty. Scunthorpe, NMBLA, 1967.

(The above titles represent a selection of those available)

Program, published quarterly by Aslib, includes reports of much of the work that is going on in this country.

2 Foskett, A C: 'Computers in libraries' (*in Five years' work in librarianship*, 1961-1965. Library Association, 1968). Now somewhat out of date, this still contains much that is relevant.

3 *Meakin, A O: Production of a printed union catalogue by computer. *Library Association record, 67* (9) 1965, 311-316.

The book catalog: a symposium. *Library resources and technical services, 8* (4) 1964, 344-407.

Dolby, J L: *Computerized library catalogues: their growth, cost and utility*. Stechert-Hafner, 1969.

4 United States. *Library of Congress*: The MARC II format: a communications format for bibliographic data. Washington, DC, Library of Congress, 1968.

*Coward, R E: 'BNB and computers'. *Library Association record, 70* (8) 1968, 198-202.

*Horner, J L: *Cataloguing*. Chapter 32.

Jeffreys, A E and Wilson, T D: *The UK MARC Project*. Oriel Press, 1970. (Report of a symposium held at Southampton, 1969.)

BNB MARC Documentation Service *publications* include one on UK MARC and one on PRECIS.

5 *Austin, C J: MEDLARS, *1963-1967*. Bethesda, Maryland, National Library of Medicine, 1968.

*Adams, S and Taine, S: 'The National Library of medicine and MEDLARS'. *Revue internationale de la documentation, 31* (3) 1964, 107-110.

6 Lancaster, F W: 'Interaction between requesters and a large mechanized retrieval system'. *Information storage and retrieval, 4* (2) 1968, 239-252.

Lancaster, F W: 'Aftermath of an evaluation'. *Journal of documentation, 27* (1) 1971, 1-10.

7 *Coates, E J: 'Computer assistance in the production of BTI'. *Library Association record, 70* (10) 1968, 255-257.

8 Batten, W: 'UKCIS: the United Kingdom Chemical Information Service'. *Chemistry in Britain, 6* (10) 1970, 420-422.

Barker, F H *and others*: *Report on the evaluation of an experimental computer-based current awareness service for chemists*. Chemical Society, 1970. (UKCIS Research reports no 1.)

9 The AIP has published a series of reports, AIP/UDC—1/9, covering the whole of this work. Some of these have been published also in the *Journal of documentation*.

14*

10 *Cayless, C and Ayres, F: 'The use of punched cards for the production of multiple copies of an alphabetical subject index in the UDC'. *Library Association record, 66* (10) 1964, 439-442.

*Ayres, F H *and others*: 'Some applications of mechanization in a large special library'. *Journal of documentation, 23* (1) 1967, 34-44.

11 *Rigby, M: 'Experiments in mechanized control of meteorological and geoastrophysical literature and the UDC schedules in these fields'. *Revue Internationale de la documentation, 31* (3) 1964, 103-106.

12 *East, H: 'The development of SDI services'. *Aslib proceedings, 20* (11) 1968, 482-491.

Hall, J L and Terry, J E: 'Development of mechanized current awareness services at Culham and Harwell.' (*in Handling of nuclear information*. International Atomic Energy Agency, 1970. 201-209).

13 Clague, P: 'The SDI study in electronics' (*in* Houghton, ref 1 above).

14 Kessler, M M: 'The MIT technical information project'. *Physics today, 18* (3) 1965, 28-36.

15 Luhn, H P: *H P Luhn: pioneer of information science. Selected works*, edited by Claire K Schultz. Macmillan, 1968. Luhn wrote several articles on statistical encoding and auto-abstracting, which will be found in this memorial volume.

Edmundson, H P: 'New methods in automatic extracting'. *Journal of the Association for Computing Machinery, 16* (2) 1969, 264-285.

16 Needham, R M and Sparck Jones, K: 'Keywords and clumps: recent work on information retrieval at the Cambridge Language Research Unit'. *Journal of documentation, 20* (1) 1964, 5-15.

Sparck Jones, K and Needham, R M: 'Automatic term classifications and retrieval'. *Information storage and retrieval, 4* (2) 1968, 91-100.

Sparck Jones, K and Jackson, D M: 'The use of automatically-obtained keyword classifications for information retrieval'. *Information storage and retrieval, 5* 1970, 175-201.

Sparck Jones, K: 'Automatic thesaurus construction and the relation of a thesaurus to indexing terms'. *Aslib proceedings, 22* (5) 1970, 226-228.

17 IBM have published a series of technical reports describing their library operations in some detail. See also the brief account by J R Davies in *Libraries and machines today* (ref 1 above).

18 Salton, G: *Automatic information organization and retrieval.* McGraw Hill, 1968.

Salton, G: 'The evaluation of automatic retrieval procedures—selected test results using the SMART system '. *American documentation, 16 (3)* 1965, 209-222.

Salton, G and Lesk, M E: 'Computer evaluation of indexing and text processing '. *Journal of the Association for Computing Machinery, 15 (1)* 1968, 8-36.

Salton, G: 'Automatic text analysis '. *Science, 168* 17 April 1970, 335-343.

19 *INTREX: report of a planning conference on information transfer experiments, September 3 1965,* edited by C F J Overhage and R J Harman. MIT Press, 1965.

20 Licklider, J C R: *Libraries of the future.* MIT Press, 1965.

21 Keen, E M: 'Search strategy evaluation in manual and automated systems '. *Aslib proceedings, 20 (1)* 1968, 65-81.

Vickery, B C: *Techniques of information retrieval.* Chapters 12 and 14.

22 Vickery, B C: 'MARLIS: a Multi-Aspect Relevance Linkage Information System '. *American documentation, 11, (2)* 1960, 97-101. Also in his *On retrieval system theory,* p 12-18.

Index

In addition to serving the normal purpose of enabling readers to find specific items quickly, this index is intended to demonstrate the principles set out in the text and discussed on pages 195-197. Certain conventions are used: *def* indicates that a term is defined; + indicates that a discussion covers more than two pages. Bibliographical references are shown by *bib*; full details of a book, in particular those cited in the bibliography for chapter 1, are usually only given once, and parentheses are used to show further citations, *eg*

Vickery, B C *bib* 18 (30, 40, 201, 203), 18 (155), 110, 254, 411

indicates that works by this author are quoted on all the pages shown, but that for full details of the work quoted on page 40 it is necessary to go back to page 18. The reason for this is that the bibliography for chapter 1 lists a number of basic works, many of which are referred to throughout the text, and it was thought unnecessary to repeat the full details at every point.

Synonyms are in general indexed fully, but in some cases this would have led to repetitive entries; in such cases, an index entry is made for the main discussion under non-preferred terms, but these are followed by the preferred term in parentheses to lead to the full set of index entries, *eg*

References (cross-references) *def* 29

which leads to page 29, but also to the index entry

Cross-references

where nineteen additional entries will be found.

Filing is word by word; abbreviations are treated as single words; hyphens are elided, so that Cross-references files *after* Crossley. Order is alphabetical within each heading or subheading; *irt* (in relation to) is filed as a word.

Figures and tables are *not* indexed, nor are spelled out forms of any of the abbreviations listed on pages 7 and 8.

BC ch 14 256+
  enumerative schedules 102
  flexibility 149
  literal mnemonics 135
  main class order 116
  MARC 392
  notation
    arbitrary symbols 148
    flexibility 149
    mnemonic features 135
    synthesis 145
BCM *Classification bib* 155
  notation non-expressive 143
  retroactive 151
Bernal, J D: classification research 363
Bias
  Eastern CC 278
  Western DC 217
    being removed 218
  see also critical classification
Bias phase 125
Bibliographic coupling 39
Bibliographic forms: common facets 112+
Bibliographic records: MARC 392
Bibliographic Systems Center 381
Bibliographies
  arrangement 193+
  importance 13
Binary coding: edge-notched cards 327
Blagden, J F *bib* 354
Bliss Classification Association 257, 267
Bliss classification bulletin 265
Bliss, H E *bib* 155 (207)
  BC ch 14 256+
  comment on notation 130
  influence on Ranganathan 267
  main class order 116+
  subject index illusion 211
BM
  guard book catalogue 193
  printed catalogue 192
  relation to BNB 233
BNB *bib* 409
  author/subject index 175
  cards available 192
  changes in 5-year cumulations 166
  CRG research 365
  dissatisfied with DC16 215
  feature headings 176

BNB *bib (contd)*
  MARC 392
  phase relations 125+
  PRECIS 67+
  relation to BM 233
  revision of practice 166
  Supplementary schedules 233, *bib* 236
  revision of BC 266
  use of DC 232+
  using DC 18 217
  verbal extensions 176
Bookform catalogues: computers 392
Books
  indexing 195+
  replaced by consoles? 407
Bourne, C P *bib* 16 (323)
Bradford, S C *bib* 254
  use of UDC 239
Brevity: notation 132
Brown, J D *bib* 128
  introduced open access 170
  main class order 115
  pervasive subjects 114
  see also SC
Browsing *def* 25
Bruin, J *bib* 237
BSI *bib* 203
  UDC 240+
BTI
  alphabetical headings 59+
  Coates' theories 59+
  computers 395
  CRG research 365
  cross-references systematic 174
  filing order 79
  open vocabulary 51
BuShips *Thesaurus* 341
Butcher, P *bib* 82

CA
  articulated indexes 76
  computers 397
  retrospective searching 194
Cambridge University Mathematical Laboratory autoindexing 404
  see also CLRU
Campbell, D J *bib* 354
Canonical order: systematic arrangement 88
Card catalogue 189+
Catalogues 172+
  arrangement one-dimensional 21, 26

415

Enumerative indexing languages (*contd*)
Sears 173
classified schedules 102
ERIC *bib* 53
Thesaurus 355+
closed vocabulary 51
Errors
correction
peek-a-boo and Uniterm 315
source of failure 20
Cranfield 367
MEDLARS 375
Euratom: SYNTOL research 379
Evolutionary order 87
Exhaustivity *def* 22
CLW research 376
Cranfield 368
Cranfield II 374
Exposition phase 126
Expressiveness: notation 138+
Extensions and corrections to the UDC 243

Facet *def* 86
Facet analysis 85+
applied to knowledge 122
BC 258
CC 269+
CRG 363
DC2 211
library science demonstrated 105+
Thesaurus of education terms 359
Facet formula (citation order) CC 270+
Facet indicators: notation 148
BC 260+
CC 278
DC uses zero 215, 220
UDC 246+
needed for synthesis 148
Facet order (citation order) 89+
Faceted classification ch 6 84+
Faceted classification: Cranfield 326
False drops: post-coordinate systems 319
edge-notched cards 326
False links: chain procedure 160
Farradane, J E L *bib* 82
CRG 364
relational indexing 74
CLW research 378
Feature cards (peek-a-boo) 311+

Feature headings
BNB 233
classified catalogue 176
FID: UDC 239+
FID/CCC 242
Fields
computer input 387
edge-notched cards 326
Filing order
alphabetical arrangement 79+
BC 262
CC 278
EJC *Thesaurus* 348
irt citation order 96+
LCSH 301
NASA thesaurus 346
systematic arrangement 95+
Thesaurofacet 348
UDC 246+
Filmsetting
computer input 385
computer output 389
Fixed field operation: computers 387
Fixed field coding: edge-notched cards 326+
Fixed location *def* 209
Fission: development of new subjects 50, 121
Flexibility
alphabetical subject catalogue 174
card catalogue 190
notation 148+
BC 258, 264, 265
lacking in CC 272
LC 292
UDC: hazards 252
Food and Agricultural Organization
List of descriptors 360
Focus (plural foci) *def* 86
Focus: PRECIS *def* 69
Food technology abstracts
articulated indexes 76
Form *irt* subject: citation order 92
Foskett, A C *bib* 18, 53, 201, 202, 323, 409
Foskett, D J *bib* 16 (110, 155, 169), 17 (82, 129), 18 128), 111 (156), 155 (202), 381
classification for occupational safety and health 97
CRG 364
rotating 185
Freeman, C B *bib* 202
Freeman, R R *bib* 254

419

Fundamental categories
alphabetical headings 58
CC 270+
citation order 93
Future part V 363+
BC 267
CC 287
DC 235
LC 294
UDC 253

Gardin, J C *bib* 53 (383)
SYNTOL 379
Garfield, E *bib* 40
General classification schemes ch 7
112+
CRG 121+, 364
Generalia class 114
CC 277
Genus-species relationships 42, 43
alphabetical subject catalogue 55
API thesaurus 345
classified catalogue 175
EJC *Thesaurus* 335, 339+
NASA thesaurus 346
post-coordinate systems 317
PRECIS 68, 72+
shown by schedule layout 108+
SYNTOL 379
systematic approach in BTI 61
Thesaurofacet 348
Gilchrist, A *bib* 354
Gore, D *bib* 156
Gradation in speciality
main class order 117
Greek alphabet
not suitable for notation 131
used by CC 141
Grogan, D J *bib* 203
Grolier, E de *bib* 128
Grose, M W *bib* 82
Group notation 140
Grouping: effect of citation order
90
Guard book catalogues 193
Guide to the UDC 252
Guiding: classified catalogue 177
systematic arrangement 144

Hall, J L *bib* 410
Halle *Schema* considered for Library
of Congress 289
Hardware: computers 385+
Harman, R J *bib* 411

Hayes, R M *bib* 202
Haykin, D J *bib* 304
Headings *def* 29
see also Indexing languages
Helpful order: systematic arrange-
ment 86+
Henley, J P *bib* 408
Heuristic searching *def* 24
computer systems 393+
Hierarchical notation *def* 138
Hille, B A *bib* 30
Hines, T C *bib* 323
Homographs: subject analysis 45
alphabetical headings 45
alphabetical indexes 157
post-coordinate indexes 317
Horner, J L *bib* 83 (169, 201, 304,
409)
Hospitality
alphabetical headings 174
notation *def* 137
conflict with expressiveness 140
in chain and array 151+
not the same as flexibility 150
Houghton, B *bib* 408
Hulme, E Wyndham 28, *bib* 30

IBM *bib* 410
Combined File Search System 398
computerized library services 404
KWIC indexing 33
SDI 399
Identifying factors *def* 14
description 29
Ideographs not suitable as notation
130
IEE: SDI 400
IIB 238
IID 239
Immroth, J P *bib* 298
Index
classified catalogues 175
systematic arrangement ch 9 157+
BC 264
CC 279
DC18 227+
LC 293
UDC 252
Index entry *def* 29
Index medicus
MEDLARS 393
MeSH 350
Index vocabulary
alphabetical headings 173

424

428